Java™ Internationalization

THE JAVA™ SERIES

Java™ Internationalization

Andrew Deitsch and David Czarnecki

O'REILLY®

Beijing · Cambridge · Farnham · Köln · Paris · Sebastopol · Taipei · Tokyo

Java™ Internationalization
by Andrew Deitsch and David Czarnecki

Published by O'Reilly & Associates, Inc., 101 Morris Street, Sebastopol, CA 95472.

Editor: Mike Loukides

Production Editor: Ann Schirmer

Cover Designer: Hanna Dyer

Printing History:

March 2001:	First Edition.

0-596-00019-7
[M]

Table of Contents

Preface

Now the whole earth had one language and few words. And as men migrated from the east, they found a plain in the land of Shinar and settled there. And they said to one another, "Come, let us make bricks, and burn them thoroughly." And they had brick for stone, and bitumen for mortar. Then they said, "Come, let us build ourselves a city, and a tower with its top in the heavens, and let us make a name for ourselves, lest we be scattered abroad upon the face of the whole earth."

And the Lord came down to see the city and the tower, which the sons of men had built. And the Lord said, "Behold, they are one people, and they have all one language; and this is only the beginning of what they will do; and nothing that they propose to do will now be impossible for them. Come, let us go down, and there confuse their language, that they may not understand one another's speech."

So the Lord scattered them abroad from there over the face of the earth, and they left off building the city. Therefore its name was called Babel, because there the Lord confused the language of all the earth and from there the Lord scattered them abroad over the face of the earth.

—Genesis

Internationalization is the process of writing applications in a way that makes localizing the application to a particular region as easy as possible. Internationalization aims to remove the burden of re-engineering an application when writing for multiple countries or regions. Programs that are written with internationalization in mind typically possess the following characteristics:

- Text resource externalization for elements such as labels and messages

- No application recompilation required for the support of new languages

- Conformation to the user's locale for the display of culturally dependent data, such as currencies, dates, times, and graphical user interface (GUI) layout

Localization deals with the translation of textual elements to a particular locale. A locale embodies both a specific language and a given cultural, geographical, and political region. Several graphical elements may also be added or removed based on locale settings to provide the user with a native look and feel for the application. Today's multimedia and graphical applications may include images and sounds that require tailoring to a specific locale. Localization may require involvement of cultural experts and can be a very time-consuming task when translating large amounts of text is necessary.

Java Internationalization examines the classes and the framework that the Java language provides for software internationalization. Together, all of these chapters will allow you to write software that realizes the Java promise of "Write Once, Run Anywhere (in the world)." Java has been able to deliver on its cross-platform capabilities; however, developers need to be aware of issues they will face in the software internationalization process. If Java is used to write software, a single application binary can carry all localizations for different locales. Which localization(s) to use can be decided by the application or the user at runtime.

Internationalization support was first introduced in JDK™ 1.1. A company called Taligent, with contributions from Justsystem, Novell, and Sun, developed much of the Java Internationalization API. IBM later bought Taligent. IBM's Center for Java Technology in California is still developing a good portion of the Java Internationalization API.

Who Should Read This Book?

This book is written for developers who would like to write truly internationalized software. This goal may apply to existing software or to a software project that is just starting. There is no assumption that you know about all the topics central to software internationalization. Those concepts will be explained along the way through discussions of facilities in the Java platform that address these issues.

Code Examples

This book contains code examples that illustrate the use of classes comprising the Java internationalization API and various internationalization concepts. If you're not inclined to type out all of the examples, you may download a package containing them at *http://www.oreilly.com/catalog/javaint/*. The authors maintain a web site *http://www.javainternationalization.com*, where you will find up-to-date examples and information from the book, articles, and other links related to software internationalization.

The examples developed in this book were tested using the Java™ 2 SDK, Standard Edition, Versions 1.2 and 1.3 from Sun Microsystems running under Windows 95/98/NT. Unless noted otherwise, all examples rely on this SDK. Also, when referring to Java or the Java Platform, we are talking about the Java™ 2 SDK, Standard Edition, Version 1.3 from Sun Microsystems. We have also tried to ensure that the examples are compatible with the JDK™ 1.1.x releases; however, some examples rely on functionality that only exists beginning with the Java™ 2 Platform.

Contents

Java Internationalization consists of 12 chapters and 5 appendixes. A brief description of each chapter and appendix follows:

Chapter 1, *Introduction*
> Discusses the general concepts of internationalization and localization and why developers choose Java for writing international applications.

Chapter 2, *Writing Systems*
> Traces the history of writing systems and covers topics such as ancient and Far East writing systems and bidirectional scripts. This chapter provides an overview of complexities associated with different writing systems.

Chapter 3, *Locales*
> Describes the locale concept and related classes in Java. It also shows how to query for locale-specific information, including country, language, and variant information, such as the use of the Euro currency for a particular locale.

Chapter 4, *Isolating Locale-Specific Data with Resource Bundles*
> Explains the use of a resource bundle and the ways developers can define locale-specific bundles and bundle loading at runtime. A discussion of how to isolate general objects in a resource bundle is also included.

Chapter 5, *Formatting Messages*
Introduces issues such as text fragmentation, agreement, date/time formats, and number formats, including currency and percentages.

Chapter 6, *Character Sets and Unicode*
Provides a brief overview of character sets and describes the Unicode™ Standard. This chapter also explains Unicode-related issues, such as unification, normalization of Unicode characters, special characters, and character set conversion.

Chapter 7, *Searching, Sorting, and Text Boundary Detection*
Explains the issues associated with collating multilingual text and demonstrates how searching and sorting through such text can be accomplished in Java. This chapter also describes how to detect character, word, and line boundaries in international text.

Chapter 8, *Fonts*
Demonstrates international font support in Java and how to use system fonts for displaying international text in your applications. This chapter also demonstrates the rendering of international text.

Chapter 9, *Graphical User Interfaces*
Describes issues associated with internationalizing graphical user interfaces, such as laying out components in a dynamic manner consistent with the target locale. The chapter includes various caveats in using graphical components.

Chapter 10, *Input Methods*
Provides a description of Java's Input Method Framework. The chapter also details how to develop applications that can accept input for languages that require more keys than can traditionally be found on a computer keyboard.

Chapter 11, *Internationalized Web Applications*
Introduces issues related to deploying Java programs as applets, servlets, and Java Server Pages. Discusses where internationalization comes into play in such situations.

Chapter 12, *Future Enhancements to the Internationalization Support in Java*
Details future enhancements in the internationalization framework for the Java™ 2 Platform, such as the character conversion Service Provider Interface (SPI) and support for complex scripts like Hindi and Thai.

Appendix A, *Language and Country Codes*
Contains a full list of the ISO Language Codes (ISO 639) and ISO Country Codes (ISO 3166).

Appendix B, *Character Encodings Supported by Java*
Lists all supported character encodings in the Java platform.

Appendix C, *Unicode Character Blocks*

Lists the Unicode 2.1 character blocks and associated code point ranges for each block.

Appendix D, *Programmer's Quick Reference*

Contains a full description of the classes related to international Java development.

Appendix E, *Internationalization Enhancements Across Versions of the JDK*

Describes bug fixes, changes, and enhancements from JDK™ 1.1; Java™ 2 SDK, Standard Edition, Version 1.2; and Java™ 2 SDK, Standard Edition, Version 1.3.

Glossary

Describes internationalization terms used throughout the book.

Bibliography

Lists external resources that readers may explore to find more detailed information on specific topics. Where applicable, such references are noted in individual chapters.

Conventions Used in This Book

Italic is used for:

- Pathnames, filenames, and program names

- New terms where they are defined

- Internet addresses, such as email addresses and URLs

Boldface is used for:

- Particular keys on the computer keyboard

- Names of user interface buttons and menus

`Constant Width` is used for:

- Anything that appears literally in a Java program, including keywords, datatypes, constants, method names, variables, class names, and interface names

- Command lines and options that should be typed verbatim on the screen

- All Java code listings

- HTML documents, tags, and attributes

Constant-Width Italic is used for:

- General placeholders that indicate an item is replaced by some actual value in your own program

Comments

In *Java Internationalization*, we have taken special care to ensure that the code examples and information presented in each chapter are up-to-date and accurate. Errors or misinterpretations may exist in the text. We apologize in advance for any discrepancies; however, we welcome any reports of bugs, errors, ambiguous or confusing statements, and other general typographic errors. You may submit these to the following email address: *bookquestions@oreilly.com.*

You can also submit feedback directly to Sun. If you find a bug in Sun's Java Runtime Environment or if you would like to request a feature, go to the Java Developer Connection Bug Parade at *http://developer.java.sun.com/developer/bugParade.* If a bug already exists or a request for a feature is already present on this site, vote for it. If not, you can submit your bug or a request for enhancement at *http://java.sun.com/cgi-bin/bugreport.cgi.* For feedback that doesn't fit into a bug or request for enhancement, you can send email to *java-intl@java.sun.com.* This email address goes directly to the internationalization team at Sun. They read all the email that is submitted to this address, but unfortunately they cannot reply to every message. Finally, you can check the Java discussion forum on internationalization. Go to *http://forum.java.sun.com* and look for "Internationalization."

Please feel free to suggest topics for future editions of *Java Internationalization.* This book was written for developers and thus requires your feedback so that we can make the book as focused and as useful as possible.

Acknowledgments

It is difficult to complete any large project without input and support from others. This book is no different.

Many thanks to Mike Loukides, our editor, who guided us through our first authorship experience; Christien Shangraw, who helped move the book into final production; Kyle Hart, for being the marketing expert she is; Rob Romano, who converted our stick figures into works of art; Lenny Muellner and Mike Sierra, who graciously left the comfort of FrameMaker to produce the book in Word 2000; and Ann Schirmer, for guiding us through the final production of the book.

We would also like to thank the following people for reviewing the book at various stages of its development: Kareem Aggour, Janet Barnett, Brian Beck, Hong Cheng, Walt Dixon III, Ginger DiDomizio, Doug Felt, Norbert Lindenberg, Steve Loomis, Osman Öksoy, Helena Shih, and Barbara Vivier. We are grateful for your corrections, comments, suggestions, and other input provided.

Andy's Acknowledgments

I would like to start off by thanking Richard Ishida, whose excitement and energy related to the topic of software internationalization inspired me to learn more and eventually write this book. A thanks also goes to Jim Farley for initially putting me in touch with our editor, Mike Loukides.

The following people, who over the years have in one way or another helped me to make this a better book than it otherwise would have been, also deserve some thanks and recognition. Thank you to my brother Gal Deitsch (גל דיטש), for providing snapshots of his Hebrew version of Windows and for correcting my Hebrew over the years. To my sister Netalie Deitsch (נטלי דיטש), who, at the age of four and unable to understand a word of English, helped teach me Hebrew through prolonged games of Charades. To Fett, a close friend who shares my interest in languages and made many dull meetings at work much more fun by speaking in various tongues and accents. A special thank you (شكرا - shokran) to Nick Chbat, who generously gave up his lunchtimes to teach me Arabic. Also, thanks to Juliana Shei, who helped me with my Japanese translations, and to Lei Shlitz, who put up with my constant questioning about Chinese ideographs during a trip to China.

Last, but certainly not least, I wish to thank my loving wife Marie, who for some reason continues to put up with my endless list of projects and wacky ideas. My career at GE has required endless hours away from home, sometimes for months at a time. In 1997 I decided to go back to school to pursue an MBA. For two years, I spent nights and weekends studying while I continued to work at GE. A week before I graduated with my MBA, I signed a contract with O'Reilly to write this book.[1] Through it all, Marie has supported me with love and encouragement. Marie is a truly wonderful wife, and I love her dearly.

---

[1] Signing a contract to write a book after two years of not spending time with my wife is not very bright. In fact, I would consider this a "wacky idea."

David's Acknowledgments

I would like to start by thanking Andy Deitsch for involving me in this project. It has certainly been a tremendous learning experience. Your guidance and mentorship over the course of writing this book has proven invaluable.

There are many friends whom I have come to rely on for support over the years. To Michelle Adams, an excellent personal trainer, who also shares my enjoyment for the finer things in life; Marc Garbiras, a friend, office mate, and the only other individual beside myself who can quote entire episodes of Seinfeld and South Park. And finally, I would like to give a very special thanks to Mark Goldstein, for making our years in high school and college worthwhile and for being a lifelong friend.

My parents, Anthony and Lorraine, and my sister, Pam, deserve the most thanks. Your love and support over the years has helped to guide me down many roads. In work and in play, your teachings and your values have always forced me strive for excellence and perfection. You are always in my thoughts, and I cannot thank you enough, especially in one paragraph, for being the perfect parents and a perfect sister.

Finally, I am dedicating this book to my sister, Pam Czarnecki. You wrote your first book, *My Pet*, while in the first grade. It contained six sentences and three illustrations. It also contained the following dedication: "I dedicate this book to my brother, David." I am sorry it has taken me so long to do the same for you.

Introduction to Internationalization

What Are Software Internationalization, Localization, and Globalization?

Conducting business in the global marketplace has been the battle cry of companies in recent years. Since the mid-1990s, the world has been consumed by an explosive growth of the Internet, driven largely by the World Wide Web (WWW). The global nature of the Web and the growing acceptance of electronic commerce have been instrumental in helping companies reach global markets. As businesses continue to expand globally and more countries become wired to the Internet, it will be increasingly important for these businesses to ensure that the products they manufacture and sell are appropriate for the world's markets.

Software engineering practices have been trailing more traditional engineering in this regard. For example, U.S. automobile manufacturers would not find much success if they attempted to sell lefthand drive cars in Australia, the United Kingdom, or Japan.[1] Likewise, clothing manufacturers that sell their products around the world must label clothing appropriately, depending on the local market.[2] In the United States washing machines are typically loaded vertically (top-loaded) even though top-loading machines consume more water and put more wear and

---

[1] Lefthand drive cars are those that have the steering wheel on the left side of the vehicle (i.e., designed to be driven on the righthand side of the road).

[2] European sizes differ from U.S. sizes, and symbols indicating cleaning directions are different around the world.

tear on the clothing. In the rest of the world, however, washing machines are typically loaded horizontally (front-loaded). Washing machine manufacturers tailor their products to their customers' needs and local market acceptance.

The Software Industry

The software development industry began in the United States, and traditionally, software that allows only English input and output has been forced upon global users. It isn't uncommon to hear developers say, "Why can't they all speak English?"[3] However, given the choice between two software products that offer similar features, most people would choose the product that is available in their native language.

In recent years, there has been a shift in where software development takes place. While the software industry remains strong in the United States, other countries, such as Australia, Germany, India, Israel, and Mexico, are creating large software development industries. As more software products are developed in different parts of the world, it will become critical for successful companies to design these products to interact with users in their native language using local conventions. Companies that continue to develop software that is adapted to monolingual and monocultural settings will not remain competitive in the global marketplace.

Global Issues

What kinds of global issues might we have to worry about as software developers? Whether a programmer is American, Israeli, Japanese, or Russian, certain cultural biases are inherently built into the software he or she writes. Given a few minutes to think about it, you would probably come up with several language issues that you don't immediately know how to tackle. For example, many languages are written using non-Latin writing systems (Arabic, Chinese, Hebrew, Hindi, Japanese, etc.). These writing systems, also known as *scripts*, have developed over thousands of years, and many have attributes requiring a much different mechanism for processing than writing systems typically used by a programmer who speaks English. We'll cover many of these non-Latin writing issues later in the book.

Even for languages that do use the Latin script, there are differences that need to be taken into account. For example, American programmers commonly assume that all letters of the alphabet exist between A and Z. The code in Example 1-1 would be quite acceptable to an American programmer unaware of the global marketplace.

---

[3] As you will soon learn, even English isn't consistent around the world.

Example 1-1. An English-Specific Way of Checking for Valid Input

```
char c;

// Get user input

if ((c >= 'A' && c <= 'Z') || (c >= 'a' && c <= 'z')) {
  // accept the input
} else {
  // handle error case
}
```

This code would not work correctly if it were used to process Danish text. In addition to the 26 letters that exist in the English alphabet, the Danish alphabet has three additional letters (æ, ø, and å) that appear after the letter z. As you can imagine, entering text into a system with this piece of code embedded in it might frustrate Danish users. Now imagine what would happen if a Korean user tried to enter data into this system![4]

Software developers, like most other employees who work for a multinational enterprise, should make themselves aware of the cultural and linguistic differences in the markets where their companies operate. Ignorance of cultural and language differences can create problems for companies. When Microsoft released its Spanish version of Word 6.0, the thesaurus suggested synonyms that were considered too derogatory to be acceptable. The company had to modify the software after media reports denounced it.[5]

Around the world, local conventions exist for formatting numbers, currency, dates and times, names, and addresses. Measurement systems also vary according to local convention. Many countries and cultures in the world use a calendar system other than the Gregorian calendar. Time zones pose another difficulty for software developers. It is often assumed that all parts of the world switch between daylight saving time and daylight standard time. But that assumption is false, even within the United States: Arizona, Hawaii, part of Indiana, Puerto Rico, the Virgin Islands, and American Samoa do not switch over to daylight saving time. Not only do different parts of the world set their own rules for this issue, they also have their own rules for when daylight saving starts and ends.

Besides language and local convention differences, a software developer must consider cultural diversity issues, such as the use of acceptable colors and numbers. In most Western countries, for example, black is generally used to denote death, while white means the same thing in Asian countries, and purple represents death

---

[4] The Korean writing system is described in Chapter 2, *Writing Systems.*

[5] Don Clark, "Hey, #@*% Amigo, Can You Translate the Word 'Gaffte'?" *Wall Street Journal,* July 8, 1996, p. B6.

in Latin America.[6] In the United States, the number 13 is considered unlucky, the number 69 has sexual connotations, and 666 is the sign of the devil. In Hong Kong, the number 7 is considered unlucky, while the number 8 is lucky.

Plan Ahead

The markets you plan to support should be considered as part of the initial software design stage. Typically, few American companies actually consider developing international software from the outset. International requirements are usually an afterthought. This situation leads to rework in both design and implementation, which ultimately delays delivery and increases product costs for foreign markets.

The decision about which markets you plan on supporting should be made with all the appropriate stakeholders: engineering, marketing, sales, the quality assurance group, the documentation department, and don't forget the customer! If you work for a global company, it is also very helpful to bring colleagues from overseas onto the decision team.

Some of the decisions you have to make are:

- What markets are we going to target?

    When designing software, it is important to think about both the initial release and what software features will be included in later versions. Early architectural decisions you make impact your ability to support certain types of internationalization features down the road. For example, your company's marketing plan may include plans to sell the product initially in North America and Western Europe. If the product is designed to support only these markets, you will probably have to do some major reengineering if, at a later stage, your marketing department decides to sell the product in Asia or the Middle East. The reason is that the software was probably not designed to handle such issues as support for non-Latin characters and, in the case of the Middle East, bidirectional text.

- Is it acceptable to internationalize only part of the application?

    Once you know your target markets, you need to make some cost tradeoffs between doing a full or partial internationalization effort. For example,

---

[6] *International Business, Environments and Operations,* Daniels and Radebaugh, Addison-Wesley, Eighth Edition, 1998, p. 78.

the extra revenue generated by building a Japanese Era[7] calendar into your product may not be enough to cover the costs of implementing such a feature.

- Is it acceptable to treat a specific language identically across all locales?

  Although many countries share the same language, spelling and vocabulary differences may not be acceptable in certain markets. For example, Table 1-1 highlights some vocabulary differences between American and British English, while Table 1-2 shows some of the spelling differences between the two versions of English. Spoken French often differs in various parts of the world, as do Spanish, German, and several other languages.

- Are the translators you choose appropriate?

  Given the nuances between different versions of the same language, it is important to choose a translator familiar with the local dialect. It would not be appropriate to use a translator with a Mexican dialect to translate a product for the Iberian Spanish market.

NOTE   Do not rely on employees who happen to be bilingual to do your translations. Translation is a skill and requires both an understanding of the region's language and the region's cultural nuances. Here are signs from hotels around the world showing what can happen if you don't have knowledgeable translators:[8]

"Please leave your values at the desk."
— France

"You are invited to take advantage of the chambermaid."
— Japan

"Because of the impropriety of entertaining guests of the opposite sex in the bedroom, it is suggested that the lobby be used for this purpose."
— Switzerland

"Ladies are requested not to have children at the bar."
— Norway

---

[7] The Japanese Era calendar counts years since the current emperor ascended the throne.

[8] *International Business, Environments and Operations,* Daniels and Radebaugh, Addison-Wesley, Eighth Edition, 1998, p. 77

Table 1-1. Some Vocabulary Differences Between U.S. and U.K. English

U.S. English	U.K. English
Elevator	Lift
Hood	Bonnet
Mutual Fund	Unit Trust
Pavement	Road
Sidewalk	Pavement
Trunk	Boot

Table 1-2. Some Spelling Differences Between U.S. and U.K. English

U.S. English	U.K. English
Aluminum	Aluminium
Center	Centre
Internationalization	Internationalisation
Flavor	Flavour
Tire	Tyre

Customized Localization

Developing a customized version of the software for each market in which the software will be sold is one way to deal with all these language, culture, and local convention issues. In other words, local country practices can be built into each software version created for a specific market. Many companies actually create separate versions for different markets, which can be very expensive to maintain. Every time a new feature needs to be added to the software, the feature must be added to each localized version. Depending on the particular market, customization may be required to support this feature. As you can imagine, the advantage of maintaining one source tree and set of application binaries for all the world's versions becomes evident as soon as you need to make a bug fix. Replicating bug fixes across several versions of source code for each combination of natural language and region your software was supporting, and then testing each version to make sure the fix worked, would be a nightmare.

Internationalization

The alternative to the customized localization approach is called internationalization. Internationalization, also known in the software industry as I18N (pronounced *EYE-EIGHTEEN-EN*), is a term used to define the architecture and design of software for which only one set of source code and binary is produced to support all the markets in which software will be sold.[9]

NOTE   Microsoft realized that maintaining their Office suite of products for all the
              major languages of the world was very costly. The Microsoft Office 97 suite was
              shipped as different binaries for each supported locale. A complete redesign
              for Office 2000 enabled most of the world's locales to be supported in one bi-
              nary with language packs available as simple add-ons. Now even an English
              version of Word can be used to edit Japanese text.

Your customers probably won't ask for internationalized software. They expect that the software works correctly in their language using their local conventions. As Tom McFarland of Hewlett-Packard stated very well in a presentation he gave at the Fourteenth Unicode Conference in Boston, Massachusetts, "Internationalization is not a feature!" He's right; it's not a feature. It is an essential part of the initial software design.

Culturally Biased Assumptions

Good internationalization practices are not normally taught in computer science curricula. As you read this book, you will see that many assumptions you typically make as a programmer are not acceptable when developing global applications. Table 1-3 lists some common assumptions and reasons why they are invalid:

Table 1-3. Common Invalid Assumptions

Assumption	Reason Why It Is Invalid
A–Z contains all letters in the alphabet.	Several languages, including Danish, have letters that appear after Z in the alphabet. Also, for languages that don't use the Latin script, such as Arabic, Korean, and Russian, this assumption does not hold true.
All scripts contain upper- and lowercase letters.	Many scripts don't have the concept of case. Examples include Han ideographs as used in Chinese, Japanese, and Korean (CJK), and other scripts, such as Arabic, Hebrew, and Thai.
Words are separated by spaces.	Scripts used to write CJK and Thai don't have the concept of word separation: asentencewouldlooklikethis.

---

[9] Internationalization begins with an I, ends with an N, and has 18 characters in between.

Table 1-3. Common Invalid Assumptions (continued)

Assumption	Reason Why It Is Invalid

Punctuation is the same.	Many languages use different punctuation symbols. For example, in English, questions end with a question mark (?), as in:
	
	    How are you?
	In Spanish, questions are surrounded by an upside-down and a right-side-up question mark, as in:
	
	    ¿Cómo está usted?
	In Greek, questions end with a semicolon (;), as in:
	
	    Πώς είσθε;

Text is written left to right.	Languages such as Arabic and Hebrew are bidirectional languages. That is, characters are written from right to left, but numbers embedded in text are written from left to right. Mongolian is written vertically from left to right. Chinese can be written either horizontally from left to right or vertically from right to left.
All calendar systems are Gregorian.	Many calendar systems exist around the world, including the Buddhist, Hebrew, Hijri (Islamic), and Japanese Era calendars. The Thai government, for example, permits only Buddhist calendar dates for use in business settings.
Characters are equivalent to bytes.	An 8-bit byte has only enough space to store a maximum of 256 characters. The number of characters in Chinese exceeds 40,000. To store all these characters, multiple bytes are used to encode a single character. In Unicode 2.x, characters are stored in 16 bits or 2 bytes.[10]
Sort order is the same for all languages that share a common script.	Languages that share a script do not always sort the same way. For example, French uses a multilevel sort, in which the first level collates words using the base characters starting from the left of the word and working toward the right (the same way it is done in English). If any characters contain diacritics, a second-level sort is performed, starting from the right and working toward the left to break any ties.
Words contain consonants and vowels.	Some scripts, such as Arabic and Hebrew don't require vowels. The vowels are implied, though they are often used in children's books and religious texts.

---

[10] Unicode provides an "escape hatch" called a surrogate pair that allows encoding of more than 1 million characters. We will discuss this concept in Chapter 6, *Character Sets and Unicode*.

Because we are unable to cover all the differences for all the locales around the world, we will focus on common types of problems encountered when internationalizing software. As the various topics of internationalization are introduced, we will provide many examples of linguistic and local convention differences.

Localization

Once a piece of software has been internationalized (either because it has been designed and implemented that way from the beginning or because it has been reengineered), it needs to be adapted or *localized* for a specific market. Typically, the product is first localized for the market where the software is developed. For example, a U.S.-based company would first localize the software to American English. At this point, the software would operate in the same way you would expect the application to run if it had been built using traditional software development methods. The advantage, however, is that you could create versions for France, Germany, and Japan without having to modify the source code or binary. This localization (L10N – pronounced *EL-TEN-EN*) process only entails translating external text files and creating locale specific bitmaps and images. [11]

Why external text files? Typically, when software needs to be localized for a given market, expert translators with knowledge of local conventions localize it in that market. Translators are not programmers and are far more effective if they don't have to sift through thousands of lines of source code to make changes. As a programmer responsible for end delivery of the code, you might find that concept rather scary! So externalizing as much of the localized data as possible to make the localization process easy for the translators is a common approach.

Globalization

The term *globalization* (G11N—pronounced *GEE-ELEVEN-EN*) is often used synonymously with internationalization. [12] Globalization, however, usually encompasses both internationalization and localization. When we use the term globalization, we refer to the entire software development process from design through implementation and localization for sale in the intended markets.

---

[11] Localization begins with an 'L,' ends with an 'N,' and has ten characters in between.

[12] Have you figured it out yet?

Multilingual Applications

Typically, applications are internationalized so they work in a single language for a specific region when they are localized. Multilingual applications go one step further and enable the user to switch locales dynamically at runtime. There are a number of reasons why an application might need to be multilingual. Imagine that you are implementing a product or service for a Swiss company. Switzerland uses four official languages: German, French, Italian, and Romansch. You might be thinking to yourself, "Why not just have four localized versions?" That option might work if the application is a desktop client. If you develop a server application (such as an electronic catalog) that needs to support networked clients (browsers), you no longer know beforehand what language a particular user understands.

Creating multilingual applications adds another dimension of complexity to the already complex task of software internationalization. Although building such an application involves additional work and planning, it can easily be accomplished using the techniques described in this book.

Why Choose Java for International Applications?

The designers of Java realized early on that support for global software development would be an important language feature. Storing all characters as 16 bits encoded in Unicode was a key Java 1.0 design decision to support internationalization. This decision facilitates software development for global markets. Unicode is covered in much more detail in Chapter 6, but for now it is sufficient to know that Unicode is a character set that supports every character for all the world's written languages.

Developing internationalized software, however, requires much more than encoding characters in Unicode. Applications rarely operate in isolation. They often import and export data and interface with the underlying operating system. Programs must be capable of converting between Unicode and various other character sets. They must also be able to handle complex writing systems, such as Arabic and Hindi, which we will cover in the next chapter. They must handle the different kinds of date, number, and monetary formats, and a host of other things to be detailed later.

Other than Unicode support, Java 1.0 lacked many features required to properly internationalize an application. In 1996, Sun Microsystems contracted with a number of companies, including Taligent, a subsidiary of IBM, to further enhance Java's internationalization features.[13]

NOTE   Since 1996, Taligent has been dissolved and various parts of IBM formally integrated the engineers and technology. The Unicode Technology Group, which is part of the IBM Center for Java Technology in Cupertino, California, now handles most of IBM's software internationalization work. IBM and Sun still work very closely together to continue developing internationalization functionality in Java.

In practice, the team at IBM builds internationalization functionality into IBM's release of the Java platform, which is usually a few steps ahead of the Java platform that Sun releases. Many of the internationalization classes that have not yet been (or may never be) integrated into Sun's release of the Java platform are available from IBM's ICU4J web site. [14] If you are interested in finding out what internationalization features might be available in upcoming versions of the Java™ 2 Platform, the ICU4J site is a good place to look. [15]

The agreement between IBM and Sun produced additional internationalization functionality, which was available in JDK™ 1.1. With the release of Java™ 2 SDK, Standard Edition, came more internationalization features. In particular, support for bidirectional languages, such as Arabic and Hebrew, became available, as did improved date handling, the input method framework, and a number of bug fixes.

Java itself is internationalized and supports approximately 100 locales, depending on the version. This internationalization means that if you use the correct classes and methods when writing your code, you get a lot of internationalized code for free. If you are currently writing some code that generates date information, for example, you might not even think about localizing the code for the Russian market. However, if you use the right APIs, the application works correctly! Support for new countries and languages, when added by the vendor of your Java runtime, is also achieved at no additional cost.

---

[13] *The Java International API, JDK 1.1 and Beyond*, Helena Shih, Fourteenth International Unicode Conference

[14] International Components for Unicode for Java

[15] *http://oss.software.ibm.com/icu4j*

What Is a Locale?

In software internationalization, we use the term *locale* when we talk about local markets. A locale embraces a specific language in combination with a given cultural, geographical, and political region. A French Canadian locale refers to the French speaking part of Canada (Quebec Province), and is associated with the language and information such as the date, currency and number formats for that particular region. A different locale would be used for the English speaking part of Canada. In addition to the language and formatting information, important data that you might not immediately associate with a locale is usually included, such as:

- Names of the months

- Days of the week

- The first day of the week

- Collation sequencing (sort order)

- Time zone information

In Java, locale information is maintained in the `java.util.Locale` object and represents:

- A language

- A country or region

- An optional variant

Chapter 3, *Locales,* provides a complete explanation of the `Locale` object. Java objects and methods that modify their behavior based on their specific locale are considered *locale-sensitive.* For example, a method displaying the days of the week should produce the output shown in Example 1-2 for a U.S. English locale, the output shown in Example 1-3 for a U.K. English locale, and the output shown in Example 1-4 for a Canadian French locale. Note that the first day of the week in the United States and Canada is Sunday, but is Monday in the United Kingdom.

Example 1-2. Days of the Week for U.S. English

```
Sunday
Monday
Tuesday
Wednesday
```

```
Thursday
Friday
Saturday
```

Example 1-3. Days of the Week for U.K. English

```
Monday
Tuesday
Wednesday
Thursday
Friday
Saturday
Sunday
```

Example 1-4. Days of the Week for Canadian French

```
dimanche
lundi
mardi
mercredi
jeudi
vendredi
samedi
```

A Simple Application

Now that you have a little background, we'll demonstrate how a simple Hello World application can be written with internationalization. First, look at Example 1-5 to see what the application would look like without internationalization:

Example 1-5. Traditional Version of HelloWorld.java

```java
public class HelloWorld {
  public static void main(String s[]) {
    System.out.println("Hello World!");
  }
}
```

The problem with this code is that the text string "Hello World!" has been hardcoded. We need a way of externalizing the hardcoded text, allowing the application to replace the text with the appropriate translated string at runtime. In Java, this replacement can be accomplished using resource bundles. We cover resource bundles in much more detail in Chapter 4, *Isolating Locale-Specific Data with Resource Bundles,* but for now just be aware that the `java.util.ResourceBundle` class allows data to be retrieved at runtime, indexed using a unique key. Example 1-6 shows what the application looks like when properly internationalized.

Example 1-6. Internationalized Version of HelloWorld.java

```java
import java.util.*;

public class HelloWorld {
  public static void main(String [] argv) {
    ResourceBundle resources;

    try {
      resources = ResourceBundle.getBundle("MyData");
      System.out.println(resources.getString("Hi"));
    } catch (MissingResourceException mre) {
      System.err.println("MyData.properties not found");
    }
  }
}
```

Example 1-7 shows the resource file containing the externalized text. Data are stored in `key = value` format, and quotes are not needed around resource bundle strings.

Example 1-7. Resource Bundle Containing Externalized Text.MyData.properties

```
Hi = Hello World!
```

We will now take you through the code step by step and explain what each key line actually does:

```java
resources = ResourceBundle.getBundle("MyData");
```

The static method `ResourceBundle.getBundle()` opens the external data contained within the resource bundle. The parameter is a `String` and is the name of the file containing the resource bundle. At this point you should notice that the file extension `.properties` is not included. As you will learn in Chapter 4, the appropriate extension is added automatically by Java when it searches for the file. The call is placed within a `try-catch` block because the method throws a `MissingResourceException` if the file isn't found. In this line of code, the `ResourceBundle.getString()` method returns a `String` containing the value found in the resource bundle indexed by the parameter: in this case, the parameter is the key value "Hi":

```java
System.out.println(resources.getString("Hi"));
```

Compiling and running the program yields the following output:

```
C:\>javac HelloWorld.java
C:\>java HelloWorld
Hello World!
```

Now we can easily localize this application to French by creating another file to store our French data. To make this file, simply create a copy of the `MyData.properties` file and name it `MyData_fr.properties`. The `_fr` appended to the first part of the filename indicates that the information inside this file is specifically French data. Java uses the two character language codes from the ISO-639 standard to identify the language. We discuss this process in much more detail in Chapter 3, *Locales*. The contents of the `MyData_fr.properties` file are modified as shown in Example 1-8.

Example 1-8. MyData_fr.properties

```
Hi = Salut tout le monde!
```

No recompilation is necessary to run the application for French. All we need to do is start the Java Virtual Machine and let it know that we want to use the French language. To do this, run the following command:

```
C:\>java -Duser.language=fr HelloWorld
Salut tout le monde!
```

NOTE   Specifying the locale on the command line is convenient; however, the feature is undocumented and is implementation dependent. There is no guarantee that a Java runtime environment will support this capability.

On Windows platforms you can also tell the Java Virtual Machine what locale you want it to use by changing the **Regional Settings** in **Control Panel**. Changing the settings also changes locale information for the operating system (look at the date and time in the lower righthand corner, for example). It is best to change the **Regional Settings** when you will be doing a lot of testing on a specific locale.

In this chapter we've introduced you to some of the issues associated with developing international software. We've defined basic terms such as internationalization, localization, globalization, and locale. Finally, we have taken you through the process of developing a simple internationalized application.

We have only skimmed the surface in covering all internationalization issues and how to address them. The rest of the book takes a closer look at the issues and provides much more detail on how they can be tackled with Java.

2

Writing Systems

It is helpful to understand the different types of writing systems that exist in the world while developing global software. This chapter gives a brief overview of the world's various writing systems. After reading it, you should have some understanding of the complexities associated with some of these writing systems.

We want to emphasize that we couldn't possibly cover all the world's writing systems in this book. We provide you with an overview of the scripts we do cover, however, so you can get a picture of the types of issues you might face in software internationalization. To learn more about a specific writing system, we encourage you to review the books in the bibliography or to look at the web sites we identify as references.

A *writing system*, or *script*, is not a language; it is a means of conveying information through written communication. Over several millennia, hundreds of scripts have been developed. Cultures have adopted scripts to represent their language in written form. Thus, there is often, but not always, a one-to-many relationship between script and language. For example, if you know how to read English, then you understand how to read the Latin script. You can also read French, but you probably don't understand what you are reading (unless you also speak French). Likewise, if you can read the Arabic script, you can read Arabic, Farsi, and Urdu, but again, you might not understand what you are reading.

Ancient Writing Systems

Cuneiform

The earliest forms of writing date back several thousand years (circa 3300 BCE) to the Sumerians of ancient Mesopotamia (now part of Iraq), who used a stylus made from a stick or reed to imprint triangular-shaped patterns onto clay tablets.[1] This form of writing is known as *cuneiform*, which comes from Latin, meaning "wedge-shaped." In its original form, cuneiform was a pictographic writing system, in which characters were drawings of objects such as a bird, a fish, or a loaf of bread. Later, abstract concepts or ideographs were added to the repertoire of characters. For example, combining the pictographs that stood for "ox" and "mountain" created the ideograph that represented "wild game." As cuneiform evolved, the pictographs changed to more abstract shapes that began to no longer look like the pictures they originally represented. Gradually, the shapes no longer represented objects, and by around 600 BCE, the symbols represented sounds that could be combined to form words. It is important to understand that cuneiform was not a language; rather it was a writing system adopted by various populations that spoke different languages. The cuneiform writing system eventually spread from the Sumerians to the Akkadians, Assyrians, Babylonians, and the Persians. Figure 2-1 shows a tablet containing a sample of cuneiform.

Hieroglyphics, Hieratic, and Demotic

The ancient Egyptians invented a writing system, which is called hieroglyphic writing from the Greek *hieros* meaning sacred, and *glyphos*, meaning inscriptions. The Egyptians may have gotten the idea of writing from the Sumerians, but recent findings suggest that the Egyptians may have invented writing independently. The first known writings in hieroglyphics date back to around 3100 BCE. Hieroglyphics were used until 396 CE, when the last hieroglyphic text was written on the walls of the temple of Isis on the island of Philae. The symbols in hieroglyphics can be used to represent both objects and sounds. Hieroglyphics also had a cursive form called *hieratic.* Hieroglyphs were typically used on hard surfaces that needed to be carved, such as limestone or plaster. The hieratic script was usually used when writing on linen or a paper-like substance made from reeds found along the Nile River called *papyrus.*

Hieratic script further evolved into a script called *demotic* sometime between 770 and 525 BCE. The name demotic comes from the Greek word *demotikos*, meaning popular. Demotic was written like hieratic with a reed brush, but the strokes were quicker and the script is much harder to discern from its hieroglyphic origins than hieratic. Demotic was mostly used in administrative texts. Hieratic and demotic

---

[1] Recent archaeological discoveries have found evidence of writing from around the same age in the Indus Valley (Pakistan).

were both written from right to left, while hieroglyphs were written in either direction as well as vertically. The Rosetta Stone, a large slab of black basalt currently housed in London's British Museum, was the key to deciphering the secrets of Egyptian hieroglyphics. The stone has a royal decree inscribed on it, praising King Ptolemy V in three scripts: Egyptian hieroglyphs, demotic, and Greek.

Figure 2-1. Cuneiform tablet

Phoenician Writing

The Phoenicians were a Semitic people who lived in the Near East, an area that is now part of Northern Israel, Lebanon, and Syria. The Greeks referred to these people as "Phoenician"; however, they are also known as Canaanites. The Phoenicians were sea traders who are credited with establishing many trade routes along the Mediterranean Sea.

By 1500 BCE, the Phoenicians had created what is believed to have been the first alphabet. Unfortunately, the Phoenicians documented most of their work on papyrus, which, being an organic material, has a tendency to decay over time. Some Phoenician inscriptions however, were written in stone. The earliest known surviving Phoenician inscription is the Ahiram epitaph at Byblos in Phoenicia, which dates back to the eleventh century BCE. The name of the town, Byblos, remains the root of many words related to writing, such as bibliography and Bible. The Phoenician alphabet consisted of 22 consonants and no vowels. This doesn't mean that vowels weren't used in speech; it was just understood that wrds cld b rd wtht vwls bsd n cntxt. Table 2-1 shows the Phoenician alphabet. The letters had a specific order and were given names. Letter names were words, and the first letter of the word was the sound the letter represented. This practice is known as *acrophony*. The shape of each letter was designed to represent the meaning of the word. For example, the Egyptian symbol for an ox head was used for the first letter Aleph and was read as "a." The symbol for the second letter was Beth, a house, and given the sound "b." The third letter Gimmel, a camel, had the sound "g," and so on.

Table 2-1. The Phoenician Alphabet

Symbol	Name	Meaning
𐤀	Aleph	Ox
𐤁	Beth	House
𐤂	Gimmel	Camel
𐤃	Daleth	Door
𐤄	He	Ladder
𐤅	Waw	Headrest
𐤆	Zayin	Sword
𐤇	Heth	Wall
𐤈	Tet	To be in
𐤉	Yodh	Arm
𐤊	Kaph	Hand
𐤋	Lamedh	Stick
𐤌	Mem	Water

Table 2-1. The Phoenician Alphabet (continued)

Symbol	Name	Meaning
𐤍	Nun	Fish (eel)
‡	Samekh	Fish
O	Ayin	Eye
7	Pe	Mouth
⌐	Tsadik	?
φ	Qoph	Monkey
◄	Resh	Head
W	Shin	Tooth
†	Taw	Sign

The Phoenician alphabet is the basis for many scripts in use today including Greek, Hebrew, Arabic, Cyrillic, and Latin. Table 2-2 shows the evolution of the Greek, Hebrew, and Latin alphabets from the Phoenician alphabet.

Table 2-2. Evolution of the Alphabet

Early Phoenician	Early Greek	Modern Greek	Hebrew	Latin
𐤀	A	A	א	A
⊴	8	B	ב	B
⌐	Λ	Γ	ג	G
◄	⊿	Δ	ד	D
𐤄	Ⅎ	E	ה	E
Y	Y		ו	F
Z	I	Z	ז	Z
‡	日	H	ח	H
•	⊗	Θ	ט	
Y	ζ	I	י	I
𐤊	Χ	K	כ	K
∠	Λ	Λ	ל	L
W	M	M	מ	M
𐤍	Ⅴ	N	נ	N
W	‡	Ξ	ס	
(	O	O	ע	O
7	Γ	Π	פ	P
⌐			צ	

Table 2-2. Evolution of the Alphabet (continued)

Early Phoenician	Early Greek	Modern Greek	Hebrew	Latin
ϙ	ϙ	Φ	ק	Q
◀	∢	P	ר	R
₩	⟨	Σ	ש	S
✝	Ⲭ	T	ת	T

Far East Writing Systems

Chinese Writing

Around 2700 BCE, the Chinese developed their own writing system. Like cunei-form, the Chinese writing system was originally written using pictographs, which gradually gave way to ideographs. Initially, the Chinese style of writing was more detailed and rounder, but with the introduction of the writing brush, Chinese characters developed a new appearance.

Chinese characters, or *hànzì* (漢字), are composed of strokes and are drawn to fit into an imaginary square.[2] There are six basic strokes. The order in which the strokes are drawn (stroke order) and the total number of strokes that produce the character (stroke count) are actually used as a mechanism for collation.[3] Table 2-3 shows some simple hànzì along with their stroke count.

Table 2-3. Simple Chinese Characters

Ideograph	Meaning	Origin	Stroke Count
人 (*rén*)	Man	A drawing of man walking.	2
木 (*mù*)	Tree	The vertical stroke represents the trunk; the horizontal stroke branches and the sweeping strokes represent the roots.	4
大 (*dà*)	Big	A man with outstretched arms.	3
天 (*tiān*)	Heaven	A big man whose head touches the sky.	4
日 (*rì*)	Sun	In ancient Chinese, the character was a circle with a line in the middle.	4
月 (*yuè*)	Moon	A picture of a crescent moon.	4

---

[2] For a more complete discussion of Chinese, Japanese, Korean, and Vietnamese writing systems, we encourage you to pick up a copy of O'Reilly's *CJKV Information Processing*, by Ken Lunde.

[3] The web site *http://www.ocrat.com/chargif* contains thousands of animated gifs for Chinese characters showing correct stroke order.

Table 2-3. Simple Chinese Characters (continued)

Ideograph	Meaning	Origin	Stroke Count
一 (*yī*)	One	A single stroke.	1
二 (*èr*)	Two	Two strokes.	2
文 (*wén*)	Writing	Pictograph of interlocking lines.	4
中 (*zhōng zhòng*)	Middle	Arrow going through a target.	4

A *radical* (部首) is a group of strokes that form a primitive used for classification. All Chinese characters contain at least one radical known as the main radical. Other radicals may exist in the character, but the main radical is used for indexing the character. In addition to stroke count and stroke order, words in Chinese may be sorted by radical. Often a combination of these collation methods is used.

Several characters can be combined together to form a more complex character called a *logical aggregate* or *compound ideograph*. The physical space for each character is the same; the individual characters are squeezed or stretched to ensure that the overall compound ideograph remains inside the boundary of the imaginary square. Table 2-4 shows some examples of logical aggregates. Without looking at the meaning, can you guess what the word could mean? Each character we list is composed of individual characters from Table 2-3. The manner in which the characters are arranged within the square is done to create visual beauty and balance. Figure 2-2 shows one, two, three, and four character combinations and their possible arrangements.

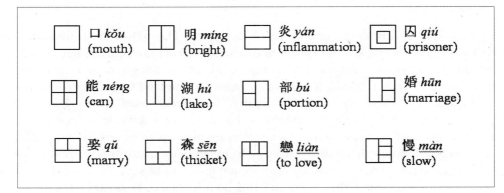

Figure 2-2. One, two, three, and four Chinese character combinations

Table 2-4. Logical Aggregate

Logical Aggregate	Meaning	Origin
明 (*míng*)	Bright	Sun 日 and moon 月 together
林 (*lín*)	Forest	Two trees 木 + 木
森 (*sēn*)	Thicket	Three trees 木 + 木 + 木
東 (*dōng*)	East	Sun 日 rising behind a tree 木
众 (*zhòng*)	Crowd	Three people 人 + 人 + 人

In addition to forming logical aggregates, Chinese characters can be combined to form more complex concepts known as *Chinese character compounds*. Table 2-5 lists some of these character compounds. See if you can figure out what the compounds mean from the individual characters.

Table 2-5. Chinese Character Compounds

Chinese Character Compound	Meaning	Origin
一月	January	One moon
二月	February	Two moons
中文	Chinese language	Middle [kingdom] + writing
中東	Middle East	Middle 中 and east 東

Some characters can be really complex. Take, for example, the 32-stroke character, 龘, which is a word meaning "the appearance of a dragon walking."

Chinese text layout

Chinese can be written in one of three directions. The older, more traditional method writes the characters vertically in columns with columns running right to left. In fact, this method is still the most common way of orienting text in Taiwan. Another way to format text, which is more common in Mainland China, is to write the characters in the same way English is written, horizontally from left to right. The problem with writing Chinese vertically is that it becomes difficult to incorporate English text, such as names and mathematical formulas. A third way to format Chinese text is to write it horizontally from right to left, although this is only done for short text—typically signs—that does not span a line. Unlike some other writing systems, such as the Latin script, words in hànzì do not need to be separated by space. This fact may make you think twice about all that code you probably wrote at some point, trying to parse words in text by looking for whitespace.

Character simplification

During the past 2,000 years, approximately 75,500 characters were added to the Chinese script. After gaining power in 1949, the new government of the Peoples Republic of China (PRC) planned to replace the hànzì characters with an alphabet similar to Latin. This idea was later dropped, and in 1956 the government instituted a plan to simplify the character set. Simplification was generally realized by eliminating some characters and reducing the number of strokes in others. Approximately 2,249 characters were simplified.

The two variants of Chinese writing are now referred to as *simplified* and *traditional* Chinese. Simplified Chinese is used in Mainland China and Singapore, while traditional Chinese is used in Taiwan and Hong Kong. In recent years, some traditional characters have made their way back to Mainland China, especially in the southern region. Table 2-6 shows both simplified and traditional Chinese characters.

Table 2-6. Traditional and Simplified Chinese Characters

Traditional	Simplified	Meaning
數	数	Number; Several; Count
國	国	Nation; Country
聲	声	Sound; Voice; Noise; Tone; Music
鑿	凿	Chisel; Bore; Pierce
語	语	Language

Transliteration methods

Languages that are not based on Chinese characters have adopted Chinese words. For example, the English words tea (茶), kung-fu (工夫), and silk (絲) were all borrowed from Chinese. The method of representing one set of characters in a foreign writing system is called *transliteration*. Several transliteration methods or phonetic scripts have been employed over the years for Chinese. In the nineteenth century, two lexicographers created the Wade-Giles (韋氏) system, which is based on the Latin alphabet. Wade-Giles is still used today, but mainly in libraries. In 1958, a different method of transliteration was adopted in the PRC, called Pinyin (拼音). The difference in the way some of the Chinese sounds were transliterated in these two methods is the reason why China's capital (北京) is now pronounced Beijing but used to be called Peking.

Pinyin uses four types of tone marks, or *diacritics*, over the Latin letters to indicate tone.[4] Sometimes a number following the Pinyin word, rather than a diacritic mark, represents tones. Table 2-7 shows the tone marks, the equivalent numbering system, and the tone that should be used. Note that the word's meaning changes completely based on tone.

Table 2-7. Pinyin Tone Marks

Tone	Number	Tone Mark	Meaning	Hànzì
dā	da1	Flat	Join together	搭
dá	da2	Rising	Attain; Reach	達
dǎ	da3	Falling-Rising	Beat; Strike	打
dà	da4	Falling	Big; Great	大

Taiwan, which is also known as the Republic of China (ROC), uses neither of these Latin-based transliteration methods. Instead, a method known as the *National Phonetic System* (注音符號), or *Zhuyin*, was invented in 1914 to help people learn to read Chinese characters. Zhuyin is not typically seen in Chinese writing. It is used to supplement Chinese characters as an aid to the reader. There are 37 characters in the Zhuyin character set, which appear in Table 2-8. The first four characters represent the sounds b, p, m, and f. This order gives Zhuyin its other common name, *Bopomofo*, much like the way the word alphabet is named after the first two letters in the Greek alphabet, alpha (α) and beta (β).

Table 2-8. Zhuyin Character Set

Zhuyin	Transliterated Sound	Zhuyin	Transliterated Sound
ㄅ	b	ㄘ	c
ㄆ	p	ㄙ	s
ㄇ	m	ㄚ	a
ㄈ	f	ㄛ	o
ㄉ	d	ㄜ	e
ㄊ	t	ㄝ	eh
ㄋ	n	ㄞ	ai
ㄌ	l	ㄟ	ei
ㄍ	g	ㄠ	au
ㄎ	k	ㄡ	ou
ㄏ	h	ㄢ	an
ㄐ	j	ㄣ	en

---

[4] The web site *http://www.uiowa.edu/~chinese/pinyin* has a Pinyin tutorial with sounds.

Table 2-8. Zhuyin Character Set (continued)

Zhuyin	Transliterated Sound	Zhuyin	Transliterated Sound
ㄑ	q	ㄤ	ang
ㄒ	x	ㄥ	eng
ㄓ	zh	ㄦ	er
ㄔ	ch	ㄧ	i
ㄕ	sh	ㄨ	u
ㄖ	r	ㄩ	iu
ㄗ	z		

Japanese Writing Systems

The Japanese adopted the Chinese characters *kanji* as their writing system beginning in 222 CE. Prior to this time, Japanese was only a spoken language. Over the next thousand years, the Japanese continued to borrow characters to add to their repertoire. In addition to the characters they borrowed from the Chinese, the Japanese created their own characters called *kokuji* (国字). Kokuji, like their Chinese counterparts, are composed of radicals and strokes, and can be combined with other Chinese characters to form logical aggregates or Chinese character compounds. In 1945, the Japanese government identified 1,850 characters for daily use. This number was increased to 1,945 characters in 1981 and was named *jōyō kanji*. The characters in jōyō kanji are taught in primary and secondary schools, and the Japanese government sanctions these characters for use in newspapers and other public documents. Kanji have multiple readings: a Japanese reading and at least one, but often two or more, Chinese readings. A reading is the manner in which a character is pronounced.

In the ninth century, two additional writing scripts were developed: hiragana (平仮名 – ひらがな) and katakana (片仮名 – カタカナ). Together, these scripts are referred to as *kana*. Kana are *syllabaries*, which means that each character represents a syllable. Hiragana and katakana both contain the same set of 46 sounds. Among these sounds are five vowels (a, i, u, e, and o). The remaining sounds are syllables combining a consonant with one of these vowels, except for the "n," which stands alone. In hiragana, the character for the syllable "sa" is さ, whereas the same sound in katakana is represented by the symbol サ.

Hiragana characters are more rounded than those in katakana. They are typically used in Japanese text as grammatical word endings, much like "ing" is added to action verbs in English. However, Japanese could theoretically be written entirely in hiragana, and many children's books are actually written this way. Table 2-9 shows the hiragana syllabary.

Table 2-9. The Hiragana Syllabary

	K	S	T	N	H	M	Y	R	W	G	Z	D	B	P
A	あ	か	さ	た	な	は	ま	や	ら	わ	が	ざ	だ	ば	ぱ
I	い	き	し	ち	に	ひ	み		り	ゐ	ぎ	じ	ぢ	び	ぴ
U	う	く	す	つ	ぬ	ふ	む	ゆ	る		ぐ	ず	づ	ぶ	ぷ
E	え	け	せ	て	ね	へ	め		れ	ゑ	げ	ぜ	で	べ	ぺ
O	お	こ	そ	と	の	ほ	も	よ	ろ	を	ご	ぞ	ど	ぼ	ぽ
N	ん														

Katakana is used to write foreign loan words, which have been incorporated into Japanese. For example, Internet (i.n.ta.-.ne.tu.to インターネット), computer (ko.n.pi.yu.-.ta コンピュータ), and web site (u.e.bu.sa.i.to ウエブサイト). The katakana syllabary is shown in Table 2-10.

Table 2-10. The Katakana Syllabary

	K	S	T	N	H	M	Y	R	W	G	Z	D	B	P
A	ア	カ	サ	タ	ナ	ハ	マ	ヤ	ラ	ワ	ガ	ザ	ダ	バ	パ
I	イ	キ	シ	チ	ニ	ヒ	ミ		リ	ヰ	ギ	ジ	ヂ	ビ	ピ
U	ウ	ク	ス	ツ	ヌ	フ	ム	ユ	ル		グ	ズ	ヅ	ブ	プ
E	エ	ケ	セ	テ	ネ	ヘ	メ		レ	ヱ	ゲ	ゼ	デ	ベ	ペ
O	オ	コ	ソ	ト	ノ	ホ	モ	ヨ	ロ	ヲ	ゴ	ゾ	ド	ボ	ポ
N	ン														

In Japanese, diacritics are used over certain kana characters. These marks, called *dakuten* (濁点) and *handakuten* (半濁点), appear over the characters on the right side of the kana matrixes displayed in Table 2-9 and Table 2-10.

A fourth script that is used in Japanese text is *rōmaji* (ローマ字), meaning Roman characters. Rōmaji contains the English alphabet and the European Arabic numbers, and is typically used for acronyms, western names, titles, and bilingual communication. It is not uncommon to see all four writing systems incorporated into the same Japanese text, as seen here:

スミスさんはＧＥ社に勤めている秘書です。

This sentence, which means "Mrs. Smith is a secretary at GE," is composed of the following segments:

Text	Writing System	Translated Meaning
スミス	Katakana	Sumisu – Smith
さんは	Hiragana	Mrs.
ＧＥ	Rōmaji	GE

Text	Writing System	Translated Meaning
社	Kanji	Company
に	Hiragana	
勤	Kanji	Work
めて	Hiragana	
いる	Hiragana	-ing
秘書	Kanji	Secretary
です	Hiragana	Is
。		Punctuation—end of sentence

Like Chinese writing, Japanese text can be oriented vertically from right to left and horizontally from left to right.

Korean Writing Systems

The Koreans also borrowed characters from the Chinese. The Korean reading for the Chinese characters is *hanja.* Prior to the fifteenth century, most people in Korea could not read the hanja, and reading was a skill reserved for nobles and scholars.

During the Yi Dynasty in 1440, King Sejong, frustrated by the fact that his own people could not communicate in writing, commissioned his court to produce a writing system that could be used by common people. The result was a text published in 1446 entitled *Hunmin chong-um,* which literally means "the correct sounds for the instruction of the people." The book describes the reason for creating a new script:

> "Being of foreign origin, Chinese characters are incapable of capturing uniquely Korean meanings. Therefore, many common people have no way to express their thoughts and feelings. Out of my sympathy for their difficulties, I have created a set of 28 letters. The letters are very easy to learn, and it is my fervent hope that they improve the quality of life of all people."

The script, which was also called Hunmin chong-um, did not become popular for several hundred years. In fact, Chinese characters were still used commonly in Korean published writings well into the twentieth century.

Today the script that is now called *Hangul* (한글) contains 40 letters composed of 19 consonants and 21 vowels. It has been said that Hangul is one of the most efficient alphabets ever designed and has been praised by linguists for its scientific design.

Individual letters in Hangul are referred to as *jamo*, the Korean word for alphabet. These consonants and vowels can be combined to form compound letters, allowing a total of 51 jamo.

Tables 2-11 and 2-12 list the jamo with their transliterated equivalents.

Table 2-11. Jamo Vowels

Jamo	Vowel	Jamo	Vowel
ㅏ	a	ㅠ	yu
ㅓ	eo	ㅒ	yae
ㅗ	o	ㅖ	ye
ㅜ	u	ㅘ	wa
ㅡ	eu	ㅙ	wae
ㅣ	i	ㅝ	weo
ㅐ	ae	ㅞ	we
ㅔ	e	ㅚ	oe
ㅑ	ya	ㅟ	wi
ㅕ	yeo	ㅢ	eui
ㅛ	yo		

Table 2-12. Jamo Consonants

Jamo	Initial	Medial	Final	Jamo	Initial	Medial	Final
ㄱ	k	g	k	ㅊ	ch	ch	t
ㄴ	n	n	n	ㅋ	k	k	k
ㄷ	t	d	t	ㅌ	t	t	t
ㄹ	r	r	l	ㅍ	p	p	p
ㅁ	m	m	m	ㅎ	h	h	t
ㅂ	p	b	p	ㄲ	kk	kk	k
ㅅ	s	sh	t	ㄸ	tt	tt	
ㅇ		ng	ng	ㅃ	pp	pp	
ㅈ	ch	j	t	ㅆ	ss	ss	t
				ㅉ	cc	cc	

Jamo cannot stand alone in hangul. They must be combined with other jamo to form a syllable according to the following three rules:

- A syllable begins with a consonant.

- A syllable has at least one consonant and one vowel.

- Each syllable must be written to fit in a square box.

For example, the word "hangul" is two syllables in which the first syllable contains the following letters (ㅎ ㅏ ㄴ) and the second syllable has the letters (ㄱ ㅡ ㄹ). When combined correctly, they form the two-syllable word 한글.[5]

Modern hangul syllables use either two or three jamo and consist of either a *consonant + vowel* or a *consonant + vowel + consonant*. Nineteen consonants can be initial consonants (*choseong*), all 21 vowels (*jungeong*) can be medial vowels, and 27 consonants can be final consonants (*jongseong*). Therefore, 399 two-jamo syllables can be formed (19*21) plus 10,733 three-jamo syllables (19*21*27), yielding a total of 11,172 modern hangul syllables. These symbols compose what is commonly called the *Johab* character set.

Bidirectional Scripts

Arabic Script

Arabic (*al arabia* - العربية), the language of the holy Qur'an, is spoken in more than 30 countries. The spread of Islam, beginning in the seventh century CE, helped ensure that the Arabic script would be adopted as far west as Spain and as far east as China. The Arabic alphabet consists of 28 letters, composed entirely of consonants. Three letters (alif, waaw, and ya) can also be used as long vowels.

The Arabic script is shown in Table 2-13. Note that some of the letters have the same basic shape and are distinguished from one another by diacritics called *nuqat* (نقط).

---

[5] The web site *http://catcode.com/kintro/index.htm* has a good tutorial on Hangul.

Table 2-13. The Arabic Alphabet

Letter Name	Glyph	Phonetic Symbol
Alif	أ	a
Ba	ب	b
Ta	ت	t
Tha	ث	th (as in "think")
Jeem	ج	j, g
Ha	ح	h (heavy)
Kha	خ	kh
Daal	د	d
Thaal	ذ	th (as in "the")
Ra	ر	r
Za	ز	z
Seen	س	s
Sheen	ش	sh
Sawd	ص	s (deep)
Dawd	ض	d (deep)
Ta	ط	t (deep)
Za	ظ	z (deep)
Ayn	ع	a (deep)
Ghayn	غ	gh
Fa	ف	f
Qaaf	ق	q
Kaaf	ك	k
Laam	ل	l
Meem	م	m
Noon	ن	n
Ha	ه	h
Waaw	و	w
Ya	ى	y

Several styles are used to write the Arabic script. The most popular style is called Naskh. An older, thicker style used in calligraphy and for writing the Qur'an is called Kufic. Urdu is typically written using a more cursive style known as Nastaliq. Arabic, as a Semitic script, is written from right to left. Numbers or Latin letters embedded in Arabic text are written from left to right, so Arabic, like Hebrew, is actually a bidirectional writing system. Whether it is handwritten, typed, or printed, Arabic is always cursive, meaning that the letters are joined. For example, the text "This is a new book," can be written in Arabic using the following sequence of letters:

هذا كتاب جديد

However, it isn't written correctly unless the letters are connected:

هذا كتاب جديد

Writing the text without connecting the letters would be considered unacceptable. An attribute of characters in Arabic is that they morph or change shape according to where they appear in a word. Table 2-14 shows the four forms of the Arabic letter ha.

Table 2-14. Four Cursive Forms of Arabic Letter Ha

Position	Glyph
Isolated	ه
Initial	ﻫ
Medial	ﻬ
Final	ﻪ

When certain characters in Arabic appear next to one another, two characters form a new shape called a *ligature.* One of the better-known Arabic ligatures is the laam-alif ligature. It is formed when the letter laam (ل) appears directly in front of the letter alif (ا). Remember, that Arabic is written from right to left, so the laam is on the right and the alif is on the left. This means that instead of seeing ل ا you would see the ligature لا. To make things even more complex, ligatures change shape based on the characters they appear next to. When the laam-alif ligature is joined by a character appearing before it (to the right of it), the ligature changes shape. So for example, the word salaam (سلام – peace) is composed of the characters seen, laam, alif, and meem. As you can see, the laam appears before the alif, which causes a ligature to be formed; however the laam is connected to the seen in front of it, which changes the shape of the ligature from لا to ﻼ. You can see this ligature more clearly in the enlarged Arabic word for peace (salaam):

Short vowels (*harakat* - حركات) are not required in written Arabic and are rarely used, though they always appear in the Qur'an and are used for elementary school books. This fact makes it difficult for people who are unfamiliar with the language to read the script correctly. For example:

$$\text{(b) } ب + \text{(n) } ن = بن$$

could be pronounced ban, bin, bun, etc. Without vowels, it is impossible to know how the word should be pronounced unless the reader understands the context in which the word appears.

When short vowels are used, they take the form of little marks that can appear above or below the letters in a word. A *fatHa* (فتحة) represents a short "a" sound, as in the word "hammer." It appears as a diagonal stroke above the letter it affects. A *kasra* (كسرة) indicates a short "i" sound, as in "lit." It appears as a diagonal stroke below the letter it affects. A *dumma* (ضمة) is a short "u" sound, as in "put." It appears as a small waaw above the letter it modifies. When no vowel sound occurs after a letter, a resting symbol, *sukoon* (سكون), is used. Finally, when a consonant appears in a word twice, it is written once and a *shadda* (شدة) symbol is placed above the character. The reader should emphasize the doubled consonant when pronouncing the word. Table 2-15 shows these symbols and provides examples of how they are used.

Table 2-15. Basic Arabic Diacritics

Vowel Name	Symbol	Sound	Example	Transliteration
FatHa	´	Short "a"	بَدر	badr
Kasra	ˏ	Short "i"	مِن	min
Dumma	˒	Short "u"	حُب	Hub
Sukoon	°	None	إبْن	ibn
Shadda	˜	Doubling	حمّة	Humma

Note also that when the *shadda* appears in combination with the *fatHa*, the *fatHa* always appears above the *shadda* (ﹼ). If the *shadda* appears in combination with the *kasra*, the *kasra* moves from below the character to above the character, but always appears below the *shadda* (ﹼ).

The Arabic script is also used to write other languages, such as Afghan, Farsi, Pashto, Sindhi, and Urdu. It has been used to write Hebrew, Spanish, and even Chinese! Some languages have sounds that aren't represented in the basic Arabic script, so other letters have been added. The basic shapes of the letters are usually the same, but additional *nuqat* (dots) are added. For example, in Farsi, the character پ represents the sound "p," which is not part of the Arabic language.

Hebrew Script

Hebrew (*Ivrit* - עברית) is one of the world's oldest languages and is the language in which the Old Testament was written. The Jews took the script with them when they were exiled from Israel to the Diaspora. For that reason, the Hebrew script has been used to write Arabic, Ladino (Judeo-Spanish), Spanish, and Yiddish (a language that is about 80 percent German), in addition to Hebrew. The alphabet contains 22 characters, which are all consonants. Five of the consonants have a different form when they appear at the end of the word. Table 2-16 shows the Hebrew alphabet. As with Arabic, the script is written from right to left and numbers embedded in a Hebrew sentence are written from left to right.

Table 2-16. Hebrew Alphabet

Dfoos (Printed)		Kteev (Cursive)		Name	Sound
Letter	Final	Letter	Final		
א		k		Aleph	a
ב		ə		Bet	b or v
ג		c		Gimmel	g
ד		ə		Dalet	d
ה		ə		Heh	h
ו		ı		Vav	v or w
ז		ɔ		Zien	z
ח		n		Chet	ch
ט		c		Tet	t
י		'		Yod	i or y
כ	ך	ɔ	ק	Chaf	ch
ל		ɣ		Lamed	l
מ	ם	N	ạ	Mem	m
נ	ן	J	ı	Nun	n
ס		o		Somach	s
ע		ﻉ		Ayn	a
פ	ף	ə	ℓ	Pay	p or f

Table 2-16. Hebrew Alphabet (continued)

Dfoos (Printed)		Kteev (Cursive)			
Letter	Final	Letter	Final	Name	Sound
צ	ץ	3	ℓ	Tsadek	ts
ק		ρ		Kuf	k
ר		ๅ		Raysh	r
ש		e		Shin	s or sh
ת		ת		Tuf	t

Modern Hebrew uses two scripts. One script called *kteev* (כתיב), a more cursive form, is used only for handwriting; the other, called *dfoos* (דפוס), a square block style, is used only for printed text.

Vowels are not required in written Hebrew (although letters are used for vowels when writing Yiddish). In fact, until about the eighth century, vowels did not exist. During that time, a system of markings was developed to indicate the vowels. These diacritical marks, *nekudot* (נקודות), appear above, in the middle, or below the letters they affect. They are used for religious texts, teaching Hebrew, poetry and spelling foreign words. Some letters in the Hebrew script can take two sounds, depending on the rules of the language for which the script is used. Typically, a reader would have to know what sound the letter makes based on the rules of grammar for the language. When diacritical marks are used, the harder of the two sounds is represented by a dot in the middle of the letter called a *dagesh* (דגש). For example, the letter pay (פ - with a dagesh), has a "p" sound, while the letter pay (פ - without a dagesh) has an "f" sound.

Greek, Latin, and Cyrillic

Greek Script

The Greek alphabet first appeared around the eighth century BCE. The alphabet was based on the Phoenician writing system, with which the Greeks had significant contact. The Greeks however, added the concept of distinct letters representing specific sounds to their alphabet, which to this point had not been included in a writing system. An earlier Greek writing system called Linear B was used around 1500 BCE but was no longer in use by approximately 1200 BCE.

Initially, Greek was written horizontally, either left to right, right to left, or *boustrophedon*. Boustrophedon is a term that literally means "as the ox turns" and comes from the alternate directions the lines are written in: first left to right (or vice versa), then upon reaching the end of the line, continuing on the line below in the reverse direction like the furrows of a plough. Interestingly, when the lines were written right to left, the letters were actually mirrored to face the opposite direction than when they were written from left to right. Additionally, early Greek writing did not have accents over letters or spaces between words. Accents were not needed because native Greek speakers knew how to pronounce words correctly. However, due in part to the spread of Greek philosophy and literature, the Greek writing system was read by more and more non-native speakers of Greek. Around 200 BCE, Aristophanes of Byzantium introduced accents and breathing marks to aid non-native speakers in reading Greek texts. Classical Greek employed a polytonic system using three accents and one or two breathings. Modern Greek, which began to develop around the ninth century CE, also used this polytonic system up until 1982.

Today, Modern Greek uses a monotonic system, which requires only one accent to indicate which syllable in a word should be stressed. The alphabet contains 24 letters, of which seven letters (alpha (α), epsilon (ε), eta (η), iota (ι), omicron (o), upsilon (υ), and omega (ω)) are vowels; however, there are only five vowel sounds. Table 2-17 shows the Greek alphabet while Table 2-18 shows the five possible Greek vowel sounds.

Table 2-17. Greek Alphabet

Upper Case	Lower Case	Letter Name	Upper Case	Lower Case	Letter Name
A	α	Alpha	N	ν	Nu
B	β	Beta	Ξ	ξ	Xi
Γ	γ	Gamma	O	o	Omicron
Δ	δ	Delta	Π	π	Pi
E	ε	Epsilon	P	ρ	Rho
Z	ζ	Zeta	Σ	ς, σ	Sigma[6]
H	η	Eta	T	τ	Tau
Θ	θ	Theta	Y	υ	Upsilon
I	ι	Iota	Φ	φ	Phi
K	κ	Kappa	X	χ	Chi
Λ	λ	Lambda	Ψ	ψ	Psi
M	μ	Mu	Ω	ω	Omega

---

[6] ς is a final form and occurs only at the end of words.

Table 2-18. Greek Vowel Sounds

English Equivalent	Greek Letters
a	α
e	ε, αι
i	ι, η, υ, ει, οι, υι
o	ο, ω
u	Ου

A couple of punctuation symbols in Greek are slightly different from what you might be used to. The symbol used for a question mark looks like a semicolon (;) as in:

Greek	English
Πώς ειόθεε;	How are you?

The symbol denoting a separator between two thoughts appears in Greek as a dot set high above the line (·).

Latin Script

In the first century CE, the Romans adapted the Greek alphabet to create their own Latin alphabet consisting of 23 capital letters. The alphabet soon evolved to include the letters J, U, and W, forming a 26-letter alphabet. Eventually people began using small letters called *minuscules* in addition to capital letters.

NOTE   The terms *upper-* and *lowercase* didn't arrive until the introduction of the print-
            ing press. The printing press operated on the concept of moveable type. No
            longer was it necessary to carve a piece of wood (with the letters in reverse) for
            each page that needed to be printed. The printer could simply select the char-
            acters needed for a given page and place them in the correct order. The let-
            ters were stored in cases arranged in alphabetical order. Capital letters were
            stored in the upper case, while small letters were stored in the lower case. This
            placement gave rise to the terms we use today.

Today the Latin script is used to write many languages in all parts of the world. What you may not realize, however, is that the 26 letters used for writing English are just a subset of the complete set of characters that make up the Latin script. For example, the Scandinavian languages have three additional letters that appear after the letter Z. Finnish and Swedish have the three letters (Å, Ä, and Ö). Danish and Norwegian also have three additional letters appearing after the letter Z but they are different letters (Æ, Ø, and Å). These languages actually have 29 letters in their alphabet.

Now let's take a look at the German letters Ä, Ö, and Ü. Two of these letters look like the same letters that appear at the end of the Swedish alphabet; however, they are not. Letters in German that have diacritics are not considered distinct letters as they are in the Scandinavian languages; they are simply characters that happen to have an accent mark. In other words, "A" and "Ä" in German represent the same letter but are read with a different sound, whereas "A" and "Ä" in Swedish are two completely different letters.

Typically, when you think of the Latin script, languages such as English, French, Spanish, and Italian come to mind. Christian missionaries have carried the Latin script to many parts of the world. For example, Vietnamese, which was once written using Chinese ideographs, now uses a Latin alphabet. Likewise, missionaries brought the Latin script to the Hawaiian Islands. The Hawaiian alphabet is the shortest alphabet in the world. It consists of 12 letters composed of five vowels (a, e, i, o, and u) and seven consonants (h, k, l, m, n, p, and w). Turkish was once written using the Arabic script; however in 1928, Turkey's President Mustafa Kemal Atatürk declared that Turkish would be written using a modified version of the Latin alphabet, consisting of 8 vowels and 21 consonants. Table 2-19 provides a sample of different languages and their alphabets.

Table 2-19. Latin Alphabets

French	Icelandic	Polish	Spanish	Turkish	Vietnamese
A a	A a	A a	A a	A a	A a
B b	Á á	Ą ą	B b	B b	Ă ă
C c	B b	B b	C c	C c	Â â
D d	C c	C c	CH ch	Ç ç	B b
E e	D d	Ć ć	D d	D d	C c
F f	Ð ð	D d	E e	E e	D d
G g	E e	E e	F f	F f	Đ đ
H h	É é	Ę ę	G g	G g	E e
I i	F f	F f	H h	Ğ ğ	Ê ê
J j	G g	G g	I i	H h	G g
K k	H h	H h	J j	I ı	H h
L l	I i	I i	K k	İ i	I i
M m	Í í	J j	L l	J j	K k
N n	J j	K k	LL ll	K k	L l
O o	K k	L l	M m	L l	M m

Table 2-19. Latin Alphabets (continued)

French	Icelandic	Polish	Spanish	Turkish	Vietnamese
P p	L l	Ł ł	N n	M m	N n
Q q	M m	M m	Ñ ñ	N n	O o
R r	N n	N n	O o	O o	Ô ô
S s	O o	Ń ń	P p	Ö ö	Ò ò
T t	Ó ó	O o	Q q	P p	P p
U u	P p	Ó ó	R r	R r	Q q
V v	Q q	P p	S s	S s	R r
W w	R r	R r	T T	Ş ş	S s
X x	S s	S s	U u	T t	T t
Y y	T t	Ś ś	V v	U u	U u
Z z	U u	T t	W w	Ü ü	Ù ù
	Ú ú	U u	X x	V v	V v
	V v	W w	Y y	Y y	X x
	W w	Y y	Z z	Z z	Y y
	X x	Z z			
	Y y	Ź ź			
	Ý ý	Ż ż			
	Z z				
	Þ þ				
	Æ æ				
	Ö ö				

Cyrillic Script

The Cyrillic alphabet is related to Greek. However, unlike Latin, which evolved over a long period of time, Cyrillic was invented. In 862 CE, Emperor Michael III sent two Greek monks, who happened to be brothers, St. Cyril and St. Methodius, to Moravia (now part of the Czech Republic) to spread the word of Christianity. The Moravians spoke a language called Slavonic, which did not have a writing system.[7] To translate the Bible into Slavonic, the missionaries created an alphabet based on Greek characters that would express the sounds of the Slavonic language.[8] The result is the Cyrillic alphabet, which bears the name of one brother, St. Cyril.

---

[7] The language today is referred to as Old Church Slavonic.

[8] Some controversy still exists over who actually invented the script. Some scholars believe that followers of St. Cyril should be credited with the work.

Today the Cyrillic script is used to write Belarusian, Bulgarian, Russian, Serbian, and Ukrainian.[9] It is also used by many non-Slavic people who once belonged to the former Soviet Union. Table 2-20 shows the Cyrillic alphabet as used in various languages.

Table 2-20. Cyrillic Alphabets

Bulgarian **Български**	**Belarusian** **Беларускі**	**Russian** **Русский**	**Serbian** **Сррпски**	**Ukrainian** **Українська**
А а	А а	А а	А а	А а
Б б	Б б	Б б	Б б	Б б
В в	В в	В в	В в	В в
Г г	Г г	Г г	Г г	Г г
Д д	Д д	Д д	Д д	Д д
Е е	Е е	Е е	Ђ ђ	Е е
Ж ж	Ё ё	Ё ё	Е е	Ж ж
З з	Ж ж	Ж ж	Ж ж	З з
И и	З з	З з	З з	И и
Й й	І і	И и	И и	Й й
К к	Й й	Й й	Ј ј	К к
Л л	К к	К к	К к	Л л
М м	Л л	Л л	Л л	М м
Н н	М м	М м	Љ љ	Н н
О о	Н н	Н н	М м	О о
П п	О о	О о	Н н	П п
Р р	П п	П п	Њ њ	Р р
С с	Р р	Р р	О о	С с
Т т	С с	С с	П п	Т т
У у	Т т	Т т	Р р	У у
Ф ф	У у	У у	С с	Ф ф
Х х	Ў ў	Ф ф	Т т	Х х
Ц ц	Ф ф	Х х	Ћ ћ	Ц ц
Ч ч	Х х	Ц ц	У у	Ч ч
Ш ш	Ц ц	Ч ч	Ф ф	Ш ш
Щ щ	Ч ч	Ш ш	Х х	Щ щ
Ъ ъ	Ш ш	Щ щ	Ц ц	Ь ь

---

[9] Prior to the collapse of Yugoslavia, the spoken language had a common name among all the republics; now each republic except Montenegro has changed the name of its national language (Serbian, Croatian, or Bosnian) to replace the name of the language once referred to as Serbo-Croatian.

Table 2-20. Cyrillic Alphabets (continued)

Bulgarian Български	Belarusian Беларускі	Russian Русский	Serbian Српски	Ukrainian Українська
Ь ь	Ы ы	Ъ ъ	Ч ч	Ю ю
Ю ю	Ь ь	Ы ы	Ц ц	Я я
Я я	Э э	Ь ь	Ш ш	Є є
	Ю ю	Э э		І і
	Я я	Ю ю		Ї ї
		Я я		

Religion often plays an important role in influencing the use of a script in writing a spoken language. This was the case with the spread of Islam and the use of the Arabic script, as we discussed earlier. Likewise, Jews in the Diaspora used the Hebrew script to write languages of the country where they happened to be living. This was also the case with Christianity. The influence of the Byzantine Church (Eastern Orthodox) resulted in languages using the Cyrillic script, while regions influenced by the Roman Catholic Church used the Latin script.

An interesting result is the phenomenon that occurs in Montenegro. Montenegrin can be written with either the Cyrillic or the Latin alphabet. Table 2-21 shows the Montenegrin alphabet in both writing systems.

Table 2-21. Montenegrin Letters in Cyrillic and Latin Alphabets

Cyrillic	Latin	Cyrillic	Latin
А а	A a	Н н	L l
Б б	B b	Њ њ	Lj lj
В в	C c	О о	M m
Г г	Č č	П п	N n
Д д	Ć ć	Р р	Nj nj
Ђ ђ	D d	С с	O o
Е е	Dž dž	Т т	P p
Ж ж	Đ đ	Ћ ћ	R r
З з	E e	У у	S s
И и	F f	Ф ф	Š š
Ј ј	G g	Х х	T t
К к	H h	Ц ц	U u
Л л	I i	Ч ч	V v
Љ љ	J j	Џ џ	Z z
М м	K k	Ш ш	Ž ž

Indic Scripts

Several writing systems exist in India today. Most of them are descendents of the ancient Brahmi script, which include Devanagari, Gujarati, Punjabi, Bengali, Oriya, Telugu, Kannada, Tamil, and Malayalam. Devanagari is the script that was used to write Sanskrit, a sacred language, and is now used to write Hindi and other languages spoken in India. Table 2-22 provides a list of consonants for a subset of the Indic writing systems.

Table 2-22. Consonants from Several Indic Scripts

Sound	Devanagari	Oriya	Tamil	Malayalam
k	क	କ	க	ക
kh	ख	ଖ	—	ഖ
g	ग	ଗ	—	ഗ
gh	घ	ଘ	—	ഘ
n'	ङ	ଙ	ங	ങ
c	क	କ	க	ക
ch	ख	ଖ	—	ഖ
j	ग	ଗ	—	ഗ
jh	घ	ଘ	—	ഘ
ñ	ङ	ଙ	ங	ങ
t	च	ଚ	ச	ച
th	छ	ଛ	—	ഛ
d	ज	ଜ	ஜ	ജ
dh	झ	ଝ	—	ഝ
n'	ञ	ଞ	ஞ	ഞ
t'	ट	ଟ	ட	ട
th	ठ	ଠ	—	ഠ
d	ड	ଡ	—	ഡ
dh	ढ	ଢ	—	ഢ
n	ण	ଣ	ண	ണ
p	त	ତ	த	ത
ph	थ	ଥ	—	ഥ
b	द	ଦ	—	ദ
bh	ध	ଧ	—	ധ
m	न	ନ	ந	ന
y	प	ପ	ப	പ
r	फ	ଫ	—	ഫ
l	ब	ଵ	—	ബ

Table 2-22. Consonants from Several Indic Scripts (continued)

Sound	Devanagari	Oriya	Tamil	Malayalam
v	भ	ଭ	—	ഭ
sh	म	ମ	ம	മ
shh	य	ଯ	ய	യ
s	र	ର	ர	ര
h	ल	ଲ	ல	ല

The Indic scripts are considered complex writing systems because, like Arabic, they contain complex ligatures. The character display order is sometimes different than the order in which they are typed. For example, in Figure 2-3, the word "Hindi" in Devanagari is typed as shown on the left, but is rendered as shown on the right.

Figure 2-3. Rendering "Hindi" in Devanagari

For a fairly intuitive set of lessons on how to read several Indic scripts, look at UK India online at *http://www.ukindia.com*. Eden Golshani also compiled a nice collection of charts on Indic scripts, which is available on his web site at *http://www.geocities.com/Athens/Academy/9594*.

Thai Script

The Thai writing system evolved from the Brahmi script. Thai is written horizontally from left to right with no spaces separating words. The reader determines word boundaries based on context. This feature adds a certain level of complexity to programs that need to parse words out of text or implement some kind of line breaking algorithm. The only way to implement text parsing correctly is by using a dictionary lookup, and even then 100 percent accuracy is not guaranteed. The alphabet consists of 44 consonants. The consonants are divided into three groups: medium, high, and low, categorized by their tonal properties as shown in Table 2-23.

Table 2-23. Thai Consonants

Medium		High		Low			
	ก ko	ข kho	ฃ kho	ค kho	ฅ kho	ฆ kho	ง ngo
	จ co	ฉ cho		ช cho	ซ so	ฌ cho	ญ yo
ฎ do	ฏ to	ฐ tho		ฑ tho		ฒ tho	ณ no
ด do	ต to	ถ tho		ท tho		ธ tho	น no
บ bo	ป po	ผ pho	ฝ fo	พ pho	ฟ fo	ภ pho	ม mo
				ย yo	ร ro	ล lo	ว wo
		ศ so	ษ so				
		ส so	ห ho	ฬ lo			
อ 'o				ฮ ho			

The vowels in the Thai script appear as diacritics before, after, above, below, or surrounding the consonant. In the latter case, the diacritic consists of multiple pieces that must surround the consonant. This feature is one reason why the Thai script is considered complex from a computing standpoint. Table 2-24 shows the vowel marks used to create the 28 vowel sounds. The consonant อ is used as a placeholder.

Table 2-24. Thai Vowel Sounds

อะ	อา	อิ	อี
อึ	อื	อุ	อู
เอะ	เอ	แอะ	แอ
โอะ	โอ	เอาะ	ออ
อัวะ	อัว	เอียะ	เอีย
เอือ	เอื้อ	เออะ	เออ
อำ	ใอ	ไอ	เอา

Thai is considered a tonal language. There are five tones representing mid, low, falling, high, and rising. The tones are indicated by one of four tone marks that appear above both the character and any vowels that may appear. The four tone marks are shown below, and again, ฤ is used as a placeholder:

In addition to the complexities mentioned earlier, Thai writing is complicated because the script has four levels associated with it, as shown in Figure 2-4.

Figure 2-4. Thai text showing four separate levels

Punctuation

The markings used to indicate punctuation differ not only between scripts, but also between languages using the same script. As an example, Table 2-25 shows some common punctuation marks and how they vary among different languages. This list is not complete, but it should give you some idea of the variations used around the world. You might think twice about using a question mark (?) to represent a help icon in your application.

Table 2-25. Punctuation in Different Languages.

Quotes	Period/Full Stop	Question Mark
"English"	English.	English?
« French »	日本語。	¿Spanish?
„German"	Hindi I	Greek;
"Swedish"		ʕcibarA[10]
»Slovenian«		
『日本語』		

---

[10] Read from right to left.

Summary

This chapter described several different writing systems. Each of these writing systems has features that create challenges for software developers who are building internationalized applications. We summarize these attributes here:

Script Type

Alphabetic

> The individual units for writing are composed of consonants, and in some cases, vowels. When combined, they spell out words phonetically. Arabic, Cyrillic, Latin, Greek, Hebrew, Indic, and Thai scripts are all examples of alphabetic scripts.

Syllabic

> The individual units for writing are composed of syllables. The Japanese kana and Korean hangul are examples of syllabic scripts.

Ideographic

> A writing system that uses pictures or symbols to represent words. Chinese is an example of an ideographic writing system.

Context-Dependent Glyph Shaping

Positional

> The shape of a character can change based on its position within a word. Characters in the Arabic, Greek, and Hebrew scripts have this attribute.

Ligatures

> Certain characters combine to form a different shape when they appear next to one another. The shape of the ligature can also depend on the characters that appear before or after it. In Arabic and Indic scripts, the use of ligatures is mandatory.

Cursive

> Arabic is an example of a writing system that requires a cursive form.

Text Direction

Left to Right

Text is written horizontally from left to right on the page.

Bidirectional

In writing systems such as Arabic and Hebrew, the text is written horizontally from right to left, except for numbers and embedded Latin text, which are written from left to right.

Vertical

In some writing systems, such as Chinese and Japanese, text can be written vertically in columns. The columns run from the right side of the page to the left.

Other Characteristics

Diacritics

Special marks used for accents, tones, and vowels, or to uniquely identify a character. In some writing systems, such as Indic and Thai, diacritics can span multiple characters.

Word Separator

Most writing systems use spaces to separate words. Exceptions to this rule include Chinese, Japanese, and Thai.

Punctuation

Marks are inconsistent within and across writing systems.

3

Locales

In this chapter we explore the concepts of the locale in Java. The documentation for the `Locale` class in Java describes a locale as "a specific geographic, political, or cultural region." Other classes use `Locale` objects to perform functions such as formatting data output in a locale-specific manner. For example, the `DateFormat` class in Java contains methods, such as `getTimeInstance(int)` and `getTimeInstance(int, Locale)`, for the application to retrieve the time formatter for the default and given locale.

You needn't worry about getting into the details of the `Locale` class. A `Locale` object provides information to other classes that need to perform locale-specific operations. The examples in this chapter focus on what methods of the `Locale` class are called and what information they return.

Defining a Locale

Locales represent a specific region or language that an application supports. Properly internationalized software uses localization features in the language to tailor the application at runtime to the particular region or language. Operations that depend on locale-specific data (e.g., text messages and GUI elements) are said to be *locale-sensitive*. In Java, locale-sensitive operations use the `Locale` class found in the `java.util` package.

A common locale-sensitive operation involves date formatting. In the United States, the string "08/10/1976" represents August 10 of the year 1976. However, Mexicans would interpret that same string as October 8 of the same year.

Working with the Locale Class

The Locale class in Java is easy to use. It is meant to be an identification class that is ultimately used by other classes performing locale-sensitive operations. Let's look at Example 3-1, a simple application that displays the days of the week using locale-specific formatting. The output of this program for U.S. English, U.K. English, and Canadian French was shown in Chapter 1, *Introduction to Internationalization.* We'll take each line step by step to illustrate the use of the Locale class.

Example 3-1. Displaying the Days of the Week for a Specific Locale

```
import java.util.*;
import java.text.*;

public class DaysOfTheWeek {

  public static void main(String argv[]) {

    Locale usersLocale;

    if (argv.length == 2)
      usersLocale = new Locale(argv[0], argv[1]);
    else if (argv.length == 3)
      usersLocale = new Locale(argv[0], argv[1], argv[2]);
    else
      usersLocale = Locale.getDefault();

    DateFormatSymbols dfs = new DateFormatSymbols(usersLocale);
    String weekdays[] = dfs.getWeekdays();

    Calendar cal = Calendar.getInstance(usersLocale);

    int firstDayOfWeek = cal.getFirstDayOfWeek();
    int dayOfWeek;

    for (dayOfWeek = firstDayOfWeek; dayOfWeek < weekdays.length; dayOfWeek++)
      System.out.println(weekdays[dayOfWeek]);

    for (dayOfWeek = 0; dayOfWeek < firstDayOfWeek; dayOfWeek++)
      System.out.println(weekdays[dayOfWeek]);
  }
}
```

We first ensure that the user passed in command-line parameters to use for the language, country, and variant. If so, we construct a Locale object with the user-supplied information; otherwise we use the default locale.

What's the default locale? Each time you invoke a Java program, the default locale is constructed from your environment, using your language and region preferences. Command-line parameters also exist to override the default locale. The user.language and user.region parameters enable the user to set the default language and country from the command line.[1] Setting the default locale in this manner is only persistent for the life of the JVM. It is not a permanent change to your environment.

Once we've got our Locale object, we use the DateFormatSymbols class, which contains methods to get data such as names of the days of the week, names of months, and the time zone. After we get the array of strings containing names of days of the week, we construct a Calendar object to iterate over the days of the week array. Finally, we print out the days of the week and there you go! You've just experienced how easy it is to write a global Java program.

Locale Constructors

Two constructors for creating Locale objects are provided. They are:

```
Locale(String language, String country)
Locale(String language, String country, String variant)
```

You'll often work with the first constructor in which you specify the ISO-639 language code (in lowercase) and the ISO-3166 country code (in uppercase). Appendix A, *Language and Country Codes*, provides a complete listing for each of these codes.

In Example 3-1, we saw how a Locale object could be constructed using a language and country code. Let's look at the code in Example 3-2 closely so you can see how this is done.

Example 3-2. Two-Argument Constructor for Locale Class

```
1: public class DaysOfTheWeek {
2:
3:     public static void main(String argv[]) {
4:
5:
6:         Locale usersLocale;
7:
8:         if (argv.length == 2)
9:             usersLocale = new Locale(argv[0], argv[1]);
10:        else if (argv.length == 3)
11:            usersLocale = new Locale(argv[0], argv[1], argv[2]);
12:        else
13:            usersLocale = Locale.getDefault();
```

---

[1] Specifying settings for the default locale using the –D argument is both undocumented and implementation-dependent.

If you look at line 9 from Example 3-2, you'll see that we grab the first two arguments from the command line and use them as language and country codes, respectively, to create a `Locale` object.

The three-argument constructor creates a `Locale` object for specifying language, country or region, and vendor- or browser-specific variant or subregion. This constructor is also the portion of the `Locale` class used to specify whether a given country uses the euro currency. For example, you could use WIN to specify Windows or MAC to specify Macintosh. The use of variants is explained in a later section of this chapter.

As we said earlier, system properties exist so users can set the default language and country from the command line. They are `user.language` and `user.region`. Here are some examples of how you'd use these properties to run the previous example to produce the results listed in Chapter 1:

```
    English in the United States
C:\>java -Duser.language=en -Duser.region=US DaysOfTheWeek

    English in the United Kingdom
C:\>java -Duser.language=en -Duser.region=GB DaysOfTheWeek

    French in Canada
C:\>java -Duser.language=fr -Duser.region=CA DaysOfTheWeek
```

Here's an interesting tidbit that you might not have known about the `user.region` property. Java allows you to set this property using the following forms: `country`, `country_variant`, or `variant`. So the following `user.region` settings would be legal: `user.region=CA`, `user.region=CA_WIN`, and `user.region=_WIN`. Although the ISO language codes are defined as lowercase and the ISO country codes are defined as uppercase, the `Locale` constructors are actually case insensitive.

Language Codes

ISO-639 defines the standard set of two-letter, lowercase codes used to identify languages from around the world. Appendix A contains a reprint of all the ISO-639 codes. One should be aware of a number of issues when referencing these codes.

The ISO-639 standard is not stable. The codes have changed over the years and there is a chance that they will change again in the future. Three languages in particular have two distinct ISO-639 codes: Hebrew, Indonesian, and Yiddish.[2] The codes in Table 3-1 are reprinted from part of the ISO-639 table in Appendix A.

---

[2] `Locale` class constructors in Java accept both the old and the new codes; however, all API calls on the `Locale` class return the old code.

Table 3-1. ISO-639 Codes for Hebrew, Indonesian, and Yiddish

Language	ISO Code
Hebrew	iw, he[3]
Indonesian	in, id
Yiddish	ji, yi

Some current programs use both variations of the ISO codes. New software should follow these simple guidelines to ensure maximum compatibility:

- When reading in data, read and interpret both variations on the ISO language code.

- When writing out data, use the oldest variation on the language. The oldest is the first instance listed in the ISO codes for each language.

All of the ISO-639 language codes are available online.[4]

Country Codes

ISO-3166 defines a standard two- and three-letter code for countries around the world. The entire table, listing country, two-letter ISO code, and three-letter ISO code, are reprinted in Appendix A.

All ISO-3166 country codes are also available online.[5]

Use of Variants

Variants are used to further differentiate locales beyond the level of country. As we mentioned before, this differentiation can tailor output for a specific browser or operating system. You could output specific messages for Windows users as opposed to Solaris users.

Variants can also differentiate dialects within a particular country or region. A New Yorker might remark, "Have a nice day," whereas a Texan might say, "Y'all come back now." Variants are a convenient way to localize your program further.

---

[3] If you request the "he" locale, it is actually an alias to the "iw" locale, and the "iw" resources are loaded. Subsequent calls to retrieve the name for that locale will return "iw."

[4] *http://www.unicode.org/unicode/onlinedat/languages.html* and *http://www.ics.uci.edu/pub/ietf/http/related/ iso639.txt*

[5] *http://www.unicode.org/unicode/onlinedat/countries.html* and *http://userpage.chemie.fu-berlin.de/diverse/doc/ ISO_3166.html*

Using the example above, you could conceive of a `Locale` object constructed for New York and Texas that might look like:

```
Locale newyorkLocale = new Locale("en", "US", "NY");
Locale texasLocale = new Locale("en", "US", "TX");
```

Java also supports fine-grained specification of a variant by separating each variant's component with an underscore (_) character. An example of this specification looks like:

```
Locale winTXLocale = new Locale("en", "US", "WIN_tx");
```

Here we have constructed a `Locale` object with the following properties: the language is English, the region is the United States, and the variant indicates Windows in Texas.

Java uses the variant portion of the `Locale` class for locales that support the Euro currency. An example of a locale string with the Euro variant applied is "de_DE_EURO." All locales that support the Euro currency use the string EURO as the variant.

Using Constants to Define Common Locales

The `Locale` class already defines a number of commonly used locales as constants. Instead of constructing a `Locale` object with the proper language and country codes, you can use these locales. Table 3-2 lists these predefined locales. They may be appropriate as a country, a language, or both, as with `Locale.FRANCE`, `Locale.FRENCH`, and `Locale.CANADA_FRENCH`, respectively.

Table 3-2. Constant Locales Defined in Locale Class

```
Locale.CANADA

Locale.CANADA_FRENCH

Locale.CHINA

Locale.CHINESE

Locale.ENGLISH

Locale.FRANCE

Locale.FRENCH

Locale.GERMAN

Locale.GERMANY

Locale.ITALIAN

Locale.ITALY

Locale.JAPAN
```

Table 3-2. Constant Locales Defined in Locale Class (continued)

Locale.JAPANESE

Locale.KOREA

Locale.KOREAN

Locale.PRC

Locale.SIMPLIFIED_CHINESE

Locale.TAIWAN

Locale.TRADITIONAL_CHINESE

Locale.UK

Locale.US

Example 3-3 uses some of the default Locale identifiers from the Locale class. Here we have an example of how to use Java's NumberFormat class to output currency in various locales. We'll take an in-depth look at date, time, and number formats in Chapter 5, *Formatting Messages*. For now, let's look at the example.

Example 3-3. Outputting Numbers Using Constant Locale Objects

```
import java.text.*;
import java.util.*;

public class ConstantLocaleUsage {

  public static void main(String [] argv) {

    NumberFormat numberFormat = NumberFormat.getInstance();
    numberFormat.setParseIntegerOnly(false);
    double usersNumber;

    if (argv.length == 1)
      try {
        usersNumber = numberFormat.parse(argv[0]).doubleValue();
      } catch (ParseException e) {
        usersNumber = 197912.29;
      }
    else
      usersNumber = 1976.0826;

    numberFormat = NumberFormat.getNumberInstance(Locale.US);
    System.out.println("User's number (US): "
      + numberFormat.format(usersNumber));
    numberFormat = NumberFormat.getNumberInstance(Locale.GERMANY);
    System.out.println("User's number (GERMANY): "
      + numberFormat.format(usersNumber));
    numberFormat = NumberFormat.getNumberInstance();
    System.out.println("User's number (DEFAULT LOCALE): "
      + numberFormat.format(usersNumber));
  }
}
```

Running the program is simple. If you're running it in the United States, you'll probably see the following output:

```
C:\>java ConstantLocaleUsage

User's number (US): 1,976.083
User's number (GERMANY): 1.976,083
User's number (DEFAULT LOCALE): 1,976.083
```

You can also run the program with your own number:

```
C:\>java ConstantLocaleUsage 1,234.56

User's number (US): 1,234.56
User's number (GERMANY): 1.234,56
User's number (DEFAULT LOCALE): 1,234.56
```

And finally, let's set the default country to France:

```
C:\>java –Duser.language=fr –Duser.region=FR ConstantLocaleUsage 1234,56

User's number (US): 1,234.56
User's number (GERMANY): 1.234,56
User's number (DEFAULT LOCALE): 1 234,56
```

Querying for Locale Information

The `getDefault()` method in the `Locale` class returns the default `Locale` object for the currently running JVM. As we said earlier, each time a JVM is invoked, the default locale is constructed from the environment.

You should also be aware that the `Locale.setDefault(Locale newLocale)` is not a thread-safe method. It should be used only to set the global default locale for the entire application. For other purposes, particularly in a multithreaded environment, use explicit `Locale` arguments.

The `Locale` class provides methods to query the ISO country and language codes that your Java runtime knows about. These static methods are `getISOCountries()` and `getISOLanguages()`. Example 3-4 demonstrates the use of these two methods.

Example 3-4. Printing Out the ISO Country and Language Codes

```
import java.util.Locale;

public class CountryLanguageCodes {

  public static void main(String [] argv) {

    String [] countries = Locale.getISOCountries();
    String [] languages = Locale.getISOLanguages();
    int i;
```

Example 3-4. Printing Out the ISO Country and Language Codes (continued)

```
    System.out.println("\nCountries:\n");
    for (i = 0; i < countries.length; i++)
      System.out.println(countries[i]);
    System.out.println("\nLanguages:\n");
    for (i = 0; i < languages.length; i++)
      System.out.println(languages[i]);
  }
}
```

The `Locale` class contains three methods that return information about the `Locale` object you're currently using: `getCountry()`, `getLanguage()`, and `getVariant()`, which return the country, language, and variant, respectively.[6] All three methods simply return the respective values of the `Locale` object.

Country Name

Example 3-5 demonstrates the use of methods in the `Locale` class that return information about the country for a given locale.

Example 3-5. Displaying Information About the Country

```
import java.util.Locale;

public class DisplayCountryOutput {

  public static void main(String [] argv) {

    Locale defaultLocale = Locale.getDefault();
    System.out.println(defaultLocale.getISO3Country());
    System.out.println(defaultLocale.getDisplayCountry());
    System.out.println(defaultLocale.getDisplayCountry(Locale.GERMAN));
  }
}
```

If you're running the example in the United States, you should see:

```
C:\>java DisplayCountryOutput

USA
United States
Vereinigte Staaten
```

The `getISO3Country()` method throws a `MissingResourceException` if the three-letter country code is not available for the `Locale` object you're working with. Since this exception is a runtime exception, it does not need to be placed in a `try-catch` block; however it is good practice to use a `try-catch` if you're not sure what locales your program will be running in. An empty string will be returned if no country is given for the current locale.

---

[6] This does not necessarily imply the default locale.

Both getDisplayCountry() and getDisplayCountry(Locale inLocale) return the country's name in a locale-dependent form. The method getDisplayCountry() tries to display the name using the default locale for the running JVM, whereas getDisplayCountry(Locale inLocale) uses the Locale object parameter to retrieve the country. As you can see from running Example 3-6, we can display the country name for the United States in German.

Language Name

Language information can be obtained by using the following methods: getISO3Language(), getDisplayLanguage(), and getDisplayLanguage(Locale inLocale). Example 3-6 demonstrates the use of these methods.

Example 3-6. Displaying Information About the Language

```
import java.util.Locale;

public class DisplayLanguageOutput {

  public static void main(String [] argv) {

    Locale defaultLocale = Locale.getDefault();
    System.out.println(defaultLocale.getISO3Language());
    System.out.println(defaultLocale.getDisplayLanguage());
    System.out.println(defaultLocale.getDisplayLanguage(Locale.CANADA_FRENCH));
  }
}
```

This program produces the following results if you're running it in the United States:

```
C:\>java DisplayLanguageOutput

eng
English
Anglais
```

As with the getISO3Country() method, getISO3Language() returns a three-letter ISO code for the language, an empty string if there is no language specified for the locale, or throws a MissingResourceException if no three-letter language code exists for the given locale.

The methods getDisplayLanguage() and getDisplayLanguage(Locale inLocale) return the name of the language that is localized for either the default locale or for the locale parameter, respectively. If this process fails for some reason, the ISO language code is used. An empty string is returned when the locale does not specify a language.

Variant Name

Because there are no standardized codes for variants, there is no getISOVariant()
method in the Locale class. If the variant is not found for that language or region,
it simply returns an empty string. Like the examples for the country and language
name, Example 3-7 shows how to use the getDisplayVariant() and getDisplay-
Variant(Locale inLocale) methods.

Example 3-7. Displaying Information About the Variant

```
import java.util.Locale;

public class DisplayVariantOutput {

  public static void main(String [] argv) {

    Locale defaultLocale = Locale.getDefault();
    System.out.println(defaultLocale.getDisplayVariant());
    System.out.println(defaultLocale.getDisplayVariant(Locale.US));
    System.out.println((new Locale("en","US","WIN_TX_Austin"))
      .getDisplayVariant());
  }
}
```

Variants constructed using the (_) character are separated by commas. For example, the variant string Variant1_Variant2_Variant3 is displayed as:

```
Variant_1, Variant_2, Variant_3
```

Running the example with different parameters (two blank lines are produced in
the second example) produces these two sets of output:

```
C:\>java -Duser.language=FR -Duser.region=FR_WIN_95 DisplayVariantOutput

WIN,95
WIN,95
WIN,TX,AUSTIN

C:\>java DisplayVariantOutput


WIN,TX,AUSTIN
```

Displaying the Entire Locale

Two variations of the getDisplayName method exist in the Locale class. The
getDisplayName() method builds an appropriate description using the default
locale. The getDisplayName(Locale inLocale) method returns a locale description
that is appropriate for the Locale object argument.

The Locale class uses information from resource bundles, discussed in the next
chapter, to build the display name that is appropriate for displaying to the user.

Depending on the information contained in the `Locale` object, the string returned by these methods is in the following form (as much information as possible is returned):

- language (country, variant)

- language (country)

- language (variant)

- country (variant)

- language

- country

- variant

If no information is available, either method returns an empty string. Example 3-8 shows how these methods are used. Using different language and region combinations creates even more interesting output.

Example 3-8. Displaying the Appropriate Name for a Locale

```
import java.util.Locale;

public class DisplayNameOutput {

  public static void main(String [] argv) {

    Locale defaultLocale = Locale.getDefault();
    System.out.println(defaultLocale.getDisplayName());
    System.out.println(defaultLocale.getDisplayName(Locale.ITALIAN));
    System.out.println(defaultLocale.getDisplayName(Locale.US));
  }
}
```

And here's the output:

```
C:\>java DisplayNameOutput

English (United States)
English (United States)
English (United States)

C:\>java -Duser.language=it -Duser.region=IT DisplayNameOutput

italiano (Italia)
italiano (Italia)
Italian (Italy)
```

Checking Available Locales

As we stated in the beginning of this chapter, the Locale class is a marker used to identify a particular locale. Note that Locale support is at the class, not at the JVM level. Hence, there may exist classes that support a certain locale, but do not support other locales. All classes that perform locale-sensitive operations should, at a minimum, support the getAvailableLocales() method:

```
public static Locale[] getAvailableLocales()
public static String getDisplayName(Locale objectLocale,
                                    Locale displayLocale)
public static final String getDisplayName(Locale objectLocale)
```

For example, if you're using the SimpleDateFormat class and you want to check if your current locale is supported, you could use code similar to Example 3-9.

Example 3-9. Checking Available Locales on the SimpleDateFormat Class

```
import java.text.*;
import java.util.*;

public class LocaleCheck {

  public static void main(String [] argv) {

    Locale [] sdfLocales = SimpleDateFormat.getAvailableLocales();
    Locale myLocale = Locale.getDefault();
    int i;

    for (i = 0; i < sdfLocales.length; i++) {
      if (myLocale.equals(sdfLocales[i]))
        break;
    }

    if (i == sdfLocales.length)
      System.out.println("Locale " + myLocale.toString()
          + ", not supported by SimpleDateFormat");
    else
      System.out.println("Hooray! " + myLocale.toString()
          + ", is supported by SimpleDateFormat");
  }
}
```

LocaleCheck displays the following output when we run it using our default locale, and also when we set a locale to a language and region that doesn't exist (at least not to our knowledge):

```
C:\>java LocaleCheck

Hooray! en_US, is supported by SimpleDateFormat

C:\>java -Duser.language=ab -Duser.region=BA LocaleCheck

Locale ab_BA, is not supported by SimpleDateFormat
```

4

Isolating Locale-Specific Data with Resource Bundles

Error messages, status messages, graphic images, and even sound clips are perfect examples of candidate elements for localization. For instance, all text messages displayed to users throughout your program first need to be translated, or localized, for the locales that you're going to support. This task can be very time consuming and costly. After completing the task, how do you package these messages together so the proper locale-specific information gets displayed to the user?

Java's ResourceBundle class provides the functionality for you to retrieve locale-specific resources. You can use resource bundles in your application to keep text messages, formatting conventions, images, sound files, etc., in a "package" targeted to different locales. It is possible to use the ResourceBundle class by providing your own subclass; however, two concrete implementations of ResourceBundle exist: PropertyResourceBundle and ListResourceBundle. These two classes provide additional functionality over the base ResourceBundle class.

Why Use Resource Bundles?

Applications need to provide locale-sensitive information to users. One approach is to hardcode locale-sensitive information or messages within the application. However, this approach is inefficient because it makes your application larger, complicates your application logic when you decide which messages to display, and requires that you change or release a new version of your application when locale-specific resources change. Another approach, Java resource bundles, provides facilities for packaging and managing collections of locale-specific elements, such as feedback or status messages. These elements may also be more complex datatypes, such as graphic images or sound files. The resource bundle facilities provide a convenient mechanism for you to separate your program code from your resource data.

Let's outline some general resource bundle properties. These properties are illustrated in Figure 4-1. Resource bundles:

- Provide facilities for storage and retrieval of all locale-specific information.

- Allow you to support multiple locales in a single application.

- Allow you to support additional locales easily in the future by simply adding more resource bundles.

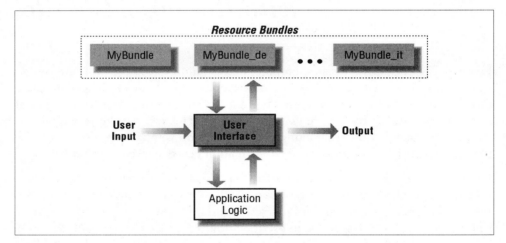

Figure 4-1. How resource bundles fit into application development

The ResourceBundle Class

The ResourceBundle class is an abstract class in the java.util package. You can provide your own subclass of ResourceBundle or use one of the subclass implementations, as in the case of PropertyResourceBundle or ListResourceBundle. We discuss each of these two classes in later sections of this chapter. For now, let's discuss some details of ResourceBundle.

Resource bundles inherit from the ResourceBundle class and contain localized elements that are stored external to an application. Resource bundles share a base name. The base name SimpleResourceBundle might be selected because of the resources it contains. We talk about design considerations for resource bundles in the last section of this chapter. Locale information further differentiates a resource bundle. For example, `SimpleResourceBundle_it` means that this resource bundle contains locale-specific items for Italian. The exact naming convention for resource bundles is detailed in the next subsection.

Example 4-1 is a simple subclass of `ResourceBundle`.

Example 4-1. Simple Resource Bundle

```
import java.util.Enumeration;
import java.util.ResourceBundle;
import java.util.StringTokenizer;

public class SimpleResourceBundle extends ResourceBundle {

  private String keys = "AMMessage PMMessage";

  public Object handleGetObject(String key) {
    if (key.equals("AMMessage")) return "Good morning";
    if (key.equals("PMMessage")) return "Good evening";

    return null;
  }

  public Enumeration getKeys() {
    StringTokenizer keyTokenizer = new StringTokenizer(keys);

    return keyTokenizer;
  }
}
```

Example 4-2 is a subclass of `SimpleResourceBundle` and contains resources specific to Italian.

Example 4-2. Simple Resource Bundle Containing Localized Strings in Italian

```
public class SimpleResourceBundle_it extends SimpleResourceBundle {

  public Object handleGetObject(String key) {
    if (key.equals("AMMessage")) return "Buona mattina";
    if (key.equals("PMMessage")) return "Buona sera";

    return null;
  }
}
```

A resource bundle is a container for key/value pairs. The key is used to identify a locale-specific resource in a bundle. If that key is found in a particular resource bundle, its value is returned. Two abstract methods must be implemented in a subclass of ResourceBundle: getKeys and handleGetObject. The handleGetObject(String key) method takes a String as its argument. This argument is used to retrieve a particular value from the resource bundle. In Example 4-1, if a key of AMMessage is passed into the handleGetObject method, a value of Good morning is returned. This method returns null to indicate that no value could be found for the given key.

The getKeys method returns an enumeration containing all keys that a particular resource bundle knows about. In Example 4-1, we only manage two keys, AMMessage and PMMessage. We return a StringTokenizer object, which implements the Enumeration interface, that parses the keys string for the SimpleResourceBundle class.

We had to override only the handleGetObject method in SimpleResourceBundle_it because only our values had changed. The keys used to retrieve those values do not change. If only the AMMessage value had changed, we would have included only the line if (key.equals("AMMessage")) return Buona mattina.

Three methods in the ResourceBundle class retrieve the value for a given key. Two of these methods are convenience methods that save you from having to cast the object returned to you. The first method, getObject(String key), takes a String used as the key and tries to retrieve a value from the resource bundle. The second method, getString(String key), also takes a String used as the key and tries to retrieve a value from the resource bundle and return the object casted to a String. The third method, getStringArray(String key), exhibits the same behavior as getObject and getString; however, this method attempts to cast the object returned to you as a String array (i.e., String []).

Example 4-3 uses SimpleResourceBundle and SimpleResourceBundle_it and demonstrates how to retrieve values from them.

Example 4-3. Demonstrating the Use of the ResourceBundle Class

```
import java.util.Enumeration;
import java.util.ResourceBundle;
import java.util.MissingResourceException;

public class SimpleResourceBundleExample {

  public static void main(String [] argv) {
    try {
      ResourceBundle rb = ResourceBundle.getBundle("SimpleResourceBundle");
```

Example 4-3. Demonstrating the Use of the ResourceBundle Class (continued)

```
        System.out.println(rb.getString("AMMessage"));
        System.out.println(rb.getString("PMMessage"));

    } catch (MissingResourceException mre) {
        mre.printStackTrace();
    }
  }
}
```

Here is the output produced by Example 4-3:

```
C:\>java SimpleResourceBundleExample

Good morning
Good evening

C:\>java -Duser.language=it SimpleResourceBundleExample

Buona mattina
Buona sera
```

Our next section describes how to retrieve resource bundles for use in an application and how resource bundles are named. We've already seen this process in Example 4-3 by using the getBundle method in the ResourceBundle class and by providing a localized resource bundle for Italian.

How Resource Bundles Are Discovered and Named

You must make resource bundles explicitly available in your applications. You can achieve this by using one of three static getBundle() methods in ResourceBundle that allow you to retrieve a resource bundle:

```
public final static getBundle(String baseName)
public final static getBundle(String baseName, Locale locale)
public final static getBundle(String baseName, Locale locale,
                          ClassLoader loader)
```

Using getBundle(String baseName) returns a resource bundle using the default locale for the running JVM. This method is useful if you allow users to select or set their locale before runtime while not allowing them to change the locale during runtime. However, we recommend that you always use the static method, getBundle(String baseName, Locale locale). This method is an easy way to eliminate debugging headaches. If your application uses its own class loader, you can use the `getBundle(String baseName, Locale locale, ClassLoader loader)` method and pass in the class loader used by your application.

The `ResourceBundle` class uses a particular lookup mechanism to find the individual resource bundles you request through one of the `getBundle` methods. Resource bundles can be thought of as having parents and children. The resource bundle naming hierarchy forms a tree structure. The name given to resource bundles is a combination of the base name and locale information. The base name you've picked for your bundles is at the root of the tree. In Example 4-1, this name was `SimpleResourceBundle`.

You further differentiate at the next level with language specific resources. We provided such a bundle in Example 4-2 with `SimpleResourceBundle_it`, to identify resources specific to Italian. Below that level, bundles are differentiated by country, and beyond that by the locale variant. Therefore, we could have provided `SimpleResourceBundle_it_IT` to localize Italian language resources for the country of Italy. Finally, we could have provided `SimpleResourceBundle_it_IT_Capri` to identify localized resources in Italian that are specific to the island of Capri.

The `getBundle` method searches for a particular resource bundle in the following order:

1.   The desired or requested locale passed to the `getBundle` method

2.   The default locale for the running JVM

3.   The root resource bundle, or `baseName`, that you supply

The search proceeds in the following order from a lower, more specific level in the resource bundle name hierarchy to a higher, more generic level. The order is as follows:

1.   baseName + "_" + desiredLocale.language + "_" + desiredLocale.country + "_" + desiredLocale.variant

2.   baseName + "_" + desiredLocale.language + "_" + desiredLocale.country

3.   baseName + "_" + desiredLocale.language

4.   baseName + "_" + defaultLocale.language + "_" + defaultLocale.country + "_" + defaultLocale.variant

5.   baseName + "_" + defaultLocale.language + "_" + defaultLocale.country

6.   baseName + "_" + defaultLocale.language

7.   baseName

Suppose that someone running Example 4-3 is interested in obtaining the `SimpleResourceBundle` for the locale "fr_FR." Further, suppose that the default locale is "en_US." The resource bundle lookup will search for the following classes:

```
SimpleResourceBundle_fr_FR
SimpleResourceBundle_fr
SimpleResourceBundle_en_US
SimpleResourceBundle_en
SimpleResourceBundle
```

The resource bundles you use in your application must be available from a directory in the classpath of the JVM. If not, the bundles will not be found and an exception will be thrown when one of the `getBundle` methods is called.

The `ResourceBundle` class also provides a convenience method called `getLocale()`. This method should be called when you want to explicitly check the locale of the resource bundle that is returned to you after calling one of the `getBundle()` methods. This way, you can determine whether the returned resource bundle matches the desired locale exactly or if one of the fallback resource bundles is in the bundle hierarchy.

Package names also affect how resource bundles are found. The name you supply as `baseName` in the `getBundle()` methods is the name of the class containing the resources, and this name must be fully qualified. Therefore, you must also supply the package name when retrieving a resource bundle that exists in a package. Imagine the class hierarchy illustrated in Figure 4-2.

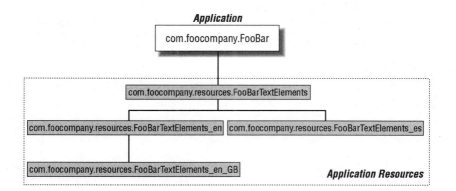

Figure 4-2. Resource bundle hierarchy using packages

Your application contains a class called `FooBar` in the com.foocompany package. This class uses the `getBundle(String baseName, Locale locale)` method to obtain resource data from the `FooBarTextElements` class for different locales. You've also provided a number of resource bundles for text elements in the com.foocompany.resources package. If the method call in the `FooBar` class looks like `ResourceBundle.getBundle("FooBarTextElements", userLocale)` a MissingResourceException is going to be thrown because the fully qualified name (package name and class name) needs to be passed into the `getBundle()` method.

The proper way to get the resource bundle in this situation is to use `ResourceBundle.getBundle("com.foocompany.resources.FooBarTextElements", userLocale)`.

Example 4-4 illustrates this point.

Example 4-4. Proper Retrieval of a Resource Bundle in a Package

```
package com.foocompany;

import java.util.Locale;
import java.util.ResourceBundle;
import java.util.MissingResourceException;

public class FooBar {

  public static void main(String [] argv) {

    ResourceBundle textResources = null;

    try {
      textResources = ResourceBundle.getBundle("FooBarTextElements",
          Locale.getDefault());
      System.out.println(textResources.getString("CompanyName"));
    } catch (MissingResourceException e) {
      System.out.println("Unqualified resource bundle name");
    }

    try {
      textResources = ResourceBundle.getBundle(
          "com.foocompany.resources.FooBarTextElements",
          Locale.getDefault());
      System.out.println(textResources.getString("CompanyName"));
    } catch (MissingResourceException e) {
    }
  }
}
```

Example 4-5 illustrates the resource bundle used in Example 4-4.

Example 4-5. Resource Bundle Used in Example 4-4

```
package com.foocompany.resources;

import java.util.Enumeration;
import java.util.Locale;
import java.util.ResourceBundle;
import java.util.StringTokenizer;
import java.util.MissingResourceException;

public class FooBarTextElements extends ResourceBundle {

  private String keys = "CompanyName";

    public Object handleGetObject(String key) {
      if (key.equals("CompanyName")) return "Foo Bar Company";

      return null;
    }

    public Enumeration getKeys() {
      StringTokenizer keyTokenizer = new StringTokenizer(keys);

      return keyTokenizer;
    }
}
```

Running Example 4-4 produces the following results:

```
C:\>java com.foocompany.FooBar
Unqualified resource bundle name
Foo Bar Company
```

You do not need to replicate elements in a resource bundle if they exist in another bundle within the resource bundle hierarchy. Example 4-6 demonstrates the lookup of the key "Hello." Examples 4-7, 4-8, and 4-9 are the resource bundles used by Example 4-6.

Example 4-6. Demonstrates That You Do Not Have to Replicate Keys and Values in All Resource Bundles

```
import java.util.Enumeration;
import java.util.Locale;
import java.util.ResourceBundle;
import java.util.MissingResourceException;

public class HelloResourceBundleExample {
```

Example 4-6. Demonstrates That You Do Not Have to Replicate Keys and Values in
All Resource Bundles (continued)

```java
  public static void main(String [] argv) {
    try {
      Locale frenchLocale = new Locale("fr", "FR");
      ResourceBundle rb =
        ResourceBundle.getBundle("HelloResourceBundle", frenchLocale);

      System.out.println(rb.getString("Hello"));
      System.out.println(rb.getString("Goodbye"));

    } catch (MissingResourceException mre) {
      mre.printStackTrace();
    }
  }
}
```

Example 4-7. Fallback Resource Bundle

```java
import java.util.Enumeration;
import java.util.ResourceBundle;
import java.util.StringTokenizer;

public class HelloResourceBundle extends ResourceBundle {

  private String keys = "Hello Goodbye";

    public Object handleGetObject(String key) {
      if (key.equals("Hello")) return "Hello";
      if (key.equals("Goodbye")) return "Goodbye";

      return null;
    }

    public Enumeration getKeys() {
      StringTokenizer keyTokenizer = new StringTokenizer(keys);

      return keyTokenizer;
    }
}
```

Example 4-8. French Resource Bundle Containing the Key "Hello"

```java
import java.util.Enumeration;
import java.util.ResourceBundle;
import java.util.StringTokenizer;
```

Example 4-8. French Resource Bundle Containing the Key "Hello" (continued)

```
public class HelloResourceBundle_fr extends HelloResourceBundle {

  public Object handleGetObject(String key) {
    if (key.equals("Hello")) return "Bonjour";

    return null;
  }
}
```

Example 4-9. French Resource Bundle Containing the Key "Goodbye"

```
import java.util.Enumeration;
import java.util.ResourceBundle;
import java.util.StringTokenizer;

public class HelloResourceBundle_fr_FR extends HelloResourceBundle_fr {

  public Object handleGetObject(String key) {
    if (key.equals("Goodbye")) return "Au Revoir";

    return null;
  }
}
```

Example 4-9 uses the locale "fr_FR," so the search for a resource matching the key of "Hello" starts in HelloResourceBundle_fr_FR. The key does not exist in this bundle, so the search proceeds up the hierarchy. The key is found in HelloResourceBundle_fr, and the value is printed to the screen. Likewise, the search for a resource matching the key of "Goodbye" starts in HelloResourceBundle_fr_FR. The search begins and ends here, since the key exists in this resource bundle.

The first time you search for a particular resource bundle, Java starts a lookup process and either returns the specific resource bundle you requested or throws a MissingResourceException if the resource is not found. Searching for a particular resource bundle (after that bundle was found) results in the bundle being cached in memory. Java stores the resource bundle in a hashtable for quick lookup. Requests made for a particular resource bundle at a later point in your application result in use of the cached bundle. Had such design considerations not been made, this situation could have been a huge bottleneck in programs that rely on resource bundle facilities. Think of how slow programs would be if each time you request a resource from a bundle, the system must go through the steps of searching the resource bundle hierarchy, loading the bundle from disk, and returning the data for a particular resource.

Property Resource Bundles

A property resource bundle is a collection of text elements in a properties file format stored in a *.properties* file. The `PropertyResourceBundle` class provides all code necessary for you to access these resources in a locale-dependent manner.

Example 4-10 illustrates basic property file formatting. The `Properties` class in the `java.util` package handles reading and writing properties files. Both the keys to lookup a value and the values returned are Java `Strings`. Example 4-10 shows a simple properties file.

Example 4-10. A Properties File

```
# Sample properties file for demonstrating PropertyResourceBundle class
#
# Text that will appear in the title bar of our application
ApplicationTitle=Demonstrating the use of PropertyResourceBundle
#
# Text that will be displayed on OK buttons
OKButtonLabel=OK
#
# Text for display on a button to cancel current operation
CancelButtonLabel=Cancel
#
#
```

A property in a properties file is specified in the following format:

```
Key=Value
```

In most properties files, you see that the separator between key and value is the equals sign (=) character. Java also allows use of the colon (:) character as a separator between key and value, as in:

```
Key:Value
```

We won't go into all the details about how Java deals with properties files, but here are a few general comments on how properties files are structured: lines starting with an exclamation (!) or a pound (#) character are ignored when the properties file is read. These characters indicate that the line is a comment line. Keys are case sensitive. Finally, you can specify values in a properties file that span multiple lines by using a backslash (\) to indicate line continuation. Example 4-11 illustrates this point.

Example 4-11. Properties File Where Values Span More Than One Line (AnimalResources.properties)

```
# Sample properties file with keys whose values span more than one line
#
Animals=Cat, Dog, Giraffe, \
    Shark, Dolphin, Bird, \
    Bear, Moose
```

If you retrieved the "Animals" key, you'd get back the value `Cat, Dog, Giraffe,`
`Shark, Dolphin, Bird, Bear, Moose`. All the leading whitespace on any continuation line is discarded. You could then, for example, break up the value returned to you by using the `java.util.StringTokenizer` class.

Example 4-12 uses the properties file from Example 4-11 to print a list of animal
names.

Example 4-12. Printing a List of Animals Stored in a Properties Resource File

```java
import java.util.Locale;
import java.util.ResourceBundle;
import java.util.MissingResourceException;

public class Animals {

  public static void main(String [] argv) {

    ResourceBundle animalResources;

    try {
      animalResources = ResourceBundle.getBundle(
          "AnimalResources", Locale.getDefault());
      System.out.println(animalResources.getString("Animals"));
    } catch (MissingResourceException mre) {
      mre.printStackTrace();
    }
  }
}
```

Here is the output produced after running Example 4-12:

```
C:\>java Animals

Cat, Dog, Giraffe, Shark, Dolphin, Bird, Bear, Moose
```

List Resource Bundles

The `ListResourceBundle` class takes its name from the fact that it manages a list of
resources. Those resources are stored in a class file, allowing you to provide local-

ized resources for any datatype. Resources in a `ListResourceBundle` are not limited to text strings, as are the resources in a `PropertyResourceBundle`. For example, images are one example of resources that can be localized, but can't be stored as text strings. The company logo is one common image important to most companies. Companies pride themselves on, and can earn hefty profits from, logo recognition alone. Logos can be associated with a company or a particular product.

`ListResourceBundle`, an abstract subclass of `ResourceBundle` stores its keys and values in a two-dimensional `Object` array. This mechanism allows you to create resources of arbitrary datatypes unlike the `PropertyResourceBundle`, in which both the keys and values must be strings. When you use a `ListResourceBundle`, the only restriction is that the keys must be specified as strings.

When you create a subclass of `ListResourceBundle`, you must override the `getContents()` method that returns a two-dimensional `Object` array. The first element is a key (a `String`) used to access the value. The second element of the pair can be of any datatype, such as an AWT `Button`, an `Integer` number, or a `String`. Example 4-13 shows a simple `ListResourceBundle` called `SampleResourceBundle` and illustrates how to create a subclass of `ListResourceBundle`.

Example 4-13. A Subclass of ListResourceBundle Called SampleResourceBundle

```java
import java.awt.*;
import java.util.*;

public class SampleResourceBundle extends ListResourceBundle {

  public Object [][] getContents() {
    return contents;
  }

  static final Object [][] contents = {
      {"okButton", new Button("OK")},
      {"negativeInteger", new Integer(-1)},
      {"textString", "Thank you for reading our book"}
  };
}
```

The `ResourceBundle` class provides a method called `getObject(String key)`. When you retrieve a value from your resource bundle, you must cast it to its proper type. To retrieve the key `okButton` from the resource bundle in Example 4-13, we would pass the `okButton` string to the `getObect` method. This method would return an `Object`, which would then be cast to `Button` to use the `Button` object.

Example 4-14 illustrates the power of the `ListResourceBundle` class. Examples 4-15 and 4-16 show a resource bundle for this applet and the HTML in which the applet is embedded. We display the O'Reilly & Associates logo to the user, but the logo displayed depends on the locale. If the parameter `url` is set to `yes` in the applet's HTML file, the logo will contain the URL for that country's O'Reilly website. We don't show all resource bundles for this example because they're so large; instead, we show a relevant portion of the German resource bundle in Example 4-15.

Example 4-14. Applet Used to Display O'Reilly & Associates Logo Depending on the Set Locale

```
import java.applet.*;
import java.awt.*;
import java.util.*;

public class OReillyLogoApplet extends Applet {
  private ImageArea imageArea;
  private Image logo;
  private Button okButton;
  private ListResourceBundle appletElements;
  private Locale logoAppletLocale;
  private boolean displayURLLogo;
  public void init()   {

    // Get the parameters to set the locale for the applet
    logoAppletLocale = new Locale(getParameter("language"),
                                  getParameter("country"));
    if (getParameter("url") != null &&
        getParameter("url").equalsIgnoreCase("yes"))
      displayURLLogo = true;
    else
      displayURLLogo = false;

    try {

      setLayout(new BorderLayout());

      imageArea = new ImageArea();
      imageArea.setBackground(Color.white);
      imageArea.setSize(getSize().width, getSize().height);

      appletElements = (ListResourceBundle)ResourceBundle.
         getBundle("OReillyResources", logoAppletLocale);
      if (displayURLLogo)
        logo = Toolkit.getDefaultToolkit()
               .createImage((byte [])appletElements
               .getObject("OReillyLogoURL"));
      else
```

Example 4-14. Applet Used to Display O'Reilly & Associates Logo Depending on the Set Locale (continued)

```
        logo = Toolkit.getDefaultToolkit()
              .createImage((byte [])appletElements
              .getObject("OReillyLogo"));

    add("North", imageArea);

    imageArea.displayImage(logo);

  } catch (MissingResourceException e) {
  }
 }
}

class ImageArea extends Canvas {

  Image image;

  public void displayImage(Image image) {
    this.image = image;
    repaint();
  }

  public void paint(Graphics g) {
    if (image != null)
      g.drawImage (image, 0, 0, Color.lightGray, this);
  }
}
```

Example 4-15. A Partial Listing of the Resource Bundle for Example 4-14 for Germany

```
import java.util.ListResourceBundle;

public class OReillyResources_de extends ListResourceBundle {

    public Object [][] getContents() {
        return contents;
    }

    static byte [] OReillyLogo = {
    (byte)71,
    (byte)73,
    (byte)70,
    (byte)56,
    (byte)57,
    (byte)97,
```

Example 4-15. A Partial Listing of the Resource Bundle for Example 4-14 for Germany (continued)

```
    ...
    (byte)59
    };

    static final Object [][] contents = {
        {"OReillyLogo", OReillyLogo},
        {"OReillyLogoURL", OReillyLogoURL}
    };
}
```

You can change the value in the language parameter in HTML to see a different logo displayed in the applet, as shown in Example 4-16. If the value for the url parameter is not yes, no URL is displayed in the logo. For example, to create Figure 4-3, set the language parameter to fr and the url parameter to no. To create Figure 4-4, set the language parameter to de and the url parameter to yes.

Figures 4-3 and 4-4 show the applet running in the French language (no URL) and the German language (with URL), respectively.

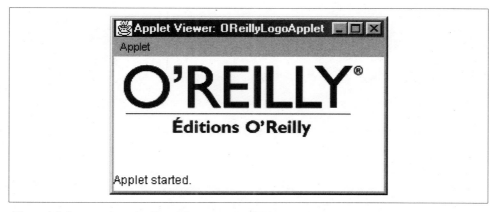

Figure 4-3. Logo applet using French language (no URL)

Figure 4-4. Logo applet using German language (with URL)

Example 4-16. HTML Used to Run the O'Reilly Logo Display Applet

```
<HTML>

<HEAD>
<TITLE>O'Reilly Logo Applet</TITLE>
</HEAD>

<BODY>

<APPLET CODE="OReillyLogoApplet" WIDTH=270 HEIGHT=115>
<PARAM NAME="country" VALUE="">
<PARAM NAME="language" VALUE="fr">
<PARAM NAME="url" VALUE="yes">
</APPLET>

</BODY>

</HTML>
```

Example 4-17 shows a utility we've used in this chapter to create a `ListResourceBundle` class automatically, using data from an image or a sound file. You can use any data file you like. You'll find that adding this type of data to your resource bundles, specifying each byte manually, is very time consuming! This program takes three arguments: the data file to include in the resource bundle; the key used to retrieve the resource from the bundle; and the name of the class you subclass from `ListResourceBundle`. Specify the class name with no *.java* extension. The proper *.java* source file is created from the name you supply.

Here's how you might use this utility:

```
C:\>java ListResourceBundleCreator oreilly_logo_germany.gif
        OReillyLogoGerman
        OReillyLogoResources_de
```

Example 4-17. Utility Program to Create a ListResourceBundle Using Data from a User-Supplied Data File

```java
import java.io.*;
import java.util.Vector;

public class ListResourceBundleCreator {

  public static void main(String [] argv) throws Exception{
    FileInputStream inputFileReader = new FileInputStream(argv[0]);
    DataInputStream dis = new DataInputStream(inputFileReader);
    long fileSize;

    ByteArrayOutputStream baos = new ByteArrayOutputStream();
    Vector myVector = new Vector();

    while (true) {
      try {
        myVector.addElement(new Integer(dis.readUnsignedByte()));
      } catch (EOFException e) {
        break;
      }
    }

    fileSize = myVector.size();
    FileWriter outputFileWriter = new FileWriter(argv[2] + ".java");
    outputFileWriter.write("import java.util.ListResourceBundle;\n\n");
    outputFileWriter.write("public class " + argv[2] +
                        " extends ListResourceBundle {\n\n");
    outputFileWriter.write("    public Object [][] getContents() {\n");
    outputFileWriter.write("        return contents;\n");
    outputFileWriter.write("    }\n\n");

    outputFileWriter.write("    static byte [] " + argv[1] + " = {\n");
    for (int i = 0; i < fileSize; i++) {
        outputFileWriter.write("\t(byte)");
        outputFileWriter.write(((Integer)myVector.elementAt(i)).toString());
        if (i < fileSize - 1)
            outputFileWriter.write(",\n");
    }
    outputFileWriter.write("\n\t};\n\n");
```

Example 4-17. Utility Program to Create a ListResourceBundle Using Data from a User-Supplied Data File (continued)

```
    outputFileWriter.write("        static final Object [][] contents = {\n");
    outputFileWriter.write("           {\"" + argv[1] + "\", " + argv[1] + "}\n");
    outputFileWriter.write("        };\n");
    outputFileWriter.write("}\n");
    outputFileWriter.close();
  }
}
```

Resource Bundle Caveats

This section details information you need to consider when using resource bundles in your application.

What to Localize in a Resource Bundle

Certain strings should not be localized and placed into a resource bundle in any application. Consider the strings that specify the region that a component is placed in for the BorderLayout class in the java.awt package. Java allows you to specify five regions on the border layout, namely, "North," "South," "East," "West," and "Center." Strings like these are used as *program identifiers* and must not be localized. Localizing would create programs that either do not work at all or behave incorrectly. This situation also holds true for keys used to retrieve a specific element from a resource bundle; you would not localize keys used to retrieve values from a PropertyResourceBundle.

Character Encoding Issues for Resource Bundles

Java source files are most commonly written and saved as ASCII text files with escape sequences for non-ASCII characters. File editors used to create your source files may also allow you to use a regional character encoding. The javac compiler supports the –encoding directive, which allows you to specify the regional encoding of the file you're trying to compile. Appendix B, *Character Encodings Supported by Java*, contains a complete listing of all supported languages and converters that can be specified for your specific regional encoding. Chapter 6, *Character Sets and Unicode*, explains encodings in more detail.

You need to be aware of the character encoding when you use a `ListResourceBundle`. In a `ListResourceBundle`, your resources are stored in a class file, which is created by compiling a *.java* source file. Say we compile a source file using a Polish character encoding. We'd compile our resource bundle as follows:

```
C:\>javac —encoding iso8859_2 ProgramResources.java
```

Using the `PropertyResourceBundle` class, we must also worry about the character encoding of the individual properties files. Properties files must use an ISO 8859-1 encoding or contain Unicode escape sequences to represent Unicode characters. Unicode escape sequences are specified as \uxxxx, for which xxxx represents the hexadecimal value of the specific character.

Java provides a utility called `native2ascii`, which takes a file written in a given character encoding and converts non-ASCII characters to the appropriate Unicode escape sequences. `native2ascii` also takes an `-encoding` option like `javac`, through which you can specify the character encoding of the file to be converted. If this option is not specified, it uses the default character encoding of the platform on which the program is running. The command-line option `-reverse` allows you to convert a file containing Unicode escape sequences to a native character encoding. You must specify an input file and you may also specify an optional output file where the converted file will be written. If the output file is not specified, standard output is used:

```
C:\>native2ascii —encoding SJIS ProgramResources_ja.java
    ProgramResources_ja.java.converted
```

Property Resource Bundle Caveats

We should point out a few things to watch for now that you're aware of how to use `PropertyResourceBundles`.

Using the `PropertyResourceBundle` class is very convenient when all you have to localize are textual elements. If you have other datatypes that you'd like to localize in a resource bundle, the `ListResourceBundle` class allows you that flexibility. In the next subsection of this chapter, we'll discuss a problem that could arise when using both `PropertyResourceBundles` and `ListResourceBundles`.

Unlike the `ListResourceBundle` class, which must be subclassed, the `PropertyResourceBundle` class is a concrete subclass of `ResourceBundle`. Therefore, to add more resources using a `PropertyResourceBundle`, simply create the appropriate properties files. You do not have to compile these resource bundles, as you must with a `ListResourceBundle`.

Properties files that are found by one of the `getBundle` methods must end with a *.properties* extension. If one of your properties files is missing this extension, it will not be found; this situation causes problems when performing a resource bundle lookup. The *.properties* extension is added automatically for you during the lookup process, so you do not need to add one to the name passed to the `getBundle` method.

Resource Bundle Lookup Caveats

An age-old philosophical musing states, "Which came first, the chicken or the egg?" A similar, and maybe equally puzzling, question arises when we speak about using class files or properties files for our resource bundles. It becomes an issue when you think about mixing the two types of bundles within an application.

Let's rephrase our philosophical question in resource bundle terms, "When looking for resource bundles, which is found first, a class file or a properties file?" If both a class file and a properties file exist at the same level in the resource bundle hierarchy, any calls to retrieve resources are retrieved from the class file. In this situation, the class file "hides" the properties file.

Example 4-18 demonstrates this behavior; Examples 4-19 through 4-23 are the resource bundles used with this example.

Example 4-18. Demonstration of Finding a Class Resource File Before a Properties Resource File

```
import java.util.ResourceBundle;
import java.util.MissingResourceException;

public class WhichBundleComesFirstExample {

  public static void main(String [] argv) {
    try {
      ResourceBundle resources =
        ResourceBundle.getBundle("WhichBundleComesFirstResources");
      System.out.println(resources.getString("Message3"));
      System.out.println(resources.getString("Message2"));
      System.out.println(resources.getString("Message1"));
    } catch (MissingResourceException mre) {
      mre.printStackTrace();
    }
  }
}
```

Example 4-19. WhichBundleComesFirstResources_en_US in ListResourceBundle Format

```
import java.util.ListResourceBundle;

public class WhichBundleComesFirstResources_en_US extends
    ListResourceBundle {

    public Object [][] getContents() {
        return contents;
    }

    static final Object [][] contents = {
        {"Message3",
         "Message 3: From WhichBundleComesFirstResources_en_US \
         (ListResourceBundle)"}
    };
}
```

Example 4-20. WhichBundleComesFirstResources_en_US in PropertyResourceBundle Format
(WhichBundleComesFirstResources_en_US.properties)

```
# Properties file for WhichBundleComesFirstResources_en_US
#
# English language in the United States
#
Message3=Message 3: From WhichBundleComesFirstResources_en_US \
  (Properties file)
```

Example 4-21. WhichBundleComesFirstResources_en in PropertyResourceBundle Format
(WhichBundleComesFirstResources_en.properties)

```
# Properties file for WhichBundleComesFirstResources_en
#
# English language in the United States
#
Message2=Message 2: From WhichBundleComesFirstResources_en (Properties file)
```

Example 4-22. WhichBundleComesFirstResources in ListResourceBundle Format

```
import java.util.ListResourceBundle;

public class WhichBundleComesFirstResources extends ListResourceBundle {

  public Object [][] getContents() {
    return contents;
  }

  static final Object [][] contents = {
```

Example 4-22. WhichBundleComesFirstResources in ListResourceBundle Format (continued)

```
        {"Message1",
         "Message 1: From WhichBundleComesFirstResources (ListResourceBundle)"}
    };
}
```

Example 4-23. WhichBundleComesFirstResources in PropertyResourceBundle Format
(WhichBundleComesFirst.properties)

```
# Properties file for WhichBundleComesFirst
#
# English language in the United States
#
Message1=Message 1: From WhichBundleComesFirstResources (Properties file)
```

The following is outputted when Example 4-18 is executed:

```
Message 3: From WhichBundleComesFirstResources_en_US (ListResourceBundle)
Message 2: From WhichBundleComesFirstResources_en (Properties file)
Message 1: From WhichBundleComesFirstResources (ListResourceBundle)
```

As you can see, the messages are retrieved from the class file resource bundle for
Message3 and Message1, which are contained in both a class file resource bundle
and a properties file resource bundle.

Why even bring this topic up? If you wish to use the ListResourceBundle class to
localize objects such as GUI widgets and images, and if you use a
PropertyResourceBundle to handle all of the text messages displayed to users using
your application. You could retrieve your images and widgets correctly, but a lot of
MissingResourceExceptions would be thrown when your application tries to
retrieve any text messages.

Example 4-24 is a utility that converts a properties file into a ListResourceBundle
class. This utility can convert your existing PropertyResourceBundles to
ListResourceBundles, given that ListResourceBundles are found before
PropertyResourceBundles. The utility takes one command-line parameter, the
name of the properties file, to convert to a ListResourceBundle.

Example 4-24. PropertyToListResourceBundle Utility

```
import java.io.FileInputStream;
import java.io.FileWriter;
import java.io.IOException;
import java.io.OutputStreamWriter;
import java.util.Enumeration;
import java.util.Locale;
import java.util.Properties;
```

Example 4-24. PropertyToListResourceBundle Utility (continued)

```java
import java.util.MissingResourceException;

public class PropertyToListResourceBundle {

  public static void main(String [] argv) {
    if (argv.length < 1) {
      System.exit(1);
    }

    try {
      String bundleName = argv[0] + "_" + Locale.getDefault().toString();
      Properties propertiesFile = new Properties();
      propertiesFile.load(new FileInputStream(bundleName + ".properties"));
      FileWriter fw = new FileWriter(bundleName + ".java");
      String key;

      fw.write("import java.util.ListResourceBundle;\n\n");

      fw.write("public class " + bundleName +
               " extends ListResourceBundle {\n\n");
      fw.write("    public Object [][] getContents() {\n");
      fw.write("        return contents;\n");
      fw.write("    }\n\n");

      fw.write("    static final Object [][] contents = {\n");

      Enumeration e = propertiesFile.propertyNames();
      while (e.hasMoreElements()) {
        key = (String)e.nextElement();
        fw.write("        {\"" + key + "\", " + "\""
                 + propertiesFile.getProperty(key) + "\"},\n");
      }

      fw.write("        {\"PropertyToListResourceBundleCreator\", "
               + "\"O'Reilly\"}\n");
      fw.write("    };\n");
      fw.write("}\n");

      fw.close();
    } catch (MissingResourceException mre) {
      mre.printStackTrace();
    } catch (IOException ioe) {
      ioe.printStackTrace();
    }
  }
}
```

We demonstrate the utility on the `PropertyResourceBundle` in **Example 4-25.**

Example 4-25. Test Resource Bundle

```
# Test properties file (TestProperties_en_US.properties)
#
Key1=This is the value for Key 1
Key2=This is the value for Key 2
Key3=This is the value for Key 3
```

The utility is run as follows:

```
C:\>java -Duser.language=en -Duser.region=US PropertyToListResourceBundle TestProperties
```

Example 4-26 shows the `ListResourceBundle` **created by the utility.**

Example 4-26. ListResourceBundle Created by the PropertyToListResourceBundle Utility

```
import java.util.ListResourceBundle;

public class TestResources_en_US extends ListResourceBundle {

    public Object [][] getContents() {
        return contents;
    }

    static final Object [][] contents = {
        {"Key3", "This is the value for Key 3"},
        {"Key2", "This is the value for Key 2"},
        {"Key1", "This is the value for Key 1"},
        {"PropertyToListResourceBundleCreator", "O'Reilly"}
    };
}
```

Deploying Resource Bundles with Applets

Applets can use resource bundles just like other applications. In this section, we show you how to package an entire applet (both program code and resource files) into a single JavaARchive (JAR) file for deployment. Two advantages of using a JAR file for deploying applets are:

- A single HTTP request is made to the web server hosting the applet to retrieve the program code and resources, which reside in a single JAR file.

- A JAR can compress the files it contains, making the request size for an application and its resources smaller than if the files were uncompressed.

There's really not much difference to deploying an applet packaged in a JAR file. We only have to specify the JAR file that contains all required *.class* and *.properties* files that hold the necessary resources required to run your applet. When running your applet, the browser tries to pull the resource files from the JAR file instead of pulling the resource from the web server. This feature helps save download time for your users and makes your application self-contained.

Like resource bundles, JAR is a convenient bundling mechanism for Java code. You can use JAR files to package and deploy applets and applications. JAR files (ending with a *.jar* extension) are similar to the ubiquitous ZIP file (ending with a *.zip* extension), a popular compressed file format. JAR and ZIP files differ because JAR files can contain an optional `Manifest` entry. A manifest entry is used to specify meta-information about the entire JAR file or individual files in the JAR file.[1]

JAR files are created using the `jar` command-line utility provided with the Java Development Kit. The syntax is fairly straightforward and the utility is very easy to use. If you have all your *.class* and *.properties* files in a single directory, run the jar utility by entering:

```
C:\>jar cvf DemonstrationApplet.jar *.class *.properties
```

The `c` option tells the jar program that you're *creating* a JAR file. The `v` option specifies *verbose* output while creating the archive file. The `f` option lets the program know that you're specifying the archive *file name* as the next parameter. Once you created a JAR file successfully, how do you deploy your applet? This step should require few modifications to the *.html* file containing your applet's `<APPLET></APPLET>` tag. Suppose your HTML file looked like Example 4-27.

Example 4-27. HTML File for Running an Applet Not Contained in a JAR File

```
<HTML>

<HEAD>
<TITLE>My Test Applet</TITLE>
</HEAD>

<BODY>

Here is my applet...<P>
<APPLET code="MyTestApplet.class" width=300 height=400>
<PARAM name="User" value="Pamela Ann">
</APPLET>

</BODY>
</HTML>
```

---

[1] You can read more about the manifest format online at *http://java.sun.com/products/jdk/ 1.3/docs/guide/jar/manifest.html*

Let's assume that you've called the JAR file containing this applet and its associated *.properties* files *MyTestApplet.jar*. The HTML used to run your applet would now look like Example 4-28.

Example 4-28. HTML File for Running an Applet Contained in a JAR File

```
<HTML>

<HEAD>
<TITLE>My Test Applet</TITLE>
</HEAD>

<BODY>

Here is my applet...<P>
<APPLET archive="MyTestApplet.jar" code="MyTestApplet.class" width=300 height=400>
<PARAM name="User" value="Pamela Ann">
</APPLET>

</BODY>
</HTML>
```

Design Considerations for Resource Bundles

The resource bundle facilities in Java allow you to decouple user-displayed messages from your actual program code and user interface. That is, resources like messages are not hardcoded directly into the application. You may also want to differentiate your resources further by packaging similar types of resources together. You do not need to restrict yourself to using only one set of resource bundles. Examples of these considerations might be:

```
UserExceptionResources
UserExceptionResources_de
UserExceptionResources_de_DE
UserExceptionResources_es
StatusMessageResources
StatusMessageResources_es
StatusMessageResources_es_ES
... and so on
```

Another good practice is to give your resource bundles meaningful names. They should be easily identified as being specific to your application. If you decided to develop a spreadsheet application, starting out with SpreadsheetApplicationResources would be a good choice for naming your bundles. A base name such as

`ProgramResources` for your resource bundles is not bad, but from a development standpoint, it does not adequately identify the resources as being specific to your spreadsheet application.

One advantage of using resource bundles is that you can support new locales by adding more resource bundles. If you have taken the proper steps to internationalize your application, you just need to make new resource bundles available. Your users don't have to download a new version of the entire application. They just have to install the new resource bundles in the proper location.

5

Formatting Messages

Several problems can occur when building text messages that need to be displayed to a user. The rules of grammar that apply to one natural language are often quite different from those that apply to other natural languages. You may not have thought about it before, but most programmers unintentionally hardcode these rules into messages as they are dynamically built.

Messages often have embedded data, such as dates, times, and numbers that must be formatted correctly according to local conventions. In this chapter, we examine issues associated with formatting messages. We will show you how you can take advantage of the built-in Java classes that enable you to handle complex message formatting. Finally, we will help you become aware of some classes and methods you should stay away from because they are not internationalized.

Date and Time Formats

The format for displaying date and time information varies according to local conventions. An American would interpret the date 03/10/1999 as March 10, 1999. A British reader, however, would interpret the same date as October 3, 1999. Obviously, formatting the date correctly is important to convey the correct message you intend to send. In this example, the delimiter (/) is the same in both locales; however, delimiters also vary depending on the locale. Additionally, each locale typically has several different formats that can be used. The following date formats are acceptable in the United States:

10/4/99
October 4th, 1999
Monday, October 04, 1999

Mon, Oct 4, 1999
4-OCT-99

You can probably come up with a few more examples yourself. Now compare those date formats with the same date formatted for France:

04/10/99
4 octobre 1999
lundi 4 octobre 1999
lun. 4 octobre 1999
4-oct.-99

The American and French formats differ in obvious ways. Notice how the order for the first date format is month/day/year for the United States and day/month/year for France. Other differences are the names for the day of the week (Monday versus lundi) and the month of the year (October versus octobre). You might also have seen that names for the weekdays or months don't necessarily have to start with a capitalized letter. English grammatical rules don't apply to the rest of the world!

Besides the names of weekdays and months, the ordering of fields, and the delimiters used between the fields, dates differ around the world based on the calendar system used. While the Western world largely uses the Gregorian calendar (named after Pope Gregory XIII, who instituted it), parts of the world rely on other calendar systems. We will cover these systems later. Finally, when formatting a date for a given locale, the appropriate time zone must be considered. Table 5-1 shows the same date formatted differently for various countries.

Table 5-1. Date Formats Around the World

Country	Date
United States	Monday, October 4, 1999
Saudi Arabia (Western)	الاثنين ٤ تشرين الاول ١٩٩٩
Saudi Arabia (Hijri)	الاثنين ٢٤ جمادى الثانية ١٤٢٠
France	lundi, 4 octobre 1999
Germany	Montag, 4. Oktober 1999
Italy	lunedì 4 ottobre 1999
Japan (Emperor)	平成11年10月4日
Japan (Western)	1999年10月4日 (月)
Israel (Western)	יום שני 04 אוקטובר 1999
Israel (Hebrew)	יום שני כ"ד תשרי תש"ס
Korea	1999년 10월 4일 월요일

Table 5-1. Date Formats Around the World (continued)

Country	Date
China	1999年10月4日星期一
Greece	Δευτέρα, 4 Οκτωβρίου 1999
Russia	Понедельник, 4 октября 1999 г.
Turkey	04 Ekim 1999 Pazartesi

Thinking about how to handle all these different date formats can make even the greatest programmers feel a little weak in the knees. Fortunately, Java comes to the rescue with some nice date and time handling functionality.

NOTE   When manipulating dates in Java, do not use methods of java.util.Date, such as Date.getMonth() or Date.getYear(), to build a String. These functions have been deprecated since JDK 1.1 and can get you into trouble if you use them. They have been deprecated because they assume that all users would want a Gregorian calendar. Besides this pitfall, using the methods would require you to handle all date formats for different locales yourself. You should also avoid using Date.toString() and Date.toLocaleString(). Instead, you should use the java.text.DateFormat class.

`DateFormat` is an abstract class that handles date and time formatting for any locale. Java defines four default date/time formats that can display locale-sensitive date/time strings: FULL, LONG, MEDIUM, and SHORT. Each style is interpreted slightly differently based on the locale; however, the following general rules can be used to determine what each style means:

- SHORT is always a numeric style.

- MEDIUM is slightly longer than SHORT and may include abbreviated names.

- LONG is a longer form of the MEDIUM style. For dates, names of months are typically spelled out; however, names of days are usually not included.

- FULL is more completely specified than LONG.

Additionally, there is a DEFAULT style, which is typically the MEDIUM style. It is not always MEDIUM, though, and you should not assume it is. If no style is specified when calling a factory method, the DEFAULT style is used. Table 5-2 shows several date/time formats using different styles and locales.

Table 5-2. Effects of Styles When Used with getDateTimeInstance()

Style	Locale	Format
SHORT	England	16/10/99 13:03
	France	16/10/99 13:03
	US	10/16/99 1:03 PM
	Germany	16.10.99 13:03
	Italy	16/10/99 13.03
	Israel	13:03 16/10/99
MEDIUM	England	16-Oct-99 13:03:01
	France	16 oct. 99 13:03:01
	US	Oct 16, 1999 1:03:01 PM
	Germany	16.10.1999 13:03:01
	Italy	16-ott-99 13.03.01
	Israel	13:03:01 16/10/1999
LONG	England	16 October 1999 13:03:01 GMT-04:00
	France	16 octobre 1999 13:03:01 GMT-04:00
	US	October 16, 1999 1:03:01 PM EDT
	Germany	16. Oktober 1999 13:03:01 GMT-04:00
	Italy	16 ottobre 1999 13.03.01 GMT-04:00
	Israel	13:03:01 GMT-04:00 16 1999 אוקטובר
FULL	England	16 October 1999 13:03:01 o'clock GMT-04:00
	France	samedi 16 octobre 1999 13 h 03 GMT-04:00
	US	Saturday, October 16, 1999 1:03:01 PM EDT
	Germany	Samstag. 16. Oktober 1999 13.03 Uhr GMT-04:00
	Italy	sabato 16 ottobre 1999 13.03.01 GMT-04:00
	Israel	13:03:01 GMT-04:00 1999 אוקטובר 16 שבת

A few items regarding this table are worth mentioning. First, these date and time formats were generated by running a simple program that called the static factory method `getDateTimeInstance()`, passing each of the styles as parameters. It then calls `format()` to generate a formatted result. For example, here is a snippet of code that formats the current date and time using the FULL style for the default locale:

```
DateFormat df;
df = DateFormat.getDateTimeInstance(DateFormat.FULL, DateFormat.FULL);
String result = df.format(new Date());
```

The second point to note in Table 5-2 is that all the times are based on the default time zone, in this case eastern daylight time (EDT), which is four hours behind Greenwich mean time (GMT). Time zones are covered a little later in this chapter.

Another point worth mentioning can be seen by comparing the FULL style for England and the United States in Table 5-2. Notice that for England, the day is not spelled out as it is for the United States. Also notice that "o'clock," used for the British time format, is left out of the U.S. format.

Finally, if you don't like the formats for a given style and locale combination, you can always create your own customized formats. We discuss this option later in this chapter.

The `DateFormat` class has several static factory methods that allow instantiation of a `DateFormat` object for the default locale or a given locale and/or a formatting style. Essentially, all the factory methods are variations of the following four points:

- `getInstance()` is equivalent to calling `getDateTimeInstance()` and passing SHORT as the style for both the date and time.

- `getDateInstance()` returns a date formatter only.

- `getTimeInstance()` returns a time formatter only.

- `getDateTimeInstance()` returns a date and time formatter.

For example, if you wanted to format a date for the default locale using a LONG style, you could use the following piece of code:

```
String result;
GregorianCalendar bday = new GregorianCalendar(1965,Calendar.JUNE,16);
result = DateFormat.getDateInstance(DateFormat.LONG).format(bday.getTime());
```

Notice that we create the date by instantiating a `GregorianCalendar` object and not using `Date`. In JDK 1.1 and higher, creating dates from individual fields (year, month, day, etc.) should be handled via the `Calendar` class or one of its subclasses.

When formatting multiple dates using the `DateFormat` object, first assign the `DateFormat` object to a variable. This way, you avoid a performance hit for each call to the factory method that instantiates a new object:

```
String result;
DateFormat df = DateFormat.getDateInstance(DateFormat.LONG);

GregorianCalendar cal = new GregorianCalendar(1965,Calendar.JUNE,16);
result = df.format(cal.getTime());

cal.set(1978, Calendar.JUNE, 24);
result = df.format(cal.getTime());
```

In this example we not only reused the `DateFormat` object, but we also reused the `Calendar` object by calling `Calendar.set()`, rather than instantiating a whole new `GregorianCalendar`.

If you want to format a date for a locale other than the default locale, you can pass the `Locale` to the factory method. For example:

```
DateFormat df;
df = DateFormat.getDateInstance(DateFormat.LONG, Locale.FRANCE);

GregorianCalendar cal = new GregorianCalendar(1965, Calendar.JUNE, 16);
String result = df.format(cal.getTime());
```

`DateFormat` can also parse strings containing date and time information. Do not use the `Date.parse()` method for this purpose. Parsing strings into `Date` objects using the `DateFormat` class is useful, for example, when your program must interpret a date that a user typed in. The following code snippet accepts user input from the console, parses it (assuming it to be in mm/dd/yy format), and then reformats it into a FULL style, writing the result back out to the console: [1]

```
InputStreamReader isr = new InputStreamReader(System.in);
BufferedReader in = new BufferedReader(isr);

DateFormat dfi = DateFormat.getDateInstance(DateFormat.SHORT);
DateFormat dfo = DateFormat.getDateInstance(DateFormat.FULL);

String s;
try {
  while ((s = in.readLine()) != null) {
     Date theDate = dfi.parse(s);
     System.out.println(dfo.format(theDate));
  }
} catch (ParseException e) {
   System.out.println("error in parsing date");
} catch (IOException e) {
   System.out.println("io exception " + e);
}
```

If we run the program and enter sample dates, we get the following results:

```
2/28/49
Monday, February 28, 1949
02/28/49
Monday, February 28, 1949
```

---

[1] Making an assumption like this is risky because the SHORT format is not necessarily mm/dd/yy. It could just as easily be dd.mm.yy. To be absolutely sure about the format of the date you intend to parse, you need to use a customized format pattern. Format patterns are described in the next section.

Notice that `DateFormat.parse()` handles both "2" and "02" correctly. Now let's look at what happens if we enter a date that doesn't exist. 1949 was not a leap year, so February 29, 1949 is not a valid date:

```
2/29/49
Tuesday, March 1, 1949
```

The date is parsed and converted into the day after February 28, 1949. Java assumes that is what we want. If you don't want Java to make such assumptions, you can turn this feature off by calling the `DateFormat.setLenient()` method. If we add the following line of code to our program immediately after getting the Date-Format instance:

```
dfi.setLenient(false);
```

When we compile it and run it again with the same erroneous date, we see that a `java.text.ParseException` is thrown instead:

```
2/29/49
error in parsing date
```

Finally, if a date is entered in a format other than the format `DateFormat` expects, a `java.text.ParseExecption` is thrown:

```
2-feb-49
error in parsing date
```

Of course, `DateFormat.parse()` can also convert between formats of different locales. Example 5-1 generates a date in the French locale using a LONG style. It then parses the string, converting it into a `Date`, and reformats the date into the default locale using a FULL style.

Example 5-1. Parsing a Date

```java
// instantiate a GregorianCalendar with a given date
GregorianCalendar cal = new GregorianCalendar(1965, Calendar.JUNE, 16);

// get a DateFormat object using a LONG style and French locale
DateFormat df;
df = DateFormat.getDateInstance(DateFormat.LONG, Locale.FRANCE);

// format the date
String frDate = df.format(cal.getTime());

// parse must be called inside a try block.
try {
  // parse the French formatted date using the DateFormat object
  // we instantiated earlier.
  Date theDate = df.parse(frDate);

  // format the Date object using the default locale and a FULL style
  String result;
  result = DateFormat.getDateInstance(DateFormat.FULL).format(theDate);
} catch (ParseException e) {
  System.out.println("Error parsing date");
}
```

Defining Your Own Date and Time Formats

Using SimpleDateFormat

You can also define your own date and time formats if you feel that the formats provided by the JDK are insufficient. This definition is accomplished by supplying a pattern to SimpleDateFormat. When you call the factory methods on DateFormat, the object you get back is a SimpleDateFormat instance cast to a DateFormat. You can cast the object back to a SimpleDateFormat object. Then apply a pattern to that object and use the format() method, as we described earlier. You can also instantiate a SimpleDateFormat object directly. Table 5-3 shows the symbols that can be used in a pattern.

Table 5-3. Symbols for Defining Your Own Date Patterns

Symbol	Meaning	Presentation	Value for U.S. Locale
G	Era designator	Text	AD
y	Year	Number	1999
M	Month in year	Text or Number	6, 06, Jun., or June
d	Day in month	Number	10
h	Hour in AM/PM (1 – 12)	Number	12
H	Hour in day (0 – 23)	Number	0
m	Minute in hour	Number	30
s	Second in minute	Number	55
S	Millisecond	Number	821
E	Day in week	Text	Sunday
D	Day in year	Number	322
F	Day of week in month	Number	3 (i.e., 3rd Mon. in June)
w	Week in year	Number	26
W	Week in month	Number	2
a	AM/PM marker	Text	PM
k	Hour in day (1 – 24)	Number	24
K	Hour in AM/PM (0 – 11)	Number	0
z	Time zone	Text	Eastern standard time
'	Escape for text	Delimiter	(None)
"	Single quote	Literal	'

SimpleDateFormat is locale-sensitive; the output can vary based on the combination of pattern provided and the default locale or the locale passed to the constructor. Example 5-2 shows a code snippet that instantiates a SimpleDateFormat object with a pattern and then formats a date using the formatter.

Example 5-2. Sample Code Showing SimpleDateFormat Usage

```
// Instantiate the formatter using a pattern
SimpleDateFormat sdf = new SimpleDateFormat("EEEE, MMMM d yyyy G");

// Define a date using the GregorianCalendar.
GregorianCalendar anniv = new GregorianCalendar(1999,Calendar.OCTOBER,4);

// format the date using the SimpleDateFormat formmatter
String theDate = sdf.format(anniv.getTime());

// print the output to standard out
System.out.println(theDate);
```

If we run this program using several locales, we get some interesting results:

Locale	Output
en_US	Monday, October 4 1999 AD
fr_FR	lundi, octobre 4 1999 ap. J.-C.
it_IT	lunedì, ottobre 4 1999 dopo Cristo
de_DE	Montag, Oktober 4 1999 n. Chr.

The number of consecutive times the symbol is used in the pattern and the presentation type (as shown in Table 5-3) for a particular symbol determines the data format. The general rules are presented in Table 5-4.

Table 5-4. Rules for Symbol Occurrences in Patterns

Presentation	Occurrences	Result
Number	≥ 1	If more symbols than digits occur, the number is padded with zeros. For years, 1 – 3 symbols displays a two-digit year; ≥ 4 symbols displays a four-digit year.[2]
Text	1 – 3	Abbreviated form
Text	≥ 4	Full form
Text or Number	1 – 2	Numeric form
Text or Number	≥ 3	Text form

For example, Table 5-5 shows some patterns and results for a few locales.

---

[2] Note that the actual behavior we describe for formatting years is inconsistent with the documentation in the javadocs. This inconsistency is a known bug and is filed as bug 4358730.

Table 5-5. Effect of Symbol Occurrences Combined with Locales

Pattern	Locale	Result
EEEE, MMMM d yyyy	en_US	Monday, October 4 1999
	de_DE	Montag, Oktober 4 1999
	it_IT	lunedì, ottobre 4 1999
EEE, MMM ddd yy	en_US	Mon, Oct 004 99
	de_DE	Mo, Okt 004 99
	it_IT	lun, ott 004 99
EE, MM d yyy	en_US	Mon, 10 4 99
	de_DE	Mo, 10 4 99
	it_IT	lun, 10 4 99

When using a `SimpleDateFormat` object, you can employ the `applyPattern()` method to reuse the object without having to instantiate a new one. For example:

```
SimpleDateFormat sdf = new SimpleDateFormat();
Date today = new Date();

sdf.applyPattern("EE, MM d yy");
System.out.println(sdf.format(today));

sdf.applyPattern("yyyy.MMMM.dd G");
System.out.println(sdf.format(today));
```

generates the output:

```
Mon, 07 31 00
2000.July.31 AD
```

Patterns used with `SimpleDateFormat` are invariant across locales from the programmer's standpoint. Remember that some patterns (for example, displaying "d" to represent "day") probably won't make sense in other locales. In French, the word "day" is "jour," so the user might expect to see "j" for the representative symbol. To solve this problem, you can use localized pattern symbols in addition to the invariant pattern symbols we have already discussed. To determine what the equivalent localized pattern for a specific locale is, you can use the `toLocalized-Pattern()` method. For example, the following code:

```
SimpleDateFormat sdf = new SimpleDateFormat("yyyy.MMMM.dd",
                                            Locale.FRANCE);
System.out.println(sdf.toLocalizedPattern());
```

generates the following output:

```
aaaa.nnnn.jj
```

To use a localized pattern to format a date/time, call `applyLocalizedPattern()` instead of `applyPattern()`. You can also change characters for localized patterns via the `DateFormatSymbols` class, which we talk about next.

Using DateFormatSymbols

The data used when formatting date and time information using patterns can also be customized. All information is encapsulated in a `DateFormatSymbols` object within the `DateFormat` object. The data are accessed via get and set methods. The majority of the get and set methods deal with arrays. Tables 5-6 and 5-7 show the data contained in these arrays for the U.S. locale. The index column indicates the index into the array. So if you had code that looked like this:

```
SimpleDateFormat sdf = new SimpleDateFormat();
DateFormatSymbols dfs = sdf.getDateFormatSymbols();

String weekdays[] = dfs.getWeekdays();
String months[] = dfs.getShortMonths();
```

then in the U.S. locale, the value of `weekdays[3]` is Tuesday according to Table 5-6 and the value of `months[5]` is Jun according to Table 5-7.

Table 5-6. DateFormatSymbols Array Contents for en_US

Index	AmPmStrings	Eras	Weekdays	ShortWeekdays
0	AM	BC		
1	PM	AD	Sunday	Sun
2			Monday	Mon
3			Tuesday	Tue
4			Wednesday	Wed
5			Thursday	Thu
6			Friday	Fri
7			Saturday	Sat

Table 5-7. DateFormatSymbols Array Contents for en_US

Index	Months	ShortMonths
0	January	Jan
1	February	Feb
2	March	Mar
3	April	Apr
4	May	May
5	June	Jun
6	July	Jul
7	August	Aug

Table 5-7. DateFormatSymbols Array Contents for en_US (continued)

Index	Months	ShortMonths
8	September	Sep
9	October	Oct
10	November	Nov
11	December	Dec
12		

NOTE For ShortWeekdays and Weekdays, a null `String` is the first element in the array. For Months and ShortMonths, 13 elements are in the array. For most locales, the 12th index (13th element) is a null `String`. This string is needed to support calendars that have 13 months in the year.

To change a symbol or set of symbols, call the appropriate set method. One way to make this call is to call the corresponding get method, modify the return value and call the set method, passing the modified return value back in. You can also build the array yourself, making sure that the elements are indexed correctly, and then calling the appropriate set method.

Depending on the locale, for example, using BC (Before Christ) and AD (Anno Domini) as eras may not be the most appropriate choice.[3] You might decide to replace these letters with the more modern acronyms BCE (Before the Common Era) and CE (Common Era). Example 5-3 demonstrates symbol substitution:

Example 5-3. Using DateFormatSymbols to Change the Era Acronyms

```java
public class ChangeEra {

  public static void main(String s[]) {
    SimpleDateFormat sdf = new SimpleDateFormat();
    DateFormatSymbols dfs = sdf.getDateFormatSymbols();

    String era[] = { "BCE", "CE" };
    dfs.setEras(era);
    sdf.setDateFormatSymbols(dfs);

    sdf.applyPattern("MMMM d yyyy G");
    System.out.println(sdf.format(new Date()));
  }
}
```

---

[3] Anno Domini is Latin and means "in the year of our Lord." Many people mistakenly believe that AD stands for "After Death." If that were the case, we would have to use an acronym to refer to the era during Jesus' life, which of course we don't have.

Running the program yields the following output:

```
October 17 1999 CE
```

Notice that we got the `DateFormatSymbols` instance from the `SimpleDateFormat` object, changed the symbols, and set the `DateFormatSymbols` object on the `SimpleDateFormat` object again.

In addition to the symbols shown in Tables 5-6 and 5-7, `get` and `set` methods change the localized pattern characters. Unlike the other customizable symbols, the pattern characters are stored in one string rather than an array. If we call `DateFormatSymbols.getLocalPatternChars()` for the U.S. locale, a `String` containing the following data is returned:

```
GyMdkHmsSEDFwWahKz
```

Changing the pattern characters to something else is a simple matter of calling `DateFormatSymbols.setLocalePatternChars()`, passing in the new `String`:

```
SimpleDateFormat sdf = new SimpleDateFormat();
DateFormatSymbols dfs = sdf.getDateFormatSymbols();

dfs.setLocalePatternChars("EsxyShdpPBbQvVbiRm");
sdf.setDateFormatSymbols(dfs);
```

`SimpleDateFormat` also has methods to get and set time zone display names; however this functionality is not needed in Java 2 and later, since similar methods now exist on the `TimeZone` class.

Calendar Systems

Most of the Western world has standardized use of the Gregorian calendar. In the latter half of the sixteenth century, Pope Gregory XIII appointed a commission led by Christopher Clavius, a Jesuit mathematician and astronomer, to fix the Julian calendar. It was well known at that time that Easter was not celebrated on the correct day. In fact, it had gradually become a summer celebration. The Julian calendar had been in use since Julius Caesar adopted it in 45 BCE, and it included leap years every four years. Clavius however, was able to calculate the exact transit time of the earth around the sun and adjusted his calendar to omit leap years if the year occurs at the beginning of the century (1800, 1900, 2000, etc.), unless that year is divisible by 400. So, for example, 1600 and 2000 are leap years, while 1900 was not. Clavius published his results in an 800-page document and Thursday, October 4, 1582 became the last day of the Julian calendar. The following day was Friday, October 15, 1582 of the Gregorian calendar.

Not all countries accepted the calendar immediately. The Orthodox Church was rather offended by the Roman intrusion, and Protestant countries rarely accepted any decree from a pope. As a result, the exact cutover date from the Julian to Gregorian calendar is different among countries. For example, England didn't adopt the Gregorian calendar until 1752. Russia didn't accept the change until the Bolshevik revolution.[4]

Parts of the world today, however, use other types of calendars. In Japan, the Gregorian calendar is used beside a calendar system called Japan Emperor. The Japan Emperor calendar counts years that the current Japanese emperor has been reigning, so the year 1999 is actually 11 Heisei. Table 5-8 shows the recent era names for the Japanese calendar and the dates that are associated with each era.

Table 5-8: Japanese Emperor Calendar Eras

Name of Era	Period
Meiji era (明治)	September 8, 1868 to July 29, 1912
Taisho era (大正)	July 30, 1912 to December 24, 1926
Showa era (昭和)	December 25, 1926 to January 7, 1989
Heisei era (平成)	January 8, 1989 to present

Additional calendars in use around the world that are not based on the Gregorian calendar include the Hebrew, Hijri (Islamic), Hindu, and Buddhist calendars. These calendars don't simply differ in the way they count years. The Hebrew and Hijri calendars, for example, are based on lunar months.

The Hebrew calendar has 12 months in most years, but every two or three years an additional month is added for that year. These 13-month years are called *leap years* and the month *Adar* (אדר) occurs twice; once as *Adar 1* (אדר א') and again as *Adar 2* (אדר ב'). Years in the Hebrew calendar are counted from the beginning of the world according to Judaism. The beginning of the Hebrew year is Rosh Hashana (ראש השנה), which literally translated means "head of the year." Rosh Hashana typically occurs in September or October of the Gregorian calendar. The new Hebrew year, which began on September 11, 1999 of the Gregorian calendar, was 5760.

In Java, calendar-related functionality is encapsulated in the abstract class `java.util.Calendar`. To instantiate a `Calendar` object, call `Calendar.getInstance()`, which returns a `Calendar` object appropriate for the current locale with the date and time fields set to the current date and time:

---

[4] A nice set of tables listing the cutover date for several countries can be found at *http://www.norbyhus.dk/calendar.html.*

```
Calendar cal = Calendar.getInstance();
```

To retrieve the `Date` object from `Calendar`, use the `getTime()` method, as in:

```
Date now = cal.getTime();
```

As of this writing, Java 2 does not have support for calendars other than the Gregorian calendar.[5] Therefore, calling any one of the `Calendar.getInstance()` methods currently returns an instance of the concrete subclass `java.util.GregorianCalendar`.

If you know that you definitely want a Gregorian calendar, you can call the `GregorianCalendar` constructor directly:

```
GregorianCalendar cal = new GregorianCalendar(1776, Calendar.JULY, 4);
```

In this example, we called the constructor that takes a year, month, and day as parameters. Notice that we used `Calendar.JULY` instead of an integer value. When the engineers at IBM built the `Calendar` class, they thought it would be a good idea to number months the same way they are numbered on the `Date` object, starting from 0. This process is rather confusing for most people who think of January as the first month of the year. In any event, you should use the constants shown in Table 5-9, rather than raw numbers, to make your code more readable.

Table 5-9: java.util.Calendar Month Constants

Constant	Value	Description
Calendar.JANUARY	0	January
Calendar.FEBRUARY	1	February
Calendar.MARCH	2	March
Calendar.APRIL	3	April
Calendar.MAY	4	May
Calendar.JUNE	5	June
Calendar.JULY	6	July
Calendar.AUGUST	7	August
Calendar.SEPTEMBER	8	September
Calendar.OCTOBER	9	October
Calendar.NOVEMBER	10	November
Calendar.DECEMBER	11	December
Calendar.UNDECIMBER	12	Month 13 for non-Gregorian calendars

---

[5] International calendar classes are available for download however, from IBM's ICU4J site *http://oss.software.ibm.com/icu4j*.

The GregorianCalendar class correctly handles all dates since March 1, 4 CE. This date was the first year when leap years were applied uniformly. Prior to that year, leap years were added arbitrarily and, as we discussed earlier, the Julian calendar didn't exist before 45 BCE.

Dates prior to the cutover date of October 15, 1582 will be handled correctly. If you want to adjust the cutover date for countries that adopted the calendar later, do so by calling setGregorianChange(). For example, the cutover date for England was September 14, 1752. The following piece of code effects the appropriate change:

```
GregorianCalendar cutover;
cutover = new GregorianCalendar(1752, Calendar.SEPTEMBER, 14);

// 1700 should not be a leap year under the Gregorian calendar
// because it is not divisible by 400.
System.out.println(cutover.isLeapYear(1700));

// change cutover date to September 14th, 1752
cutover.setGregorianChange(cutover.getTime());

// 1700 should be a leap year now, because the date occurs
// prior to the cutover date and is thus calculated using
// Julian calendar rules.
System.out.println(cutover.isLeapYear(1700));
```

The output from this code results in:

```
false
true
```

which is exactly what we would expect.

The Calendar class has two abstract methods, set() and get(), which can be used to manipulate fields within the calendar. For example:

```
int year = Calendar.getInstance().get(Calendar.YEAR);
```

gets a Calendar instance in the current locale with the date and time set to the current time and then returns the year piece of the date. Likewise, the following code:

```
Calendar cal = Calendar.getInstance();
cal.set(Calendar.YEAR, 2001);
```

gets a Calendar instance and then modifies the year portion of it by calling set(), which takes two parameters. The first parameter indicates the time field that will be modified, and the second parameter is the integer value the field should be changed to.

Table 5-10 lists the fields of `Calendar` that can be used in the `get()` and `set()` methods. Some fields in the table are designated with an asterisk (*). Tables 5-11 through 5-13 show constants (defined on the `Calendar` class) that should be used instead of raw numbers. The number to the right of the asterisk is the table in this book that contains the valid constants for this field.

Table 5-10. java.util.calendar Fields Used by get() and set()

Field	Description
`AM_PM (* Table 5-11)`	Indicates whether the hour is before or after noon
`DATE`	Indicates the day of the month
`DAY_OF_MONTH`	Synonymous with DATE
`DAY_OF_WEEK (* Table 5-12)`	Indicates the day of week
`DAY_OF_WEEK_IN_MONTH`	Indicates the ordinal number of the day of the weekday within the current month
`DAY_OF_YEAR`	Indicates the day number within the year
`DST_OFFSET`	Indicates daylight saving offset in milliseconds
`ERA (* Table 5-13)`	i.e., AD or BC in the Gregorian U.S. locale
`HOUR`	Used for the 12-hour clock
`HOUR_OF_DAY`	Used for the 24-hour clock
`MILLISECOND`	Indicates milliseconds within the current second
`MINUTE`	Indicates minutes within the current hour
`MONTH (* Table 5-9)`	Indicates the ordinal month within the year
`SECOND`	Indicates seconds within the current minute
`WEEK_OF_MONTH`	Indicates week number within the current month
`WEEK_OF_YEAR`	Indicates the week number within the year
`YEAR`	Indicates the year
`ZONE_OFFSET`	Raw offset of time zone from GMT in milliseconds

Table 5-11. Constant Values for Calendar.AM_PM Field

Constant	Description
`Calendar.AM`	The period of the day from midnight to just before noon
`Calendar.PM`	The period of the day from noon to just before midnight

Table 5-12. Constant Values for Calendar.DAY_OF_WEEK Field

Constant	Description
Calendar.SUNDAY	Sunday
Calendar.MONDAY	Monday
Calendar.TUESDAY	Tuesday
Calendar.WEDNESDAY	Wednesday
Calendar.THURSDAY	Thursday
Calendar.FRIDAY	Friday
Calendar.SATURDAY	Saturday

Table 5-13. Constant Values for Calendar.ERA Field

Constant	Description
GregorianCalendar.BC	The period of time before the common era (before Christ).
GregorianCalendar.AD	The period of time during the common era (after the birth of Christ, or Anno Domini).

As you may recall from Example 3-1 in Chapter 3, *Locales,* we provided a sample program that displays days of the week in the correct order. The program used DateFormatSymbols to get the names of the days of the week and used the Calendar.getFirstDayOfWeek() method to determine the day on which the week began. While the United States starts the week on Sunday, most of Europe considers the first day of the week to be Monday, and most Middle Eastern countries consider Saturday the first day of the week.

Example 5-4 creates calendar instances for three different locales (Jordan, France, and Canada). It then writes the first day of the week for each local to standard output.

Example 5-4. Showing the First Day of the Week in Three Locales

```
Calendar JO_cal = Calendar.getInstance(new Locale("ar", "JO"));
Calendar FR_cal = Calendar.getInstance(Locale.FRANCE);
Calendar CA_cal = Calendar.getInstance(Locale.CANADA);

DateFormatSymbols dfs = new DateFormatSymbols();
String weekdays[] = dfs.getWeekdays();

System.out.println(weekdays[JO_cal.getFirstDayOfWeek()]);
System.out.println(weekdays[FR_cal.getFirstDayOfWeek()]);
System.out.println(weekdays[CA_cal.getFirstDayOfWeek()]);
```

Running this program generates the following output:

```
Saturday
Monday
Sunday
```

Another nice feature of the `Calendar` class is the ability to add and roll dates. You can change the `Calendar` date to move forward or backward in time by a given unit (day, month, week, year, etc.). You might have seen this type of capability in a graphical calendar widget. Adding or rolling dates manually is difficult because it requires the programmer to worry about things such as month and year boundaries, leap years, and, of course, non-Gregorian calendars! Adding and rolling in the `Calendar` class are handled in an internationalized way so that if new calendars are added in the future, adding and rolling will still work correctly.

To add a time unit to the current date, call the abstract `Calendar` method `add(int field, int amount)`. The field parameter can be any of the fields from Table 5-10. For example, the following code snippet adds eight days to the current date:

```
Calendar cal = Calendar.getInstance();
cal.add(Calendar.DATE, 8);
```

To subtract an amount, simply use a negative parameter. The following piece of code subtracts four hours from the current time:

```
Calendar cal = Calendar.getInstance();
cal.add(Calendar.HOUR, -4);
```

To help you understand how these manipulations affect the date, look at the program in Example 5-5.

Example 5-5. Manipulating Fields on the Calendar Class via the add Method

```
public class CalendarManipulation {
  public static void main(String s[]) {
    Calendar cal = Calendar.getInstance();
    DateFormat df = DateFormat.getDateTimeInstance(DateFormat.FULL,
                                                   DateFormat.MEDIUM);

    // print out the current date and time
    System.out.println(df.format(cal.getTime()));

    // add 8 days to the current date and print out the date and time
    cal.add(Calendar.DATE, 8);
    System.out.println(df.format(cal.getTime()));

    // subtract 4 hours from the time and print out the date and time
    cal.add(Calendar.HOUR, -4);
    System.out.println(df.format(cal.getTime()));
```

Example 5-5. Manipulating Fields on the Calendar Class Via the add Method (continued)

```
      // add 12 hours to the current time and print out the date and time
      cal.add(Calendar.AM_PM, 1);
      System.out.println(df.format(cal.getTime()));

      // add another 12 hours and print out the date and time
      cal.add(Calendar.AM_PM, 1);
      System.out.println(df.format(cal.getTime()));
   }
}
```

The output of this program looks something like this:

```
Sunday,    October 24, 1999 1:03:41 PM
Monday,    November 1, 1999 1:03:41 PM
Monday,    November 1, 1999 9:03:41 AM
Monday,    November 1, 1999 9:03:41 PM
Tuesday, November 2, 1999 9:03:41 AM
```

Rolling is similar to adding, except the behavior is slightly different if a boundary is encountered. The mechanism by which dates are rolled in Java is almost identical to that of adding:

```
Calendar cal = Calendar.getInstance();
cal.roll(Calendar.DATE, 8);
```

In this case, if the current date is October 24, the result of this code causes the date to be October 1, whereas if we had used add(), it would be November 1. Dates can also be rolled backward. If we had the following code:

```
Calendar cal = new GregorianCalendar(2000, Calendar.JANUARY, 1);
cal.roll(Calendar.MONTH, -1);
```

the date is rolled back from January 1, 2000 to December 1, 2000. If we had used add(), the date would be December 1, 1999. The following code is almost identical to the code we just showed, except that we changed the field parameter on roll() from Calendar.MONTH to Calendar.DATE:

```
Calendar cal = new GregorianCalendar(2000, Calendar.JANUARY, 1);
cal.roll(Calendar.DATE, -1);
```

In this case, the date is pushed forward from January 1, 2000 to January 31, 2000.

Time Zones

The world is divided into 24 longitudinal regions called time zones, where each time zone is approximately 15° wide. The 0° longitudinal line, also known as a *meridian,* passes through Greenwich, England. Each time zone is given an offset from the time in Greenwich, which is referred to as *Greenwich mean time* (GMT). For example, the east coast of the United States is in the eastern standard time zone, which is –5 hours from GMT, or GMT-5. Israel, on the other hand, is +2 hours from GMT, or GMT+2. In general, the 12 zones to the east of Greenwich increase by one hour for each zone while the 12 zones to the west of Greenwich decrease by one hour. At least that is how time zones would work in a perfect world. In reality, the lines move in different parts of the world to satisfy political and geographical boundaries. In fact, you may be surprised to find out that the time can differ between two zones by 30 or even 45 minutes.[6] Figure 5-1 shows the world time zone table.

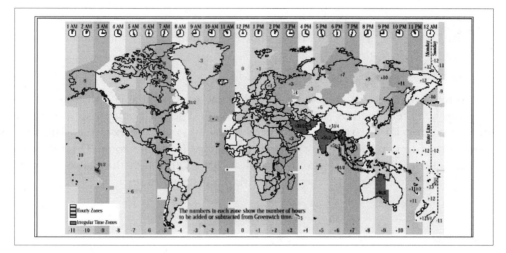

Figure 5-1: World time zones

To take advantage of more daylight hours, some locations compensate for the shorter days in winter by moving the clocks back an hour in autumn and forward an hour in spring. During the summer months, the time zone runs on *daylight saving time*. During the rest of the year, the time zone runs on *standard time*. Determining time zones is actually a bit more complex than that, however. Not all time zones switch between standard time and daylight saving time simultaneously. In the United States, Arizona, Hawaii, part of Indiana, Puerto Rico, the Virgin Islands, and American Samoa never switch to daylight saving time. To make matters even more complicated, some regions within the same time zone don't always adhere to the switch over. In the United States, Albuquerque, New Mexico and Phoenix, Arizona both lie in the mountain standard time zone, or GMT-7. However, Phoenix does not make the switchover, so during the summer months Phoenix is an hour behind Albuquerque!

---

[6] The offsets for every time zone worldwide can be found at *http://www.worldtimeserver.com*.

The addition of `java.util.TimeZone` was new in JDK 1.1. This class, along with its concrete subclass `java.util.SimpleTimeZone`, encapsulates the obscurities of dealing with these time zone issues. Internally, the `TimeZone` class maintains a raw offset from GMT in seconds. Rules for when daylight saving begins and ends are also taken care of, but these rules can be overridden using the `setStartRule()` and `setEndRule()` methods on `SimpleTimeZone`.

To determine the default time zone for the host the program is running on, simply call the static method `TimeZone.getDefault()`, as in:

```
TimeZone tz = TimeZone.getDefault();
```

You can also get a specific time zone by calling the static method `Time-Zone.getTimeZone(String ID)`, as in:

```
TimeZone tz = TimeZone.getTimeZone("GMT");
```

which returns a `TimeZone` object set to GMT. The list of available time zone identifiers can be determined by calling the static method `getAvailableIDs()`. Typically, the time zone ID is structured in terms of region/city, for example, America/New_York. In many cases, more than one ID maps to a time zone. The following IDs are all in the same time zone region as GMT (although they have different behavior with respect to how they observe daylight saving time):

```
Africa/Ouagadougou
Africa/Abidjan
Africa/Accra
Africa/Banjul
Africa/Conakry
Africa/Bissau
Atlantic/Reykjavik
Africa/Monrovia
Africa/Casablanca
Africa/Timbuktu
Africa/Nouakchott
Atlantic/St_Helena
Africa/Freetown
Africa/Dakar
Africa/Sao_Tome
Africa/Lome
UTC
Atlantic/Faeroe
Atlantic/Canary
Europe/Dublin
Europe/Lisbon
Europe/London
```

It is understandable that people in Lisbon would not want to refer to their time zone as Africa/Timbuktu. You might wonder how we got these time zone names. The following code generated the list:

```
int millisInHour = 60 * 60 * 1000;

// change this value for different time zones
int gmtOffset = 0;

String zones[] = TimeZone.getAvailableIDs(gmtOffset * millisInHour);

for (int i=0; i < zones.length; i++) {
  System.out.println(zones[i]);
}
```

In this sample code, we use another getAvailableIDs() method, except that this one takes a raw offset from GMT. This means that you need to pass it the offset from GMT in milliseconds. Only the list of time zone IDs for that offset is returned.

We referred to Table 5-2 earlier in this chapter and noted that all dates were in the same time zone, even though we had used a DateFormat object with different locales. The reason for this situation is that in JDK 1.2 and later, DateFormat uses the time zone from the host system.[7] To change the time zone, you need to call the DateFormat.setTimeZone() method. The following code instantiates a Date with the current date and time and creates a DateFormat object. It then prints out the formatted date and time before setting the time zone and again after setting the time zone to Australia/Sydney, which happens to be GMT+10:

```
Date now = new Date();
DateFormat df = DateFormat.getDateTimeInstance(DateFormat.FULL,
                                              DateFormat.FULL);
System.out.println(df.format(now));
df.setTimeZone(TimeZone.getTimeZone("Australia/Sydney"));
System.out.println(df.format(now));
```

If run on a machine with the system time zone set to eastern daylight time, the code's output would be:

```
Sunday, October 24, 1999 8:43:58 PM EDT
Monday, October 25, 1999 10:43:58 AM GMT+10:00
```

---

[7] In earlier versions of the JDK, the time zone was determined from the DateFormat's locale, which was often confusing.

The `TimeZone` class can also make queries about daylight saving time. You can find out if the time zone uses daylight saving time by calling `useDaylightTime()`:

```
TimeZone tz = TimeZone.getDefault();
boolean usesDLT = TimeZone.useDaylightTime();
```

To determine if a given date is in daylight saving time for a specific time zone, use the method `inDaylightTime()`. For example:

```
TimeZone tz = TimeZone.getDefault();
boolean dlt = tz.inDaylightTime(new Date());
```

Number Formats

To display a number, it must be converted to a `String` and formatted according to local conventions before it is displayed to the user. A few locale-specific issues need to be addressed when we present numbers in a globally aware manner. The main formatting issues are:

- Group and decimal separators
- Numeric shapes (Arabic, European, Indic, Thai, Chinese, etc.)
- Negative numbers
- Currency symbols and placement
- Percentage symbols and placement

Group and Decimal Separators

In the United States, the decimal separator (the delimiter that separates the whole and fractional parts of a number) is a period (.), and the character used for grouping is the comma (,). An American can easily read 1,234.56 as one thousand, two hundred thirty four and 56 one hundredths. In Germany, however, the decimal separator is a comma (,) and the grouping character is a period (.). In other words, a German would expect the same number to be formatted as 1.234,56. In Russia, the number is formatted as 1.234 56 and in France the number is formatted as 1 234,56.

Numeric Shapes

Numeric shapes used in the Western hemisphere are well known internationally. However, shapes of numbers used in other parts of the world vary radically. The decimal numbering system was developed in India (१ २ ३ …) and was later adopted by the Arabs, who modified the glyph forms slightly (١٢٣…). Later, the

Europeans adopted the decimal numbers from the Arabs and again altered the character shapes (123...). European shapes were adopted in various parts of the world and are even used in many parts of the Arabic-speaking world. This adoption has led to some confusion in the names of different numbering systems. The forms used by the Europeans are called "Arabic digits." The forms used in the Arab world are called "Hindi digits." The forms used in India are also called "Hindi digits." To avoid confusion, we use the naming scheme termed by the Unicode™ Standard; the forms used in Europe and many other parts of the world are referred to as *European*. The digits used in the Arabic world are called *Arabic*. The forms used in Iran and Pakistan are referred to as *Eastern Arabic Indic*, while those used in the Indian sub-continent are called *Indic*. Several Indic variants exist, including Devanagari, Bengali, Gurmukhi, Oriya, and Tamil.

Besides the number forms mentioned, different numeric forms exist for ideographic numbers. Table 5-14 shows several numeric glyph shapes.

Table 5-14. Number Forms

European	Arabic	Eastern Arabic Indic	Indic-Devanagari	Indic-Bengali	Thai	Ideographic
0	٠	٠	०	০	๐	零
1	١	١	१	১	๑	一
2	٢	٢	२	২	๒	二
3	٣	٣	३	৩	๓	三
4	٤	۴	४	8	๔	四
5	٥	۵	५	৫	๕	五
6	٦	۶	६	৬	๖	六
7	٧	٧	७	৭	๗	七
8	٨	٨	८	৮	๘	八
9	٩	٩	९	৯	๙	九

Negative Numbers

The manner in which negative numbers are represented changes both between locales and among domains within a locale. For most locales, the minus sign indicates a negative number. A Romanian would expect to see negative one million two hundred thirty four thousand, five hundred sixty seven represented as:

-1.234.567

An American would expect to see the same negative number written as:

-1,234,567

In this case, it looks like the grouping separator that we mentioned earlier in this chapter is the only difference. However, an accountant in the United States would want to see the same number represented as:

($1,234,567)

Finally, the placement of the negative sign could change. Look at what happens when the same number is displayed to an Arabic reader:

1,234,567- or ١,٢٣٤,٥٦٧-

Currency Symbols and Placement

Typically when numbers are formatted for a currency, additional formatting rules must be considered. Besides the decimal and grouping separators, the correct currency symbol must be displayed and the location of the currency symbol must be correct for the given locale. The currency symbol can be a special character ($, £, €, ¥, ฿), one or more alphabetic characters (F, DM, SFr, رس), or a combination of both (NT$, Cz$).

The local currency symbol is typically used within a locale when referring to monetary amounts in that locale's currency. Outside the locale, a three-letter code or international currency symbol is often used to represent the currency. The ISO 4217 standard specifies the three-letter codes.[8] For example, within the U.S, monetary amounts are shown using the dollar sign ($). In other parts of the world, U.S. monetary amounts are denoted with the three-letter code "USD."[9] Table 5-15 shows numbers formatted for various currencies with their three-letter codes.

Table 5-15. Currency Formats Around the World

Country	Format	ISO 4217	Currency
Argentina	$1.234,56	ARS	Peso
China	¥ 1,234.56	CNY	Yuan
France	1 234,56 F	FRF	Franc
France	1 234,56 €	EUR	Euro
Germany	1.234,56 DM	DEM	Deutsche Mark
Israel	ש"ח 1,234.56	NIS	New Shekel
Italy	L. 1.235	ITL	Lira
Italy	€ 1.234,56	EUR	Euro

---

[8] The ISO 4217 codes can be found at http://currency.xe.net/gen/iso4217.htm.

[9] The ISO 4217 codes are needed because a currency symbol is ambiguous (i.e., $ is used for Argentina, Australia, Canada, and the United States).

Table 5-15. Currency Formats Around the World (continued)

Country	Format	ISO 4217	Currency
Japan	¥ 1,234.56	JPY	Yen
Portugal	1.234$56 Esc.	PTE	Escudo
Russia	1 234,56p.	RUR	Ruble
Saudi Arabia	1,2345.56 رس	SAR	Riyal
Sweden	1 234,56 kr	SEK	Krona (plural—kronor)
Switzerland	SFr. 1'234.56	CHF	Franc
Taiwan	NT$1,234.56	TWD	New Dollar
United Kingdom	£1,234.56	GBP	Pound Sterling
United States	$1,234.56	USD	Dollar

There are a few interesting items that should be pointed out in Table 5-15:

- First, currency symbols may take up more than one character! Look at the Israel symbol for new shekel (ש"ח).

- Second, the currency symbol can appear either to the left of the number (e.g., Argentina), to the right of the number (e.g., France), or in the middle of the number (e.g., Portugal).

- Some currencies don't show fractional units; look at how the currency is formatted in the first entry for Italy.[10]

Another important aspect related to currency (that isn't directly related to formatting but is important to understand) is the use of terminology. In the United States, 1 billion is equivalent to 1,000 million. In the United Kingdom, 1 billion is equivalent to 1,000,000 million (a trillion US). It takes a lot more to become a billionaire in the U.K. than it does in the U.S.!

With the introduction of the euro among member countries of the European Community, software must now have the ability to handle both local country currency as well as euro currency. Table 5-15 shows two entries for France and Italy. The first entry for each country shows the French franc and Italian lira, respectively, while the second entry shows the euro. Notice that the number format for both entries with respect to decimal and grouping characters is the same and that the currency symbol for the euro (€) moves, depending on locale.

Finally, you want to be careful when handling the formatting of currencies that you don't arbitrarily replace currency symbols simply based on the locale. For example, if you had currency data in U.S. dollars, you wouldn't want to just change

---

[10] At the time of this writing, 1 USD = 1,814 ITL.

the currency symbol to Japanese yen if you were running the application in Japan. You would either need to make sure your users understood that the amount was in U.S. dollars (probably by using the ISO 4217 code USD) or by performing a currency conversion from U.S. dollars to yen and displaying the correct amount in yen. Of course, doing the currency conversion accurately requires access to up-to-date online information.

Percentage Symbol and Placement

The symbol used for percentage and placement of the symbol can also vary from one locale to another.

```
45 %
45%
45 pct
.45
%45
٪٤٥
```

Number Formatting in Java

All issues we just discussed related to formatting numbers can be handled easily in Java. Remember that you should not use the toString() methods on the classes that extend java.lang.Number, such as Integer or Double, to display numbers to a user. These methods aren't aware of internationalization requirements. Instead, use the abstract class java.text.NumberFormat and its concrete subclass java.text.DecimalFormat. For even more customization, you might need to use java.text.DecimalFormatSymbols, which we describe a little later.

To get a NumberFormat object for the default locale, call:

```
NumberFormat numFormatter = NumberFormat.getInstance();
```

To get a NumberFormat object for a specific locale, call:

```
Locale austria = new Locale("de","AT");
NumberFormat numFormatter = NumberFormat.getInstance(austria);
```

Once you have a NumberFormat object, simply call format(), which returns a formatted String for the appropriate locale:

```
String formattedOutput = NumFormatter.format(1234.56);
```

formattedOutput contains the text "1.234,56," if formatted using the NumberFormat we just created for Austria. The getNumberInstance() method on NumberFormat is identical to getInstance().

Additional factory methods are available on NumberFormat. To format a currency for the default locale, use the factory method:

```
NumberFormat numFormatter = NumberFormat.getCurrencyInstance();
```

To format a percentage for the default locale, use the factory method:

```
NumberFormat numFormatter = NumberFormat.getPercentInstance();
```

As with getInstance(), these factory methods come in two forms. One uses the default locale, and the second one allows you to pass in a Locale and returns a NumberFormat object appropriate for that locale.

When formatting currencies in Java, you should be aware of a couple of things. In JDK 1.1.7b and higher, Java supports the euro for countries that have adopted the euro currency. There is no support in Java for countries that are part of the EC but have not yet adopted the euro (e.g., the United Kingdom). To specify that you want euro currency formatting, you must instantiate the Locale with a EURO variant. If you don't specify the variant as EURO, the local country currency is used. For example, the following code snippet instantiates two NumberFormat objects for Luxembourg. One object formats the output in euro currency and the other formats the output in Luxembourg francs:

```
Locale lu = new Locale("de","LU");
Locale luEuro = new Locale("de","LU", "EURO");

NumberFormat formatter1 = NumberFormat.getCurrencyInstance(lu);
NumberFormat formatter2 = NumberFormat.getCurrencyInstance(luEuro);

double amount = 1234.56;

System.out.println(formatter1.format(amount));
System.out.println(formatter2.format(amount));
```

The output from this code looks like:

```
1.234,56 F
1.234,56 €
```

If you run the program from a DOS window or a Unix command line, you probably won't see the euro symbol (€) correctly. It works fine when displayed in a Swing component. We just show it this way for simplicity's sake.

When formatting currencies in Java, make sure you qualify your locales fully. If you use the following code to get a NumberFormat object, you run into problems:

```
NumberFormat.getCurrencyInstance(new Locale("en",""));
```

These problems occur because English is a language. It certainly isn't sufficient to determine what currency to use, as the currency might be New Zealand dollars, British pounds sterling, U.S. dollars, etc. Thus, you need to include the region specifier for the particular locale. Formatting currencies with an incomplete locale results in use of the currency sign (¤).

Parsing numbers

You can also use `NumberFormat` to parse numbers. You should not use methods such as `Integer.parseInt()` or `Double.parseDouble()` because they cannot deal with formatting differences associated with various locales.

To parse a number, instantiate a `NumberFormat` object using the appropriate factory method and locale and then call `parse()`, as shown in Example 5-6.

Example 5-6. Parsing a Number Using NumberFormat

```
String parseMe = "1.234,56";
NumberFormat numParser = NumberFormat.getInstance(Locale.GERMANY);

try {
  Number result = numParser.parse(parseMe);
  System.out.println(result);
} catch(ParseException e) {
  // handle error condition
}
```

The output of this program is:

```
1234.56
```

Parsing with `NumberFormat` also works nicely when you have a `String` that contains numbers other than European digits. The following program is a good example:

```
// The Malayalam digits ൧൨൩൪ (1234)
String parseMe = "\u0f21\u0f22\u0f23\u0f24";
NumberFormat numParser = NumberFormat.getInstance();

try {
  Number result = numParser.parse(parseMe);
  System.out.println(result);
} catch(ParseException e) {
  // handle error condition
}
```

In this program, `parseMe` contains the Unicode code points for the characters ൧൨൩൪, the numbers 1234 in the Malayalam script.[11]

Notice that the call to `getInstance()` does not specify a `Locale`. Since we do not have formatting characters (i.e., grouping or decimal separators) embedded in our

---

[11] The Malayalam script is a South Indian script used to write the Malayalam language, which is spoken in the Kerala state of India.

string, getting a `NumberFormat` for any locale works. Running this program results in the following output:

```
1234
```

Using the DecimalFormat class

If you want more control over your number formatting, you need to use the `Deci-malFormat` class. `DecimalFormat` allows you to format numbers in the decimal numbering system for Western, Arabic, and Indic languages. If you want to format numbers that are not base-10, or if you want to format ideographic numbers, such as those used in Chinese and Japanese, you cannot use this class.[12]

Do not instantiate a `DecimalFormat` object directly since it essentially hardcodes the decimal numbering system into your program. It is better to call the factory methods on `NumberFormat` and then make any changes through that object after first confirming that the object returned is, in fact, a `DecimalFormat`. The following code demonstrates this:

```
NumberFormat nf = NumberFormat.getInstance();
if (nf instanceof DecimalFormat) {
  DecimalFormat df = (DecimalFormat)nf;

  // customize your decimal formatting here...
  df.setGroupingSize(2);
}
```

Methods that change how numbers are formatted belong to the `DecimalFormat` class. If you want to change the number of digits that are grouped together by the grouping character, make a call to `setGroupingSize()`. By default, the grouping size is set to 3. In the US, the number 123456789 is formatted as:

123,456,789

If we change the grouping size to 2, as we did in the previous code snippet, the number is formatted as:

1,23,45,67,89

You can also change the minimum and maximum number of digits that should be displayed on either side of the decimal, force the addition of a prefix or suffix, or change the multiplier. The multiplier scales the number for a particular reason. When formatting a number to be shown as a percentage, the multiplier is 100.

---

[12] JDK 1.3 does not support ideographic number formatting; however, IBM does. You can download a class called `RuleBasedNumberFormat` on the ICU4J site at *http://oss.software.ibm.com/icu4j*.

DecimalFormat uses patterns to determine how format() and parse() should operate. You can customize these patterns by calling applyPattern() on DecimalFormat passing in your own pattern string. In fact, NumberFormat manages the formatting rules for all the locales it handles by reading the patterns for each locale from ResourceBundles. The symbols you put in a pattern and their function are shown in Table 5-16.

Table 5-16. DecimalFormat Pattern Symbols

Symbol	Description
0	Indicates a digit; will pad if necessary
#	Indicates a digit; zero shows as absent
.	Indicates placeholder for decimal separator
,	Indicates placeholder for grouping separator
E	Separates mantissa and exponent for exponential formats
;	Separates positive and negative patterns
-	Indicates default negative prefix
%	Multiplies by 100 and shows as percentage
‰ (\u2030)	Multiplies by 1,000 and shows as per mille
¤ (\u00a4)	Indicates currency sign; replaced by the locale currency symbol; if doubled, replaced by international currency symbol; if present in a pattern, the monetary decimal separator is used instead of the decimal separator
X	Indicates that any other characters can be in the prefix or suffix
'	Used to quote special characters in a prefix or suffix

The following code in Example 5-7 shows how a customized pattern is used. After we confirm that the object we get back from calling getInstance() is an instance of DecimalFormat, we call applyPattern(), providing a pattern string. In this example, the pattern string contains patterns for both a positive and negative number. A semicolon in the pattern string separates the two patterns. The pattern's currency symbol (¤) is replaced during formatting by the local currency symbol.

Example 5-7. Patterns in DecimalFormat

```
double d = 1234567.89;
double n = -1234567.89;

// a pattern for both positive and negative numbers
// that displays the local currency symbol and formats
// using both local group and decimal separators.
String pattern = "¤#,###.##;(¤#,###.##)";
```

Example 5-7. Patterns in DecimalFormat (continued)

```
NumberFormat nf = NumberFormat.getInstance();
if (nf instanceof DecimalFormat) {
    DecimalFormat df = (DecimalFormat)nf;

    df.applyPattern(pattern);

    System.out.println(df.format(d));
    System.out.println(df.format(n));
}
```

Running this code on a machine with the locale defined as the U.S. generates the following output:

```
$1,234,567.89
($1,234,567.89)
```

To provide you with a little more help in understanding how the pattern string works, Table 5-17 shows the result of applying different values to various patterns for different locales. We encourage you to modify the code in Example 5-7 and see what happens when you change key values, such as the value of the formatted number, the pattern string, and the locale.

Table 5-17. Combination of Input Value, Pattern, and Locale

Value	Pattern	Locale	Output
1234567.89	#,###.##;(#,###.##)	en_US	1,234,567.89
-1234567.89	#,###.##;(#,###.##)	en_US	(1,234,567.89)
1234567.89	#,###,###.## ¤	pt_PT	1.234.567$89 PTE
1234567.89	#,###,###.## ¤	de_CH	1'234'567.89 CHF
1234567.89	#,###,###.## ¤	de_DE_EURO	1.234.567,89 EUR
123.45	000000.000	en_US	000123.450
1234567.89	$###,###.###	de_CH	$1'234'567.89
1234567.89	¤#,###,###.##	de_CH	SFr. 1'234'567.89

Using DecimalFormatSymbols

Number formats can be customized even further using the `DecimalFormatSymbols` class, which encapsulates all symbols used by `DecimalFormat`. The values that are inserted into a pattern when a number is formatted, with the symbols used in the pattern, can be tailored to suit your needs. The following types of parameters can be modified using `DecimalFormatSymbols`.

Parameter	Methods
The currency symbol ($, ¥, €, NT$, etc.)	`getCurrencySymbol()` `setCurrencySymbol()`
The decimal separator	`getDecimalSeparator()` `setDecimalSeparator()`
The character used for digits in a pattern (#)	`getDigit()` `setDigit()`
The grouping separator	`getGroupingSeparator()` `setGroupingSeparator()`
The string used to show infinity	`getInfinity()` `setInfinity()`
The international currency symbol (USD, JPY, EUR, etc.)	`getInternationalCurrencySymbol()` `setInternationalCurrencySymbol()`
The symbol used for the minus sign (-)	`getMinusSign()` `setMinusSign()`
The decimal separator to use when formatting currencies	`getMonetaryDecimalSeparator()` `setMonetaryDecimalSeparator()`
The string to use for NaN	`getNaN()` `setNaN()`
The character used to separate positive and negative patterns (;)	`getPatternSeparator()` `setPatternSeparator()`
The symbol used for percentage (%)	`getPercent()` `setPercent()`
The symbol used for per mille (‰)	`getPerMill()` `setPerMill()`
The characters that should be used for digits (i.e., 123, ١٢٣)	`getZeroDigit()` `setZeroDigit()`

The best way to get a `DecimalFormatSymbols` object is by calling `getDecimalFormatSymbols()` on the `DecimalFormat` object, making necessary changes, and calling `setDecimalFormatSymbols()` to put the object back. Example 5-8 illustrates this process.

Example 5-8. Modifying Values on DecimalFormatSymbols

```
NumberFormat nf = NumberFormat.getInstance();
if (nf instanceof DecimalFormat) {
    DecimalFormat df = (DecimalFormat)nf;

    // get the DecimalFormatSymbols from DecimalFormat
    DecimalFormatSymbols dfs = df.getDecimalFormatSymbols();

    // modify some parameters on DecimalFormatSymbols
    dfs.setCurrencySymbol("AD$");
```

Example 5-8. Modifying Values on DecimalFormatSymbols (continued)

```
            // put the DecimalFormatSymbols object back again
            df.setDecimalFormatSymbols(dfs);

            // apply a pattern - remember \u00a4 == ¤
            df.applyPattern("\u00a4#,###.##");
        }

        System.out.println(nf.format(1234.56));
```

In this example we got the `DecimalFormatSymbols` object and we then called `setCurrencySymbol()`, passing in the new symbol "AD$" (the currency that one of the authors will institute on the island he will buy from the royalties of this book). We then called `applyPattern()`, passing in a pattern that uses the new currency symbol.[13] Finally, we format a number and print it to test the code. The output from this program is:

```
AD$1,234.56
```

Let's take a look at one more example, Example 5-9, in which we change the numeric shapes to use the Arabic digits (٠١٢٣٤٥٦٧٨٩) when formatting our numbers. In Unicode, the European digits 0...9 are encoded in the range `\u0030` through `\u0039`. The digits for other scripts are located in various parts of the Unicode character map; however they are always encoded in order from 0 to 9 in a contiguous block. For example, the Arabic digits are encoded in the range `\u0660` through `\u0669`. To change the type of digits that `DecimalFormat` uses, you simply need to point Java to the beginning of the contiguous range. The method that allows you to do this is `setZeroDigit()`, which tells Java where the beginning of the digit range is.

Example 5-9. Formatting Numbers Using Arabic Digits

```
public class ArabicDigits extends JPanel {
  static JFrame frame;

  public ArabicDigits() {
    NumberFormat nf = NumberFormat.getInstance();

    if (nf instanceof DecimalFormat) {
      DecimalFormat df = (DecimalFormat)nf;
      DecimalFormatSymbols dfs = df.getDecimalFormatSymbols();

      // set the beginning of the range to Arabic digits
      dfs.setZeroDigit('\u0660');
      df.setDecimalFormatSymbols(dfs);
    }
```

---

[13] The patterns that Java retrieves from the resource bundles for each locale have the currency symbol hardcoded as part of the pattern (i.e. $#,###.## or #,##0.00 F), so we need to create our own pattern if we want our newly created currency symbol to appear.

Example 5-9. Formatting Numbers Using Arabic Digits (continued)

```
    // create a label with the formatted number
    JLabel label = new JLabel(nf.format(1234567.89));

    // set the font with a large enough size so we can easily
    // read the numbers
    label.setFont(new Font("Lucida Sans", Font.PLAIN, 22));
    add(label);
  }

  public static void main(String [] argv) {
    ArabicDigits panel = new ArabicDigits();
    frame = new JFrame("Arabic Digits");
    frame.addWindowListener(new WindowAdapter() {
    public void windowClosing(WindowEvent e) {System.exit(0);}});
    frame.getContentPane().add("Center", panel);
    frame.pack();
    frame.setVisible(true);
  }
}
```

Running the program produces the output displayed in Figure 5-2.

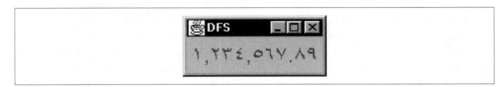

Figure 5-2. Formatted Arabic digits

Message Formats

If all text strings in your application are static, then simply externalizing them into a `ResourceBundle` as we showed in Chapter 4, *Isolating Locale-Specific Data with Resource Bundles*, is sufficient. Unfortunately life isn't that simple. We often have pieces of variable data that we need to insert into the middle of text before we can display it to the user. In the following messages, the variable data are **emphasized**:

Flight number **4106** will begin boarding from gate **2** at **10:05 p.m.**
Last login: **Fri Sep 24 09:51:37** from **calvin**
You are visitor **#9,238** to this web site since **January 1, 1999**
Volume Serial Number is **1F6E-16F1**

Text Fragmentation

A common programming mistake when forming messages of this type is concatenating fragments of text together to build a complete text string, which we did in Example 3-9 in Chapter 3. We reproduced the guilty code in Example 5-10. (Ignore the fact that the hardcoded strings have not been externalized; we did that for simplicity's sake).

Example 5-10. A ResourceBundle Containing the English Warning Message

```
// Our locale is not supported
if (i == sdfLocales.length)
  System.out.println("Locale " + myLocale.toString() +
                   ", not supported by SimpleDateFormat");
// Our locale is supported!
else
  System.out.println("Hooray! " + myLocale.toString() +
                   ", is supported by SimpleDateFormat");
```

The problem with this approach is that different languages form sentence structure differently. If we were to build a string as follows:

```
System.out.println("There were " + spellingMistakes +
                " spelling mistakes in file " + filename);
```

we would be in trouble when we tried to translate this message into German. The reason for this problem becomes clear when you see the same sentence shown in both English and German below:

English	German
There were **3** spelling mistakes in file **foo**.	Datei **foo** enthält **3** Rechtschreibfehler.

The **emphasized** pieces of the text indicate the variable arguments that would be dynamically inserted at runtime. Note that the order of the arguments in these two translations is reversed. Concatenating the text fragments together in a hardcoded manner as we did causes all sorts of localization problems down the road.

Problems also occur when programmers use "clever" string manipulation techniques in an attempt to save space, not realizing that they make future software localization more difficult. The following messages might need to be displayed to the user based on certain error conditions:

An error occurred *opening* file *filename*
An error occurred *reading* file *filename*
An error occurred *deleting* file *filename*

You might think taking shortcuts to generate these messages is appropriate. As you can see, there are only two variables in each of the messages: the action and the name of the file. We could externalize the words *opening, reading,* and *deleting* into a `ResourceBundle` and then retrieve the appropriate action based on the message we want to generate. One problem with fragmenting your text strings in this manner is that at localization time, your translators are asked to translate the text fragments without any context associated with them. In other words, all the translator might see in the `ResourceBundle` is:

```
action1 = opening
action2 = reading
action3 = deleting
```

This issue deserves attention because translation from one language to another doesn't have a one-to-one mapping. The verb "to open" in English can be used in reference to various objects such as a file, a window, and a connection. However, the same words in another language might require different verbs to be used with them. Unless the translator has some context in which to translate a snippet of text, an inappropriate translation could occur. Of course, a simple solution to this problem is the use of comments within the `ResourceBundle`; however, that solution won't solve all the problems.

Another problem with fragmenting your text strings is the issue of agreement. Agreement is a grammatical rule within a language that requires use of the correct form of the verb based on the subject's gender and plurality. English is one of few languages that do not apply the concept of gender to parts of speech, such as verbs and nouns. Most languages distinguish between masculine and feminine words, and some languages, such as German, also have the concept of neutral words. To make things even more complex, English has only the notion of singular and plural, while some languages also include the concept of dual. Each of these modalities must then be combined with gender when conjugating verbs. Here are three messages that an application localized in English might display to a user:

The printer is *enabled.*
The modem is *enabled.*
The network is *enabled.*

You don't want to externalize the word *enabled* into one key within a `ResourceBundle` and reuse it everywhere the enabled word appears in English. This externalization just won't work for other languages. To demonstrate this issue, here are the same three messages translated into French:

L'imprimante *activée.*
Le modem *activé .*
Le réseau *activé.*

Notice how the verb "activer," literally meaning "to activate" in French, is conjugated differently for the first message than for the second and third messages. Java's solution to all these problems is to use the MessageFormat class.

NOTE   It is acceptable to share an externalized string in some cases. For example, if you want to have a cancel button on all dialog boxes in your application, you could externalize all these strings as one key in a ResourceBundle since they will all be used in the same context. If, however, you want to use the word "cancel" elsewhere in your application, say to cancel a print job, then you should not assume that you could share the externalized string between its use in the dialog box and its use for the print job. In this case, you are better off having two keys in your ResourceBundle as follows:

```
CancelDialogBox = Cancel
CancelPrintJob = Cancel
```

Working with the MessageFormat Class

The MessageFormat class, contained within the java.text package, provides a way of inserting arguments into a string, independent of the order in which the arguments appear to the user. This process is accomplished by building a string (also known as a "pattern") and embedding within it digits surrounded by curly brackets to indicate the dynamic parts. Typically the pattern is stored in a resource bundle, as shown in Example 5-11, and retrieved dynamically at runtime.

Example 5-11. A ResourceBundle Containing the English Warning Message

```
WarningMsg = There were {0} spelling mistakes in file {1}.
```

Before we explain what the embedded symbols in the pattern string mean, we'll first take the example we used earlier and rewrite it to use the MessageFormat class. See Example 5-12.

Example 5-12. Using the MessageFormat Class

```
1: String fileName = "foo";
2: int spellingMistakes = 3;
3:
4: Object[] arguments = { new Integer(spellingMistakes), fileName };
5: String out = MessageFormat.format(resources.getString("WarningMsg"), arguments);
6: System.out.println(out);
```

Let's look at this example more closely. Lines 1 and 2 contain our variable arguments, the pieces of the text we want to insert into the pattern that might appear in a different order, depending on the language's sentence structure. Typically, these arguments are generated programmatically and aren't normally declared this way; otherwise, we wouldn't need to use MessageFormat in the first place!

Line 4 creates an array of objects in which we store our arguments. For this example, we have chosen to make the number of spelling mistakes the first argument and the name of the file the second argument. Note that since we create an array of objects, it is illegal to simply pass spellingMistakes as the first argument. We must convert it into an object first using the Integer class.

What order you choose to place the arguments inside the object is up to you. Once you choose the order, however, you must always refer to the objects inside the array using the correct index in the pattern. The first argument is referenced as {0}, the second as {1}, and so on up to a maximum of {9}.[14] So, in our example, new Integer(spellingMistakes) is referenced as argument {0} and fileName is referenced as argument {1}. You can rearrange the arguments any way you like in the pattern string. In fact, you can choose to not use an argument, or even use the same argument more than once. The following pattern strings are all valid:

```
There were {0} spelling mistakes in file {1}.
File {1} had {0} spelling mistakes.
There were one or more spelling mistakes in file {1}.
File {1} had {0} mistakes. That's {0} spelling mistakes!
There were spelling mistakes in the file.
```

Line 5 calls the static method format() on the MessageFormat class. This method is a convenience method because it doesn't require you to instantiate a MessageFormat object. For simple cases, the static format() method works fine. A little later, we'll explain how to use the MessageFormat class in its full glory to take advantage of more complex situations.

The static format(String pattern, Object[] arguments) method takes two arguments. The first parameter is the pattern string in which the arguments are placed. In this case, we retrieve the pattern from a resource bundle. The second parameter is the array of objects containing the arguments. The method returns a String that can then be displayed to the user.

Example 5-13 shows the warning message from Example 5-11 translated into German. Again, notice that the arguments {0} and {1} have been reversed. The code doesn't change and the output is correct when run in the German locale. This flexibility is highly desirable in an internationalized piece of code.

---

[14] This reference means that you are limited to a maximum of ten arguments in any given MessageFormat pattern.

Example 5-13. A ResourceBundle Containing the German Warning Message

```
WarningMsg = Datei {1} enth\u00e4lt {0} Rechtschreibfehler.
```

Notice that the word embedded between the {1} and {0} in Example 5-13, enth\u00e4lt, looks a little strange. This is the word "enthält," the German word for "contains," but we represent the letter ä using its Unicode value 00e4, which is expressed in Java as \u00e4. We cover Unicode in more detail in Chapter 6, *Character Sets and Unicode*.

MessageFormat checks to see if each object in the argument array is a String. If it is, it inserts the data from the String directly into the appropriate locations within the pattern string. If it is a Date or a subclass of Number, it invokes DateFormat or NumberFormat, respectively, to format the data according to the appropriate Locale. Example 5-14 shows a small program that has a pattern string with embedded date and number data. As with all correctly internationalized programs, the pattern should be externalized in a resource bundle, but we place it in the code for simplicity.

Example 5-14. Date and Number Data Inserted into a Pattern String.

```java
import java.text.*;
import java.util.*;

public class DateNumberSample {
  public static void main(String args[]) {
    Double kb = new Double(3.5);
    Date today = new Date();
    String pattern = "{0}K was deleted on {1}.";

    Object[] arguments = { kb, today };
    System.out.println(MessageFormat.format(pattern, arguments));
  }
}
```

The output is shown for different locales:

```
C:\>java DateNumberSample
3.5K was deleted on 10/3/99 1:21 PM.

C:\>java -Duser.language=fr DateNumberSample
3,5K was deleted on 03/10/99 13:22.

C:\>java -Duser.language=ru DateNumberSample
3,5K was deleted on 03.10.99 13:23.

C:\>java —Duser.language=sl DateNumberSample
3,5K was deleted on 99.10.3 13:23.
```

Notice that the decimal separator in French, Russian, and Slovenian is a comma and that the dates and times are formatted differently.

Using the static `format()` method of `MessageFormat` is fine for simple cases; however, you might want to instantiate a `MessageFormat` object for more complex situations. Some reasons why you might want to do this include:

- You want to format the message using a locale different from the default.

- You want to change the pattern string to format other messages (it is more efficient to create the `MessageFormat` object once and change the pattern, rather than instantiate a `MessageFormat` object multiple times indirectly by calling the static `format()` method).

- You want to call any of the other `set` or `get` methods on `MessageFormat`.

Example 5-15 shows a program that uses the `MessageFormat` constructor and demonstrates how the pattern and locale can be changed, allowing reuse of the instance.

Example 5-15. A Program That Reuses a MessageFormat Object

```
import java.text.*;
import java.util.*;

public class MessageFormatReuse {
  public static void main(String args[]) {
    // create the pattern and instantiate the formatter
    String pattern = "{0}K was deleted on {1}.";
    MessageFormat formatter = new MessageFormat(pattern);

    // build the argument array
    Double kb = new Double(3.5);
    Date today = new Date();
    Object[] arguments = { kb, today };

    // set the locale to US
    formatter.setLocale(Locale.US);

    // format the message and print it out
    System.out.println(formatter.format(arguments));

    // set the locale to France
    formatter.setLocale(Locale.FRANCE);

    // format the message and print it out
    System.out.println(formatter.format(arguments));

    // modify the pattern string
    pattern = "On {1}, {0}K was deleted.";
    formatter.applyPattern(pattern);
```

Example 5-15. A Program That Reuses a MessageFormat Object (continued)

```
      // format the message (using the French locale)
      System.out.println(formatter.format(arguments));

      // set the locale back to US
      formatter.setLocale(Locale.US);

      // format the message and print it out
      System.out.println(formatter.format(arguments));
   }
}
```

Running this code generates the following output:

```
3.5K was deleted on 1/3/01 8:22 PM.
3,5K was deleted on 03/01/01 20:22.
On 03/01/01 20:22, 3,5K was deleted.
On 1/3/01 8:22 PM, 3.5K was deleted.
```

Setting the locale on `MessageFormat` may not be necessary in all cases. However, if the array of arguments contains date, time, or number data, as it does in this case, you should set the locale appropriately.

In Example 5-15, the `format()` method is not the static method used in previous examples. It is the method that `MessageFormat` inherits from the `Format` class.

Parameterized patterns

So far, our examples have limited arguments in the pattern string to digits. `MessageFormat` allows additional parameters to be supplied inside the curly brackets that provide more formatting information. Table 5-18 shows the parameters that can be provided to further specify the type of data to be formatted.

Table 5-18. MessageFormat Parameter Values

Element Format	Element Style
time	short
	medium
	long
	full
	pattern
date	short
	medium
	long
	full
	pattern

Table 5-18. MessageFormat Parameter Values (continued)

Element Format	Element Style
number	currency
	percent
	integer
	pattern
choice	pattern

For each element format type, the element style is optional, except in the case of choice, when the pattern is mandatory. In the case of time and date, if no element style is provided, then the data are formatted using the default format as obtained by DateFormat.getTimeInstance() and DateFormat.getInstance(), respectively. Similarly, in the case of number, if no element style is provided, then the data are formatted using the default format as obtained by NumberFormat.getInstance(). The syntax for using the additional formatting parameters is:

```
{argNumber, elementFormat, elementStyle}
```

Let's use some different formatting parameters in several pattern strings so you can get an idea as to how this all works. First, we'll create an array of pattern strings:

```
String[] pat = { "{0} was born at {1} on {1}.",
                 "{0} was born at {1,time} on {1,date}.",
                 "{0} was born at {1,time,short} on {1,date,long}.",
                 "{0} was born at {1,time,long} on {1,date,short}." };
```

Now, we'll build a simple argument array and instantiate a MessageFormat object, setting the locale to US:

```
Object[] arguments = { "John", new Date() };

// instantiate the MessageFormat object
MessageFormat formatter = new MessageFormat("");
formatter.setLocale(Locale.US);
```

The next piece of code simply iterates through each pattern string in our array, applies the pattern, formats the message, and prints it out:

```
for (int i = 0; i < pat.length; i++) {
   formatter.applyPattern(pat[i]);
   System.out.println(formatter.format(arguments));
}
```

The output appears as follows:

```
John was born at 10/3/99 8:59 PM on 10/3/99 8:59 PM.
John was born at 8:59:12 PM on Oct 3, 1999.
John was born at 8:59 PM on October 3, 1999.
John was born at 8:59:12 PM EDT on 10/3/99.
```

Now we set the locale to France and repeat the loop again so we can see the difference in date and time formatting between France and the United States:

```
formatter.setLocale(Locale.FRANCE);

for (int i = 0; i < pat.length; i++) {
    formatter.applyPattern(pat[i]);
    System.out.println(formatter.format(arguments));
}
```

Here is the output with the locale set to France:

```
John was born at 03/10/99 20:59 on 03/10/99 20:59.
John was born at 20:59:12 on 3 oct. 99.
John was born at 20:59 on 3 octobre 1999.
John was born at 20:59:12 GMT-04:00 on 03/10/99.
```

6

Character Sets and Unicode

As mentioned in the first chapter, a big factor in Java's ability to support internationalized programs results from the choice the designers made in selecting Unicode as the internal representation for text. So far, we have only said that Unicode was an important design decision without providing much information about it. This chapter covers character sets and encoding methods and gives the reader a deeper understanding of the Unicode Standard and its relation to Java. This chapter is not intended to provide exhaustive coverage of the Unicode Standard; rather the chapter aims to provide the reader with enough information to leverage the Unicode features available in Java. For a complete understanding of Unicode, we refer you to The Unicode Standard, available from The Unicode Consortium.[1]

What Are Character Sets?

A *character set* is a collection of characters that have been grouped together for a particular purpose. You can think of the English alphabet as a character set that contains 52 upper- and lowercase letters. Since the character set is relatively small, we don't have a committee that maintains the English alphabet standard; however, this situation is not the case for Asian languages. Tens of thousands of Chinese characters exist, but only a subset of them is required to communicate with people effectively. The Japanese government has defined a character set that contains what they consider to be the most important characters to learn. The set called *jōyō*

---

[1] Certain parts of the Unicode Standard, including technical reports and electronic copies of the Unicode character database, are available online at *http://www.unicode.org*.

kanji contains 1,945 characters. Similar character sets exist in China and Korea. A collection of characters that are grouped together for a specific purpose is typically referred to as a *noncoded character set.*

In the computer world, simply grouping characters together is not sufficient. The character data must be stored electronically in the computer's memory as binary digits, and thus the individual characters must be assigned unique values so they can be distinguished from each other. A character set that has assigned values for each character is termed a *coded character set* or *code set*. Each character within the code set has a unique assigned value and is referred to as a *code point.*

ASCII

The code set that most programmers know is the American Standard Code for Information Interchange (ASCII). ASCII is a 7-bit code set, meaning that all characters contained within the set are assigned a unique value between 0 and 127. ASCII contains:

- Control characters (NUL, BEL, CR, etc.)

- Upper- and lowercase English letters (A – Z and a– z)

- European digits (0–9)

- Punctuation and other symbols (!"#$%&'()*+,-/:;<=>?@[\]^_`{|}~)

The ASCII code set is shown in Table 6-1. To determine the hexadecimal value of a character, find the character in the table and read the column heading first, then read the row heading. For example, the value of the character (@) is 0x40 and the value of the character (a) is 0x61.

Table 6-1. ASCII Code Set

	0	1	2	3	4	5	6	7
0	NUL	DEL		0	@	P	`	p
1	SOH	DC1	!	1	A	Q	a	q
2	STX	DC2	"	2	B	R	b	r
3	ETX	DC3	#	3	C	S	c	s
4	EOT	DC4	$	4	D	T	d	t
5	ENQ	NAK	%	5	E	U	e	u
6	ACK	SYN	&	6	F	V	f	v
7	BEL	ETB	'	7	G	W	g	w
8	BS	CAN	(	8	H	X	h	x
9	TAB	EM	)	9	I	Y	i	y

Table 6-1. ASCII Code Set (continued)

	0	1	2	3	4	5	6	7
A	LF	SUB	*	:	J	Z	j	z
B	VT	ESC	+	;	K	[	k	{
C	FF	FS	,	<	L	\	l	|
D	CR	GS	-	=	M	]	m	}
E	SO	RS		>	N	^	n	~
F	SI	US	/	?	O	_	o	DEL

The characters included in the ASCII code set are sufficient for English, but even then their use is limited. Notice that the only currency symbol included in the code set is the dollar sign ($). A programmer could not use ASCII to encode British English text that contained the pound sterling currency symbol (£). The code set also does not contain any characters with diacritics, so it is not suitable for encoding most other European languages, such as French, Italian, or German.

ISO 8859 Series

Most computers operate on an 8-bit byte, so people began to take advantage of the extra space made available by the additional bit. The International Standards Organization (ISO) created a series of 8-bit code sets to handle a much larger selection of languages than does ASCII. The code sets known as ISO-8859 are a superset of ASCII; thus, they each provide backward compatibility for legacy data encoded in ASCII. In addition to the characters found in ASCII, each set includes an additional 96 slots, which each code set in the series uses to encode its own set of characters. Table 6-2 shows the fourteen ISO-8859 code sets and some of the languages each code set supports. You might be familiar with the first code set in the series, ISO-8859-1, which happens to be the default code set for HTML.

Table 6-2. ISO-8859 Code Set Series

Code Set	Nickname	Languages
ISO-8859-1	Latin 1	Afrikaans, Albanian, Basque, Catalan, Danish, Dutch, English, Faroese, Finnish, French, German, Icelandic, Irish, Italian, Norwegian, Portuguese, Rhaeto-Romanic, Scottish, Spanish, Swahili, Swedish
ISO-8859-2	Latin 2	Albanian, Croation, Czech, German, Hungarian, Irish, Polish, Romanian, Slovak, Slovenian, Sorbian
ISO-8859-3	Latin 3	Afrikaans, Albanian, Basque, Catalan, Dutch, English, Esperanto, German, Irish, Maltese, Spanish, Turkish

Table 6-2. ISO-8859 Code Set Series (continued)

Code Set	Nickname	Languages
ISO-8859-4	Latin 4	Danish, English, Estonian, Finnish, German, Greenlandic, Hawaiian, Lappish, Latvian, Lithuanian, Swedish, Norwegian
ISO-8859-5	Latin/Cyrillic	Bulgarian, Byelorussian, English, Macedonian, Russian, Serbian, Swahili, Ukrainian
ISO-8859-6	Latin/Arabic	Arabic
ISO-8859-7	Latin/Greek	Greek
ISO-8859-8	Latin/Hebrew	Hebrew, Yiddish
ISO-8859-9	Latin 5	Afrikaans, Albanian, Basque, Catalan, Danish, Dutch, English, Faeroese, Finnish, French, German, Irish, Italian, Norwegian, Portuguese, Rhaeto-Romanic, Scottish, Spanish, Swahili, Swedish, Turkish
ISO-8859-10	Latin 6	Danish, English, Estonian, Faeroese, Finnish, German, Greenlandic, Hawaiian, Icelandic, Irish, Lappish, Latvian, Lithuanian, Swedish, Norwegian
ISO-8859-11	Latin/Thai	Thai
ISO-8859-12	Undefined	
ISO-8859-13	Latin 7	Estonian, Finnish, Hawaiian, Latvian, Lithuanian
ISO-8859-14	Latin 8	Afrikaans, Albanian, Basque, Catalan, Dutch, English, German, Gaelic, Irish, Portuguese, Spanish, Welsh
ISO-8859-15	Latin 9 or Latin 0	Identical to Latin 1, except for the following changes:

Latin 1	Latin 9
¤	€
¦	Š
¨	š
´	Ž
¸	ž
¼	Œ
½	œ
¾	Ÿ

The introduction of ISO-8859-15 was meant to replace ISO-8859-1, but the huge number of existing web pages makes the conversion a slow process. The two code sets ISO-8859-6 (Arabic) and ISO-8859-7 (Greek) do not fully handle all capabilities of their respective languages. If you need to write programs for writing systems that have a relatively small alphabet, the ISO-8859 series might be sufficient.

Multibyte Code Sets

The maximum number of characters that can be represented in an 8-bit code set is 256, which is not enough to handle the tens of thousands of characters used in languages such as Chinese, Japanese, and Korean (CJK). To solve this problem, multibyte code sets were developed. In a multibyte code set, one character can be represented in 8-bits, 16-bits, 24-bits, or 32-bits. There is no reason why more bytes couldn't be used, except that 4,294,967,296 (2^{32}) slots are more than adequate to handle even CJK languages! Table 6-3 shows some multibyte code sets used in the CJK countries.

Table 6-3. CJK Code Sets

Code Set	Country	Characters
GB 8565.2-88	China	8,150
Big Five	Taiwan	13,494
GB 2312-80	China[2]	7,445
JIS X 0208:1997	Japan	6,879
KS X 1001:1992	Korea	8,224

Many multibyte code sets vary the number of bytes needed to represent a particular character. If a text stream contains mixed Latin and Japanese characters, it might contain some characters that are one byte in length and other characters that are two bytes in length in the same stream. This process can be very confusing when you need to parse the text to determine whether you are on a character boundary. If you want to delete a character, first determine if the character you want to delete is represented by one or two bytes. Deleting only one byte of a two-byte character causes all kinds of problems. For this reason, many programmers who use multibyte code sets convert the data into a fixed length per character as it comes into a program.

What Are Encoding Methods?

A coded character set specifies what integer values or code points each character in the character set will have. An *encoding method* or *character encoding* specifies how the character's code point (integer value) is mapped to a sequence of octets.[3] For code sets whose code points do not exceed 255, such as ASCII and ISO-8859, the mapping is relatively straightforward. The characters are usually encoded using

---

[2] GB 2312 is also used in Singapore.

[3] An octet is eight bits, which in most, but not all, cases is identical to a byte.

their code point values. For example, to encode the string "Hi World!" simply take the code point values for each character and store them contiguously in memory:

H	i		W	o	r	l	d	!
0x48	0x69	0x20	0x57	0x6F	0x72	0x6C	0x64	0x21

For multibyte code sets, the encoding methods are more complex. While many characters need more than one byte to be represented, many others can be represented using a single byte, such as Japanese half-width hiragana and katakana, numerals, and Latin text. To save space, the encoding method uses one byte for characters that only require one byte, and multiple bytes for characters that require more space. Additionally, some encoding methods allow use of more than one code set at a time, allowing different combinations of languages or sets of characters in a text stream.

Encoding methods are either *modal* or *nonmodal*. In a modal encoding method, such as the Japanese encoding method JIS, special escape sequences indicate how many bytes are used in each character following the escape sequence. Whenever the number of bytes used to represent a character changes, another escape sequence must appear in the text stream. Table 6-4 shows the characters sets and their corresponding escape sequences.

Table 6-4. JIS Encoding Escape Sequences

Character Set	Bytes per Character	Escape Sequence
JIS-Roman	1	0x1B 0x28 0x4A
ASCII	1	0x1B 0x28 0x42
Half-width katakana	1	0x1B 0x28 0x49
JIS C 6226-1978	2	0x1B 0x24 0x40
JIS X 0208-1983	2	0x1B 0x24 0x42
JIS X 0208-1990	2	0x1B 0x26 0x40 0x1B 0x24 0x42
JIS X 0208:1997	2	0x1B 0x26 0x40 0x1B 0x24 0x42
JIS X 0212-1990	2	0x1B 0x24 0x28 0x44

The following table is an example of how the escape sequences and characters are used in the text stream:

0x1B	0x28	0x42	0x48	0x69	0x20	0x1B	0x28	0x49	0x6B
Shift to ASCII			H	i		Shift to half-width katakana			カ

A nonmodal encoding method defines specific ranges for characters. For example, in Shift-JIS, a popular Japanese encoding method created by Microsoft, the following ranges are used: an ASCII or romaji character in the range 0x21 to 0x7E; a half-width katakana character in the range 0xA1 to 0xDF; any double-byte character requires that the first byte be in the range 0x81 to 0x9F, or 0xE0 to 0xEF, and the character's second byte must be in the range 0x40 to 0x7E or 0x80 to 0xFC. Unlike a modal encoding method, the value of the character unambiguously indicates what type of character it is and how many bytes it consumes in the encoding.

If you are confused by the difference between character set, code set, and encoding methods, you are not alone. This confusion is aggravated by inaccurate use of the terms. For example, HTML provides a keyword to define a page's encoding method. Unfortunately, HTML uses the term "charset," which as you now know, doesn't define an encoding at all.

To help clarify things, try to remember that a code set can be encoded using more than one encoding method, while an encoding method can be applied to more than one code set.

What Is Unicode?

The Unicode Standard defines a code set with a fixed-width, 16-bit character-encoding scheme. The current version of the Unicode Standard is Version 3.0; however, Java 2 supports only Version 2.1.[4] When we refer to Unicode in this book, we refer to Version 2.1, unless specifically stated otherwise. The advantage of Unicode is that characters from all the world's major scripts are uniformly supported. Thus it is possible to combine Arabic, French, Japanese, and Russian characters all in the same string. Internally, Java's primitive character type is a 16-bit entity. As a programmer, you don't have to worry about any of the difficulties in managing variable length datatypes.

The Unicode Standard has assigned each character within the Standard a unique code point in the hexadecimal range of 0x0000 to 0xFFFF, thus, unlike ASCII, providing 65,536 unique slots. Actually, the Standard has a back door that cannibalizes 2048 slots to make room for an additional 1,048,576 characters. Together with the remaining 63,448 slots, this cannibalization allows a total of 1,112,064 characters. The total number of individual markings that humans have made since the beginning of time is estimated at roughly 500,000, so we shouldn't need to upgrade to a new encoding scheme anytime soon.

---

[4] The Unicode Standard™ is available online at *http://www.unicode.org*.

Unicode characters are referenced in Java using the escape sequence "\u" followed by the hexadecimal value of the character. When specifying hexadecimal numbers, the case does not matter. The following strings are examples of how Unicode characters can be used:

```
char  middle = '\u4E2D'; // Chinese character 中
String str1 = "ab\u0063"; // abc
String str2 = "\u0061\u0062\u0063"; // abc
String str3 = "\u05e9\u05dC\u05d5\u05DD";  // shalom in Hebrew
String str4 = "espa\u00F1ol"; // español
```

In this example, `str1` and `str2` are equivalent. Throughout the book, whenever we refer to a Unicode code point, we use the \uXXXX syntax.

Each character in Unicode is also given a unique name. Names are always spelled out in uppercase letters. The names are identical to those used in the ISO/IEC 10646 code set. We sometimes use the character's name when referring to a character. Examples of character names include:

Unicode Name	Value	Glyph
LATIN CAPITAL LETTER A	\u0041	A
LATIN CAPITAL LIGATURE OE	\u0152	Œ
CYRILLIC SMALL LETTER DE	\u0434	д
ARABIC LETTER KAF	\u0643	ك
ALMOST EQUAL TO	\u2248	≈

Character Blocks

Characters in Unicode are organized into clusters called *blocks*. Typically, each block encapsulates the characters for a particular script, with the exception of general punctuation, which is contained in its own block. The punctuation characters in that block can be used with various scripts.

In Java, the blocks and their ranges are encapsulated in the `Character.UnicodeBlock` class. We include the block names and ranges in Appendix C, *Unicode Character Blocks*. Detailed information about each block is available in the Unicode Standard.

It is possible to determine to which block a given character belongs using the static method `Character.UnicodeBlock.of()`. The method returns a `Character.UnicodeBlock` object. In the following code snippet, we rely on the object's `toString()` method to print the appropriate block name:

```
import java.lang.Character.* ;
...
System.out.println(UnicodeBlock.of('\u0436'));
```

```
System.out.println(UnicodeBlock.of('\u05D6'));
System.out.println(UnicodeBlock.of('\u9A3C'));
```

Running this code results in the following output:

```
CYRILLIC
HEBREW
CJK_UNIFIED_IDEOGRAPHS
```

Design Principles

Unicode was designed with the following ten principles in mind:

1. Sixteen-bit characters
2. Full encoding
3. Characters, not glyphs
4. Semantics
5. Plain text
6. Logical order
7. Unification
8. Dynamic composition
9. Equivalence sequence
10. Convertibility

In the next few sections, we'll look at how Unicode implements these principles.

Sixteen-bit characters

In Unicode, characters are 16 bits in length no matter what script the character comes from.[5] The following string, which consists of five characters from five different writing systems, is 10 bytes in length:

```
String str = "\u0041\u03b2\u062c\u5927\u044d";
```

A	β	ج	大	э
\u0041	\u03B2	\u062C	\u5927	\u044D

Notice that even the first character in the string "A" is two bytes long. Characters from the ASCII code set maintain their original values with the most significant byte having the value 0.

Full encoding

Unlike some other encoding methods, such as ISO-2022 and Shift JIS, Unicode does not have the notion of shift states or escape sequences to access certain characters. In other words, no special programming is needed to reference a character

---

[5] The introduction of surrogate pairs (see the section "Full Encoding") violates this principle, but for the majority of characters in Unicode and for all current versions of Java, it still holds.

other than its 16-bit value. This advantage makes iterating back and forth through a text stream extremely easy compared to some other encoding schemes.

We mentioned earlier that the Unicode Standard provides a back door that allows support of over 1,000,000 characters. A block called the "Surrogates Area" has been set aside for this future expansion. The idea is that two 16-bit values, called *surrogate pairs*, are used to reference one character. The first two bytes of the pair are known as the *high surrogate* and can be in the range \uD800 to \uDBFF. The second two bytes of the pair are the *low surrogate*, and can be in the range \uDC00 to \uDFFF. The low and high surrogate ranges each contain 1,024 values, allowing an additional 1,048,576 characters (1024^2). As of this writing, no characters have been assigned to the surrogates area, although this situation is expected to change in the near future. Java does not support surrogate pairs and no decision has been made at this point as to how it will support them in the future.

Characters, not glyphs

Unicode specifies the characters in the standard and the properties associated with each character, but it does not define what the character's shape, or *glyph*, should look like. In most cases, the font vendor determines what the glyph should look like for a given character. Thus, the small Latin letter g has different shapes, depending on the font style, as shown in Table 6-5.

Table 6-5. Glyphs Versus Characters

Glyph	Unicode Value	Unicode Name
g g g	\u0067	LATIN SMALL LETTER G
ه ه ه ه	\u0647	ARABIC LETTER HEH
لا	\u0644\u0627	ARABIC LETTER LAM + ARABIC LETTER ALEF

In some complex scripts, such as Arabic and Devanagari, the glyph changes shape based on the location of a character in a word and the characters that appear next to it. Table 6-5 shows the four shapes of the Arabic letter ha.[6] In Unicode, the character has one value (\u0647) and the rendering engine (in our case, the Java rendering engine) is responsible for displaying the appropriate glyph.

As you may recall from Chapter 2, *Writing Systems*, ligatures are combinations of characters that appear as one glyph. An example of this combination is the laam-alif ligature in Arabic. Although the character appears to be one glyph, it is still

---

[6] The Arabic letter ha corresponds with the Unicode Name "ARABIC LETTER HEH," and the laam-alif ligature corresponds with the Unicode name "ARABIC LETTER LAM + ARABIC LETTER ALEF."

composed of and stored as two separate characters (\u0644 and \u0627). The rendering engine is responsible for displaying the correct glyph when these characters appear next to one another.

Ligatures also exist in the Latin script. They were originally introduced by typesetters, who used them to improve the æsthetics of printed text. For example, two common ligatures are the fi (\uFB01) and fl (\uFB02) ligatures. Look at the following words with and without the ligatures:

No Ligature	Using a Ligature
float	float
file	file

Notice how without the ligature, the "f" and "l" collide at the top in the word "float," as does the "f" and the dot from the "i" in the word "file."

In many cases, ligatures exist as separate characters in Unicode, allowing systems that don't have sophisticated rendering engines to fall back on these presentation forms of the characters for displaying the glyphs. Sun's implementation of Java renders Arabic ligatures in this way; IBM's version of Java relies on the rendering engine to do the work.

Semantics

Unicode is different from other code sets, such as ASCII and ISO-8859; the Unicode Standard not only defines the characters and their code point, but it also associates properties with each character.

Case (uppercase, lowercase or titlecase)

Not all writing systems differentiate between upper- and lowercase letters, but for those that do, this property is applied to the characters. The Unicode Standard provides mappings from lowercase to uppercase letters. The mappings are not necessarily the same between languages sharing the same writing system. In Turkish, the lowercase letter i maps to an uppercase letter İ with a dot. The uppercase letter I without a dot maps to the lowercase letter ı without a dot.

To convert characters to lowercase in Java, use the following methods: `String.toLowerCase()` returns a copy of the `String` in lowercase using the default locale; `String.toLowerCase(Locale)` returns a copy of the `String` in lowercase using the locale provided as a parameter.

`Character.toLowerCase(char)` is a static method that returns a lowercase copy of the character parameter.

In most cases, the methods on `String` actually make calls to the static `Character` method. The one exception is if the locale language is Turkish. In this instance, the case mapping rules are hardcoded into the methods on `String` where the following mappings occur:

```
I (\u0069) → ı (\u0131)
İ (\u0130) → i (\u0049)
```

If characters in the `String` do not have a case property, the original character is returned. Let's look at the following code:

```
String test = "ABC\u05DD";
String result = test.toLowerCase();
```

The content of result contains "abc\u05DD." To determine if a character is lowercase, call the static method `Character.isLowerCase(char)`. The return value will be true if the Unicode Standard considers the character to be lowercase.

Similar functionality exists for converting to uppercase letters. `String.toUpperCase()` returns a copy of the `String` in uppercase using the default locale. `String.toUpperCase(Locale)` returns a copy of the `String` in uppercase using the locale provided as a parameter.

`Character.toUpperCase(char)` is a static method that returns an uppercase copy of the character parameter.

As is the case with the lowercase methods, the `toUpperCase()` methods on `String` make calls to `Character.toUpperCase()` to do the work with a couple of exceptions. The first exception is if the locale language is Turkish. In this situation, the following hardcoded mappings are built into the `String` methods:

```
ı (\u0131) → I (\u0069)
i (\u0049) → İ (\u0130)
```

The second exception exists for the sharp s character ß (\u00DF), also known as the German "Eszett." In this situation, the character is mapped to two uppercase S letters (\u0053\u0053). The following code demonstrates this process:

```
String street = "stra\u00DFe"; // straße
System.out.println(street.toUpperCase());
```

The output from this code snippet is:

```
STRASSE
```

NOTE	An interesting bug prevents ß (`\u00DF`) from being converted to uppercase if no other lowercase characters are in the string. `String.toUpperCase()` first checks to see if any characters need to be converted to uppercase. It checks by calling `Character.toUpperCase()` and seeing if the return value is different from the value passed in. However, `Character.toUpperCase()` doesn't handle the ß to SS mapping because it returns a single char, and SS obviously requires two chars. `Character.toUpperCase()` simply returns the value passed to it. If no other characters in the string require conversion, then `String.toUpperCase()` returns the string passed to it and the ß remains unconverted.[7]

To determine if a character is uppercase, call the static method `Character.isUpperCase(char)`. If the character is uppercase according to the Unicode Standard, the method returns true; otherwise, it returns false.

In languages such as Serbo-Croatian, one-character letters exist that are actually composed of two letters. When these characters appear at the beginning of a word that should be capitalized, the first of the character's two letters should be capitalized. The Unicode Standard defines this special case as *titlecase*. Examples of these characters are shown in Table 6-6.

Table 6-6. Titlecase Characters

Lowercase	Uppercase	Titlecase
dž \u01C6	DŽ \u01C4	Dž \u01C5
lj \u01C9	LJ \u01C7	Lj \u01C8
nj \u01CC	NJ \u01CA	Nj \u01CB
dz \u01F3	DZ \u01F1	Dz \u01F2

To convert a character to titlecase, call the static method `Character.toTitleCase()`. If no Unicode mapping for the character from lowercase to titlecase exists, but the character does have a mapping from lowercase to uppercase, the method returns the uppercase version of the character. Look at the following code sample:

```
char a = 'a';
char lj = '\u01C9';
```

---

[7] This bug was apparently fixed for the Java 2 Standard Edition Version 1.4 code named Merlin.

```
System.out.println(Integer.toHexString(Character.toTitleCase(a)));
System.out.println(Integer.toHexString(Character.toTitleCase(lj)));
```

The output of this code is:

```
41
1c8
```

Unlike the functions for lowercase and uppercase conversions, the `String` class does not have methods for conversion to titlecase. To determine if a character is in titlecase, call the method static `Character.isTitleCase()`. The method returns true only if the character is a titlecase character according to the Unicode Standard.

Numeric value

Characters that can represent a numeric value are designated with a numeric value property in Unicode. Examples of characters that contain this property are shown in Table 6-7.

Table 6-7. Examples of Characters with Numeric Values

Glyph	Unicode Value	Unicode Name
1	\u0031	DIGIT ONE
¼	\u00BC	VULGAR FRACTION ONE QUARTER
٣	\u0663	ARABIC-INDIC DIGIT THREE
㉃	\u3283	CIRCLED IDEOGRAPH FOUR
VIII	\u2167	ROMAN NUMERAL EIGHT

It is possible to retrieve the numeric value for a Unicode character containing the numeric value property by calling the static method `Character.getNumericValue(char)`. The method returns an integer value for the character. If the character passed in does not have a numeric value property according to Unicode, the method returns –1. If the character passed in has a numeric value but it can't be represented in integer form (e.g., a fraction), the method returns –2. The following code snippet demonstrates the functionality:

```
char a = '\u0031'; // DIGIT ONE
char b = '\u00BC'; // VULGAR FRACTION ONE QUARTER
char c = '\u0663'; // ARABIC-INDIC DIGIT THREE
char d = '\u3283'; // CIRCLED IDEOGRAPH FOUR
char e = '\u2167'; // ROMAN NUMERAL EIGHT
char f = '\u05DD'; // HEBREW LETTER FINAL MEM

System.out.println(Character.getNumericValue(a));
System.out.println(Character.getNumericValue(b));
```

```
System.out.println(Character.getNumericValue(c));
System.out.println(Character.getNumericValue(d));
System.out.println(Character.getNumericValue(e));
System.out.println(Character.getNumericValue(f));
```

The output from this code is:

```
1
-2
3
4
8
-1
```

Directionality

In Unicode, characters are either left to right (i.e., Latin characters, Kanji characters), right to left (i.e., Arabic or Hebrew characters), switch based on context (i.e., digits, punctuation)—also known as weak, or are independent of direction—also known as neutral. Java does not provide a mechanism to determine the directionality of a character. The information is available in the Unicode Standard. For the most part, you do not need to know this information, as the Java rendering engine takes care of rendering text properly.

Mirrored

A character property related to directionality is mirroring. Certain characters visually change to a mirrored image of themselves, depending on the text's direction flow. A good example of this property is the use of parenthesis. When text flows from left to right as it does in English, an open parenthesis looks like (. When the text flows right to left, an open parenthesis looks like). Again, there is no way in Java to determine whether a character contains the mirrored property. The Java rendering engine automatically uses the appropriate character based on the Unicode bi-directional algorithm.

Letters

Another Unicode character property determines if the character is a letter. This category has alphabetic and ideographic subtypes. From Java's standpoint, the static method Character.isLetter(char) returns true if the character is an alphabetic or ideographic character according to the Unicode Standard.

Plain text

This design principle implies that Unicode encodes only text, not formatting information. For example, no codes or tags are embedded in a Unicode text stream to indicate the language of the text. Unicode assumes that higher-level protocols should be used to handle rich text.[8]

Logical order

When characters in English are typed into the computer's keyboard or stored in memory, they appear on the screen in the same order; the string "Green eggs and ham." would be stored in memory with the characters in sequential order as:

G	r	e	e	n		e	g	g	s		a	n	d		h	a	m	.
\u0047	\u0072	\u0065	\u0065	\u006E	\u0020	\u0065	\u0067	\u0067	\u0073	\u0020	\u0061	\u006E	\u0064	\u0020	\u0068	\u0061	\u006D	\u002E

As mentioned in Chapter 2, languages such as Arabic and Hebrew are actually bi-directional languages. Text flows from right to left, but numbers and embedded Latin text flow from left to right. For example, look at the following Hebrew sentence:

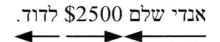

The sentence reads "Andy paid $2500 to David." It begins from the right and flows to the left ("Andy paid"—"אנדי שלם"). Where the text "$2500" appears, it starts flowing from left to right. Text then continues flowing from right to left ("to David"—"לדוד"). That's how it looks visually. Now let's look at how the characters are stored in memory. The following characters should be read from left to right:

א	נ	ד	י		ש	ל	ם		$	2	5	0	0		ל	ד	ו	ד	.
\u05D0	\u05E0	\u05D3	\u05D9	\u0020	\u05E9	\u05DC	\u05DD	\u0020	\u0024	\u0032	\u0035	\u0030	\u0030	\u0020	\u05DC	\u05D3	\u05D5	\u05D3	\u002E

The order in which the characters are stored in memory is known as *logical order*. The order in which the characters appear visually is its *visual order*. Logical order is also the order the characters are typed into the keyboard and, in the case of Hebrew, the order in which the characters are read.

---

[8] Rich text is text that is marked up to include formatting information.

Unicode's sixth design principle states that characters will be stored in logical order. From a programming standpoint, this principle is important for you to understand so that you can construct and parse text correctly.

In Java, the Hebrew sentence we just created could be stored in a string as follows:

```
String str = "\u05D0\u05E0\u05D3\u05D9 \u05E9\u05DC\u05DD $2500 "+
             "\u05DC\u05D3\u05E0\u05D9.";
```

Unification

Character unification is one of Unicode's fundamental design principles. To assure maximum compatibility with previously defined code sets, the Unicode Standard referenced the world's code sets as a starting point to determine code points for each character. To minimize duplicate entries for characters with essentially the same form, but from different scripts or code sets, the process of character unification was necessary. Unification means that all characters sharing a common form are given one slot within the code set. The advantage of this process becomes apparent if you imagine trying to search through a piece of text for all instances of a specific character. If that character had multiple values in the code set, it would require a much harder search than if the character had one unique value.

The basis for unification went beyond just unifying characters sharing a common form. The characters also needed to share properties and behaviors. For example, the capital letter "A" in the Latin script looks similar to the capital letter alpha in Greek. If you look at their lowercase equivalents, as shown in Table 6-8, you see that lowercase Latin "a" looks completely different from lowercase Greek alpha "α." For this reason, the characters were not unified.

Table 6-8. Nonunified Characters

Glyph	Unicode Value	Unicode Name
A	\u0041	LATIN CAPITAL LETTER A
a	\u0061	LATIN SMALL LETTER A
B	\u0042	LATIN CAPITAL LETTER B
b	\u0062	LATIN SMALL LETTER B
A	\u0391	GREEK CAPITAL LETTER ALPHA
α	\u03B1	GREEK SMALL LETTER ALPHA
B	\u0392	GREEK CAPITAL LETTER BETA
β	\u03B2	GREEK SMALL LETTER BETA

A major undertaking occurred with the unification of Chinese characters (known in Unicode circles as *Han Unification*). As described in Chapter 2, many characters used in Japanese and Korean writing were borrowed from Chinese. Several of these characters evolved over time to become different enough that they could no longer be considered the same as the original Chinese character they evolved from. Other characters did not change at all, or were changed only slightly over the years.

As a result, the Chinese, Japanese, and Korean (CJK) countries have each developed several code sets over the past several decades that include their own collection of Chinese characters. If you were to look at the characters in each of these code sets, you would see that some characters in each set are the same, while others are quite different. Table 6-3 lists a few of these code sets. The complete list is actually quite large.

The challenge for the Unicode Consortium was to examine all these code sets and determine which characters were, in fact, the same character, and which characters needed their own unique code point. To stay true to the tenth design principle, convertibility, a rule known as *source set separation* prevented unification of characters within the same code set. The Han Unification process took several years, involving teams of experts from the CJK countries, the United States, and Canada.

To understand the complexity of the unification process, let's look at some examples. Table 6-9 shows two characters that look similar to a naïve reader of Chinese ideographs. In fact, these characters not only have different meanings, but the length of the horizontal strokes on each character differs (look closely). As a result, these characters were not unified.

Table 6-9. Nonunified Han Characters

Unicode Value	Glyph	Meaning
\u571F	土	soil; earth
\u58EB	士	scholar; gentleman, soldier

Table 6-10 shows a list of characters as they are rendered in different countries. Notice that for some of these characters, particularly \u4E0E and \u9AA8, the glyph varies considerably between locales. Even so, these characters are considered the same character, so they have been unified.

Table 6-10. Unified Characters Requiring Different Glyphs

Unicode Value	Taiwan	China	Japan	Korea	Meaning
\u4E0E	与	与	与		To; and; for; give; grant
\u5B57	字	字	字	字	Character; word; letter
\u6587	文	文	文	文	Writing; literature; culture
\u9AA8	骨	骨	骨	骨	Bone; skeleton; frame

Some controversy has developed over the Han Unification process. Understandably, people feel strongly about their cultural heritage and don't want years of orthographical history to be wiped out by a few years of work undertaken by a consortium. In reality, Han Unification does not prevent a computer program from displaying the correct national glyphs for a given locale. Dealing with unification is simply a matter of choosing a font that contains the glyphs appropriate for that country.

Dynamic composition

When we said earlier that characters in Unicode are 16 bits, we didn't tell the whole truth. What we should have said is that a *code element* in Unicode is encoded in 16 bits. A code element is the smallest unit defined in the Unicode Standard and is equivalent to a code point. Dynamic composition allows the combination of multiple code elements to form a single text element or character.

As we saw in Chapter 2, many writing systems have the concept of diacritics, vowels, or other markings that can be applied to base characters. For some scripts, the number of possible character and diacritic marking combinations is so large that including them all in the code set isn't practical. Instead, the *base characters* and *combining diacritical marks*, which are also called *nonspacing marks* in the Unicode Standard, are given their own code points in the Unicode Standard. The combining diacritical marks for Latin and Greek are located in the character block "Combining Diacritical Marks," and are in the range \u0300 to \u036F. Nonspacing marks specific to other scripts are located within that script's block. For example, Hebrew vowels and cantillation marks are located in the Hebrew block.[9]

Dynamic composition, illustrated in Figure 6-1, allows combination of a base character with one or more nonspacing marks to produce the needed character. To produce the character Ã, we can combine the base character A (LATIN CAPITAL LETTER A—\u0041) with the combining diacritic (˜) (COMBINING TILDE—\u0303). To produce the character Ā, we can combine the base character "A" (LATIN CAPITAL LETTER A—\u0041) with the combining diacritic (˙) (DOT ABOVE—\u0307) and the combining diacritic (¯) (MACRON—\u0304).

When composing characters, the base character must come first, followed by the nonspacing marks. Thus, ˜ followed by A would not be a valid composition. The tilde could be combined with the character preceding it, resulting in an unintended character composition.

---

[9] Cantillation marks are used with biblical texts to indicate precise punctuation and to help the cantor (reader) read the text aloud correctly.

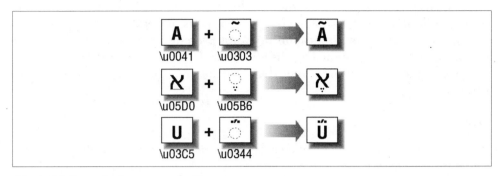

Figure 6-1. Dynamic character composition

When more than one nonspacing mark is combined with a base character, the order in which the nonspacing marks are combined is also important. If two nonspacing marks interact (that is, they both appear in the same location relative to the base character), then the marks are stacked outward from the base character according to the order in which they were combined, as shown in Figure 6-2.

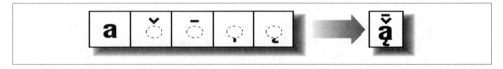

Figure 6-2. Stacking nonspacing marks

To create a character using dynamic composition in Java, simply combine the characters in the `String`:

```
String str = "A\u0303" // Ã
```

As of this writing (JDK 1.3), the Java rendering engine does not display glyphs of dynamically composed characters very well. The engineers at IBM are working on improving the rendering engine for complex text output. We hope these efforts will eventually be incorporated into Sun's implementation of the JVM, although there are no guarantees. Only the rendering engine, however, is of limited value. From a text-processing standpoint, characters created using dynamic composition are handled correctly in Java.

Equivalence sequence

In addition to the endless number of characters that can be created using dynamic composition, Unicode provides a large set of *precomposed* characters. Most of these characters appear in the following character blocks:

Character Block	Code Range
C1 Controls and Latin-1 Supplement	\u0080 → \u00FF
Latin Extended-A	\u0100 → \u017F
Latin Extended-B	\u0180 → \u024F
Latin Extended Additional	\u1E00 → \u1EFF
Greek Extended	\u1F00 → \u1FFF

Unicode mandates that a precomposed character is equivalent to its dynamic composition sequence. The rules for these equivalences are defined by the Unicode Standard and are built into Java. Table 6-11 shows a few examples of precomposed characters and their equivalent sequence.

Table 6-11. Precomposed Characters and Equivalent Sequence

Glyph	Unicode Value	Unicode Name	Equivalent Sequence
ä	\u00E4	LATIN SMALL LETTER A WITH DIAERESIS	\u0061\u0308
ù	\u00F9	LATIN SMALL LETTER U WITH GRAVE	\u0075\u0300
Ę	\u0118	LATIN CAPITAL LETTER E WITH OGONEK	\u0045\u0328
Ǖ	\u01D5	LATIN CAPITAL LETTER U WITH DIAERESIS AND MACRON	\u00DC\u0304

To take advantage of the equivalent sequence rules, you must use the `Collator` class to compare strings. The `Collator` class is typically used for searching and sorting, and we discuss it in detail in Chapter 7, *Searching, Sorting, and Text Boundary Detection*. For now, look at the following code snippet:

```
// Define two strings that are equivalent
String a1 = "\u0061\u0308"; // a + diaeresis
String a2 = "\u00E4";       // precomposed ä

// Use the factory to get a Collator instance
Collator collate = Collator.getInstance();

// Use Collator.equals to compare the two strings for equivalence
System.out.println(collate.equals(a1, a2));
```

```
// Use String.equals to compare the two strings for equivalence
System.out.println(a1.equals(a2));
```

The output from this code is:

```
true
false
```

This example demonstrates that Java does support equivalent sequence rules and indicates that you shouldn't use `String.equals()` to compare natural language strings.

Convertibility

The tenth and final Unicode design principle requires that text data can be converted between Unicode and other major code sets. This convertibility is critical because of the vast amount of legacy data that exists, and providing a new code set without a way to convert to and from legacy code sets and encoding methods just adds to the mess. According to the Unicode Standard, "convertibility is guaranteed between the Unicode Standard and other standards in wide usage as of May 1993."

As we discussed in the section on unification earlier in this chapter, the ability to convert between characters played a key role in determining whether characters could be unified. Remember that Unicode attempts to incorporate as many code set standards as possible. Two characters in the same legacy code set that were considered the same based on etymology and meaning may still not have been unified because of the requirement for round-trip conversion.

Java easily converts between Unicode and other code sets. There are essentially two mechanisms: one converts the data in memory using the `String` class and the other converts the data as it is being read from or written to a file. We'll cover this process later in this chapter.

Compatibility characters and presentation forms

Many characters in Unicode would not be necessary were it not for the requirement that all characters must be mapped back to their source standard. Relying on character composition and smart rendering engines to deal with these additional characters might have been sufficient. However, we don't live in a perfect world and more data are encoded in other code sets than in Unicode; we must have a way to perform round-trip conversion between these code sets.

The Unicode Standard specifies the compatibility between characters. Many of the characters are actually useful, especially for rendering engines that haven't quite gotten it all together yet (including Java). Examples of these characters include the precomposed accented letters, presentation forms for the Arabic letters (i.e., initial, medial, final, and ligatures), and precomposed Hangul syllables.

Unicode Encoding Methods

The default encoding method for Unicode, and the one used internally within Java, is known as the Universal Character Set (UCS-2). Since UCS-2 does not have any shift states or escape sequences, the encoding is as easy to use as ASCII. UCS-2 is fine for use if your application can work in isolation, but if you need to send and receive data from systems that can only deal with 7- or 8-bit data, you need to use another encoding scheme.

The Unicode Standard supports several encoding schemes known as Unicode transformation formats (UTF). UTF-7 is a modal encoding method that encodes the data into 7-bit bytes, leaving the high-order bit clear. This method is useful if you need to transmit your data through an application that ignores the high-order bit, as do some email programs.

Outside of UCS-2, UTF-8 has become the most common encoding scheme for Unicode data. Most popular web browsers and email clients support data in UTF-8. UTF-8 is an 8-bit variable length encoding, meaning that one, two, or three bytes could represent a Unicode code point. Table 6-12 shows the UCS-2 code point ranges and the number of bytes to use for each range. Except for characters in the ASCII range (\u0000 to \u007F), the number of high-order bits set to 1 in the first byte indicates the number of bytes used to encode the character. For example, the high-order byte used for characters in the range \u0800 to \uFFFF is 1110xxxx.[10] The three high-order bits indicate that three bytes are necessary to encode the character in this range. An "x" in the pattern indicates bits that are replaced during conversion.

Table 6-12. UTF-8 Encoding Ranges and Bit Patterns

UCS-2 Encoding Range	UTF-8 Bit Pattern
\u0000 to \u007F	0xxxxxxx
\u0080 to \u07FF	110xxxxx 10xxxxxx
\u0800 to \uFFFF	1110xxxx 10xxxxxx 10xxxxxx

One nice feature of UTF-8 is that characters in the range \u0000 to \u007F map to ASCII. In other words, if you had Unicode data that fell only in the ASCII range,

---

[10] This feature of UTF-8 makes it easy to find character boundaries in a UTF-8 data stream.

its UTF-8 encoding would be identical to encoded ASCII data. Table 6-13 shows what the text string "I speak 日本語" ("I speak Japanese") looks like encoded in both UCS-2 and UTF-8.

Table 6-13. Example of UCS-2 and UTF-8 Encoding

Text String	UCS-2 Encoding	UTF-8 Encoding
I speak 日本語	0049 0020 0073 0070 0065 0061 006B 0020 65E5 672C 8A9E	49 20 73 70 65 61 6B 20 E6 97 A5 E6 9C AC E8 AA 9E

To better explain how UTF-8 works, we provide a working example. Figure 6-3 takes the first character in the word 日本語 (Japanese) and converts it to UTF-8. The UCS-2 encoding for the character 日 is \u65E5. The code point fits in the range \u0800 to \uFFFF, so we use the 3-byte pattern from Table 6-12. Converting 0x65E5 to binary we get 110010111100101. Starting from the least significant bit, break the binary value into a two 6-bit chunks and one 4-bit chunk to match the x's in the bit patterns. We get 110 010111 100101 in our example. Notice that we don't have enough bits to fill out the x's in the most significant byte. In this case, simply pad the value with zeros so we end up with 0110 010111 100101.

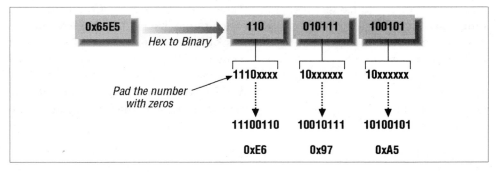

Figure 6-3. Converting from UCS-2 to UTF-8

Code Set Conversion

Prior to the release of JDK 1.1, the classes in the java.io package that read from and wrote to files consisted solely of byte streams. These classes were capable of reading only a single byte, or 8 bits, at a time. However, characters in the Unicode character set consist each of a double byte, or 16 bits. This deficiency in the Java class libraries was addressed starting in JDK 1.1 with the enhancements made to the `java.io` package.

Java makes converting data from one encoding method to another very simple. The conversion can be done either during file I/O or in memory using the `String` class. This section demonstrates the simplicity of character code conversion in Java.

File I/O Conversion

The `java.io` package offers two classes that act as a bridge between byte streams and character streams. The `InputStreamReader` allows you to read bytes from an input stream and convert those bytes into a particular character encoding. Conversely, the `OutputStreamWriter` takes character stream data and outputs it to a byte stream. The characters written are converted, according to a specific encoding, into the proper bytes.

The value of the system property, `file.encoding`, determines the default character encoding used by the character stream classes.[11] This property gives you the name of the character encoding from the list in Appendix B, *Character Encodings Supported by Java*. The following code shows how to get the default character encoding for your system:

```
System.out.println(System.getProperty("file.encoding"));
```

Running this code on a U.S. version of Windows 98 yields the following output:

```
Cp1252
```

Since the string returned in `file.encoding` is determined by the host system, it may or may not match one of the names of the Java encoding converters. The default encoding can be overridden by using class methods that take the encoding as a parameter.

Using java.io.InputStreamReader

Let's look at the `InputStreamReader` class first. An `InputStreamReader` knows how to read in byte stream data in a particular character encoding and convert that data into Unicode. Two constructors are available to create an `InputStreamReader`:

```
InputStreamReader(InputStream in)
InputStreamReader(InputStream in, String enc)
    throws UnsupportedEncodingException
```

---

[11] `file.encoding` is not part of the Java specification, and is therefore an implementation-dependent feature.

The first constructor creates an `InputStreamReader` object with a given `Input-Stream` using the platform's default encoding. You may also specify the encoding that should be used to convert bytes from the underlying `InputStream` by using the second constructor. An `UnsupportedEncodingException` is thrown if no converter that can handle the encoding passed into the constructor is available.

The following piece of code opens a file called *foo.in* encoded in Shift-JIS and creates a `BufferedReader` object to read the file:

```
FileInputStream fis = new FileInputStream(new File("foo.in"));
BufferedReader in =
    new BufferedReader(new InputStreamReader(fis,"SJIS"));
```

To read the file, simply use the `BufferedReader` object the way you would normally. To read a character, call:

```
char c = in.read();
```

The data are automatically converted to Unicode (UCS-2) as they are read. What could be easier?

Using java.io.OutputStreamWriter

Converting data from Unicode to another character encoding method when writing out a text stream is just as easy. We use the `OutputStreamWriter` class, which has two constructors:

```
OutputStreamWriter(OutputStream out)
OutputStreamWriter(OutputStream out, String enc)
    throws UnsupportedEncodingException
```

The functionality of the `OutputStreamWriter` is exactly opposite to that of the `InputStreamReader`. This class takes character data and converts it to its byte representation using a given character encoding. Like the `InputStreamReader` class, the first constructor creates an `OutputStreamWriter` object using the default character encoding of the host platform. The second constructor allows you to specify the encoding that should be used to convert characters when they are written to the stream. If we wanted to output characters in Shift-JIS, a popular Japanese character encoding, we would construct an `OutputStreamWriter` in the following manner:

```
FileOutputStream fos = new FileOutputStream(new File("foo.out"));
BufferedWriter out =
    new BufferedWriter(new OutputStreamWriter(fos, "SJIS"));
```

To write data to the file, just use one of the `BufferedReader` methods:

```
out.write("Japanese is \u65E5\u672C\u8A9E");
```

This method converts "Japanese is 日本語" to Shift-JIS as it writes to the file.

The `InputStreamReader` and `OutpuStreamWriter` both have a `getEncoding()` method that returns the name of the character encoding used by the class. However, the `getEncoding()` method may return a character encoding name different from the one used to create the `InputStreamReader` or `OutputStreamWriter` object. This different name occurs because the `getEncoding()` method returns the canonical name of the character converter, which may differ from the name passed to the constructor. The following code demonstrates this behavior:

```
import java.io.*;

class EncodingNameTest {

    public static void main(String args[]) throws Exception {
        FileOutputStream fos =
            new FileOutputStream(new File("foo.out"));
        OutputStreamWriter osw = new OutputStreamWriter(fos, "CP1006");

        System.out.println(osw.getEncoding());
    }
}
```

In this example, the value printed out to the screen would be `Cp1006`, which differs only in that the p is not capitalized. This method returns the `null` string if the stream has been closed.

Combining input and output together

Example 6-1 combines import and export conversion to demonstrate how to convert a file from Shift-JIS to UTF-8. The program could be modified slightly to accept the encoding methods as parameters, which would make the utility rather useful. We leave that utility as an exercise to the reader.

Example 6-1. Conversion Utility

```
import java.lang.*;
import java.io.*;

class Converter {
  public Converter(String input, String output) {
    try {
      FileInputStream fis = new FileInputStream(new File(input));
      BufferedReader in = new BufferedReader(new InputStreamReader(fis, "SJIS"));

      FileOutputStream fos = new FileOutputStream(new File(output));
      BufferedWriter out = new BufferedWriter(new OutputStreamWriter(fos, "UTF8"));
      // create a buffer to hold the characters
```

Example 6-1. Conversion Utility (continued)

```
    int len = 80;
    char buf[] = new char[len];

    // read the file len characters at a time and write them out
    int numRead;
    while ((numRead = in.read(buf, 0, len)) != -1)
      out.write(buf, 0, numRead);

    // close the streams
    out.close();
    in.close();
  } catch (IOException e) {
    System.out.println("An I/O Exception Occurred: " + e);
  }
}

public static void main(String args[]) {
  new Converter(args[0], args[1]);
}
}
```

String Conversion

Another facility that converts between non-Unicode data and Unicode character representation is constructing a `String` object with the appropriate byte data. A number of methods in the `String` class convert the Unicode string into a non-Unicode byte array.

Converting legacy encoding methods to Unicode

Six different constructors are provided in the `String` class to convert a byte array into a Unicode string:

```
String(byte[] bytes)
String(byte[] bytes, int offset, int length)
String(byte[] ascii, int hibyte)
String(byte[] ascii, int hibyte, int offset, int count)
String(byte[] bytes, int offset, int length, String enc)
      throws UnsupportedEncodingException
String(byte[] bytes, String enc) throws UnsupportedEncodingException
```

Let's first mention two deprecated methods that should not be used. The `hibyte` argument is used to fill in the high-order byte of a two-byte character:

```
String(byte[] ascii, int hibyte)
String(byte[] ascii, int hibyte, int offset, int count)
```

Both of these constructors were present in JDK 1.0.2 and were deprecated with the release of JDK 1.1. The following two constructors should be used instead. They convert a byte array that you provide as the first argument to a String using the host platform's default encoding:

```
String(byte[] bytes)
String(byte[] bytes, int offset, int length)
```

As mentioned before, the system property, file.encoding, gives the host platform's default character encoding. The first constructor converts the entire byte array to the platform's encoding. In the second constructor, you specify an offset to be the starting position in the byte array from which conversion begins. From this position, conversion occurs for length bytes.

Finally, the last two String constructors allow you to provide an encoding into which the byte array will be converted:

```
String(byte[] bytes, int offset, int length, String enc)
     throws UnsupportedEncodingException
String(byte[] bytes, String enc) throws UnsupportedEncodingException
```

If the conversion is not possible because the encoding is not supported on your platform, the constructor throws an UnsupportedEncodingException. The following code snippet creates a byte array encoded in Shift-JIS containing the Japanese word "日本語" (nihongo), which means Japanese. The code then converts the array to Unicode using the String constructor:

```
try {
   byte[] nihongo_sjis = {(byte)0x93, (byte)0xfa,
                          (byte)0x96, (byte)0x7b,
                          (byte)0x8c, (byte)0xea};
   String nihongo_unicode = new String(nihongo_sjis, "SJIS");
} catch (UnsupportedEncodingException e) {
   System.out.println("An UnsupportedEncodingException: " + e);
}
```

Converting Unicode to legacy encoding methods

Java also allows you to go from a Unicode String to a resulting byte array by using one of the following three methods on the String class:

```
public byte[] getBytes()
public byte[] getBytes(String enc)
public void getBytes(int srcBegin, int srcEnd, byte[] dst, int destBegin)
```

The first method takes the String object and converts it to a byte array using the platform's default encoding. The second method, getBytes(String enc), allows you to specify the character encoding for use in the conversion process. An UnsupportedEncodingException is thrown by this method if the converter is not available on the current platform. The last method is a deprecated method and should not be used because it strips off the high-order 8 bits and only copies the corresponding character's low-order 8 bits.

The following code snippet creates a string containing the word "日本語" encoded in Unicode and converts it to Shift-JIS:

```
try {
  String nihongo = "\u65E5\u672C\u8A9E";
  byte[] nihongo_sjis = nihongo.getBytes("SJIS");
} catch (UnsupportedEncodingException e) {
  System.out.println("An UnsupportedEncodingException: " + e);
}
```

We demonstrated data conversion using Shift-JIS, but any of the valid encoding methods listed in the table in Appendix B could be used.

Deprecated Functionality

In addition to the deprecated methods we discussed earlier in this chapter, we should point out other deprecated features of the java.io package.

java.io.DataInputStream

Do not use the readLine() method in the DataInputStream class. This class reads a single line from the input stream; however, it does not convert bytes to characters properly. You can change your existing code to be I18N compliant as follows, assuming your code looks something like this:

```
FileInputStream fis = new FileInputStream("foo.txt");
DataInputStream dis = new DataInputStream(fis);
String myString = dis.readLine();
```

The code should be changed to:

```
FileInputStream fis = new FileInputStream("foo.txt");
BufferedReader br = new BufferedReader(new InputStreamReader(fis));

String myString = br.readLine();
```

The BufferedReader class contains a readLine() method that reads a single line from the underlying input stream and properly converts bytes to characters.

java.lang.Runtime

Two methods in the `java.lang.Runtime` class have been deprecated due to improper conversion of bytes to characters:

```
Runtime.getLocalizedInputStream(InputStream in)
Runtime.getLocalizedOutputStream(OutputStream out)
```

If you need to create a localized `InputStream` or `OutputStream`, you should use the `InputStreamReader` or `OutputStreamWriter` classes that we discussed earlier.

The sun.io Package

Implementations of the Java Runtime Environment support different converters because they can exist on many different host operating systems. Therefore, certain converters may not be present in all releases of the JRE. In Sun's implementation, the converters live in the `sun.io` package. In early alpha and beta releases of JDK 1.1, the character conversion engine was part of the `java.io` package. The classes that handle character conversion, such as `java.io.Reader` and `java.io.Writer` (and their subclasses), invoke classes from the `sun.io` package. Sun puts a disclaimer in the JDK documentation stating that programs that reference the `sun.*` packages directly are not guaranteed to run correctly, or even at all, on all platforms. The classes in the `sun.*` packages may be replaced with other classes or they may not be present in future releases of the JDK.

Consequently, the available character converters may differ from vendor to vendor, or certain converters may not be present in a release of the JDK. We therefore recommend that you only invoke the converters indirectly through the documented API's we described in this chapter.

In this section, we illustrated how effortless it is to convert data between one encoding method and another in Java. If you have had to convert this data in a programming language other than Java, you would realize just how wonderful Java's capabilities in this area are!

7

Searching, Sorting, and Text Boundary Detection

Almost every introductory class in computer science teaches a section on sorting algorithms. Typically, students are taught how to sort a collection of English words using a number of algorithms, such as bubble sort, heap sort, merge sort, or quick sort. These algorithms are fine, except that at the heart of them is some comparison logic that checks if one word should appear before or after another in the list. Typically, students are taught that it is safe to assume that the encoded values of the letters in the alphabet are in numerical order. Thus a < b < c assumes that the encoded value of a is less than the encoded value of b, which is less than the encoded value of c. Unfortunately, this assumption falls apart when trying to sort other languages.

Collation Issues

As a very simple example, let's look at what happens if we try to sort the two Spanish words "pipa" and "piña," meaning pipe and pineapple, respectively. If we sort these words correctly, "piña" sorts before "pipa." The problem is that the character "ñ" has a value of \u00F1, while the character "p" has a value of \u0070, so "pipa" is incorrectly sorted before "piña."

Even within English, sorting using a character's encoded value doesn't always produce the desired results. Some users might expect to see capitalized words segregated from lowercase words, while others would expect to see all words combined. Implementing a typical ASCII-based sort would result in the case-sensitive list that follows; but if you wanted to look these words up in a dictionary, you would expect them to appear in the case-insensitive order shown on the right column of the following table:

Case Sensitive	Case Insensitive
Albany	Albany
December	android
Zulu	apple
android	brick
apple	cell
brick	December
cell	dinner
dinner	doctor
doctor	Zulu

Phone book order requires yet another kind of collating sequence. If you look in a U.S. phone book, you will find that "St." is sorted alphabetically between "Sains-" and "Saint." "St." is the abbreviation for saint, and people are used to finding the abbreviation as if it were spelled out fully. Similarly, you will find "Dr." sorted in the "Doc" section.

Another issue that crops up often in English and in other languages is the question of how to handle ignorable characters. For example, should the words e-mail and email be sorted together (can the hyphen be ignored)? Loan words from other languages, such as French, sometimes have diacritics such as café, résumé or déjà-vu. Most English-speaking users would expect to see these words sorted as if the diacritics didn't exist.

These examples demonstrate that, even in English, collation is based on the domain in question. Simply sorting by code point value isn't sufficient for most purposes. The issues associated with collating English are trivial compared to those in some other languages, as you will see in a moment.

One-to-Two Character Mappings

Some languages, such as German, treat single characters as if they were two characters. This treatment is sometimes referred to as *expansion*. The German letter ß (pronounced Eszett) only appears in the lower case and is equivalent to a double s (ss). When capitalized, "SS" replaces Eszett (e.g., straße becomes STRASSE). Swiss German abandoned ß several decades ago; however, it is still in use in Austria and Germany. In recent years, the German language has undergone a spelling reform (Rechtschreibreform), not without controversy, and some places now require the use of ss where ß was once used. The new rules (Neuregelung) for determining when to use ß and ss are somewhat complicated. Full adoption of the rules by all German-speaking countries will take effect on July 31, 2005.

In German, characters with an umlaut (ä, ö, ü) are treated as the base character followed by e, so they are equivalent to ae, oe, and ue for sorting purposes.

Two-to-One Character Mappings

Some languages treat two characters as if they are one. This treatment is sometimes referred to as *contraction*. In traditional Spanish, ch is considered one letter that sorts between c and d. Likewise ll is a letter that sorts between l and m. Modern Spanish no longer uses these contractions, but other languages still have the requirement. In Czech, ch is also treated as a single character, but it sorts between h and i.

Diacritics

The order of characters, even in the same writing system, can change from one language to another. In German, a-umlaut (ä) should be sorted with the letter a, but the same letter sorts after the letter z in Swedish.

In French, as in English, words are sorted using the base characters. Then a second-level sort is made, breaking any ties based on accents. The second sort is right to left, starting at the end of the word, working toward the beginning. In other words, accents that appear later in the word are more important from a collation standpoint than accents appearing earlier in the word. The following example demonstrates this behavior. The French word pêche, meaning "peach," sorts before the French word péché, meaning "indiscretion," even though the letter ê sorts after the letter é. Starting from the end of the words, a character with no accent sorts before the same character with an accent.

CJK Sorting

Chinese ideographs add another complication to the topic of sorting. Ideographic characters can be sorted using a number of techniques, and each locale that uses the characters typically applies a different collation sequence.

In Chapter 2, *Writing Systems*, we learned that each Chinese character is composed of a distinct number of strokes. Stroke count sorting collates characters according to the number of basic strokes required to draw the character. Another common sorting method is to collate characters according to their main radical, similar to an English word root. Often a first-level sort using either the radical or stroke count method is used, followed by a second-level sort using the other method.

Ideographic characters can also be sorted based on their pronunciation. Simplified Chinese, for example, is often sorted using Pinyin sort order. This order is equivalent to an alphabetical ordering based on pronunciation.

It is common practice for CJK languages to sort according to the character order as listed in certain character sets. In fact, the collation rules provided by the JDK for the CJK languages are as follows:

Locale	Character Set Used for Collation Sequence
Japan	SJIS
Taiwan	Big5
China	GB
Korea	KSC

Sorting in Java

In Java, all of these different issues can be handled quite easily by using the appropriate classes and methods. You should not use the methods `String.equals()` or `String.compareTo()` for comparing strings, as they simply perform a bitwise comparison. This comparison won't work for most languages. The simplest solution is to use the abstract class `java.text.Collator`. As with many of the other abstract classes we've discussed, use the `getInstance` factory methods to retrieve an instance of the class, rather than instantiating the object directly. Two `getInstance` methods are available. The first method takes no parameters and returns a `Collator` object for the default locale. The second method takes a `Locale` object and returns an instance of `Collator` for that particular locale. Here is an example of how to create a collation object for German:

```
Collator collate = Collator.getInstance(new Locale("de", ""));
```

Once you have a `Collator` instance, use either the `Collator.compare()` or `Collator.equals()` method to compare two strings. The compare method takes two strings as arguments and returns an integer. The returned value is either less than, equal to, or greater than zero, depending on if the first argument is less than, equal to, or greater than the second argument:

```
if (collate.compare(String1, String2) > 0)
```

Example 7-1 shows a small program that sorts a list of Swedish words. Table 7-1 displays the words in unsorted order, Swedish sort order, and German sort order.

Notice how the letter ä in Swedish collates after the letter z. Figure 7-1 displays the output from Example 7-1.

Figure 7-1. Output from Example 7-1

Table 7-1. Swedish Versus German Sort Order

Unsorted	Swedish	German
päron	banan	äpple
äpple	orange	banan
orange	päron	orange
banan	äpple	päron

Example 7-1. Sorting Strings Using Collator

```
class Sort extends JPanel {
    static JFrame frame;

    public Sort() {
        Vector list = new Vector();
            list.add("\u00e4pple");
            list.add("banan");
            list.add("p\u00e4ron");
            list.add("orange");

            // Obtain a Swedish collator
        Collator collate = Collator.getInstance(new Locale("sv", ""));

            Collections.sort(list, collate);

        StringBuffer result = new StringBuffer();
        for (int i= 0;i < list.size(); i++) {
          result.append(list.elementAt(i));
          result.append("  ");
        }
        add(new JLabel(result.toString()));
    }

    public static void main(String s[]) {
        Sort panel = new Sort();

        frame = new JFrame("Sort");
```

Example 7-1. Sorting Strings Using Collator (continued)

```
    frame.addWindowListener(new WindowAdapter() {
      public void windowClosing(WindowEvent e) {System.exit(0);}
    });
    frame.getContentPane().add("Center", panel);
    frame.pack();
    frame.setVisible(true);
  }
}
```

Collator Strength

The `Collator` object allows you to specify a parameter known as *strength*. Strength determines how the collator should interpret differences between two characters. These differences are locale specific, so rules could differ between locales. The four strength types are:

Strength	Description	Example
Collator.PRIMARY	The base letters themselves are different.	A versus B
Collator.SECONDARY	The base characters are the same, but the accents are different.	A versus Â
Collator.TERTIARY	The letters are the same, but differ by case.	A versus a
Collator.IDENTICAL	The letters are identical.	A versus A

The least restrictive strength is primary and the most restrictive is identical. By default, the strength of the Collator object is set to `Collator.TERTIARY`. This setting means that the collator takes primary, secondary, and tertiary differences into account when comparing characters. If you change the strength to `Collator.SECONDARY`, only primary and secondary differences are considered. If you change the strength to `Collator.PRIMARY`, only primary differences are evaluated. Finally, if you change the strength to `Collator.IDENTICAL`, all distinctions between characters are considered a difference. This consideration includes differences between precomposed and composed characters such as Â and `A\u0302` (as long as *decomposition* is set to `Collator.NO_DECOMPOSITION`. We discuss decomposition a little bit later in this chapter.) [1]

The two methods `Collator.setStrength()` and `Collator.getStrength()` allow you to get and set the strength of the `Collator` object. Let's look at how we might use the strength parameter to our advantage. In English, the word "cafe" can also be

---

[1] See Chapter 6, *Character Sets and Unicode*, to learn more about character composition.

spelled the French way, "café." If we were to use the default tertiary strength, the U.S. English collator would say that these two words are different. The following code sample demonstrates this idea:

```
String str1 = "cafe";
String str2 = "caf\u00e9";  // café

Collator collate = Collator.getInstance(Locale.US);
if (collate.equals(str1, str2))
    System.out.println(str1 + " is equal to " + str2);
else
    System.out.println(str1 + " is NOT equal to " + str2);
```

The output from this code is:

```
cafe is NOT equal to café
```

The following code sample is identical to the previous one, except that we changed the strength to primary. This change tells the collator that it should ignore accents and only make a distinction using base character differences:

```
String str1 = "cafe";
String str2 = "caf\u00e9";  // café

Collator collate = Collator.getInstance(Locale.US);
collate.setStrength(Collator.PRIMARY);
if (collate.equals(str1, str2))
    System.out.println(str1 + " is equal to " + str2);
else
    System.out.println(str1 + " is NOT equal to " + str2);
```

The output from this code is:

```
cafe is equal to café
```

As we discussed in Chapter 6, Unicode provides a set of compatible characters to enable roundtrip conversion between Unicode and legacy code sets. Unless the strength is set to `Collator.IDENTICAL`, compatible characters are considered equivalent for the purposes of collation. As an example, the character "Å" has two code points in the Unicode Standard. It is found in the C1 Controls and Latin-1 Supplement block at location \u00C5—LATIN CAPITAL LETTER A WITH RING ABOVE and in the Letterlike Symbols block at location \u212B—ANGSTROM SIGN. The following code demonstrates this functionality:

```
// E LATIN CAPITAL LETTER A WITH RING ABOVE
String str1 = "\u00c5";
// E ANGSTROM SIGN
String str2 = "\u212b";
Collator collate = Collator.getInstance(Locale.US);
if (collate.equals(str1, str2))
    System.out.println("The strings are equal.");
else
```

```
    System.out.println("The strings are NOT equal.");
// Set the strength to IDENTICAL
collate.setStrength(Collator.IDENTICAL);
if (collate.equals(str1, str2))
    System.out.println("The strings are equal.");
else
    System.out.println("The strings are NOT equal.");
```

The output from this code is:

```
The strings are equal.
The strings are NOT equal.
```

Collator Decomposition

The Collator class allows you to specify the level of *decomposition* used when comparing strings. In Chapter 6 we described the Unicode concepts of dynamic composition and equivalence sequences. We stated that characters could be composed dynamically by combining a base character with at least one combining mark. We also said that a dynamically composed character is equivalent to its precomposed version (if one exists). Decomposition converts precomposed characters into their primitive parts, as shown in Figure 7-2.

NOTE   In CJK languages, each ideographic character fills a squared area called a cell. The cell's width is roughly twice the width of a Latin character. The term *full-width*, or *zenkaku* (全角) in Japanese, refers to a character that fills the complete width of the cell. Characters that take up half the width of the cell are referred to as *half-width*, or *hankaku* (半角) in Japanese. For historical reasons, legacy encodings such as Shift-JIS contain both half- and full-width versions of kana and Latin letters. To support roundtrip conversion, the half-width kana characters and the full-width ASCII (Latin) characters have their own code points in the Unicode Standard.

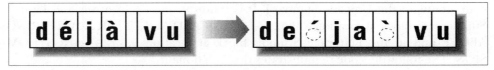

Figure 7-2. Precomposed versus decomposed characters

Text is said to be *normalized* if it is transformed so that all characters are either in their precomposed form or are decomposed. Once text is normalized it is much easier to search and sort. Typically, decomposition rather than precomposed text is recommended for normalization; normalization based on precomposed characters does not guarantee uniqueness due to compatible characters (e.g., Å could be either \u00C5 or \u212B). Another reason for this recommendation is that new precomposed characters may be added to the Unicode Standard. Text that has been normalized prior to the new version might contain decomposed characters that didn't have a precomposed equivalent previously, but now do.

The Collator class supports two forms of decomposition. The first form, known as *canonical decomposition*, recursively decomposes each precomposed character in a string, using the canonical decomposition mapping rules found in the Unicode Standard, until no further decomposition can occur.

The second form of decomposition used by the Collator class is called *full decomposition*. Full decomposition recursively decomposes each precomposed character in a string, using the canonical decomposition mapping rules and the compatibility decomposition mapping rules found in the Unicode Standard, until no more decomposition can occur. Compatible characters are included in the Unicode Standard to ensure roundtrip conversion between Unicode and legacy code sets. When the compatibility decomposition mapping rules are used, compatible characters, such as half- and full-width katakana or half- and full-width ASCII, are considered equivalent. Selected half- and full-width characters are shown in Table 7-2.

Table 7-2. Examples of Half-Width and Full-Width Characters

	Half-Width	Full-Width
Latin	ABCDEF	ＡＢＣＤＥＦ
Katakana	ｱｲｳｴｵ	アイウエオカ

Two methods on Collator allow you to set and get the decomposition value:

```
void setDecomposition(int decompositionMode)
int getDecomposition()
```

The decomposition values are:

```
Collator.NO_DECOMPOSITION
Collator.CANONICAL_DECOMPOSITION
Collator.FULL_DECOMPOSITION
```

Example 7-2 demonstrates the effects of applying different levels of decomposition to the collator with three different pairs of strings. Notice that we initially set the collator strength to Collator.IDENTICAL to ensure that we test the decomposition levels and not let the strength parameter interfere with the results. The first pair of strings (half-width A—\u0041 and full-width A—\uFF21) are only equal using full decomposition because these characters are only normalized using the compatibility decomposition mapping rules. The second and third pairs of strings are equal using either canonical or full decomposition.

Example 7-2. Effects of Decomposition on Comparison

```
import java.text.*;
import java.util.*;
import java.lang.*;
import java.io.*;

class Decomposition {
  public void compare(Collator c, String a, String b) {
    switch(c.getDecomposition()) {
      case Collator.NO_DECOMPOSITION:
        System.out.print(" NO DECOMPOSITION: ");
        break;
      case Collator.CANONICAL_DECOMPOSITION:
        System.out.print(" CANONICAL DECOMPOSITION: ");
        break;
      case Collator.FULL_DECOMPOSITION:
        System.out.print(" FULL DECOMPOSITION: ");
        break;
      default:
        System.out.print(" UNKNOWN DECOMPOSITION: ");
    }

    if (c.equals(a, b))
      System.out.println("The strings are equal.");
    else
      System.out.println("The strings are NOT equal.");
  }

  public Decomposition() {
    String pairs[][] = new String[3][3];
    pairs[0][0] = "Half-Width and full-width A";
    pairs[0][1] = "A";
    pairs[0][2] = "\uFF21"; // full-width A
    pairs[1][0] = "A with Ring and Angstrom Sign";
    pairs[1][1] = "\u00c5"; // A with ring
    pairs[1][2] = "\u212b"; // Angstrom
    pairs[2][0] = "a + umlaut and precomposed a-umlaut";
    pairs[2][1] = "a\u0308";
    pairs[2][2] = "\u00e4";

    for (int i = 0; i < 3; i++) {
      Collator collate = Collator.getInstance(Locale.US);
      collate.setStrength(Collator.IDENTICAL);
```

Example 7-2. Effects of Decomposition on Comparison (continued)

```
      System.out.println("Comparing " + pairs[i][0]);
      collate.setDecomposition(Collator.NO_DECOMPOSITION);
      compare(collate, pairs[i][1],pairs[i][2]);

      collate.setDecomposition(Collator.CANONICAL_DECOMPOSITION);
      compare(collate, pairs[i][1],pairs[i][2]);

      collate.setDecomposition(Collator.FULL_DECOMPOSITION);
      compare(collate, pairs[i][1],pairs[i][2]);
      System.out.println("");
    }
  }

  public static void main(String s[]) {
    new Decomposition();
  }
}
```

The output from Example 7-2 is:

```
C:\>java Decomposition
Comparing Half-Width and full-width A
   NO DECOMPOSITION: The strings are NOT equal.
   CANONICAL DECOMPOSITION: The strings are NOT equal.
   FULL DECOMPOSITION: The strings are equal.

Comparing A with Ring and Angstrom Sign
   NO DECOMPOSITION: The strings are NOT equal.
   CANONICAL DECOMPOSITION: The strings are equal.
   FULL DECOMPOSITION: The strings are equal.

Comparing a + umlaut and precomposed a-umlaut
   NO DECOMPOSITION: The strings are NOT equal.
CANONICAL DECOMPOSITION: The strings are equal.
FULL DECOMPOSITION: The strings are equal.
```

Tailoring Collation

Even within the same language, many ways to collate text exist, depending on the application. The collator for each locale in Java provides default rules for how to sort text in that locale. This section shows how to create customized rules.

When you call the factory method `getInstance` on `Collator`, the string containing the locale-specific key `CollationElements` is loaded from a system resource bundle (called `LocaleElements`) and used to construct a `RuleBasedCollator`. It is possible to create your own customized collator by instantiating a `RuleBasedCollator` object directly. First, you must understand how to define collation rules. The rules are specified using a special syntax; the rules are passed to the `RuleBasedCollator` constructor as a `String`. The following simple rule states that d should sort after c, which should sort after b, which should sort after a:

```
String simpleRule = "< a < b < c < d";
RuleBasedCollator simpleCollator = new RuleBasedCollator(simpleRule);
```

The less-than sign (<) indicates that the relationship between the text arguments on either side of it is a primary difference, as explained earlier in this chapter.

Appending Rules

Often you might want to add to already existing rules. To do so, use a reset character (&). What the reset character does is difficult to explain in words, and much easier to describe by example. Look at the rules in the following table.

Example	Rule	Definition	Result
1	< a < b < c	c sorts after b, which sorts after a	a < b < c
2	< a < b & b < c	b sorts after a, then c sorts after b	a < b < c
3	< a < c & a < b	c sorts after a, then b sorts after a	a < b < c
4	< a < b & a < c	b sorts after a, then sorts c after a	a < c < b
5	< b < c & a < b	Invalid	Invalid

Notice that the rules in Examples 1 through 3 produce the same result. The order in which resets are placed matters. This order is demonstrated in Example 4, where the relation a < c overrides the relation defined prior to the reset and places c directly after a.

The rule in Example 5 is invalid because the reset is trying to put b immediately after a in the rule, but a has not been defined yet. Attempting to use this rule would result in a `ParseException` being thrown.

So far we have used the less-than sign (<) to indicate primary differences between text arguments. It is also possible to specify secondary (;) and tertiary (,) differences as well as equivalence (=), as shown in Table 7-3.

Table 7-3. Relations

Relation	Meaning	Example
<	Primary difference	A versus B
;	Secondary difference	A versus Ä
,	Tertiary difference	A versus a
=	Equal	A versus A

To support both upper- and lowercase letters, change the simple rule we defined earlier to look like this:

```
String simpleRule = "< a,A < b,B < c,C < d,D";
```

All rules must begin with a relation character. In the examples shown so far, we simply use the less-than-sign (<) to begin the rule.

When specifying rules, text arguments can be any character sequence, except for whitespace characters (\u0009–\u000D, \u0020) and rule syntax characters (\u0021–\u002F, \u003A–\u0040, \u005B–\u0060, \u007B–\u007E). If one of these characters is needed, it must be placed in single quotes:

```
String simpleRule = "< '&' < a,A < b,B < c,C";
```

If a special character is not placed in single quotes, a `ParseException` is thrown.

Let's look at a real example. In traditional Spanish sort, the characters ch are treated as if they were only one character, which sorts between the letters c and d. Likewise, the characters ll are treated as one character, which sorts between the letters l and m. If you called the factory method `Collator.getInstance(new Locale("es", "ES"))`, the object returned would handle only modern Spanish sort, which ignores the contractions. The program in Example 7-3 shows how to add traditional Spanish sort capability.

Example 7-3. Adding Traditional Spanish Sort Capability

```
01: class SpanishSort {
02:
03:   public SpanishSort() {
04:
05:     Vector v = new Vector();
06:     v.add("musa");
07:     v.add("chic");
08:     v.add("llama");
09:     v.add("dela");
10:     v.add("chocolate");
11:     v.add("banana");
12:     v.add("crispa");
13:     v.add("luzca");
14:
15:     Collator esCollator = Collator.getInstance(new Locale("es","ES"));
16:     String spanishRules = ((RuleBasedCollator)esCollator).getRules();
17:
18:     try {
19:       String traditionalRules = "& C < ch, cH, Ch, CH " +
20:                                  "& L < ll, lL, Ll, LL";
21:       RuleBasedCollator collate =
22:             new RuleBasedCollator(spanishRules + traditionalRules);
23:
```

Example 7-3. Adding Traditional Spanish Sort Capability (continued)

```
24:      Collections.sort(v, collate);
25:    } catch (ParseException e) {
26:      System.out.println("Error parsing rules " + e.toString());
27:    }
28:    StringBuffer result = new StringBuffer();
29:    for (int i= 0;i < v.size(); i++) {
30:      result.append(v.elementAt(i));
31:      result.append("\n");
32:    }
33:    System.out.println(result);
34:    }
35:
36:    public static void main(String [] args) {
37:      new SpanishSort();
38:    }
39: }
```

Lines 5 through 13 instantiate a `Vector` and add the words to be sorted to that `Vector` object. Line 15 calls the factory method `getInstance` and passes in a locale specifying Spanish as spoken in Spain.

Line 16 relies on the fact that the returned object is really a `RuleBasedCollator` object. On this line, we cast it to a `RuleBasedCollator` and call the `getRules()` method to return a `String` containing the default rules for this `Collator`.

On lines 18 and 25 we surround the next bit of code in a `try-catch` block. This step is required because the `RuleBasedCollator` constructor throws a `ParseException` if the rules are invalid.

On line 19 we define a `String` that adds the rules for traditional Spanish. Notice how we use the reset character to append to the collation rules.

On lines 21 and 22 we instantiate a `RuleBasedCollator` passing in the rules we retrieved from line 16 and concatenated with the traditional Spanish rules we defined on line 19.

Line 24 sorts the vector. Lines 28 through 33 simply iterate through the vector and write out the results.

Compiling and running this program produces the following output:

```
banana
crispa
chic
chocolate
dela
luzca
llama
musa
```

Handling Expansion

In some languages, a character is treated as equivalent to two characters. In German, the following character sequences are equivalent for the purposes of sorting:

ä ≡ ae

ö ≡ oe

ü ≡ ue

To configure the collator to understand these expansion rules, use the following syntax:

```
& ae ; a\u0308
& oe ; o\u0308
& ue ; u\u0308
```

The character represented by \u0308 is the Unicode character COMBINING DIAERESIS. The code in Example 7-4 demonstrates the functionality. It creates two collators, one that uses simple collation rules and another that includes the expansion rules we just described. It then compares the two strings Mueller and Müller, which are both common spellings for a German surname. Notice that we set the strength to primary in each case. If we didn't set this strength, both comparisons would return false.[2]

Example 7-4. Comparing Strings Using German Expansion Rules

```
String a = "Mueller";
String b = "Mu\u0308ller";

// define the basic collation rules
String basicRules =
            "< a < b < c < d < e < f < g < h < i " +
            "< j < k < l < m < n < o < p < q < r " +
            "< s < t < u < v < w < x < y < z ";

// Define the rules for German Expansion.
String deExpansion = "& ae ; a\u0308 & oe ; o\u0308 & ue ; u\u0308";

RuleBasedCollator collator;
try {
  // Create a collator with the basic rules.
  // Don't forget to set the strength to PRIMARY.
  collator = new RuleBasedCollator(basicRules);
  collator.setStrength(Collator.PRIMARY);
  System.out.println("Basic Rules: " + collator.equals(str1, str2));
```

---

[2] Refer to the section "Collator Strength" to learn more information.

Example 7-4. Comparing Strings Using German Expansion Rules (continued)

```
    // Create a collator with the basic rules with German Expansion.
    collator = new RuleBasedCollator(basicRules + deExpansion);
    collator.setStrength(Collator.PRIMARY);
    System.out.println("Expansion Rules: " + collator.equals(str1, str2));
} catch (ParseException e) {
    System.out.println("Error parsing rules " + e.toString());
}
```

The output from this program is:

```
Basic Rules: false
Expansion Rules: true
```

The Modifier

A special relation called a *modifier* specifies that accents should be sorted in reverse. The at sign character (@) represents the modifier. The modifier was added specifically for French, which requires a secondary ordering of accents starting from the back of the word. When present, the modifier affects the entire collator object.

Ignorable Characters

Sometimes ignoring certain characters when sorting words is desirable. Consider the word "e-mail," which is sometimes written as "email." It would be nice to sort these two words together, even though the hyphen generally sorts either before a or after z, depending on the specified collation rules.

The following rule shows how to order words alphabetically in English:

```
String enAlphabetical = "< a,A < b,B < c,C < d,D < e,E < f,F < g,G " +
                        "< h,H < i,I < j,J < k,K < l,L < m,M < n,N " +
                        "< o,O < p,P < q,Q < r,R < s,S < t,T < u,U " +
                        "< v,V < w,W < x,X < y,Y < z,Z";
```

Characters not specified in the rules sort after the last character defined in the rules in the numerical order in which the Unicode Standard defines them. In our example, the word "e-mail" would be sorted after "entity" because the hyphen character does not appear in the rules, so it is sorted after the letter Z (the last character defined in our rules list).

When defining rules for the `RuleBasedCollator`, any character that appears before the first < is considered an ignorable character. If we wanted a hyphen to be ignored, we would use the following rule:

```
String ignoreHyphen = ", '-' < a,A < b,B < c,C < d,D < e,E < f,F " +
                      "< g,G < h,H < i,I < j,J < k,K < l,L < m,M " +
                      "< n,N < o,O < p,P < q,Q < r,R < s,S < t,T " +
```

```
                    "< t,T < u,U < v,V < w,W < x,X < y,Y < z,Z";
RuleBasedCollator ignoreCollator = new RuleBasedCollator(ignoreHyphen);
```

Remember, we stated earlier that all rules must begin with a relation (one of the characters in Table 7-3). Since ignorable characters appear in the rule before the < relation, we must choose another relation to appear first. In this example, we chose a comma. Table 7-4 shows the same list of unsorted words, words sorted using the English alphabetical rules we defined earlier, and words sorted using the customized collator to ignore the hyphen.

Table 7-4. Sorting Ignorable Characters

Unsorted	English Alphabetical	Ignoring Hyphens
e-business	dog	dog
dog	ebony	ebony
ebony	email	e-business
end	embassy	email
email	end	e-mail
entity	entity	embassy
fruit	e-business	end
e-mail	e-mail	entity
embassy	fruit	fruit

Characters such as the hyphen, em-dash, en-dash, their Unicode compatible characters, and the combining diacritic characters are ignorables in the rules defined in the locales in the JDK.

Improving Performance

Sorting strings can be costly in terms of performance. When you call `Collator.compare` or `Collator.equals`, one character in each string is examined at a time according to the locale specific rules. If the sorting algorithm you use compares the same strings repeatedly, it may make sense to use the `CollationKey` object instead.

A `CollationKey` represents a decomposed `String` as a sequence of integers known as *collation elements*. Typically, a one-to-one mapping between characters in the `String` and collation elements does not exist. Characters such as the German Eszett "ß" are represented by two collation elements, while the "ch" in Spanish are represented by one collation element. The mapping between characters and collation elements depends on the collation rules provided by the `Collator` object. Once all the `CollationKey` objects are created, comparing the strings is simply a matter of doing a bitwise comparison between the `CollationKey`s. Creating `Colla-tionKey` objects is expensive, so the performance benefit exists only if the same strings are compared repetitively.

To instantiate a `CollationKey`, simply call the method `Collator.getCollationKey` and pass in the string to be represented. The method has the following signature:

```
CollationKey getCollationKey(String source)
```

The following code snippet shows how the method is used:

```
Collator collator = Collator.getInstance();
CollationKey bananaKey = collator.getCollationKey("banana");
CollationKey kiwiKey = collator.getCollationKey("kiwi");
```

Once we have the `CollationKey` objects, we can compare them using either the `CollationKey.compareTo` or the `CollationKey.equals` methods shown here:

```
int compareTo(CollationKey target)
int compareTo(Object o)
boolean equals(Object o)
```

In the second `compareTo` method, the `Object` passed as the parameter must be a `CollationKey` object. If it is not, the method throws a `ClassCastException`. Continuing with our example, we could compare the keys as follows:

```
if (bananaKey.equals(kiwiKey))
  // do something
```

or:

```
if (bananaKey.compareTo(kiwiKey) == 0)
  // do something
```

The value returned from the `compareTo` methods is negative if the `CollationKey` is less than the target, zero if the `CollationKey` objects are identical, or positive if the `CollationKey` object is greater than the target. This behavior is similar to that of the `compare` method on `Collator`.

NOTE   CollationKey objects are comparable only if they originate from the same Collator object.

To retrieve the original string from the `CollationKey` object, use the `getSourceString` method as follows:

```
String kiwi = kiwiKey.getSourceString();
```

Example 7-5 consolidates all these steps by showing how to sort a list of words using `CollationKey` objects and displaying the results.

Example 7-5. Sorting Using CollationKeys

```
class SortWithCollationKeys {
  public static void main(String [] args) {
    // Build a vector of words to be sorted
    Vector list = new Vector();
    list.add("mocha");
    list.add("chocolate");
    list.add("espresso");
    list.add("cappuccino");

    // Obtain a collator
    Collator collate = Collator.getInstance();

    // Create an array to hold the CollationKey objects
    CollationKey[] keys = new CollationKey[list.size()];

    // Fill the array
    for (int k = 0; k < list.size(); k ++)
      keys[k] = collate.getCollationKey((String)list.elementAt(k));

    // Use a standard bubble sort to collate the keys
    CollationKey tmp;
    for (int i = 0; i < keys.length; i++) {
      for (int j = i + 1; j < keys.length; j++) {
        // Compare the keys
        if ( keys[i].compareTo( keys[j] ) > 0 ) {
          // Swap keys[i] and keys[j]
          tmp = keys[i];
          keys[i] = keys[j];
          keys[j] = tmp;
        }
      }
    }

    // Display the sorted results
    StringBuffer result = new StringBuffer();
    for (int l= 0;l < keys.length; l++) {
      System.out.println(keys[l].getSourceString());
    }
  }
}
```

Searching

Like sorting, searching through text is much more complicated when we have to worry about locale-sensitive rules. In addition to the complexities of natural languages, Unicode allows different ways of encoding characters. If we want to search for the surname "Müller" in a block of German text, we need to be able to handle the following situations:

- The character ü may substitute for ue. This substitution means that the word in the block of text might appear as "Mueller." Similarly, the word in the block of text might appear as "Müller" and the search pattern could be entered as "Mueller."

- The character ü can be represented as the 16-bit Unicode value \u00FC or as the two 16-bit Unicode values \u0075 and \u0308.

Not all methods on the String class are internationalized, so methods such as compareTo, indexOf and lastIndexOf are not able to handle these situations. Java does not supply simple internationalized compliant replacements for these methods, although it does provide infrastructure to allow you to build your own matching routines.

The support comes in the form of the CollationElementIterator class. This class enables you to iterate through collation elements. Performing a search requires that you match collation elements between the text in which you search and the pattern for which you search. Once you have found a match, you can use the CollationElementIterator.getOffset() method to map the collation element back to an offset within the original String.

The code in Example 7-6 implements a simple indexOf method.

Example 7-6. A Simple Implementation of indexOf

```
01:class Search {
02:  public static int indexOf(String source, String pattern) {
03:    // Obtain a collator
04:    RuleBasedCollator rbc=(RuleBasedCollator)Collator.getInstance();
05:    rbc.setStrength(Collator.SECONDARY);
06:
07:    CollationElementIterator textCEI;
08:    CollationElementIterator patCEI;
09:    textCEI = rbc.getCollationElementIterator(source);
10:    patCEI = rbc.getCollationElementIterator(pattern);
11:
12:    // e1 will contain the collation element for the source
13:    // e2 will contain the collation element for the pattern
14:    int e1, e2;
15:    int startMatch = -1;
16:
17:    // initialize e2 with the first collation element in the pattern
18:    e2 = patCEI.next();
19:
20:    while ((e1 = textCEI.next())!=CollationElementIterator.NULLORDER) {
21:      if (e1 == e2) { // if the elements match
22:        if (startMatch == -1) startMatch = textCEI.getOffset();
23:        e2 = patCEI.next(); // increment to the next element
24:        if (e2 == CollationElementIterator.NULLORDER)
```

Example 7-6. A Simple Implementation of indexOf (continued)

```
25:            break;
26:        } else { // elements do not match
27:          if (startMatch != -1) {
28:            patCEI.reset();
29:            e2 = patCEI.next();
30:            startMatch = -1;
31:          }
32:        }
33:      }
34:      return startMatch;
35:    }
36:
37:    public static void main(String [] args) {
38:      String text = "Wie hei\u00DFen Sie?"; // Wie heißen Sie?
39:      String pattern = "heissen";
40:
41:      int index = indexOf(text, pattern);
42:      if (index != -1)
43:        System.out.println("Found a match at: " + index);
44:      else
45:        System.out.println("No match found!");
46:    }
47:}
```

Here we break the code down into simple steps and explain what is happening:

```
01:class Search {
02:  public static int indexOf(String source, String pattern) {
03:    // Obtain a collator
04:    RuleBasedCollator rbc=(RuleBasedCollator)Collator.getInstance();
05:    rbc.setStrength(Collator.SECONDARY);
```

On line 2 we define the method. The source string contains the text in which we search and the pattern string contains the text for which we look.

On line 4 we get a `Collator` object and cast it to a `RuleBasedCollator` because the `getCollationElementIterator` method exists only on `RuleBasedCollator`.

On line 5 we set the strength to `Collator.SECONDARY` because, in the pattern we are matching, we want to make sure that the characters ss match the character ß. Remember that the default strength is `Collator.TERTIARY`:

```
07:    CollationElementIterator textCEI;
08:    CollationElementIterator patCEI;
09:    textCEI = rbc.getCollationElementIterator(source);
10:    patCEI = rbc.getCollationElementIterator(pattern);
```

On lines 7 through 10 we retrieve the `CollationElementIterator` objects for both the source string and the pattern string:

```
12:     // e1 will contain the collation element for the source
13:     // e2 will contain the collation element for the pattern
14:     int e1, e2;
```

As the comments claim, the variables e1 and e2 hold the collation element for the source and pattern, respectively, as we iterate through them:

```
15:     int startMatch = -1;
```

On line 15 we declare the variable `startMatch`, which indicates if we have started matching any of the collation elements in the pattern. We initialize it with a value of −1 to mean that no match was found yet. Any value other than −1 indicates the offset in the source string where the pattern begins:

```
18:     e2 = patCEI.next();
```

On line 18 we retrieve the first collation element from the pattern and store it in e2:

```
20:     while ((e1 = textCEI.next()) != CollationElementIterator.NULLORDER) {
```

On line 20 we define the while loop to iterate through each collation element in the source string until we have reached the last collation element:

```
21:        if (e1 == e2) { // if the elements match
22:          if (startMatch == -1) startMatch = textCEI.getOffset();
23:          e2 = patCEI.next(); // increment to the next element
24:          if (e2 == CollationElementIterator.NULLORDER)
25:            break;
26:        } else { // elements do not match
27:          if (startMatch != -1) {
28:            patCEI.reset();
29:            e2 = patCEI.next();
30:            startMatch = -1;
31:          }
32:        }
```

On line 21 we check to see if the elements from the source and pattern match. If they do, then on line 22 we check to see if we aren't already matching part of the sequence. If we aren't, then e1 is the first "character" of a potential match and we should remember the beginning of the sequence by saving it in `startMatch`.

On line 23 we increment to the next collation element in the pattern and then check line 24 to make sure we aren't at the end of the pattern. If we are, then we exit the loop on line 25, successfully matching the pattern.

If the elements did not match on line 21, we check line 27 to see if we had started to match the pattern partially. We know if the pattern is partially matched because `startMatch` would have a value other than −1. If we did match the pattern partially, we need to reset the `CollationElementIterator` for the pattern to the beginning and reinitialize `startMatch` to –1. We do this reset on lines 28 through 30:

```
34:    return startMatch;
```

On line 34 we return the value of `startMatch`. If the value is something other than –1, it means a match was found and the value is the index into the source string where the pattern begins:

```
37:  public static void main(String [] args) {
38:    String text = "Wie hei\u00DFen Sie?"; // Wie heißen Sie?
39:    String pattern = "heissen";
40:
41:    int index = indexOf(text, pattern);
42:    if (index != -1)
43:      System.out.println("Found a match at: " + index);
44:    else
45:      System.out.println("No match found!");
46:  }
47:}
```

We use `main()` as the test driver for the `indexOf` function, which begins on line 37. On line 38 we define the text we search in as "Wie heißen Sie?," which in German means, "What is your name?" or literally, "how are you called?" The pattern we look for is "heissen," which we define on line 39. Remember that in German, the characters "ss" should match the character "ß."

On line 41 we call the function and save the result in a variable called `index`. Finally, on lines 42 through 45, we display the results.

There are several methods missing from JDK 1.1 that were added in JDK 1.2. These methods include `getOffset()`, `setOffset()`, `previous()`, `setText()`, `isIgnorable()`, and `getMaximumExpansion()`. Searching can be handled without these methods, but it makes life a lot more difficult.

NOTE   IBM has developed a robust class that implements a fast Boyer-Moore search algorithm. The class is called `StringSearch` and is available for free download from the ICU4J site at *http://oss.software.ibm.com/icu4j*.

Detecting Text Boundaries

Sometimes it is necessary to find character, word, line, or sentence boundaries when searching through text. One possible application for this capability is in an information retrieval system. The discipline of Information Retrieval (IR) requires that text be broken into units that can be indexed. This process is known as *segmentation*. Locating these boundaries, however, can be trickier than it may seem. In

English, words are contiguous characters separated by whitespace. In some languages, such as Korean and Chinese, the concept of whitespace doesn't exist. What constitutes a word in one language can be very different in another.

Java provides a class called `BreakIterator` that is specifically designed to handle text boundary issues. Like the other internationalized classes, `BreakIterator` provides a set of factory methods that you should call rather than instantiate the object directly. In this case, the methods are:

```
getCharacterInstance()
getCharacterInstance(Locale where)
getWordInstance()
getWordInstance(Locale where)
getLineInstance()
getLineInstance(Locale where)
getSentenceInstance()
getSentenceInstance(Locale where)
```

These methods return one of four types of `BreakIterator` objects (character, word, line, or sentence). Once you have an object of one type, you can use it only to segment text for the unit for which it was designed. If you want to perform boundary analysis for another type of unit, you must use a different `BreakIterator` instance.

Methods that take no parameters return a `BreakIterator` for the default locale. You can specify a different locale by calling the methods that take a specific locale as a parameter.

Each `BreakIterator` object must be told the text over which to iterate. To give the iterator its text, use the `setText()` method as follows:

```
BreakIterator bi = BreakIterator.getWordInstance();
bi.setText("A rose by any other name would smell as sweet.");
```

To iterate over the text, simply use a loop mechanism as follows:

```
01: int boundary = bi.first();
02:
03: while (boundary != BreakIterator.DONE) {
04:   // do something...
05:   boundary = bi.next();
06: }
```

On line 1 we call the method `first()` to retrieve the first boundary in the text. The method returns an integer value indicating the position in the text where the boundary was detected. A special value, `Breakiterator.DONE`, is returned if no boundary exists.

On line 3 we begin a `while` loop that continues iterating through boundaries (line 5) until no more exist.

It is also possible to iterate through text backward using the last(), previous() and preceding() methods, although from a performance standpoint, iterating forward through text is faster.

The methods following(int offset) and preceding(int offset) find a boundary closest to the offset passed as a parameter. If you were writing an application that allowed a user to double click in a random location on a page of text, you could use these methods to select the word or sentence they clicked on.

Character Boundaries

A character BreakIterator allows you to step through text one character at a time in a locale-sensitive manner. Thus, the iterator doesn't simply step through Unicode code points. Instead, it uses locale specific rules to determine what a character is. For example, the Finnish word "ymmällä" could be represented as ymma\u0308lla\u0308 in Java. The character BreakIterator object treats a\u0308 as one character. You might need to use character boundary detection if you were building an editor that allowed a user to move the cursor through text one character at a time or to select individual characters.

Let's look at a practical example. Suppose we wanted to build a word processor to handle Korean text. As we discussed in Chapter 2, Korean writing is based on syllables, which are combined to form words. Each syllable is composed of two to four individual units known as jamo. When users enter text, they will want to type in the jamo and have the word processor build the syllables automatically. For example, to type the word "Hangul," the user would enter the following six jamo: ㅎ ㅏ ㄴ ㄱ ㅡ ㄹ and the word processor should automatically stack the jamo into the two syllables한글 to form the word. Although the user enters jamo, the actual base unit (or character) of Korean text is the syllable. Jamo are not allowed to stand alone. Suppose we had a feature in our word processor that let us move the cursor through the text either one character or one word at a time. It isn't sufficient to simply count characters because, in this example, a character is composed of three Unicode code points and one word is composed of six Unicode code points.

In Figure 7-3 we show the one Korean word composed of two syllables on the left and the individual jamo used in this word laid out horizontally on the right. The arrows indicate boundaries before the word, between syllables and after the word. Notice that though the syllables are each composed of three jamo, from a boundary perspective, the jamo are ignored.

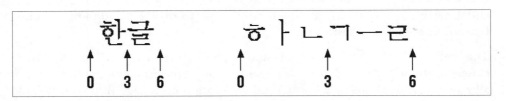

Figure 7-3. Character and word boundaries in Hangul

In other words, if our cursor were at the arrow marked 0 and we wanted to move one syllable (character) to the right, we would be positioned at the arrow marked 3. The `BreakIterator` object must be smart enough to skip over three Unicode characters. If we were positioned at the arrow marked 0 and we wanted to move one word to the right, the `BreakIterator` must skip over six Unicode characters and we would be positioned at the arrow marked 6.

To implement this functionality, we create two `BreakIterator` objects (one for character and one for word boundary detection) in Example 7-7 to demonstrate how to detect these boundaries.

Example 7-7. Detecting Text Boundaries in Hangul

```
class HangulTextBoundaryDetection {
  // A helper function to print out the boundary positions
  static void printBoundaries(String source, BreakIterator bi) {
    bi.setText(source);
    int boundary = bi.first();

    while (boundary != BreakIterator.DONE) {
      System.out.print(boundary + " ");
      boundary = bi.next();
    }
  }

  public static void main(String s[]) {
    // we create a string composed of 6 jamo
    String hangul = "\u1112\u1161\u11ab\u1100\u1173\u11af";

    // Retrieve a character and a word BreakIterator object
    // that is locale-sensitive for Korean text.
    BreakIterator ci = BreakIterator.getCharacterInstance(Locale.KOREAN);
    BreakIterator wi = BreakIterator.getWordInstance(Locale.KOREAN);

    System.out.print("Character Boundaries: ");
    printBoundaries(hangul, ci);
    System.out.print("\nWord Boundaries:");
    printBoundaries(hangul, wi);
  }
}
```

Running the program correctly produces the following output:

```
Character Boundaries: 0 3 6
Word Boundaries: 0 6
```

Word Boundaries

A word `BreakIterator` distinguishes words within text in a locale sensitive manner. When a piece of text is broken up into things that are words and things that are not, the things that are not (punctuation marks or symbols) have boundaries on either side of them. To extract words from text, use the `String.substring()` method once you have the beginning and ending boundaries:

```
String text = "Four score and seven years ago. ";
BreakIterator bi = BreakIterator.getWordIterator();

int start = bi.first();
int end = bi.next();
String word;

if (end != BreakIterator.DONE)
    word = text.substring(start, end);
```

Line Boundaries

Use a line `BreakIterator` when you need to determine where line breaks are legally allowed to occur in text. The class is locale sensitive, so it knows that in English, lines can break on hyphens and after colons and, in Chinese, lines can break after any ideographic character, with exceptions around punctuation.

Sentence Boundaries

A sentence `BreakIterator` should be used to determine sentence boundaries in text. The class is smart enough to know that it shouldn't simply look for periods to determine boundaries. Look at the following string that contains two sentences:

```
String text = "One imperial gallon is equal to 1.201 U.S. gallons. " +
              "That is a fact!";
```

An "ignorant" boundary detection algorithm would get confused by "1.201" and "U.S.," but `BreakIterator` can handle this situation without a hitch. The following code prints out each sentence in the text on its own line:

```
BreakIterator bi = BreakIterator.getSentenceIterator();
bi.setText(text);
int start = bi.first();
int end = bi.next();
```

```java
while (end != BreakIterator.DONE) {
  String sentence = text.substring(start, end);
  System.out.println(sentence);
  start = end;
  end = bi.next();
}
```

The output from this code is:

```
One imperial gallon is equal to 1.201 U.S. gallons.
That is a fact!
```

The `BreakIterator` class provided with the JDK has the rules for locales hardcoded within it. If you want to extend the behavior for locales not supported by the JDK, none of the code can be leveraged. Most locales are supported; however, Thai, which requires a dictionary lookup capability, is not. IBM has a rule-based `BreakIterator` class that is not only extensible, but also handles Thai. It is available for download from the ICU4J web site located at *http://oss.software.ibm.com/icu4j*.

8

Fonts and Text Rendering

As discussed in Chapter 6, *Character Sets and Unicode,* Java provides a robust set of classes and mechanisms for handling internationalized text in your applications. As we will see in this chapter, that text can be output in a number of different ways. The first, and probably the most obvious, way is to display the text to the user on the screen. Text will be output to the screen in a particular font or graphical representation for a particular language.

Computers often distinguish individual character attributes—for example, the information about a character and the shape of the character, or glyph. Distinguishing between this information allows us to distinguish operations that are specific to the individual attributes. In Chapter 7, *Searching, Sorting, and Text Boundary Detection*, we discussed string comparison and different search and sort methods for internationalized text. These examples illustrate operations specific to the character information.

By rendering text in a graphical user interface (GUI), we consider an entirely different set of operations on the characters such as their display (e.g., bidirectional text) and the format (e.g., different glyphs rendered depending on the context). We can also think of operations between the two views, such as character-to-glyph mappings and character recognition of glyphs. In other words, the character view is concerned with content processing and the glyph view is concerned with presentation processing.

In this chapter, we explore the font support that exists in the Java platform. This support has evolved significantly since the initial release of Java. We consider Java's view of fonts and the classes that are provided to interface with and manipulate fonts. We also discuss how to work with the *font.properties* files. We cover the addition of new fonts to your system. Starting with Version 1.2, Sun's Java 2 Runtime Environment includes a number of TrueType fonts for use in your applications. We show you how to use these and other TrueType fonts from your applications.

Characters, Glyphs, and Fonts

Chapter 6 outlined many details of the Unicode Standard. A script is a system for writing a variety of different languages (that may be related or unrelated). We've already come across a script used daily in both written and electronic form in the United States, the Latin script. This script can be used to write many different languages such as English and French. The Arabic script can be used to write languages like Arabic and Kurdish. The Cyrillic script can be used to represent several eastern European languages, such as Ukrainian, Serbian, and Russian.

Characters

A significant benefit of using scripts is that many different languages can utilize the same "character" from a given script. One example is the letter L. A *character* is an abstract representation of this letter, but this character can be used in French, German, and Spanish writing.

Glyphs

How do characters and glyphs relate to each other? A *glyph* is a particular manifestation or representation of a given character or symbol. As mentioned in Chapter 6, characters are the basic semantic unit in a writing system. They do not necessarily have a particular appearance and can be rendered in several different forms.

Figure 8-1 shows a number of glyphs for the character A.

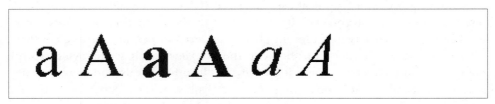

Figure 8-1. A number of glyphs for the character A

We are not implying that a one-to-one correspondence exists between a character and a glyph. When talking about fonts, a glyph refers to an encoded image in the font. This glyph may represent part of a character, a whole character, or multiple characters.

Ligatures

A specific type of glyph with which you'll want to familiarize yourself is a ligature. A *ligature* is the combination of two or more characters into a single glyph. One of the most widely used ligatures in the electronic mail world is the "at" symbol, represented by @. The "at" symbol derives its meaning from the Latin word "ad," meaning "at." Another common symbol used sometimes in URLs is the ampersand symbol, which is represented by &. This symbol is an abbreviation for the Latin word "et," which means "and." Arabic and Indic languages can have many ligatures. Some are required (like laam-alif, (ﻻ)) and are not typographic "options."

A few other common ligatures are "fi," "fl," "ffi ," and "ffl ." Ligatures are useful for representing two or more characters with a single graphical representation, or glyph. However, you don't always see ligatures in use when words are printed on a page or on a screen. Figure 8-2 shows some common words with and without ligatures.

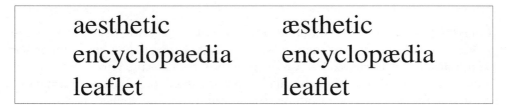

Figure 8-2. Some common words with and without ligatures

Fonts

We now draw our distinction of what we call a font. Just as a character set is an ordered collection of characters, we refer to a *font* as an ordered collection of glyphs. Usually fonts contain other information, such as glyph widths, advances, and other information useful in rendering text using the font. A font is comprised of two principal components: a character encoding, or font table, and a set of glyphs. A character encoding maps the individual code points to the particular glyphs that are to be displayed or printed when that code point is discovered in a stream of data. The glyphs are the actual symbols that will be rendered on a computer display or printed to a page.

Fonts may use different mechanisms to map characters to glyphs. This mapping is almost exclusively represented as a table, which maps character code points to particular glyphs. See Table 8-1.

Table 8-1. Examples of Locations for Font Mapping Tables

Type of Mapping	Examples
Internal mapping table: the mapping table associating particular characters with glyphs is included in the font itself.	TrueType and OpenType fonts
Rendering engine mapping table: the mapping table is part of the engine that is responsible for rendering the font.	PostScript Type-1 fonts
External mapping table: the mapping table is external to the font itself.	Fonts in use by the Bell Labs Plan-9 operating system

Complex and simple fonts

We need to differentiate between complex and simple fonts. *Complex fonts* contain associative information or rules. These associations may specify an association between other glyphs. One example is the glyph index for the ﬃ ligature—\ufb03. In a complex font, information within the font would associate this code point with the combination of the three glyphs: two f's (\u0066) followed by the i character (\u0069). Fonts without such associative information are called *simple fonts*.

Complex fonts contain two different types of glyphs: *character glyphs* and *rendering forms*. Character glyphs are simpler because of their one-to-one correspondence with individual character codes. A rendering form contains the information associating glyphs with other glyphs and rules governing their combination. Examples of rendering forms in fonts are ligatures, contextual forms, and applied marks.

Marks

Marks, or more properly, diacritical marks, are individual marks added to either a single glyph or a number of glyphs. Common marks applied to glyphs are dots, umlauts, tildes, and other accents. Figure 8-3 shows examples of glyphs with marks.

Figure 8-3. Examples of glyphs with marks

Marks sometimes indicate the presence of a vowel. One example of a writing system in which marks are present is the Arabic script. Arabic contains a form with vowels that many children read and a form without vowels that adults read. The Thai language uses tone marks, and the tone must be correct for a word to be understood correctly.

Now that we've looked at font characteristics, we're ready to look at Java's Font class and other classes that support the manipulation and rendering of text in different fonts.

Java's Font-Related Classes

The java.awt.Font class contains information on the particular typeface that should be used when rendering characters and the size of the glyphs rendered to a display. This class has changed significantly since the release of JDK 1.0 and even since JDK 1.1. The newest features allow you to query typographic information such as whether the font can render all the characters in a particular string or determine how many glyphs are contained in the font.

The java.awt.Font Class

The most straightforward way of constructing a font for rendering text is to use the following constructor:

```
public Font(String name, int style, int size)
```

The first argument is the font's name, which can be any one of the five logical font names (`Dialog`, `DialogInput`, `Monospaced`, `Serif`, or `SansSerif`) or a physical font name.[1] A logical font may encompass a number of actual or physical fonts on the host system. Logical and physical fonts are discussed in more detail later. The `Font` class defines three different styles of fonts: bold, italic, or plain. In your code, you may pass in one of the predefined style constants from the `Font` class into the `Font` constructor: `Font.BOLD`, `Font.ITALIC`, and `Font.PLAIN`. You may also OR the `Font.BOLD` and `Font.ITALIC` style constants to create a font that is both bold and italicized. The `size` parameter refers to the font's point size. TrueType fonts can use this parameter because they do not contain predefined glyphs of certain sizes: they calculate the appropriate size and shape of the glyph, depending on the point size chosen, scaling the characters appropriately for any chosen point size.

To create a Dialog 20-point bold font, use the following code:

```
Font dialogFont = new Font("Dialog", Font.BOLD, 20);
```

You may also want a font that is both bold and italicized. To construct the appropriate font, use the `Font.BOLD | Font.ITALIC` bitmask as shown:

```
Font bolditalicFont = new Font("Dialog", Font.BOLD | Font.ITALIC, 20);
```

Obtaining fonts

Several static methods in the `Font` class are available for retrieving fonts by name or by a system property.

NOTE   All these methods require the string input parameter to be one of the following forms:

```
fontname-style-pointsize
fontname-pointsize
fontname-style
```

where `fontname` describes the name of the font as in `dialog`, `style` can be one of the following values: `bold`, `italic`, or `bolditalic`, and `pointsize` is a valid integer value.

---

[1] The ability to specify a physical font name for this argument was introduced in Sun's Java 2 Platform, Standard Edition, Version 1.2.

The method:

```
static Font decode(String str)
```

returns a `Font` object described by the `str` argument. Unlike the `decode(String str)` method, the `getFont()` methods treat the first parameter as a key to retrieve a font name from the system properties, as in `System.getProperty(nm)`. Another method you can use is:

```
static Font getFont(String nm)
```

which also returns a `Font` object described by the `nm` argument.

The method:

```
static Font getFont(String nm, Font font)
```

also returns a `Font` object, but if the proper object cannot be created, it returns the input parameter `font` as a default `Font` object. For both `getFont()` methods, the default style is `PLAIN` and the default size is 12.

We recommend using one of the `getFont` methods over the `decode` method. When reading through code samples, it is not entirely clear what the `decode` method actually does until after consulting the javadocs for the `Font` class. Using this method helps make your code more understandable to others.

Retrieving font name information

Each font on your system belongs to a font family. Font families contain fonts with similar characteristics. To retrieve the family name of a font, use one of the `getFamily()` methods. The first method:

```
public String getFamily()
```

returns a string containing the font family name in the default locale. If used a Courier New Bold Italic font, this method would return the string, "Courier New." Another method returns the font family name localized for a given locale:

```
public String getFamily(Locale l)
```

As we will see, the *font.properties* file groups different physical fonts under a logical font name. You can retrieve the logical font name by calling the method:

```
public String getName()
```

If you're looking for the actual font face name, one of the following two methods should suffice:

```
public String getFontName()
public String getFontName(Locale l)
```

The `getFontName(Locale l)` method returns a localized version of the font face name.

Finally, you can retrieve the Postscript name for your font by calling the following method:

```
public String getPSName()
```

Example 8-1 demonstrates displaying this value for all fonts available on your system. This method returned the same name as returned by `getFontName()` on the machines where we tested the example.

Example 8-1. Displaying the Postscript Name for the Fonts on a System

```java
import java.awt.Font;
import java.awt.GraphicsEnvironment;

public class FontPostscriptNames {

  public static void main(String [] argv) {
    GraphicsEnvironment ge = GraphicsEnvironment.getLocalGraphicsEnvironment();
    Font [] fonts = ge.getAllFonts();

    for (int i = 0; i < fonts.length; i++)
      System.out.println(fonts[i].getPSName());
  }
}
```

A portion of the output from this code is printed here:

```
C:\>java FontPostscriptNames

Arial Bold
Arial Bold Italic
Arial Rounded MT Bold
Arial Unicode MS
Baskerville Old Face
```

Font class utility methods

A number of methods in the `Font` class perform utility functions you can use in your code to perform error checking on a particular font. The `canDisplay(char c)` method returns a `boolean` value that indicates whether the particular font contains a glyph for the character. To check whether an entire string of characters can be rendered using a given font, use one of the following methods:

```
canDisplayUpTo(char[] text, int start, int limit)
canDisplayUpTo(CharacterIterator iter, int start, int limit)
canDisplayUpTo(String str)
```

Each of these methods returns an `int` value, indicating the first character in the text that cannot be displayed with the given font. A value of −1 indicates that all the characters can be displayed properly. Suppose we had the following string, which contains both English and Japanese characters, and that we used a font capable of displaying characters from only the English alphabet:

```
englishjapanese = "English and \u65E5\u672C\u8A9E together.";
int englishStop = englishFont.canDisplayUpTo(englishjapanese);
```

`englishStop` would now contain the value `12`.

You can also derive a new `Font` object from an existing one using one of the six `deriveFont()` methods. We will describe the most straightforward methods here. The `deriveFont(float size)` method takes an existing `Font` object and creates a new one with a different font size as specified in the input parameter, `size`:

```
Font size12Font = new Font("Monospaced", Font.PLAIN, 12);
Font size20Font = size12Font.deriveFont((float)20.0);
```

Notice how we typecast the value in the call to create the 20-point size font; a method called `deriveFont(int style)`, which applies a different style to an existing `Font` object also exists, as in the following code:

```
Font boldFont = new Font("Sans", Font.BOLD, 20);
Font italicizedFont = boldFont.deriveFont(Font.ITALIC);
```

You might also want to apply a new style and create a `Font` object of a different size so you can use the `deriveFont(int style, float size)` method as shown:

```
Font plain12PtFont = new Font("Sans", Font.PLAIN, 12);
Font bold20PtFont = plain12PtFont.deriveFont(Font.BOLD, (float)20.0);
```

Finally, the method `getNumGlyphs()` returns the number of glyphs contained in the given `Font` object.

Components for Rendering Complex Text

Complex text is just that: complex. Examples of languages that contain complex text are Arabic, Hebrew, and Thai. Characteristics that make these languages complex include bidirectionality (running right to left and left to right), letters that may change shape depending on the characters that appear before or after (context sensitivity), and characters that may combine to form ligatures.[2] We saw an example of this combination in Chapter 6, which described ligatures as combinations of characters that appear as one glyph. Horizontal and vertical spacing

---

[2] Numbers in bidirectional text run from left to right.

used to align characters are also an issue, as characters in these complex scripts may fall well above or below the character baseline.

The complex text APIs in Java allow you to do a variety of things, from displaying complex text to providing capabilities for you to write your own word processor.

Enhanced Support for Complex Text

The Java 2 platform introduced a number of enhancements to support the rendering of complex text. We discuss the areas individually.

Graphics.drawString()

This method is useful for displaying single lines of text, and especially for displaying text that can be used as a message or a title. It has been updated to support the scripts supported in the Java 2 platform; if you use this method, you automatically inherit the new functionality.[3]

Example 8-2 shows the use of the drawString() method.

Example 8-2. Writing Out Text Using drawstring()

```
import java.awt.*;
import java.awt.event.*;
import javax.swing.*;

public class DrawStringDemo extends JFrame {

  String message =
      "David says, \"\u05E9\u05DC\u05D5\u05DD \u05E2\u05D5\u05DC\u05DD\"";
  public DrawStringDemo() {
    super("DrawStringDemo");
  }

  public void paint(Graphics g) {
    Graphics2D graphics2D = (Graphics2D)g;
    GraphicsEnvironment.getLocalGraphicsEnvironment();
    Font font = new Font("LucidaSans", Font.PLAIN, 40);
    graphics2D.setFont(font);
    graphics2D.drawString(message, 50, 75);
  }
```

---

[3] The scripts supported in the Java 2 platform vary by vendor.

Example 8-2. Writing Out Text Using drawstring() (continued)

```
public static void main(String[] args) {
  JFrame frame = new DrawStringDemo();
  frame.addWindowListener(new WindowAdapter() {
    public void windowClosing(WindowEvent e) {System.exit(0);}
  });

  frame.pack();
  frame.setVisible(true);
  }
}
```

Running Example 8-2 produces Figure 8-4. One limitation of this method is that its context is a single line of text. In complex text, what follows one line of text affects how the first line of text is displayed. By drawing strings on the screen independently of one another, you cannot change the text. This method has another limitation: it is meant only for unstyled text; that is, text without attributes, such as bold or italic. Unstyled text is commonly used in a password field or a text field.

Figure 8-4. The string, "David says, "Hello World" (in English and Hebrew)

JTextComponent

The JTextComponent supports rendering of complex text. This support means that direct subclasses of JTextComponent, such as JEditorPane, JTextArea, JTextField, and JTextPane, inherit this new functionality.[4] These components provide both the functionality and the interface to edit styled and unstyled documents. However, the functionality and architecture are somewhat limited, which is why the complex text APIs were introduced in the Java 2 platform. The use of JTextArea is demonstrated in Example 8-3.

---

[4] In the initial release of Java 2, Java 2 SDK, Standard Edition, Version 1.2, bidirectional text is supported only in the styled text components JEditorPane and JTextPane; however, in the Java 2 SDK, Standard Edition, Version 1.3 release, bidirectional text is also enabled in the plain text components, JTextArea and JTextField.

Example 8-3. Demonstration of the Use of a JTextArea

```java
import java.awt.*;
import java.awt.event.*;
import javax.swing.*;

public class JTextAreaDemo extends JFrame {

  String davidMessage =
      "David says, \"\u05E9\u05DC\u05D5\u05DD \u05E2\u05D5\u05DC\u05DD\" \n";
  String andyMessage =
      "Andy also says, \"\u05E9\u05DC\u05D5\u05DD \u05E2\u05D5\u05DC\u05DD\"";

  public JTextAreaDemo() {
    super("JTextAreaDemo");
    GraphicsEnvironment.getLocalGraphicsEnvironment();
    Font font = new Font("LucidaSans", Font.PLAIN, 40);
    JTextArea textArea = new JTextArea(davidMessage + andyMessage);
    textArea.setFont(font);
    this.getContentPane().add(textArea);
    textArea.show();
  }

  public static void main(String[] args) {
    JFrame frame = new JTextAreaDemo();
    frame.addWindowListener(new WindowAdapter() {
      public void windowClosing(WindowEvent e) {System.exit(0);}
    });

    frame.pack();
    frame.setVisible(true);
  }
}
```

Notice that in Figure 8-5 the `JTextArea` supports *logical highlighting*. Logical highlighting selects a block of text contiguous in memory, even if it appears as separate highlight regions when rendered. This feature explains why in Figure 8-5 you see the gap in the highlighted region. *Visual highlighting*, on the other hand, is when a block of text is selected that is one continuous highlight region on the screen, but may be a discontinuous selection in memory. Let's digress for a second and discuss logical and visual highlighting in some more detail.

Logical highlighting uses logical order. The logical order refers to the way a block of text is actually stored in memory, as in an array of characters. This ordering may differ from the way in which the text is rendered in your application. This feature is the case with bidirectional text. The actual direction in which text is displayed is referred to as the visual order. Figures 8-6 and 8-7 demonstrate this order with the sentence, "Andy speaks Hebrew well." English text is marked in black, while the Hebrew text is marked in light gray.[5]

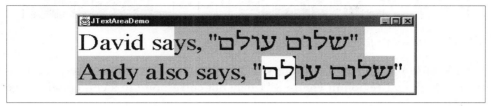

Figure 8-5. Logical highlighting of bidirectional text using a JTextArea

Figure 8-6. The sentence "Andy speaks Hebrew well." in logical order, as it would be stored in memory

Figure 8-7. The sentence "Andy speaks Hebrew well." in visual order, as it would be rendered

Figures 8-8 and 8-9 demonstrate the logical highlighting of "speaks Hebrew." Although the highlight region is contiguous in memory, the highlight region as it would appear on the screen is not contiguous.

Figure 8-8. In-memory highlight region for logical highlighting of "speaks Hebrew"

---

[5] We use English text instead of actual Hebrew text for demonstration.

Figure 8-9. On-screen highlight region for logical highlighting of "speaks Hebrew"

Figures 8-10 and 8-11 demonstrate visual highlighting. As you can see, the contiguous highlight region in Figure 8-11 may not correspond to a contiguous range in memory.

Figure 8-10. In-memory highlight region for visual highlighting of "speaks well"

Figure 8-11. On-screen highlight region for visual highlighting of "speaks well"

Look carefully at Figure 8-5 and you will see the flag-like entity on the cursor. The entity points in the direction that the text runs. Since we are in the middle of highlighting a block of Hebrew text, which runs from right to left, the flag points to the left. This flag indicates the direction of the character the caret is next to logically and where the next character will be inserted. When the cursor is positioned between characters that run in different directions, the flag can have a different position, depending on the character it is "stuck" to.

Notice in Figure 8-12 that the cursor is in a block of English text and the flag points to the right.

An example of the flag indicating the character the cursor is "stuck" to is shown in Figure 8-13. If you position the cursor between the last Hebrew character and the double quotes, and then hit the left arrow key, the flag points to the right. This act indicates that its directionality is determined by the double quotes. If you started to type, your text would begin to run from left to right.

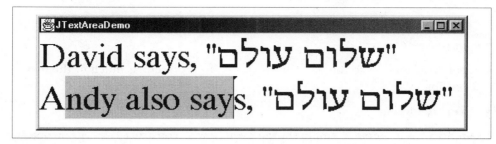

Figure 8-12. Logical highlighting of bidirectional text demonstrating the cursor's direction

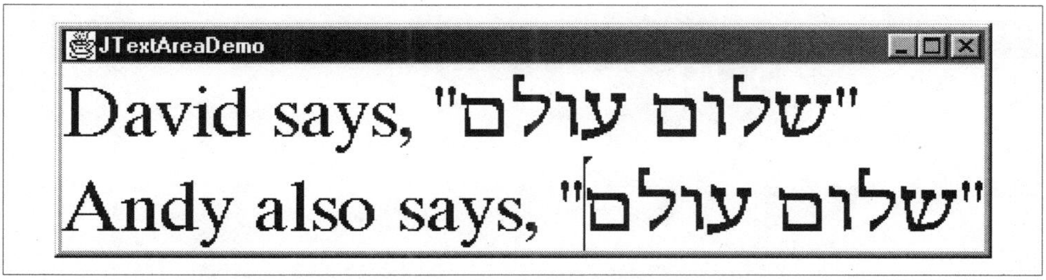

Figure 8-13. The cursor's position indicates that its directionality is determined by the quotation mark

New APIs That Support Complex Text

All new APIs that were added in the Java 2 platform to support complex text live in the `java.awt.font` package. They are meant to be a set of classes and interfaces that allow you to write your own word processor.[6] A number of classes related to the manipulation and querying of information from glyphs exist that break up lines of text, take measurements on text, and obtain different attribute types that can occur in complex text.

The `TextLayout` class is one of the important classes in this package. It is the most comprehensive and powerful way to support editable and rendered complex text. This class supports a number of capabilities, such as:

- Rendering and reordering of bidirectional text

- Cursor manipulation and positioning; support for multiple cursors in bidirectional text

---

[6] IBM's alphaWorks site contains a styled text editor that supports many languages, such as English, Arabic, Hebrew, and Thai. It is available at *http://www.alphaworks.ibm.com/tech/bidi.*

- Logical and visual highlighting

- Hit testing to determine the offset of where a user clicked in a piece of text

- Justification of text

- Font substitution so the best font is chosen to represent as much of the text as possible

- Text rendering

Example 8-4 is a simple example showing you how to construct `TextLayout` objects to render a multiline, bidirectional message.

Example 8-4. Use of TextLayout to Render a Piece of Complex Text

```java
import java.awt.*;
import java.awt.event.*;
import java.awt.font.*;
import java.text.*;
import javax.swing.*;

public class TextLayoutDemo extends JFrame {

  String davidMessage =
    "David says, \"\u05E9\u05DC\u05D5\u05DD \u05E2\u05D5\u05DC\u05DD\" ";
  String andyMessage =
    "Andy also says, \"\u05E9\u05DC\u05D5\u05DD \u05E2\u05D5\u05DC\u05DD\" ";
  String textMessage = davidMessage + andyMessage + davidMessage + andyMessage +
                       davidMessage + andyMessage + davidMessage + andyMessage +
                       davidMessage + andyMessage + davidMessage + andyMessage +
                       davidMessage + andyMessage + davidMessage + andyMessage;

  public TextLayoutDemo() {
    super("TextLayoutDemo");
  }

  public void paint(Graphics g) {
    Graphics2D graphics2D = (Graphics2D)g;
    GraphicsEnvironment.getLocalGraphicsEnvironment();
    Font font = new Font("LucidaSans", Font.PLAIN, 14);
    AttributedString messageAS = new AttributedString(textMessage);
    messageAS.addAttribute(TextAttribute.FONT, font);
    AttributedCharacterIterator messageIterator = messageAS.getIterator();
    FontRenderContext messageFRC = graphics2D.getFontRenderContext();
    LineBreakMeasurer messageLBM =
        new LineBreakMeasurer(messageIterator, messageFRC);

    Insets insets = getInsets();
    float wrappingWidth = getSize().width - insets.left - insets.right;
    float x = insets.left;
    float y = insets.top;
```

Example 8-4. Use of TextLayout to Render a Piece of Complex Text (continued)

```
    while (messageLBM.getPosition() < messageIterator.getEndIndex()) {
      TextLayout textLayout = messageLBM.nextLayout(wrappingWidth);
      y += textLayout.getAscent();
      textLayout.draw(graphics2D, x, y);
      y += textLayout.getDescent() + textLayout.getLeading();
      x = insets.left;
    }
  }

  public static void main(String[] args) {
    JFrame frame = new TextLayoutDemo();
    frame.addWindowListener(new WindowAdapter() {
      public void windowClosing(WindowEvent e) {System.exit(0);}
    });

    frame.pack();
    frame.setVisible(true);
  }
}
```

Running this example produces the screen shown in Figure 8-14. As you can see from the figure, you must do more work to wrap the text properly; but if you write your own text editor or word processor, you have to worry about those nuances.

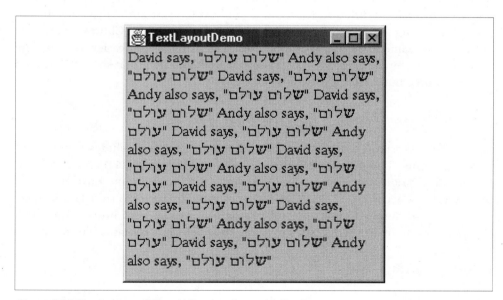

Figure 8-14. Rendering multiline, bidirectional text with TextLayout

Font Size in Complex Text

While designing internationalized user interfaces, more complex character sets (rather, more complex glyphs) require you to think about font size and screen resolution for your application, as shown in Figure 8-15.

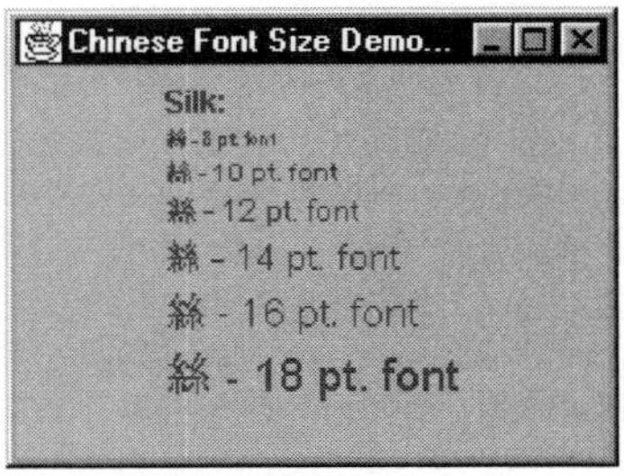

Figure 8-15. Demonstrating the importance of font size in complex text

Traditionally, one way that developers have dealt with glyphs that are taller and wider than the display line is by reducing the font size for the internationalized text. Smaller font sizes can lead to headaches for your users from frustration at trying to discern the different words, and will lead to eyestrain. As you'll notice in Table 8-15, using an 8-point font makes strokes on some of the Chinese characters illegible. The same word in larger font sizes makes things a bit easier to read. The font size for different languages is certainly a candidate item that should be added to the resource bundle for a particular locale.

TrueType Font Support in Java

Starting with Version 1.2, Sun's Java 2 Runtime Environment includes a number of TrueType fonts. These files can be found in a directory called `lib/fonts` of your Java installation directory or the directory where the Java Runtime Environment is installed. Usually the $JAVA_HOME environment variable points to your Java installation. Twelve different fonts from the Lucida font family were initially included. Java provides three different classes of fonts, and each class contains four fonts:

Bright Fonts

```
LucidaBrightDemibold
LucidaBrightDemiItalic
LucidaBrightItalic
LucidaBrightRegular
```

Sans Fonts

```
LucidaSansDemiBold
LucidaSansDemiOblique
LucidaSansOblique
LucidaSansRegular
```

Typewriter Fonts

```
LucidaTypewriterBold
LucidaTypewriterBoldOblique
LucidaTypewriterOblique
LucidaTypewriterRegular
```

Figures 8-16, 8-17, and 8-18 show text rendered in the `LucidaBrightRegular`, `LucidaSansRegular`, and `LucidaTypewriterRegular` fonts, respectively.

Figure 8-16. "Java Internationalization" in the LucidaBrightRegular font

Figure 8-17. "Java Internationalization" in the LucidaSansRegular font

Figure 8-18. "Java Internationalization" in the LucidaTypewriterRegular font

These fonts can provide more variety in the typefaces you use in your applications. The set of `Sans` and `Typewriter` fonts are also capable of rendering Arabic and Hebrew characters. Java also provides a mechanism to load TrueType Fonts directly from your applications.

Example 8-5 demonstrates how you can import existing TrueType fonts for use in Java applications. This example was also used to create Figures 8-16, 8-17, and 8-18.

Example 8-5. Importing Your Own TrueType Fonts in Java

```java
import java.awt.*;
import java.awt.event.*;
import javax.swing.*;

public class TrueTypeTest extends JFrame {

  private String textMessage = "Java Internationalization";

  public TrueTypeTest() {
    super("TrueType Font Demonstration");

    GraphicsEnvironment ge = GraphicsEnvironment.getLocalGraphicsEnvironment();
    ge.getAllFonts();

    Font font = new Font("Jokerman", Font.PLAIN, 35);
    JLabel textLabel = new JLabel(textMessage);
    textLabel.setFont(font);

    getContentPane().add(textLabel);
    show();
  }

  public static void main(String[] args) {
    JFrame frame = new TrueTypeTest();
    frame.addWindowListener(new WindowAdapter() {
      public void windowClosing(WindowEvent e) {System.exit(0);}
    });

    frame.pack();
    frame.setVisible(true);
  }
}
```

Jokerman is a font included with Windows 98. After running this program with the Jokerman font, the text "Java Internationalization" is output, as Figure 8-19 shows. In Example 8-5, the call to create the proper Font object is as follows:

```java
Font font = new Font("Jokerman", Font.PLAIN, 35);
```

If you'd like to use your own TrueType fonts, be sure that your application executes the following code during initialization:

```java
GraphicsEnvironment ge =
    GraphicsEnvironment.getLocalGraphicsEnvironment();
ge.getAllFonts();
```

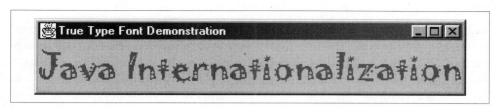

Figure 8-19. Jokerman font demonstration

This code discovers the available fonts on your system. If you don't check these fonts, your application will not display the proper font.

NOTE   This code is a workaround for a bug in the Java Runtime Environment.[7] It should be placed at the beginning of your application if your system contains a large number of TrueType fonts. This step is necessary because Java needs to read through all the fonts to obtain font information. However, this reading only happens once.

Be cautious when developing applications that call TrueType fonts this way. You're not guaranteed that the TrueType font you call in your application will exist on the host system to which your application is deployed. A common application feature you may want to provide would be a font menu that shows users all available fonts in an application and allows them to choose any one of them. Hardcoding the names of fonts whose presence you can't guarantee isn't a good idea.

Working with the font.properties File

Prior to the release of JDK 1.1, programs written in Java could render characters only from the Latin-1 script. This act made displaying text in other languages or scripts a bothersome, if not impossible, task. After the release of JDK 1.1, the Java font architecture now allows your programs to render text in any font that exists on the host platform.

The *font.properties* files contain mappings specifying which fonts should be used by your application to display certain characters. The mappings group a number of

---

[7] This bug seems to be fixed when using Sun's Java 2 SDK, Standard Edition, Version 1.3 under Windows; however, the bug still existed for us when using Sun's Java 2 SDK, Standard Edition, Version 1.2.2 under Windows.

fonts under one logical name; as we said earlier in the chapter, a logical font may encompass a number of actual or physical fonts on the host system.

Technically, the use of *font.properties* files is an implementation detail. They are used in Sun's Java 2 Runtime Environments and provide a mapping from virtual or logical font names to physical font names. Be aware that these files will not necessarily exist for your Java runtime implementation (e.g., the Macintosh Runtime for Java does not use them at all); they differ significantly from implementation to implementation (e.g., Sun's Windows and Solaris implementations) and they have changed from JDK 1.1 to Java 2 SDK, Standard Edition, Version 1.2. The examples using *font.properties* files in this chapter are from an installation of Sun's Java 2 SDK, Standard Edition, Version 1.2 under Windows 95.

Physical and Logical Fonts

Physical fonts

On a typical Windows platform, you can check the *\Windows\Fonts* directory to see a number of fonts installed on your system. These fonts were installed either when you installed the operating system or when you installed third-party applications. On Windows, the fonts in this directory typically end with a .TTF file extension. This extension specifies that the font is a TrueType font. The typical fonts installed on most U.S. English systems include Arial, Courier New Bold, and Times New Roman.

Each font typically contains glyphs for a subset of the Unicode character set. They contain a subset of the glyphs because a font that contains a full Unicode character set would be very large, and average users may never need to display a large range of the characters in that font.

We call these fonts *physical fonts* because they exist physically on your computer system. However, because of the size of fonts that contain all the Unicode characters, it is desirable to have some way of grouping fonts together so that all the characters can be displayed, while the information and size of any one font is kept to a minimum. This step allows you to use various fonts at different times in your application, depending on the text you need to display.

Logical fonts

Logical fonts fill the role of grouping together a number of physical fonts under a logical or virtual font name. This role means that these fonts can be used in your Java applications, but do not actually exist on your system as physical fonts. Figure 8-20 illustrates the relationship between logical and physical fonts, which is a one-to-many relationship. For a single logical font name, one or more physical fonts may be used to support the application in displaying or printing characters.

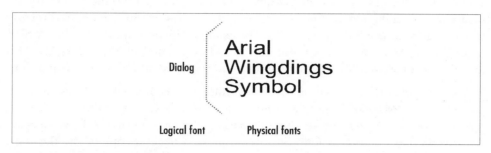

Figure 8-20. Relationship between logical and physical fonts

Java currently supports five generic logical font names, which can map to a number of physical fonts on your system: `Dialog`, `DialogInput`, `Monospaced`, `Serif`, and `SansSerif`. The following code is a portion of the *font.properties* file showing you how the `Monospaced` logical font name is mapped to a number of physical system fonts:

```
monospaced.0=Courier New,ANSI_CHARSET
monospaced.1=WingDings,SYMBOL_CHARSET,NEED_CONVERTED
monospaced.2=Symbol,SYMBOL_CHARSET,NEED_CONVERTED
```

Now we discuss one of the less-understood components of the Java font architecture, the *font.properties* files.

The font.properties File

You will often encounter situations in which you'll want to display certain characters from other writing systems, such as Arabic, Chinese, or Japanese. By setting up your *font.properties* file correctly, you can rest assured that your application will display multilingual text correctly.

An example of what the *font.properties* file looks like from an installation of Sun's Java 2 SDK, Standard Edition, Version 1.2 under Windows 95 is as follows:

```
# @(#)font.properties          1.10 98/10/09
#
# AWT Font default Properties for Windows
#

dialog.0=Arial,ANSI_CHARSET
dialog.1=WingDings,SYMBOL_CHARSET,NEED_CONVERTED
dialog.2=Symbol,SYMBOL_CHARSET,NEED_CONVERTED
```

The *font.properties* files exist in the */lib* directory of the Java 2 Runtime Environment. In a typical installation of the Java 2 SDK, these files are in the */jre/lib* directory from where you install the Java 2 SDK. For example, if you installed the Java 2 SDK in *C:\jdk1.2.2* under Windows, these files would be located in *C:\jdk1.2.2\jre\lib*. This location varies, depending on the environment you have set up on your computer.

The *font.properties* file is broken up into seven different sections. We will discuss each part of the *font.properties* file here and how it is used by Java. A word to the wise: before you begin editing any of the *font.properties* files or one of the locale-specific *font.properties* files on your system, be sure to make a backup copy of the file. This backup helps ensure that you can "undo" any changes.

Logical font mapping

The first section in the *font.properties* file defines the logical font mapping for your system. The five logical font names supported by Java may map to a number of physical system fonts:

```
# @(#)font.properties          1.10 98/10/09
#
# AWT Font default Properties for Windows
#

dialog.0=Arial,ANSI_CHARSET
dialog.1=WingDings,SYMBOL_CHARSET,NEED_CONVERTED
dialog.2=Symbol,SYMBOL_CHARSET,NEED_CONVERTED

dialog.bold.0=Arial Bold,ANSI_CHARSET
dialog.bold.1=WingDings,SYMBOL_CHARSET,NEED_CONVERTED
dialog.bold.2=Symbol,SYMBOL_CHARSET,NEED_CONVERTED

dialog.italic.0=Arial Italic,ANSI_CHARSET
dialog.italic.1=WingDings,SYMBOL_CHARSET,NEED_CONVERTED
dialog.italic.2=Symbol,SYMBOL_CHARSET,NEED_CONVERTED
```

The format of each line is as follows:

```
<logical font>.<style>.<order>=<physical font>,<charset>,<conversion info>
```

`<logical font>` refers to one of the five logical font names mentioned earlier: `Dialog`, `DialogInput`, `Monospaced`, `Serif`, and `SansSerif`. You cannot create a new logical font name. When using logical fonts, you should use one of these five names to instantiate a `Font` object.

If you run your application using a version of the Java platform developed before the 1.2 releases, you probably won't see the `<style>` element used in *font.properties*. In JDK 1.2, we see an example of this element in use, as shown in the next code block. This element is used to describe the four different styles that may be applied to a font when a `Font` object is constructed. Valid values for `<style>` are `plain`, `bold`, `italic`, and `bolditalic`.

If you omit the `plain` style from an entry, Java assumes that the style is `plain`. Therefore, the following two lines are equivalent. However, if you choose to explicitly write out the `plain` style, we recommend that you stick with the convention throughout your *font.properties* file:

```
dialog.0=Arial,ANSI_CHARSET
dialog.plain.0=Arial,ANSI_CHARSET
```

All entries corresponding to the different styles must be present in your *font.properties* files. For example, the `dialog` logical font name must have entries for `dialog.plain`, `dialog.bold`, `dialog.italic`, and `dialog.bolditalic`.

You must also define a preference for the order in which fonts are searched when using a particular logical font name. Java looks at the `<order>` tag to determine which physical font to check first. Java first searches for a particular glyph in the font, starting with 0 in the `<order>` tag, followed by 1, 2, and so on. Let's say, for example, that you had the following section in your *font.properties* file for the `Serif` logical name. Suppose that you were trying to display the Unicode character \u6587, 文, and that this character was not available in `serif.0` (i.e., the Times New Roman font):

```
serif.0=Times New Roman,ANSI_CHARSET
serif.1=WingDings,SYMBOL_CHARSET,NEED_CONVERTED
serif.2=Symbol,SYMBOL_CHARSET,NEED_CONVERTED
```

Java would first search `serif.0`, and then search the `serif.1` and `serif.2` entries, in that order, to find a font that could render the character correctly. This step is also how Java maps many physical fonts to one logical font name. Any new fonts that you add to your system should be added to this section. Be sure that when adding physical fonts to a logical font name that the numbers are in sequence.

The `<physical font>` element refers to the name of the physical font that you installed on your system. This might be a name like `Century Schoolbook Italic`. Just make certain that you type the typeface name of the font that you have installed and not the actual filename of the font.

As far as the `<charset>` element goes, if you're adding a new font to your system, the value of `DEFAULT_CHARSET` should suffice. Other values commonly used in this element of the *font.properties* file are `ANSI_CHARSET` and `SYMBOL_CHARSET`.

Finally, an optional parameter, `<conversion info>`, can take only one value, `NEED_CONVERTED`. This parameter tells Java that your physical font does not use Unicode indexing, but some other indexing mechanism. If you add a font and specify `NEED_CONVERTED`, you also need to add a line to the character conversion information section. This part of the *font.properties* file is described later on in this section.

Font alias mapping for backward compatibility

Unfortunately, remnants of the first major release of Java still linger in the *font.properties* file. The following section from the *font.properties* file shows how these old font names are mapped to the logical font names that should now be used:

```
# name aliases
#
alias.timesroman=serif
alias.helvetica=sansserif
alias.courier=monospaced

# for backward compatibility
zapfdingbats.0=WingDings,SYMBOL_CHARSET
```

Because this section is included for backward compatibility, it should not be removed.

Font filenames mapping

The *font.properties* file establishes a mapping between logical and physical font names:

```
# font filenames for reduced initialization time
#
filename.Arial=ARIAL.TTF
filename.Arial_Bold=ARIALBD.TTF
filename.Arial_Italic=ARIALI.TTF
filename.Arial_Bold_Italic=ARIALBI.TTF
```

```
filename.Courier_New=COUR.TTF
filename.Courier_New_Bold=COURBD.TTF
filename.Courier_New_Italic=COURI.TTF
filename.Courier_New_Bold_Italic=COURBI.TTF
```

The format of this section is as follows:

```
filename.<logical name>_<style>=<physical filename>
```

The name you supply for `<logical name>` must have underscores in place of spaces, like in the font name, `Courier_New_Bold`. All different values for `<style>` must be present. Notice, though, that the style for Bold and Italic is `Bold_Italic`.

Including these lines reduces the amount of time your Java application spends trying to find a physical font corresponding to the particular font name.

Default character information

If you've ever used an application in which the fonts on your system cannot be used to render all characters correctly, you may see a default character displayed. Usually this character is the Unicode LOWER RIGHT SHADOWED WHITE SQUARE (\u2751) ❑ character. This section of the *font.properties* file specifies the character that should be used in the situation when no font on the system can display a given character:

```
# Default font definition
#
default.char=2751
```

The default character should be a character that can be distinguished from characters you would normally encounter in your application to help you debug your applications.[8]

Figure 8-21 shows the display of Example 8-6; the example displays the Japanese phrase for "Hello," which is Konnichi wa. Notice all the squares indicating that the Japanese glyphs are unavailable in this font (which happens to be Arial Bold).

Example 8-6. Hello in Japanese—Konnichi wa

```
import java.awt.*;
import java.awt.event.*;
import javax.swing.*;

public class HelloInJapanese extends JPanel {

  static JFrame frame;
```

---

[8] We have not been able to get this feature to work. If you are able to get this feature working, please contact us.

Example 8-6. Hello in Japanese—Konnichi wa (continued)

```
static String helloInJapanese =
    "Hello in Japanese is konnichi wa, \u4eca\u65e5\u306f.";

public HelloInJapanese(String characters) {
   Font theFont = new Font("Bitstream Cyberbit", Font.PLAIN, 20);
   JTextArea area = new JTextArea(characters, 2, 30);
   area.setFont(theFont);
   area.setLineWrap(true);
   JScrollPane scrollpane = new JScrollPane(area);
   add(scrollpane);
}

public static void main(String argv[]) {

   HelloInJapanese japanesePanel = new HelloInJapanese(helloInJapanese);

   frame = new JFrame("Hello in Japanese");
   frame.addWindowListener(new WindowAdapter() {
     public void windowClosing(WindowEvent e) {System.exit(0);}
   });
   frame.getContentPane().add("Center", japanesePanel);
   frame.pack();
   frame.setVisible(true);
  }
}
```

Later on in this chapter, after adding a font capable of displaying the Japanese, you'll see that the squares indicating that a glyph is not found in the font will be replaced by the proper glyphs.

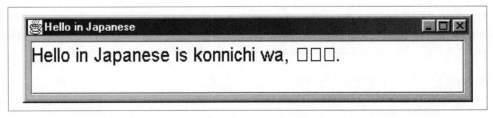

Figure 8-21: An application unable to display Japanese characters

Character conversion information

Earlier in this chapter we mentioned that some fonts use the Unicode indexing scheme and some fonts do not. Unicode indexing only means that you can request a particular glyph from the font by specifying the Unicode code point. In a font using Unicode indexing and supporting the Latin-1 script, for example, the Unicode character LATIN CAPITAL LETTER A (A) is indexed as `\u0065`. Fonts not using the Unicode indexing scheme must contain the NEED_CONVERTED tag in the logical font mapping section of the *font.properties* file.

The structure of the lines in this section is as follows:

```
fontcharset.<logical font>.<order>=<converter>
```

An example character conversion section from a *font.properties* file is shown below:

```
# Static FontCharset info.
#
fontcharset.dialog.1=sun.awt.windows.CharToByteWingDings
fontcharset.dialog.2=sun.awt.CharToByteSymbol

fontcharset.dialoginput.1=sun.awt.windows.CharToByteWingDings
fontcharset.dialoginput.2=sun.awt.CharToByteSymbol

fontcharset.serif.1=sun.awt.windows.CharToByteWingDings
fontcharset.serif.2=sun.awt.CharToByteSymbol
```

Recall our earlier example showing the logical font mapping section of the *font.properties* file: the second and third entries under the `dialog` logical name contain the NEED_CONVERTED tag. This tag implies that entries must be present in this section of *font.properties* for proper character conversion to take place. Both `<logical font>` and `<order>` must match the corresponding entries from the logical font mapping section of the file. Most fonts do use Unicode indexing, but you can check with the font vendor if you are unsure.

Exclusion range information

As you install more fonts on your system, you'll find that certain fonts contain individual or ranges of characters that overlap. You may prefer that certain characters be displayed with a certain font if several fonts overlap. *font.properties* provides a section that allows you to define exclusions. A portion of the *font.properties* file that deals with this issue is shown as follows:

```
# Exclusion Range info.
#
exclusion.dialog.0=0100-20ab,20ad-ffff
exclusion.dialoginput.0=0100-20ab,20ad-ffff
exclusion.serif.0=0100-20ab,20ad-ffff
```

This section tells the rendering engine which individual or ranges of characters to exclude from display by a particular font. The previous example says that any characters encountered in the range `\u0100` to `\u20ab`, and in the range `\u20ad` to `\uffff`, for the `dialog.0`, `dialoginput.0`, and `serif.0` fonts, should be excluded. If, for example, `dialog.0` was in use and Java were to encounter a character in one of the ranges above, it would search the fonts `dialog.1`, `dialog.2`, of the ranges above, it would search the fonts dialog.1, dialog.2, and so on for the proper glyph to be displayed. If, after searching each font, the glyph is not found, the default character is displayed. Note that you do not need to add the "\u" substring to the beginning of the range values.

You can specify exclusion of multiple ranges or individual characters on a single line; simply separate the range values or the individual characters by a comma. A range is specified by placing a dash (-) between two values. Be sure to check the Unicode code point values if you edit this section yourself.

Character set for text input

Certain applications allow users to enter text information. A number of GUI components allow you to enter text such as text boxes and text fields. The value specified in the inputtextcharset field, as shown here, tells Java to use the specified character set in these components:

```
# charset for text input
#
inputtextcharset=ANSI_CHARSET
```

Other values we have seen are CHINESEBIG5_CHARSET, EASTEUROPE_CHARSET, HANGEUL_CHARSET, RUSSIAN_CHARSET, and SHIFTJIS_CHARSET. The localized versions of the *font.properties* files contain the correct value for this property.

Not only does a *font.properties* file exist, but so do several locale-specific *font.properties* files. These files include *font.properties.ko*, *font.properties.ru*, and *font.properties.zh*, which are used in Korean, Russian, and Chinese locales, respectively.

NOTE   Notice that localized versions of the *font.properties* files do not follow the same naming convention as property resource files. Recall from Chapter 4, *Isolating Locale-Specific Data with Resource Bundles*, that property resource files must end with a *.properties* extension. For the *font.properties* files, the convention used in naming the file is as follows:

    font.properties.<locale>.<osVersion>

The format of <locale> is:

    <language>_<region>_<encoding>

Also note that the *font.properties* files are not resource bundles. They are simply properties files. Their lookup strategy differs from that of resource bundles, and if they're missing entries, they don't inherit those entries from other files. Finally, Java reads the *font.properties* file on startup of the virtual machine. Therefore, if you make changes to any of the *font.properties* files, you need to restart your application for the changes to take effect.

How Java discovers the font.properties files

In addition to a different naming convention from resource bundles, Java searches for the proper *font.properties* file in the following order:

```
font.properties.<language>_<region>_<encoding>.<osVersion>
font.properties.<language>_<region>_<encoding>
font.properties.<language>_<region>.<osVersion>
font.properties.<language>_<region>
font.properties.<language>_<encoding>.<osVersion>
font.properties.<language>_<encoding>
font.properties.<language>_<osVersion>
font.properties.<language>
font.properties.<encoding>.<osVersion>
font.properties.<encoding>
font.properties.<osVersion>
font.properties
```

Here the following values are used:

```
<osVersion> is the value returned from the system property, os.version
<encoding> is the value returned from the system property, file.encoding
<region> is the value returned from the system property, user.region
<language> is the value returned from the system property, user.language
```

Each property could be retrieved by calling `System.getProperty(<property name>)`, as in `System.getProperty("user.language")`.

For example, if the language of your current locale is "ko" (Korean), Java would search for *font.properties.ko*. If this file did not exist, it would then search for *font.properties*. Another difference between the way in which Java deals with *font.properties* files and resource bundles is that the *font.properties* do not support each other in the hierarchy. For example, if Java uses the *font.properties.ko* file and you write code in which Java cannot get the proper information from this file, it will not default to search *font.properties* for this information.

Adding New Fonts to Your System

In this section we'll show you how to install a popular Unicode font so you can start developing multilingual applications. The font we're going to install is called the Bitstream Cyberbit font. This font is popular and freely available on the Internet.[9] It's a big font, weighing in at just over 12.5 MB. This font contains approximately 30,000 glyphs and is capable of rendering text in languages such as Arabic,

---

[9] The Bitstream Cyberbit can be found on Netscape's FTP site at *ftp://ftp.netscape.com/pub/communicator/extras/fonts/windows*.

Hebrew, and Thai. Another popular font that comes with either Microsoft Office 2000 or FrontPage 2000 is the Arial Unicode MS font. Almost 52,000 glyphs are included in this font. However, this font takes up about 23 MB of hard disk space.[10]

After you've obtained the font you want to install, open the Control Panel in Windows and open the Fonts folder. You should see an option off the File menu titled `Install New Font`, as shown in Figure 8-22.

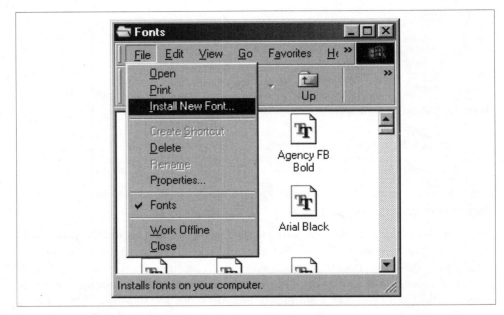

Figure 8-22. Installing a new font from the Windows Control Panel

After you select this option, a dialog opens, as shown in Figure 8-23. Here you should navigate to the directory where you downloaded and extracted the Bitstream Cyberbit font file.

That's it. You've installed the font successfully and now you can use this font in Windows applications such as Microsoft Word. But we still need to set up the *font.properties* file so that your Java applications can use the font. Let's step through each part of the *font.properties* file that we covered earlier in this chapter and add the relevant information for the Bitstream Cyberbit font.

---

[10] Both the Bitstream Cyberbit and Arial Unicode MS fonts support Chinese, Japanese, and Korean glyphs. Arabic and Hebrew are supported in the Lucida fonts that ship with Sun's Java 2 Runtime Environment.

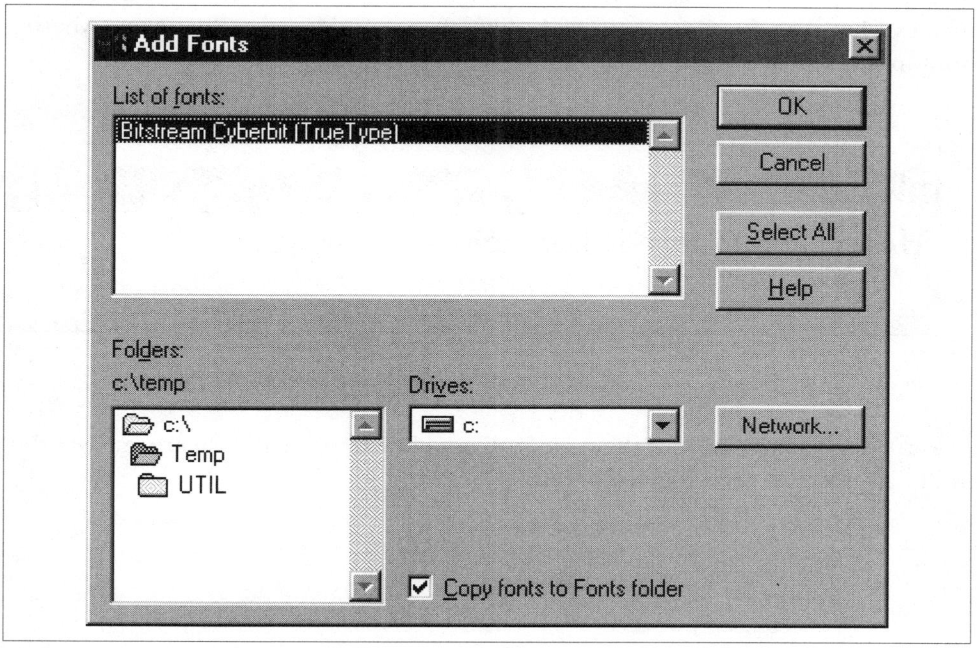

Figure 8-23. Adding the Bitstream Cyberbit font from the download folder

Let's first look at the logical font mapping section. For this example, we're only going to install the Bitstream Cyberbit font under the dialog logical name. We'd like to make Bitstream Cyberbit the default font, the font first chosen for rendering text. Remember that the numbering of fonts indicates the order in which fonts are searched for particular glyphs; 0 indicates the first font searched:

```
dialog.0=Bitstream Cyberbit,DEFAULT_CHARSET
dialog.1=Arial,ANSI_CHARSET
dialog.2=WingDings,SYMBOL_CHARSET,NEED_CONVERTED
dialog.3=Symbol,SYMBOL_CHARSET,NEED_CONVERTED
```

The next section of the *font.properties* file is the font alias mapping. We don't need to worry about this particular section. You also don't have to add the font to the font filenames section, but let's do it anyway. In the font filenames mapping section, add the entry for the Bitstream Cyberbit font as follows. Don't forget to add the underscores in the name:

```
# font filenames for reduced initialization time
#
filename.Arial=ARIAL.TTF
filename.Bitstream_Cyberbit=CYBERBIT.TTF
```

That's all there is to it. Remember Figure 8-21, where we showed you an application that was not capable of displaying Japanese characters. Figure 8-24 demonstrates what that same program looks like after we added the Bitstream Cyberbit font to the *font.properties* file.

Figure 8-24. Displaying Japanese characters after installing the Bitstream Cyberbit font

We can also change part of the code in Example 8-6 to use the Bitstream Cyberbit font directly. The code is given here:

```
public HelloInJapanese(String characters) {
    Font theFont = new Font("Bitstream Cyberbit", Font.PLAIN, 20);
    JTextArea area = new JTextArea(characters, 2, 30);
    area.setFont(theFont);
    area.setLineWrap(true);
    JScrollPane scrollpane = new JScrollPane(area);
    add(scrollpane);
}
```

Java provides a robust set of classes that give you much control over the displayed fonts, information about individual fonts, and the characters that can be displayed using particular fonts. Adding your own fonts for use in your Java applications is relatively painless and Java's support for TrueType fonts extends the realm of possibilities for displaying multilingual text in your applications.

9

Internationalized Graphical User Interfaces

This chapter focuses on designing internationalized graphical user interfaces (GUI). Once internationalized, an application may be localized to provide a look and feel native to the region where the application is being used. This chapter highlights many of the pitfalls associated with designing internationalized graphical user interfaces; however, it does not serve as a general GUI design reference. A good general GUI design reference, *Java Swing*, by Robert Eckstein, Marc Loy, and Dave Wood, is also available from O'Reilly.

This chapter is unique because we draw upon many topics discussed in previous chapters. For example, we use locales to determine which GUI layout is appropriate and we use resource bundles to package localized text for GUI components, such as buttons and text labels. We render text from non-Latin writing systems by using fonts and Unicode. By using the Input Method Framework (discussed in Chapter 10, *Input Methods*), you can also add the ability to input text in languages such as Hebrew or Japanese in your application.

General Issues

Several issues are associated with designing internationalized user interfaces. In this section, we describe some of the most common pitfalls to avoid when developing an internationalized GUI.

Text Issues

The most common mistake made when designing an internationalized user interface is to not consider screen real estate. When text is translated from one language to another, the length of the original text can expand or shrink significantly. When translating from English to German for example, expect the text to expand by an average of 30 percent. The expansion could be up to 300 percent for short strings. Table 9-1 lists some common menu strings and their translations. As you design a GUI, ensure that components still fit correctly on the screen, independent of the length of text.

Table 9-1. Common Menu Strings Translated into Different Languages

English	German	Italian	Norwegian	Turkish
File	Datei	File	Fil	Dosya
Open...	Öffnen...	Apri...	Åpne...	Aç...
Save As...	Speichern unter...	Salva con nome	Lagre som...	Farklý Kaydet...
View	Anzeigen	Visualizza	Vis	Görünüm
Edit	Bearbeiten	Modifica	Rediger	Düzenle
Select All	Alles auswählen	Seleziona tutto	Merk alt	Tümünü Seç
Print...	Drucken...	Stampa...	Skriv ut...	Yazdýr...
Exit	Beenden	Esci	Avslutt	Çýkýþ

Avoid using colloquialisms, puns, or slang expressions in text. In many cases they are difficult to translate; in some cases they are offensive. For example, a U.S. company might think of naming a word processor "EZ Write" as a cute shortcut for "Easy Write." In other English speaking countries, such as England and Australia, however, the letter Z is pronounced "zed," so the reader would read "E-Zed Write."

Do not assume that acronyms apply for all locales. Depending on the acronym, it may not make sense in some locales. In other cases, the acronym might be different when it is translated for a given locale. For example, the English acronym NATO (North Atlantic Treaty Organization) is known as OTAN (l'Organisation du Traité de l'Atlantique Nord) in French and NAVO (Noord Atlantische Verdrags Organisatie) in Dutch. Acronyms are distinguished from other words in languages that use the Latin script by the use of uppercase letters. As we discussed in Chapter 2, *Writing Systems*, some writing systems do not have the concept of case; another mechanism is needed to inform the reader that the word is in fact an acronym. In Hebrew, a double-quote (") is used between the last two letters of the acronym. In Hebrew, the acronym for NATO is נאט"ו.

Screen Layout

Just as scripts contain orientation properties (i.e., left to right, right to left, bidirectional, or vertical), the graphical interfaces supporting these scripts also have orientation properties. For example, pull-down menus in the United States start at the top left corner of the application screen and run from left to right, as shown in Figure 9-1.

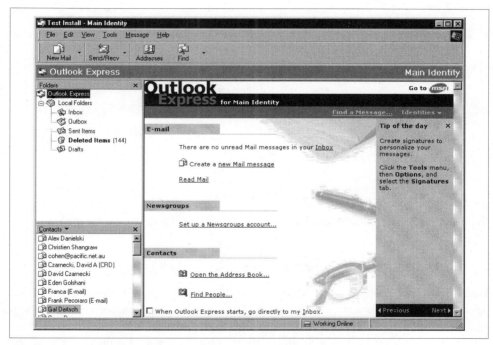

Figure 9-1. Microsoft Outlook Express application screen running on a United States version of Windows

This interface may seem familiar, but would be awkward to users in Israel. In countries such as Israel, where the language is written from right to left, applications provide GUIs that conform to this convention. Figure 9-2 demonstrates the same application running in such an environment. Notice that the pull-down menus now run from right to left.

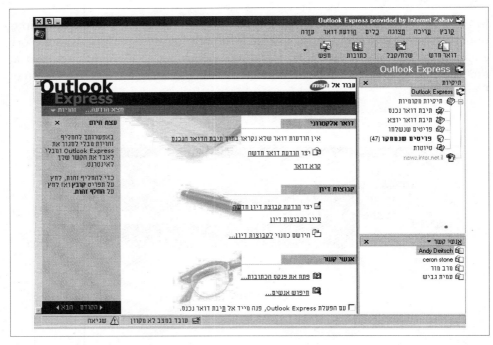

Figure 9-2. Microsoft Outlook Express application screen running on a Hebrew version of Windows

Icon and Symbol Design Issues

While internationalizing your applications, be sensitive to the proper use of images. In Chapter 4, *Isolating Locale-Specific Data with Resource Bundles*, we showed you that adding localized objects such as images and sound files into a `ListResource-Bundle` for a particular locale is appropriate. However, you should check that the images that you include in your application are appropriate for the locale in which you deploy your application. For example, if you drive down a highway in the United States and see a road sign that looks like Figure 9-3, you might say to yourself, "I can make a U-turn here."

However, in the Netherlands, this sign is interpreted as "no turning allowed."[1]

When choosing icons, do not use graphical puns. Words that take on multiple meanings in one language do not necessarily translate into another. For example,

---

[1] A red band circumscribes this sign. Red circles on traffic signs throughout Europe mean "forbidden."

in many languages, the links of a chain shown in Figure 9-4 will not help a non-English speaking user think of a hypertext link.

Figure 9-3. A Dutch highway sign indicating no turning allowed

Figure 9-4. Example of a graphical pun

Icons should be generic enough to work across all locales, or locale-specific icons should be stored in resource bundles. Choosing a mailbox to represent email, for example, is only meaningful to U.S. users. As shown in Figure 9-5, several countries use slots in the front door to receive mail, and in countries that do have mailboxes, they don't look anything like the ones used in the United States.

Figure 9-5. Examples of icons with meanings specific to a locale

Avoid using icons with pictures of national emblems, sports equipment, or other symbols that might be familiar in one culture but confusing in another. Also be cautious when using pictures of animals, hand gestures, religious artifacts, or mythological symbols. These pictures can all be offensive in some cultures.

As another example, the dialog in Figure 9-6 might be appropriate in the United States as an indication that your application is in trouble. However, if you were to localize this application for use in Greece, you would also want to localize the image displayed to the user. In Greece, this hand gesture is highly offensive.

Avoid using flags to represent languages unless you are referring to a specific locale. For example, using the French flag, as shown in Figure 9-7, to show that the user interface can switch to French could offend people from Algeria, Belgium, and Canada. Instead, provide a list of language names as words using each language's own name as the word for itself. For example, use English, Deutsch, Français, 日本語, etc.

Figure 9-6. An image appropriate in the United States, but not in Greece

Figure 9-7. Example of an icon that may not appropriately represent a language.

If you can avoid it, try not to embed text in icons, as shown in Figure 9-8. In most cases the text needs to be translated for each locale; in some cases the translated text will not fit on the image. Recreating icons with new translations also takes more time than simply changing text in a resource bundle. A better alternative is to leave icons without text and use tooltips instead.

Figure 9-8. Examples of icons with embedded text

Providing a list of all images that might be considered appropriate in certain countries is impossible. Before using any image or icon, verify it with an end-user in the country where you wish to deploy your application. You might be surprised that certain cultural icons and references are not universal. As a guide, you may want to run down the following checklist to ascertain that your application's images do not fall into any of these categories:

- Characters from fictional stories or television

- Religious or political symbols

- Culturally specific icons

- Sports icons

- Body parts or body language

Screen layout must also be considered when designing icons. Remember that the layout runs from right to left in some locales. An icon with an arrow pointing to the left to indicate "undo" will probably confuse someone using Arabic. Figures 9-9 and 9-10 represent graphics for the Tab and Enter keys, respectively.

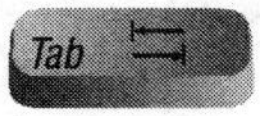

Figure 9-9. Tab key image appropriate for locales where text runs from left to right

Enter

Figure 9-10. Return key image appropriate for locales where text runs from left to right

These graphics are appropriate when your application is running in a locale where the text runs left to right. However, when you switch to a locale where text runs right to left, then Figures 9-11 and 9-12 are appropriate. They convey the appropriate direction and behavior in this type of language.

Figure 9-11. Tab key image appropriate for locales where text runs from right to left

Figure 9-12. Return key image appropriate for locales where text runs from right to left

Arabic and Hebrew books are read from right to left. Make sure your icons reflect these cultural nuances. Figure 9-13 shows an icon appropriate for right-to-left or left-to right orientation.

Figure 9-13. Icons appropriate for certain locales based on right-to-left or left-to-right orientation

The `ListResourceBundle` class allows you to localize very complex objects. In Chapter 4, we provided a utility you can use to add objects like images and sound files to a `ListResourceBundle`. A competent localization engineer understands the cultural dos and don'ts for the particular locale to which you deploy your application. And, like dealing with doctors, it can never hurt to get a second opinion.

Other Issues

Phone numbers

Depending on the country, phone numbers have varying lengths, the numbers are grouped together differently, and a diverse array of delimiters may be used. As a result, an application should not force the entry or display into a specific pattern without taking the locale into consideration. Americans are very familiar with a phone number consisting of a three-digit area code and three-digit exchange, followed by four digits. Reading the numbers grouped differently would be confusing (try reading 5185 551 212). Phone numbers generally have three components: the country code, the city code, and the number. The country code is typically prefaced with a plus symbol (+), while the remaining numbers are formatted according to local convention. In some locales, if a phone number is dialed within the same country, a national prefix is used so the number might look slightly different, depending on where it will be dialed. Table 9-2 shows how telephone numbers are formatted in different countries.

Table 9-2. Phone Number Grouping in Different Countries

Phone Number	Country
+(43)(1)58701 2136	Austria
+33 01 39 25 37 51	France
+49 (0)211 / 4560-01	Germany
+972 3-5403112	Israel
+81 052-264-1007	Japan
+44 020 7676 5534	United Kingdom
+1 (518) 555-1212	United States

When providing phone number information to a user (e.g., customer support), use digits. Some companies choose phone numbers with easily remembered mnemonics, such as 555-HELP. The problem is that in some countries, letters are not located on the phone. If you do want to provide a mnemonic, make sure you also include the digits. Also remember that if you use a toll-free number for customers, make sure it is accessible from all countries where your software is distributed, or provide an alternate phone number for users located in other countries.

People's names

Software packages designed by American programmers gather contact information fairly rigidly. If, as a user, your name doesn't match the pattern *first name, middle initial, last name*, you might be out of luck. Look at the following names:

> Walter Dixon III
> Charles Phillip Arthur George Windsor
> George Herbert Walker Bush
> F. Scott Fitzgerald

In Western cultures, people typically have a given first name and a family name that has been passed down through male heirs. In India, children have a given name and a surname, which is the given name of their father. For example,

Subramanian Venkateswaran had a daughter he named Pushkala. Her full name is Pushkala Subramanian. As in Western cultures, a female typically changes her surname to that of her husband's upon marriage. In India, however, the wife could use either her husband's surname or given name. In India names are usually written as *surname, given name*. People in India usually sign their names using the first initial of their surname followed by their given name. So Pushkala would sign her name as S. Pushkala. When Indians write their name in Western cultures, they typically use the Western practice of writing the given name followed by the surname. Clearly, software needs to be a bit more flexible and not simply ask for the first name, middle initial, and last name. An Indian user might be confused by the definition of a first and last name. When building a form, asking for a given name and family or surname is generally preferable.

Color

Adding color to your user interface is important because it makes the application more appealing to an end user and also sends a message to your users. The exact message a particular color conveys differs among cultures. Understanding the symbolism for a given color and choosing colors appropriately for each locale is thus important. Table 9-3 highlights a few colors and their meanings in different parts of the world.

Table 9-3. Cultural Meanings of Colors

Color	Cultural Meaning
Red	China: celebration, happiness, and luck India: purity United States: stop or danger
White	Eastern cultures: mourning or death United States: purity
Blue	China: immortality Hindus: the color of Krishna Jews: holiness Middle East: protection; ward off evil spirits
Green	India: the color of Islam Ireland: religious significance Some tropical countries: danger United States: safe or go; environmental awareness
Yellow	Asia: sacred, imperial Western cultures: joy; happiness; caution
Black	Western cultures: mourning or death

Component Orientation

Graphical components can be laid out in a GUI using a specific ordering. In this context, *component orientation* refers to the position of various GUI components in an application that is appropriate for the locale where the application is running. The component orientation affects the component's layout within an application and the orientation of any text rendered within that component.

Java encapsulates component orientation in the ComponentOrientation class in the java.awt package. A property in the base class of all GUI components, the component orientation property, controls this aspect of positioning components. You can set the orientation of different GUI components by using the ComponentOrientation class. This class allows you to differentiate between left-to-right and right-to-left running text or component placement. It also allows you to differentiate between text that runs vertically, as in Japanese, where the text runs top to bottom, with lines arranged right to left.

Example 9-1 determines component orientation properties for a specific locale.

Example 9-1. Determining Orientation Properties for a Given Locale

```
import java.awt.*;
import java.util.*;

public class ListLocaleOrientation {

  public static void main(String [] argv) throws Exception {

    Locale myLocale;
    if (argv.length < 2)
      myLocale = Locale.getDefault();
    else
      myLocale = new Locale(argv[0], argv[1]);
    ComponentOrientation ce =
        ComponentOrientation.getOrientation(myLocale);
    System.out.println("Is horizontal? " + ce.isHorizontal());
    System.out.println("Is left to right? " + ce.isLeftToRight());
  }
}
```

Three static ComponentOrientation objects exist to specify how text should be laid out in a given component:

```
ComponentOrientation.LEFT_TO_RIGHT
ComponentOrientation.RIGHT_TO_LEFT
ComponentOrientation.UNKNOWN
```

Table 9-4 describes component orientation in more detail.

Table 9-4. Descriptions of the Various Types of Component Orientation

ComponentOrientation. LEFT_TO_RIGHT	ComponentOrientation. RIGHT_TO_LEFT	ComponentOrientation. UNKNOWN
Indicates that text or component placement occurs from left to right	Indicates that text or component placement occurs from right to left	Indicates that text and component orientation have not been specified

The `ComponentOrientation` class also contains two methods for determining the orientation style: `isHorizontal()` and `isLeftToRight()`, described in Table 9-5.

Table 9-5. Description of Component-Orientation Style Method

isHorizontal()	IsLeftToRight()
Returns true if text is positioned horizontally. Chinese and Japanese text may run vertically, not horizontally.	Returns true when text and components are oriented from left-to-right. Arabic and Hebrew run from right-to-left, not left-to-right.

When making tests on a component's various properties, use the `isLeftToRight()` and `isHorizontal()` access methods. Try to avoid tests that test for equality against `ComponentOrientation.LEFT_TO_RIGHT`, `ComponentOrientation.RIGHT_TO_LEFT`, and `ComponentOrientation.UNKNOWN`. You should not use:

```
if (frameOrientation == ComponentOrientation.LEFT_TO_RIGHT)
    // .. do something
```

The following test is preferred:

```
if ((frame.getComponentOrientation()).isLeftToRight())
    // .. do something
```

Running Example 9-1 demonstrates the component orientation for various locales:

```
C:\>java ListLocaleOrientation en US

Is horizontal? true
Is left to right? true

C:\>java ListLocaleOrientation ar AR

Is horizontal? true
Is left to right? false
```

Querying the Component Orientation

Two methods in the `ComponentOrientation` class allow you to retrieve the component orientation for a given resource bundle or a given locale. Both methods search on a resource bundle, which must conform to two characteristics:

- The searched resource bundle must be a `ListResourceBundle` since this type of resource bundle can store objects, unlike a `PropertyResourceBundle`.

- The resource bundle must contain a key named, "Orientation," which contains a value that is one of the three static `ComponentOrientation` objects, `ComponentOrientation.LEFT_TO_RIGHT`, `ComponentOrientation.RIGHT_TO_LEFT`, or `ComponentOrientation.UNKNOWN`.

These two static methods are as follows:

```
public static ComponentOrientation getOrientation(Locale locale)
public static ComponentOrientation getOrientation(ResourceBundle bdl)
```

The first method, `public static ComponentOrientation getOrientation(Locale locale)`, uses the locale passed into the method to retrieve the orientation from a `ListResourceBundle` for that locale.

The second method, `public static ComponentOrientation getOrientation(ResourceBundle bdl)`, takes a `ResourceBundle` (remember, it must be a `ListResourceBundle`) and retrieves the `ComponentOrientation` object given by the "Orientation" key. A call to this method using the resource bundle in Example 9-2 returns a value of `ComponentOrientation.UNKNOWN`.

Example 9-2. Sample Resource Bundle for a Fictitious Locale

```
import java.awt.ComponentOrientation;
import java.util.ListResourceBundle;

public class ComponentOrientationBundle_xx_XX extends ListResourceBundle {

  public Object[][] getContents() {
    return contents;
  }

  static final Object[][] contents = {
      {"Orientation", ComponentOrientation.UNKNOWN}
  };
}
```

We recommend that you use the `getOrientation(Locale locale)` method in your applications if you need to retrieve a `ComponentOrientation` object for a given locale. This method signature follows the normal pattern used throughout java.util and java.text and is similar to NumberFormat.getCurrencyInstance(Locale inLocale). Also, the getOrientation(ResourceBundle bdl) method may be a candidate for deprecation in future versions of the Java platform.

Now that you can retrieve the component orientation for your application in a locale-dependent manner, let's put it to practical use.

NOTE   ComponentOrientation support does not exist in the following classes:

```
java.awt.GridLayout
java.awt.GridBagLayout
javax.swing.JTable
javax.swing.JSplitPane
javax.swing.JOptionPane
javax.swing.JColorChooser
javax.swing.JFileChooser
javax.swing.BoxLayout
```

The actual classes may differ depending on the version, and possibly the supplier, of your Java runtime environment.

Setting the Component Orientation for an Entire Application

Initially, the component orientation value for all components you use in your application defaults to ComponentOrientation.UNKNOWN. This default seems logical because no particular component orientation is associated with a given component. Therefore, you need to set the component orientation for all the components in your application if you plan to support bidirectional writing systems.

Doing something similar to the following block of code would be a waste of time and code:

```
JButton okButton = new JButton();
okButton.setComponentOrientation(ComponentOrientation.RIGHT_TO_LEFT);
JButton cancelButton = new JButton();
cancelButton.setComponentOrientation(ComponentOrientation.RIGHT_TO_LEFT);
...
```

At this point, you might want to abandon supporting bidirectional languages. Don't despair! The code shown in Example 9-3 will do the job for you.[2]

---

[2] We would like to thank Brian Beck of Sun Microsystems for his permission to use this code.

Example 9-3. Code to Set the Component Orientation Property for Each Component in an Application

```
/*
 * applyOrientation():
 * Borrowed from SwingApplet demo!
 */
private void applyOrientation(Component c, ComponentOrientation o) {

    c.setComponentOrientation(o);

    if (c instanceof JMenu)
      JMenu menu = (JMenu)c;
      int ncomponents = menu.getMenuComponentCount();
      for (int i = 0 ; i < ncomponents ; ++i) {
        applyOrientation( menu.getMenuComponent(i), o );
      }
    } else if (c instanceof Container) {
        Container container = (Container)c;
        int ncomponents = container.getComponentCount();
        for (int i = 0 ; i < ncomponents ; ++i) {
            applyOrientation( container.getComponent(i), o );
        }
    }
}
```

Examples 9-4 and 9-5 show the resource bundles we used in the application.

Example 9-4. ComponentOrientationBundle_en_US.java

```
import java.awt.ComponentOrientation;
import java.util.ListResourceBundle;

public class ComponentOrientationBundle_en_US extends ListResourceBundle {

  public Object[][] getContents() {
    return contents;
  }

  static final Object[][] contents = {
      {"Orientation", ComponentOrientation.LEFT_TO_RIGHT}
  };
}
```

Example 9-5. ComponentOrientationBundle_ar_AR.java

```
import java.awt.ComponentOrientation;
import java.util.ListResourceBundle;

public class ComponentOrientationBundle_ar_AR extends ListResourceBundle {

  public Object[][] getContents() {
    return contents;
  }
```

Example 9-5. ComponentOrientationBundle_ar_AR.java (continued)

```
static final Object[][] contents = {
    {"Orientation", ComponentOrientation.RIGHT_TO_LEFT}
};
}
```

Figures 9-14 and 9-15 demonstrate a simple application that uses the applyOrientation method.

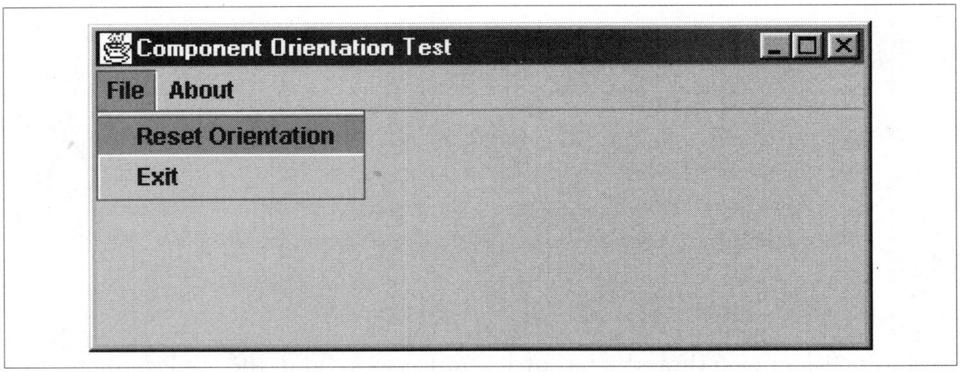

Figure 9-14. The application running where the components are laid out from left to right

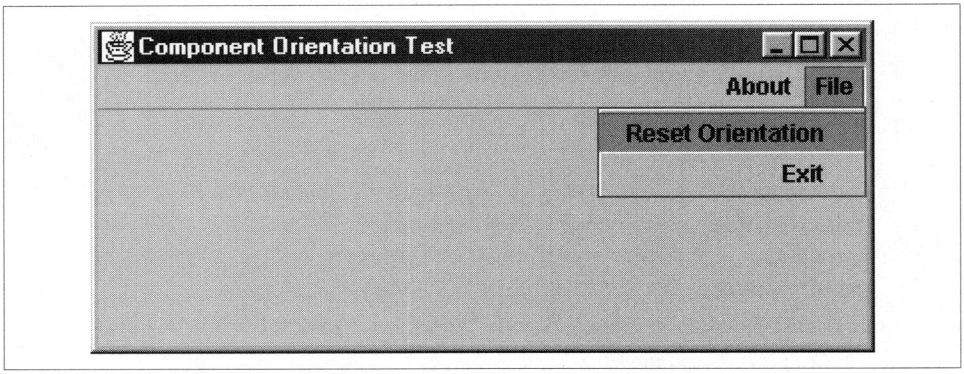

Figure 9-15. The application running where the components are now laid out from right to left

After selecting **Reset Orientation**, we see the application has changed the orientation from left to right to right to left.

You could also use the applyResourceBundle(ResourceBundle rb) method from the java.awt.Window class. However, this method will not properly update JMenu components in your application because of the way they are stored. This situation is why the `applyOrientation` method from Example 9-3 contains an explicit test for a component being a `JMenu`. This method is represented in the javadocs as a method that applies the given resource bundle's settings to the `Window` object (or a subclass of `java.awt.Window`). However, this method currently looks in the resource bundle for a key called "Orientation," which must be of the `ComponentOrientation` type. It then applies this `ComponentOrientation` object and applies it to the `Window` and all the components contained therein.

Another method, `applyResourceBundle(String rbName)`, also exists in `java.awt.Window`. This method loads the resource bundle with the name you pass in; however it uses the JVM's default locale to load the resource bundle.

We do not advocate using either `applyResourceBundle()` method in the `Window` class. For example, both methods require an "Orientation" key in your resource bundle that returns a `ComponentOrientation` object. This requirement means that you should remember to store your resources in a class file. Also, because the method `applyResourceBundle(String rbName)` uses the JVM's default locale, you may not be loading the correct resource bundle or a resource bundle that even exists. You should use the `applyOrientation` method from Example 9-3 if your application needs to set the component orientation.

Internationalization and Localization Caveats for Various Components

This section outlines some caveats one might encounter while using different Swing components. You may use certain components in your application because they are convenient and save time from writing all the "glue" code to tie a more complex component together. Some of these components may present special difficulties when you try to internationalize and localize them.[3]

JOptionPane

One example of such a component is the `javax.swing` package's `JOptionPane` component. If you use default options for this component or even if you consider using them, it's good to know where you may find problems when localizing your application. Example 9-6 shows the use of the `JOptionPane` component.

---

[3] Localization of these and other Swing components may vary, depending on the vendor supplying your Java runtime environment.

Example 9-6. Using the JOptionPane Component

```
import javax.swing.*;

public class JOptionPaneDemonstration {

  public static void main(String [] argv) {

    JOptionPane jop = new JOptionPane(
        "This is a message", JOptionPane.ERROR_MESSAGE,
        JOptionPane.YES_NO_CANCEL_OPTION);
    JDialog jopDialog = jop.createDialog(null, "This is a title");
    jopDialog.show();
    Object userSelection = jop.getValue();
    // NOTE: The return value returned by the above statement is an int
    System.exit(0);
  }
}
```

Figure 9-16 shows this application running.

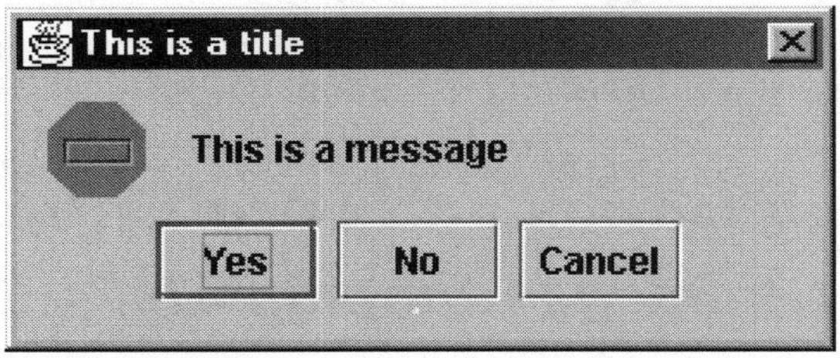

Figure 9-16. Dialog created when Example 9-6 is executed

You should notice a few things about this dialog. First, it contains the correct title and internal message that we specified when creating the dialog. Second, we didn't have to specify the text or explicitly create the Yes, No, and Cancel buttons. Those buttons were created for us by specifying the YES_NO_CANCEL_OPTION when we created the JOptionPane. This panel might be fine when writing an application used only in the United States or another English-speaking country. We did not specify the text for the buttons, so we need to move those strings into a resource bundle and use another constructor to create the JOptionPane.

Examples 9-7 and 9-8 show the modified application and resource bundle, respectively. Note that we explicitly set a font for the JOptionPane to LucidaSans, which can display both English and Hebrew.

Example 9-7. JOptionPane Demonstration with Localized Messages

```java
import java.awt.*;
import java.util.*;
import javax.swing.*;

public class JOptionPaneDemonstrationLocalized {

  public static void main(String [] argv) {

    GraphicsEnvironment ge = GraphicsEnvironment.getLocalGraphicsEnvironment();
    Font unicodeFont = new Font("LucidaSans", Font.PLAIN, 12);

    ResourceBundle bundle =
        ResourceBundle.getBundle("JOptionPaneResources", Locale.getDefault());
    if (bundle == null)
      System.exit(1);

    String [] textMessages = new String[3];
    textMessages[0] = bundle.getString("Yes");
    textMessages[1] = bundle.getString("No");
    textMessages[2] = bundle.getString("Cancel");

    JOptionPane jop =
        new JOptionPane(bundle.getString("MessageText"),
                      JOptionPane.ERROR_MESSAGE,
                      JOptionPane.YES_NO_CANCEL_OPTION,
                      null, textMessages);
    JDialog jopDialog = jop.createDialog(null, bundle.getString("TitleText"));
    jop.setFont(unicodeFont);
    jopDialog.show();
    Object userSelection = jop.getValue();
    // NOTE: The return value returned by the above statement is an int
    System.exit(0);
  }
}
```

Example 9-8. JOptionPane Resources for a Hebrew Locale (JOptionPaneResources_iw.properties)

```
# JOptionPane text resources in Hebrew
#
Yes=\u05db\u05df
No=\u05dc\u05d0
OK=\u05d0\u05d9\u05e9\u05d5\u05e8
Cancel=\u05d1\u05d9\u05d8\u05d5\u05dc
MessageText=\u05d6\u05d0\u05ea \u05d4\u05d5\u05d3\u05e2\u05d4
TitleText=\u05d6\u05d0\u05ea \u05db\u05d5\u05ea\u05e8\u05ea
```

Several valid option types are available for the JOptionPane component. DEFAULT_OPTION creates a dialog that only contains one button. It is useful for notifying the user that an operation, such as the import of a large amount of data into a database, has completed successfully. The option types are:

```
javax.swing.JOptionPane.DEFAULT_OPTION
javax.swing.JOptionPane.OK_CANCEL_OPTION
javax.swing.JOptionPane.YES_NO_OPTION
javax.swing.JOptionPane.YES_NO_CANCEL_OPTION
```

Any application that uses JOptionPane should contain localized strings that are appropriate for the various option types. Figure 9-17a shows what the application looks like when using Hebrew as the locale and running on a U.S. version of Windows. Since the example uses Locale.getDefault() to retrieve the proper resource bundle, you need to set the new language using a command-line property setting:

```
java -Duser.language=iw JOptionPaneDemonstration
```

A number of options can be passed to the JOptionPane constructor. You can pass an Icon object to use in the pane. However, be sure to read the first section of this chapter, which deals with user interface issues concerning images. For the Object [] options array, you would typically pass in an array of String objects, as we did in Example 9-7. These strings should be retrieved from a resource bundle and represent the strings displayed on the buttons.

You should note three things about the figure. First, why are there question marks (?) in the dialog title? Second, the buttons are not oriented correctly from right to left. Third, is there any way to orient the stop sign and the message text from right to left? The answers are easy, but they may not be the answers you want to hear. JOptionPane does not obey settings for component orientation. So while you may be able to create text that runs from right to left, the buttons will be laid out from left to right. The title bar for JOptionPane uses the default character set for the operating system. Therefore, even if a font capable of displaying the desired characters is set for the title bar, the correct characters display only if the underlying operating system supports them. Since we run the example on a machine running a U.S. version of Windows, the default character set is Latin-1. Figure 9-17b shows the dialog created from Example 9-7 when the example is run on a machine using a Hebrew version of Windows.

Figure 9-17a. Dialog created when Example 9-7 is executed on a U.S. version of Windows

Figure 9-17b. Dialog created when Example 9-7 is executed on a Hebrew version of Windows

JColorChooser

There are two ways of creating a JColorChooser object; neither allows localization of the button text. A static method exists called createDialog(Component c, String title, boolean modal, JColorChooser chooserPane, ActionListener okListener, ActionListener, cancelListener). This method returns a JDialog, as shown in Example 9-9. However, the buttons contain text labels already created for you. This text cannot be localized. The only text that can be localized is the dialog's title.

Example 9-9. Creating a JColorChooser Dialog

```
import java.awt.*;
import java.awt.event.*;
import javax.swing.*;
import javax.swing.event.*;
import javax.swing.colorchooser.*;

public class ColorChooserDialog extends JFrame {
  public ColorChooserDialog() {
    super("ColorChooserDialog");

    JDialog colorChooserDialog =
```

Example 9-9. Creating a JColorChooser Dialog (continued)

```
        JColorChooser.createDialog(this, "This is a sample title", true,
            new JColorChooser(),
            new ActionListener() {
                public void actionPerformed(ActionEvent e) {
                    system.exit(0);
                }
            },
            new ActionListener() {
                public void actionPerformed(ActionEvent e) {
                    system.exit(0);
                }
            }
        );
    }

  public static void main(String[] args) {
    JFrame frame = new ColorChooserDialog();
    frame.addWindowListener(new WindowAdapter() {
      public void windowClosing(WindowEvent e) {System.exit(0);}
    });

    frame.pack();
    frame.setVisible(true);
  }
}
```

If you run Example 9-9, the application looks like Figure 9-18. As you can see from the figure, the text for the buttons, "OK," "Cancel," and "Reset" are appropriate for English-speaking locales. As intuitive as they seem to native English speakers, they may not be for your users in other regions of the world.

Unfortunately, there is not a way to localize the text of the buttons, the tab title, or the border title "Preview" in the JColorChooser dialog. You can localize the title text; however, as with JOptionPane, it only supports the characters from the operating system's default character set.

JFileChooser

JFileChooser is another very useful component, but one in which much text cannot be localized. Example 9-10 shows a simple JFileChooser.

Example 9-10. Creating a JFileChooser Dialog

```
import java.awt.*;
import java.awt.event.*;
import javax.swing.*;
import javax.swing.event.*;
import javax.swing.colorchooser.*;
```

Example 9-10. Creating a JFileChooser Dialog (continued)

```
public class FileChooserDemo extends JFrame {
  public FileChooserDemo() {
    super("FileChooserDemo");

    JFileChooser fileChooser = new JFileChooser();
    fileChooser.setDialogTitle("Choose a file");
    this.getContentPane().add(fileChooser);
    fileChooser.show();
  }

  public static void main(String[] args) {
    JFrame frame = new FileChooserDemo();
    frame.addWindowListener(new WindowAdapter() {
      public void windowClosing(WindowEvent e) {System.exit(0);}
    });

    frame.pack();
    frame.setVisible(true);
  }
}
```

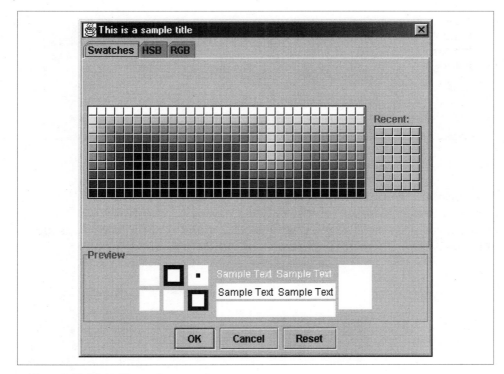

Figure 9-18. JColorChooser demonstration

We would normally want to localize the strings `Look in`, `File name`, `Files of type`, `Open`, and `Cancel`.

`JFileChooser` does provide flexibility in localizing one of these strings. In the `JFileChooser` class, you can use the `setApproveButtonText(String approveButtonText)` to set the text that would replace "Open" in Figure 9-19. When creating a `JFileChooser`, you could also use `showDialog(Component parent, String approveButtonText)` to pass in a localized string for the approve button.

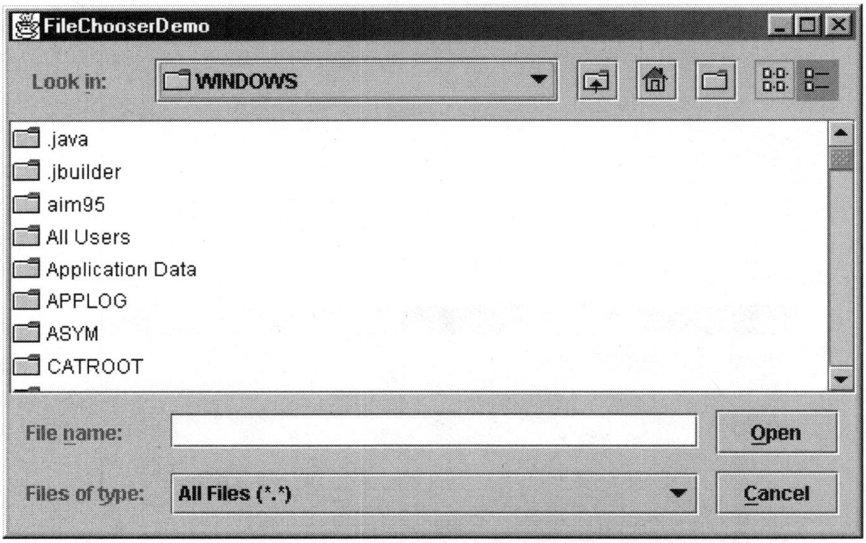

Figure 9-19. JFileChooser demonstration

As a last resort, you could try creating a `JFileChooser` object, calling the method, `setControlButtonsAreShown(boolean b)`, and passing in a value of `false`. This step creates a `JFileChooser` dialog without the "Open" and "Cancel" buttons, as shown in Figure 9-20.

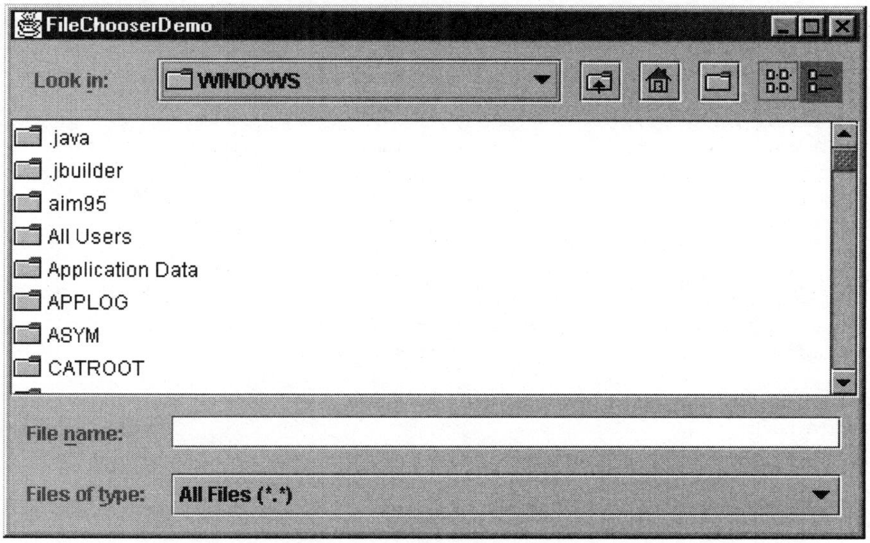

Figure 9-20. JFileChooser dialog without "Open" and "Cancel" buttons

However, creating this dialog requires you to create your own buttons and add them, along with your `JFileChooser` object, to another panel, allowing you to localize more of the dialog; the `Look in`, `File name`, and `Files of type` strings still cannot be localized.

JComboBox

As of the writing of this book, a bug exists for this component in the Swing package. When your `JComboBox` is editable, the selections do not obey the proper orientation. Example 9-11 illustrates this problem.

Example 9-11. Editable JComboBox Not Obeying Component Orientation

```
import java.awt.*;
import java.awt.event.*;
import javax.swing.*;

public class JComboBoxDemo extends JFrame {

  public JComboBoxDemo() {
    super("JComboBoxDemo");
```

Example 9-11. Editable JComboBox Not Obeying Component Orientation (continued)

```
    String [] items = {"Anthony", "Lorraine", "Marie"};
    JComboBox itemsComboBox = new JComboBox(items);
    itemsComboBox.setEditable(true);
    itemsComboBox.setMaximumRowCount(3);
    this.getContentPane().add(itemsComboBox);
    itemsComboBox.show();
    applyOrientation(this, ComponentOrientation.RIGHT_TO_LEFT);
    this.validate();
    this.repaint();
  }

  public static void main(String[] args) {
    JFrame frame = new JComboBoxDemo();
    frame.addWindowListener(new WindowAdapter() {
      public void windowClosing(WindowEvent e) {System.exit(0);}
    });

    frame.pack();
    frame.setVisible(true);
  }

  /*
  ** applyOrientation():
  ** Borrowed from SwingApplet demo!
  */
  private void applyOrientation(Component c, ComponentOrientation o)  {
    c.setComponentOrientation(o);

    if (c instanceof JMenu) {
      JMenu menu = (JMenu)c;
      int ncomponents = menu.getMenuComponentCount();
      for (int i = 0; i < ncomponents; ++i) {
        applyOrientation(menu.getMenuComponent(i), o);
      }
    } else if (c instanceof Container) {
      Container container = (Container)c;
      int ncomponents = container.getComponentCount();
      for (int i = 0; i < ncomponents; ++i) {
        applyOrientation(container.getComponent(i), o);
      }
    }
  }
}
```

Notice that the editable item and the scrollbar in Figure 9-21 obey the proper right-to-left orientation; however, the items in the pulldown selection are still aligned from left to right.

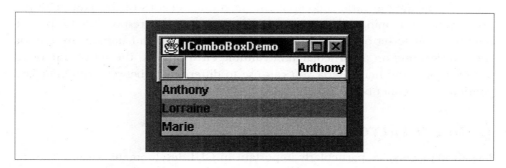

Figure 9-21. Component orientation is not followed if the JComboBox is editable

Be aware of this issue if your application uses internationalized text, especially text that runs right to left, in an editable JComboBox.

Localized Properties Files for Various Swing Components

This subsection is not meant to encourage tampering with the Java runtime archive files. We are merely detailing the circumstances when some of the various Swing components obtain default text strings.

If you look through the *rt.jar* file that ships with Java 2 SDK, Standard Edition, Version 1.3, you'll notice a few resource files in the *javax.swing.plaf.basic.resources* and *javax.swing.plaf.metal.resources* directories. In the basic resources directory, you should find the files *basic.properties*, *basic_ja. properties*, and *basic_zh.properties*. These files contain localized strings used by the JColorChooser, JFileChooser, and JOptionPane components for English, Japanese, and Chinese, respectively. Looking through Example 9-12, *basic.properties*, we see the strings used by JOptionPane.

Example 9-12. Strings from basic.properties

```
########### OPTION PANE STRINGS ############
OptionPane.yesButtonText=Yes
OptionPane.noButtonText=No
OptionPane.okButtonText=OK
OptionPane.cancelButtonText=Cancel
```

If you switch to the *javax.swing.plaf.metal.resources* directory, you'll notice *metal.properties*, *metal_ja.properties*, and *metal_zh.properties*. As with the Basic Look and Feel, Metal Look and Feel uses these files to localize strings for various components. Unlike the Basic Look and Feel, however, the only component using strings from these properties files is the JFileChooser. The Multi Look and Feel does not provide localized string resources for any of these components.

These properties files contain text reporting that Sun will address localization of these strings for the various components in future versions of the Java platform. For anyone developing software components, the vendor is responsible for providing an adequate set of localizations. Just as performance and stability are criteria used in deciding on a particular Java runtime environment, the set of supported locales is also another criteria you can use to differentiate between different Java runtime environments.

Using a Layout Manager

Layout managers are particularly important in GUI development because they allow you to position components within an application according to a scheme. Your application uses a layout manager whenever components are added to the container that uses a given layout manager. For example, the `BorderLayout` class allows you to position components in different regions of the screen designated as "North," "South," "East," "West," and "Center." Figure 9-22 demonstrates this layout manager.

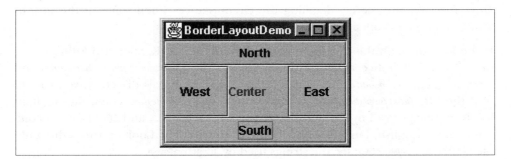

Figure 9-22. Components laid out using the BorderLayout layout manager

`FlowLayout` is one layout manager that obeys the component orientation settings in use. Example 9-13 shows how two buttons are laid out from right to left, using a flow layout manager.

Example 9-13. Using a FlowLayout

```
import java.awt.*;
import java.awt.event.*;
import javax.swing.*;

public class FlowLayoutDemo extends JFrame {
```

Example 9-13. Using a FlowLayout (continued)

```java
public FlowLayoutDemo() {
  super("FlowLayoutDemo");

  Container contentPane = getContentPane();
  contentPane.setLayout(new FlowLayout());
  contentPane.add(new JButton("OK"));
  contentPane.add(new JButton("Cancel"));

  applyOrientation(this, ComponentOrientation.RIGHT_TO_LEFT);
}

public static void main(String [] argv) {
  JFrame frame = new FlowLayoutDemo();
  frame.addWindowListener(new WindowAdapter() {
    public void windowClosing(WindowEvent e) {System.exit(0);}
  });

  frame.pack();
  frame.setVisible(true);
}

/*
** applyOrientation():
** Borrowed from SwingApplet demo!
*/
private void applyOrientation(Component c, ComponentOrientation o)  {
  c.setComponentOrientation(o);

  if (c instanceof JMenu) {
    JMenu menu = (JMenu)c;
    int ncomponents = menu.getMenuComponentCount();
    for (int i = 0; i < ncomponents; ++i) {
      applyOrientation(menu.getMenuComponent(i), o);
    }
  } else if (c instanceof Container) {
    Container container = (Container)c;
    int ncomponents = container.getComponentCount();
    for (int i = 0; i < ncomponents; ++i) {
      applyOrientation(container.getComponent(i), o);
    }
  }
}
}
```

Figure 9-23 shows that the buttons are in proper right-to-left order.

Layout Managers Without Component Orientation Support

BoxLayout, GridLayout, and GridBagLayout lack support for component orientation. Future versions of the Java platform will add this support, but as of Java 2 SDK

1.3, there was no support for component orientation in these classes. You can either use one of the other available layout managers, or, if you're really adventurous, you could write your own layout manager. For most applications, you should be able to develop a GUI that obeys proper component orientation for a given locale using the available layout managers.

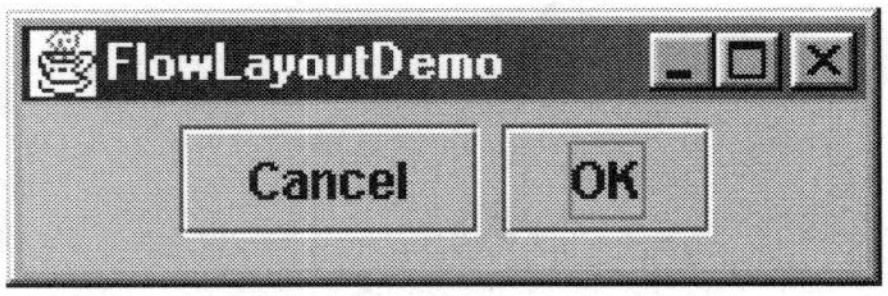

Figure 9-23. Buttons laid out from right to left using a flow layout

Copying, Cutting, and Pasting International Text

Copying, cutting, and pasting internationalized text between applications is more of a behind-the-scenes issue in terms of getting it to work correctly. Nonetheless, the ability to manipulate data in this way is a vital aspect of developing robust applications.

Copying, Cutting, and Pasting Within an Application

Example 9-14 shows how to copy and paste text within an application. Running Windows, you should be able to use the shortcut keystrokes, CTRL-C (Copy), CTRL-X (Cut), and CTRL-V (Paste) to copy, cut, and paste text within an application.

This example implements the ClipboardOwner interface that is part of the java.awt.datatransfer package. This interface defines a single method:

```
public void lostOwnership(Clipboard clipboard, Transferable contents)
```

This method is called when your application loses ownership of the clipboard. This loss occurs when another application writes to the clipboard. You get a reference to the Clipboard object that you no longer own and to the contents you had placed on the clipboard. You could buffer the content you get back or you could notify the user that the contents of the clipboard have changed.

Example 9-14. Copying and Pasting Internationalized Text Within an Application

```java
import java.awt.*;
import java.awt.datatransfer.*;
import java.awt.event.*;
import javax.swing.*;

public class CopyAndPasteDemo extends JFrame implements ClipboardOwner {

  String davidMessage = "David says, \"\u05E9\u05DC\u05D5\u05DD " +
      "\u05E2\u05D5\u05DC\u05DD\" \n";
  String andyMessage = "Andy also says, \"\u05E9\u05DC\u05D5\u05DD " +
      "\u05E2\u05D5\u05DC\u05DD\"";

  private Clipboard clipboard;

  public void lostOwnership(Clipboard clipboard, Transferable contents) {
    System.out.println("Lost clipboard ownership");
  }

  public CopyAndPasteDemo() {
    super("Copy And Paste Demonstration");

    clipboard = getToolkit().getSystemClipboard();

    GraphicsEnvironment.getLocalGraphicsEnvironment();
    Font font = new Font("LucidaSans", Font.PLAIN, 15);
    JTextArea textArea1 = new JTextArea(davidMessage + andyMessage, 5, 25);
    JTextArea textArea2 = new JTextArea("<Paste text here>", 5, 25);
    textArea1.setFont(font);
    textArea2.setFont(font);

    JPanel jPanel = new JPanel();
    jPanel.setLayout(new BoxLayout(jPanel,BoxLayout.Y_AXIS));
    jPanel.add(textArea1);
    jPanel.add(Box.createRigidArea(new Dimension(0,10)));
    jPanel.add(textArea2);

    getContentPane().add(jPanel, BorderLayout.CENTER);
  }

  public static void main(String[] args) {
    JFrame frame = new CopyAndPasteDemo();
    frame.addWindowListener(new WindowAdapter() {
      public void windowClosing(WindowEvent e) {System.exit(0);}
    });

    frame.pack();
    frame.setVisible(true);
  }
}
```

As you can see from Figure 9-24, we have selected the second sentence from the text area at the top of the screen and copied that sentence into the text area in the bottom of the screen.

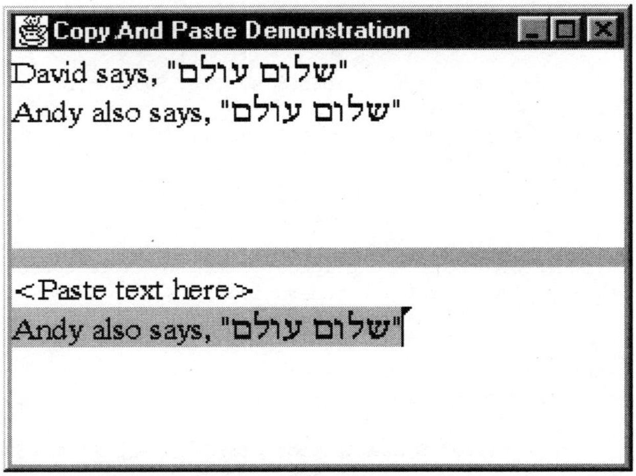

Figure 9-24. Demonstrating copy and paste of international text

Cutting and pasting text within an application also works correctly, as demonstrated in Figure 9-25.

Copying, Cutting, and Pasting Between Applications

There is no straightforward way to copy, cut, and paste international text between applications (i.e., between two different instances of your application in different virtual machines). Transferring international text works in an application that uses Drag and Drop (DnD). However, as of the Java 2 Runtime Environment, Standard Edition, Version 1.3 from Sun, if you use the clipboard, you cannot copy, cut, and paste international text between applications. This limitation exists because the clipboard and DnD use separate and independent data transfer implementations.[4] Sun will fix this problem in a later version of the Java Runtime Environment.

If you need to support the transfer of international text between instances of your application, one technique you could use is to write out the selection from a copy or cut operation to a temporary file. When the user selects the paste operation,

---

[4] Thanks to David Mendenhall of Sun Microsystems for providing valuable feedback on this issue.

read the data from the temporary file and paste it in the proper location. Note that this technique will not work with the Windows shortcut keystrokes, CTRL-C, CTRL-X, and CTRL-V, unless you override these keystrokes in your application. Example 9-15 demonstrates this technique.

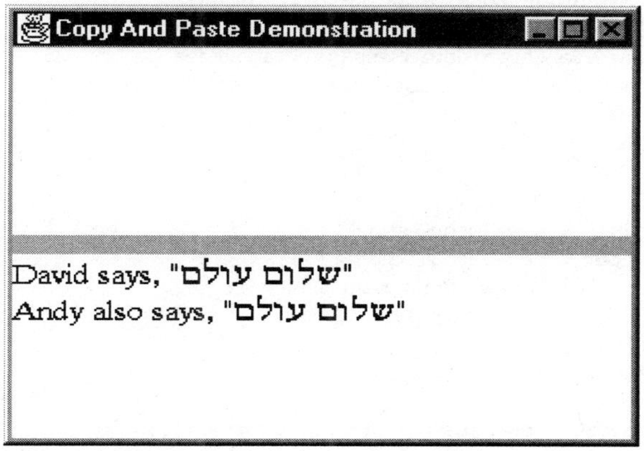

Figure 9-25. Demonstrating copy and paste of international text

Example 9-15. Cutting and Pasting Internationalized Text Between Applications

```java
import java.io.*;
import java.awt.*;
import java.awt.datatransfer.*;
import java.awt.event.*;
import javax.swing.*;

public class CutAndPasteDemo extends JFrame implements ClipboardOwner {

  private static String TEMPFILE = "CUTPASTE.TMP";

  String davidMessage = "David says, \"\u05E9\u05DC\u05D5\u05DD " +
      "\u05E2\u05D5\u05DC\u05DD\" \n";
  String andyMessage = "Andy also says, \"\u05E9\u05DC\u05D5\u05DD " +
      "\u05E2\u05D5\u05DC\u05DD\"";

  private Clipboard clipboard;

  public void lostOwnership(Clipboard clipboard, Transferable contents) {
    System.out.println("Lost clipboard ownership");
  }

  JTextArea textArea1;
  JTextArea textArea2;
```

Example 9-15. Cutting and Pasting Internationalized Text Between Applications (continued)

```
public CutAndPasteDemo() {
  super("Cut And Paste Demonstration");

  clipboard = getToolkit().getSystemClipboard();

  GraphicsEnvironment.getLocalGraphicsEnvironment();
  Font font = new Font("LucidaSans", Font.PLAIN, 15);
  textArea1 = new JTextArea(davidMessage + andyMessage, 5, 25);
  textArea2 = new JTextArea("<Paste text here>", 5, 25);
  textArea1.setFont(font);
  textArea2.setFont(font);

  JPanel jPanel = new JPanel();
  JMenuBar jMenuBar = new JMenuBar();
  JMenuItem cutItem = new JMenuItem("Cut");
  JMenuItem pasteItem = new JMenuItem("Paste");
  JMenu jMenu = new JMenu("Edit");
  jMenu.add(cutItem);
  jMenu.add(pasteItem);

  cutItem.addActionListener(new CutActionListener());
  pasteItem.addActionListener(new PasteActionListener());

  jMenuBar.add(jMenu);
  jPanel.add(jMenuBar);

  jPanel.setLayout(new BoxLayout(jPanel,BoxLayout.Y_AXIS));
  jPanel.add(textArea1);
  jPanel.add(Box.createRigidArea(new Dimension(0,10)));
  jPanel.add(textArea2);

  getContentPane().add(jPanel, BorderLayout.CENTER);
}

class CutActionListener implements ActionListener {

  public void actionPerformed (ActionEvent event) {
    try {
      if (textArea1.getSelectedText() != null) {
        BufferedWriter bw = new BufferedWriter(new OutputStreamWriter(new
            FileOutputStream(TEMPFILE), "UTF8"));
        bw.write(textArea1.getSelectedText());
        bw.close();
        textArea1.replaceSelection("");
      }
    } catch (Exception e) {
      e.printStackTrace();
    }
  }
}
```

Example 9-15. Cutting and Pasting Internationalized Text Between Applications (continued)

```
class PasteActionListener implements ActionListener {

  public void actionPerformed (ActionEvent event) {
    try {
      BufferedReader br = new BufferedReader(new InputStreamReader(new
          FileInputStream(TEMPFILE), "UTF8"));
      StringBuffer text = new StringBuffer();
      String tempString;
      while ((tempString = br.readLine()) != null) {
        text.append(tempString);
      }
      br.close();
      textArea2.replaceSelection(text.toString());
    } catch (Exception e) {
    }
  }
}

public static void main(String[] args) {
  JFrame frame = new CutAndPasteDemo();
  frame.addWindowListener(new WindowAdapter() {
    public void windowClosing(WindowEvent e) {System.exit(0);}
  });

  frame.pack();
  frame.setVisible(true);
}
}
```

Figure 9-26 shows that text from the application in the figure's upper-left portion was pasted correctly into the application in the figure's bottom-right portion.

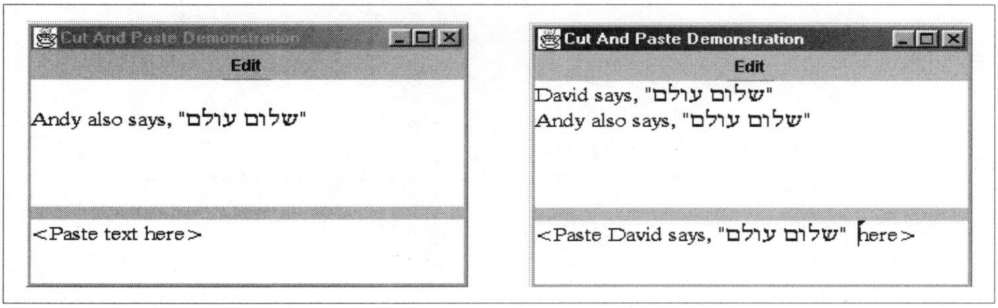

Figure 9-26. Demonstrating Cut and Paste Between Applications

A Simple Example

Example 9-16 demonstrates a simple multilingual application that compiles much of what is covered in this book into a properly internationalized GUI. The languages on the "Language" menu are the names of languages supported by the application, in the currently selected locale, collated correctly for that language. When a new language is selected from the menu, the components within the window change to reflect the new locale.

Figures 9-27 and 9-28 demonstrate Example 9-16 when run in English and in Hebrew, respectively.

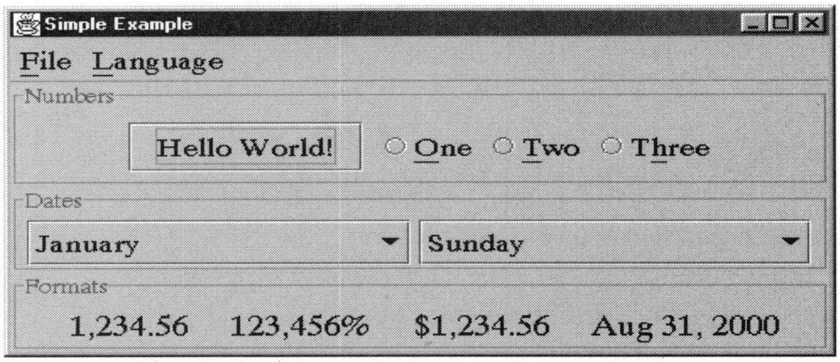

Figure 9-27. Example 9-16 when run in English

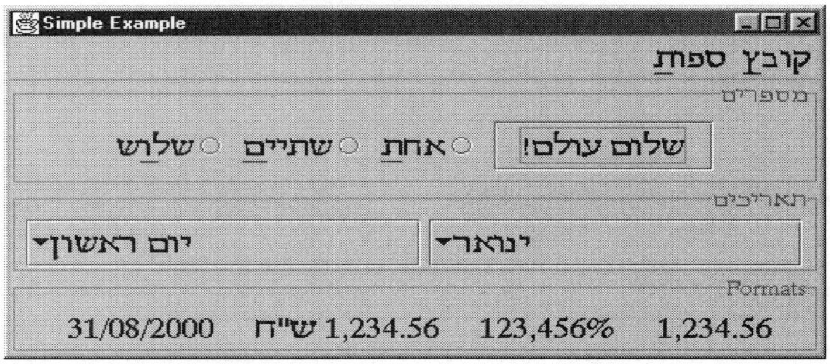

Figure 9-28. Example 9-16 when run in Hebrew[5]

---

[5] The mnemonic keys (underlined characters on the menu) are incorrect in the Hebrew version. Though the correct characters are specified in the *.properties* file (`FileMenuMnemonic` and `Language-MenuMnemonic`). The first, right-most character should be underlined, but the algorithm is obviously broken and seems to be starting from the left!

Example 9-16. Displaying Items That Adhere to Locale-Specific Conventions and Formatting

```java
import java.awt.*;
import java.awt.event.*;
import java.text.*;
import java.util.*;
import javax.swing.*;
import javax.swing.border.TitledBorder;

public class SimpleExample extends JPanel {

  static JFrame frame;
  static Font smallFont;
  static Font mediumFont;
  static Font bigFont;

  private ResourceBundle resources;
  private ComponentOrientation co;

  private static void applyComponentOrientation(Component c, ComponentOrientation o) {

    c.setComponentOrientation(o);

    if (c instanceof JMenu) {
      JMenu menu = (JMenu)c;
      int ncomponents = menu.getMenuComponentCount();
      for (int i = 0 ; i < ncomponents ; ++i) {
        applyComponentOrientation( menu.getMenuComponent(i), o );
      }
    } else if (c instanceof Container) {
      Container container = (Container)c;
      int ncomponents = container.getComponentCount();
      for (int i = 0 ; i < ncomponents ; ++i) {
        applyComponentOrientation( container.getComponent(i), o );
      }
    }
  }

  private void loadResources() {
    try {
      resources = ResourceBundle.getBundle("resources.Simple",
                      Locale.getDefault());
    } catch (MissingResourceException mre) {
      mre.printStackTrace();
      System.exit(1);
    }
  }

  private static JFrame getFrame() {
    return frame;
  }
```

Example 9-16. Displaying Various That Adhere to Locale-Specific
Conventions and Formatting (continued)

```java
public SimpleExample() {

    // Load our resource bundle
    loadResources();

    JRadioButton oneButton, twoButton, threeButton;
    JButton button;

    GraphicsEnvironment ge = GraphicsEnvironment.getLocalGraphicsEnvironment();
    ge.getAllFonts();

    // Setup the fonts
    smallFont = new Font("Bitstream Cyberbit", Font.PLAIN, 14);
    mediumFont = new Font("Bitstream Cyberbit", Font.PLAIN, 18);
    bigFont = new Font("Bitstream Cyberbit", Font.PLAIN, 20);

    co = ComponentOrientation.getOrientation(Locale.getDefault());

    setLayout(new BoxLayout(this,BoxLayout.Y_AXIS));
    String language = Locale.getDefault().getLanguage();

    // Create the buttons
    button = new JButton(resources.getString("Hello"));
    button.setToolTipText(resources.getString("HelloToolTip"));
    button.setFont(mediumFont);

    // Setup the buttons
    oneButton = new JRadioButton(resources.getString("One"));
    oneButton.setFont(mediumFont);
    oneButton.setMnemonic(resources.getString("OneMnemonic").charAt(0));
    oneButton.setHorizontalAlignment(JButton.TRAILING);
    oneButton.setHorizontalTextPosition(JButton.TRAILING);

    twoButton = new JRadioButton(resources.getString("Two"));
    twoButton.setFont(mediumFont);
    twoButton.setMnemonic(resources.getString("TwoMnemonic").charAt(0));
    twoButton.setHorizontalAlignment(JButton.TRAILING);
    twoButton.setHorizontalTextPosition(JButton.TRAILING);

    threeButton = new JRadioButton(resources.getString("Three"));
    threeButton.setFont(mediumFont);
    threeButton.setMnemonic(resources.getString("ThreeMnemonic").charAt(0));
    threeButton.setHorizontalAlignment(JButton.TRAILING);
    threeButton.setHorizontalTextPosition(JButton.TRAILING);

    // Group the radio buttons
    ButtonGroup group = new ButtonGroup();
    group.add(oneButton);
    group.add(twoButton);
    group.add(threeButton);
```

Example 9-16. Displaying Items That Adhere to Locale-Specific Conventions and Formatting (continued)

```
// Register a listener for the radio buttons
RadioListener myListener = new RadioListener();
oneButton.addActionListener(myListener);
twoButton.addActionListener(myListener);
threeButton.addActionListener(myListener);

// Setup the button panel
JPanel buttonPanel = new JPanel();
buttonPanel.setMaximumSize(new Dimension(Short.MAX_VALUE,100));
TitledBorder tb = new TitledBorder(resources.getString("Numbers"));
tb.setTitleFont(smallFont);
tb.setTitleJustification(
    co.isLeftToRight() ? TitledBorder.LEFT : TitledBorder.RIGHT);

buttonPanel.setBorder(tb);
buttonPanel.setLayout(new FlowLayout());
buttonPanel.add(button);
buttonPanel.add(oneButton);
buttonPanel.add(twoButton);
buttonPanel.add(threeButton);

add(buttonPanel, BorderLayout.CENTER);

// Setup the date panel
JPanel datePanel = new JPanel();
datePanel.setMaximumSize(new Dimension(Short.MAX_VALUE,100));
tb = new TitledBorder(resources.getString("Dates"));
tb.setTitleFont(smallFont);
tb.setTitleJustification(
    co.isLeftToRight() ? TitledBorder.LEFT : TitledBorder.RIGHT);

datePanel.setBorder(tb);
datePanel.setLayout(new BoxLayout(datePanel,BoxLayout.X_AXIS));
datePanel.add(Box.createRigidArea(new Dimension(5,1)));

DateFormatSymbols dfs = new DateFormatSymbols();

JComboBox months = new JComboBox(dfs.getMonths());
months.setFont(mediumFont);

String weekDays[] = dfs.getWeekdays();
JComboBox days = new JComboBox();
days.setFont(mediumFont);

// Determine what day is the first day of the week
GregorianCalendar cal = new GregorianCalendar();

int firstDayOfWeek = cal.getFirstDayOfWeek();
int dayOfWeek;
```

Example 9-16. Displaying Items That Adhere to Locale-Specific
Conventions and Formatting (continued)

```java
for (dayOfWeek = firstDayOfWeek; dayOfWeek < weekDays.length; dayOfWeek++)
  days.addItem(weekDays[dayOfWeek]);

for (dayOfWeek = 0; dayOfWeek < firstDayOfWeek; dayOfWeek++)
  days.addItem(weekDays[dayOfWeek]);

if (!co.isLeftToRight()) {
  datePanel.add(days);
  datePanel.add(Box.createRigidArea(new Dimension(5,1)));

  datePanel.add(months);
  datePanel.add(Box.createRigidArea(new Dimension(5,1)));
} else {
  datePanel.add(months);
  datePanel.add(Box.createRigidArea(new Dimension(5,1)));

  datePanel.add(days);
  datePanel.add(Box.createRigidArea(new Dimension(5,1)));
}
add(datePanel);

// Setup the formatting panel
JPanel formatPanel = new JPanel();
formatPanel.setMaximumSize(new Dimension(Short.MAX_VALUE,100));
tb = new TitledBorder(resources.getString("Formats"));
tb.setTitleFont(smallFont);
tb.setTitleJustification(co.isLeftToRight() ?
      TitledBorder.LEFT : TitledBorder.RIGHT);

formatPanel.setBorder(tb);
formatPanel.setLayout(new BoxLayout(formatPanel,BoxLayout.X_AXIS));
formatPanel.add(Box.createRigidArea(new Dimension(5,1)));

double theNumber = 1234.56;
NumberFormat nFormat = NumberFormat.getInstance();
NumberFormat cFormat = NumberFormat.getCurrencyInstance();
NumberFormat pFormat = NumberFormat.getPercentInstance();
DateFormat dFormat = DateFormat.getDateInstance();

JLabel numberLabel = new JLabel(nFormat.format(theNumber));
numberLabel.setForeground(Color.black);
numberLabel.setFont(bigFont);

JLabel percentLabel = new JLabel(pFormat.format(theNumber));
percentLabel.setForeground(Color.black);
percentLabel.setFont(bigFont);
```

Example 9-16. Displaying Items That Adhere to Locale-Specific
Conventions and Formatting (continued)

```java
    JLabel currencyLabel = new JLabel(cFormat.format(theNumber));
    currencyLabel.setForeground(Color.black);
    currencyLabel.setFont(bigFont);

    JLabel dateLabel = new JLabel(dFormat.format(new Date()));
    dateLabel.setForeground(Color.black);
    dateLabel.setFont(bigFont);

    formatPanel.add(Box.createRigidArea(new Dimension(25,1)));

    if (co.isLeftToRight()) {
      formatPanel.add(numberLabel);
      formatPanel.add(Box.createRigidArea(new Dimension(25,1)));
      formatPanel.add(percentLabel);
      formatPanel.add(Box.createRigidArea(new Dimension(25,1)));
      formatPanel.add(currencyLabel);
      formatPanel.add(Box.createRigidArea(new Dimension(25,1)));
      formatPanel.add(dateLabel);
    } else {
      formatPanel.add(dateLabel);
      formatPanel.add(Box.createRigidArea(new Dimension(25,1)));
      formatPanel.add(currencyLabel);
      formatPanel.add(Box.createRigidArea(new Dimension(25,1)));
      formatPanel.add(percentLabel);
      formatPanel.add(Box.createRigidArea(new Dimension(25,1)));
      formatPanel.add(numberLabel);
    }
    formatPanel.add(Box.createRigidArea(new Dimension(25,1)));

    add(formatPanel);
  }

  public JMenuBar createMenuBar() {
    JMenuBar menuBar = new JMenuBar();

    JMenu file =
      (JMenu) menuBar.add(new JMenu(resources.getString("FileMenu")));
    file.setFont(mediumFont);
    file.setMnemonic(resources.getString("FileMenuMnemonic").charAt(0));

    JMenuItem exitItem = (JMenuItem)
    file.add(new JMenuItem(resources.getString("FileMenuExit")));
    exitItem.setFont(mediumFont);
    exitItem.setMnemonic(resources.getString("FileMenuExitMnemonic").charAt(0));
    exitItem.addActionListener(new ActionListener() {
        public void actionPerformed(ActionEvent e) {
          System.exit(0);
        }
      });
```

Example 9-16. Displaying Items That Adhere to Locale-Specific
Conventions and Formatting (continued)

```java
    menuBar.add(new LocaleChanger());

    return menuBar;
  }

  public void reloadResources() {
    try {
      resources = ResourceBundle.getBundle("resources.Simple", Locale.getDefault());
    } catch (MissingResourceException mre) {
      mre.printStackTrace();
      System.exit(1);
    }
  }

  /**
   * An ActionListener that listens to the radio buttons
   */
  class RadioListener implements ActionListener {
    public void actionPerformed(ActionEvent e) {
      String lnfName = e.getActionCommand();

      Object[] options = { resources.getString("OK"), resources.getString("CANCEL") };
      Object[] arguments = { new Integer(3), lnfName };

      JOptionPane.showOptionDialog(null,
      MessageFormat.format(resources.getString("WarningMsg"), arguments),
          resources.getString("WarningTitle"),
          JOptionPane.DEFAULT_OPTION,
          JOptionPane.WARNING_MESSAGE,
          null, options, options[0]);
      try {
      } catch (Exception exc) {
        JRadioButton button = (JRadioButton)e.getSource();
        button.setEnabled(false);
      }
    }
  }

  /**
   * A class to change the locale for the application
   */
  class LocaleChanger extends JMenu implements ItemListener {

    public LocaleChanger() {
      super();
      setText(resources.getString("LanguageMenu"));
      setFont(mediumFont);
      setMnemonic(resources.getString("LanguageMenuMnemonic").charAt(0));
```

Example 9-16. Displaying Items That Adhere to Locale-Specific
Conventions and Formatting (continued)

```java
        ButtonGroup langGroup = new ButtonGroup();
        String language = Locale.getDefault().getLanguage();

        // Sort the language names according to the rules specific to each locale
        RuleBasedCollator rbc = (RuleBasedCollator)Collator.getInstance();
        ArrayList al = new ArrayList();
        al.add(resources.getString("Arabic"));
        al.add(resources.getString("Chinese"));
        al.add(resources.getString("English"));
        al.add(resources.getString("German"));
        al.add(resources.getString("Italian"));
        al.add(resources.getString("French"));
        al.add(resources.getString("Hebrew"));
        al.add(resources.getString("Japanese"));
        al.add(resources.getString("Russian"));

        Collections.sort(al, rbc);

        String langName = Locale.getDefault().getDisplayLanguage();
        for (int i = 0; i < al.size(); i++) {
          JRadioButtonMenuItem mi;
          mi = (JRadioButtonMenuItem)
            add(new JRadioButtonMenuItem((String)al.get(i)));
          mi.setFont(mediumFont);
          if (langName.equalsIgnoreCase((String)al.get(i)))
            mi.setSelected(true);
          mi.addItemListener(this);
          langGroup.add(mi);
        }
      }

      public void itemStateChanged(ItemEvent e) {
        JRadioButtonMenuItem rb = (JRadioButtonMenuItem) e.getSource();
        if (rb.isSelected()) {
          String selected = rb.getText();
          if (selected.equals(resources.getString("Arabic"))) {
            Locale.setDefault(new Locale("ar", "EG"));
            co = ComponentOrientation.RIGHT_TO_LEFT;
          } else if (selected.equals(resources.getString("English"))) {
            Locale.setDefault(Locale.US);
            co = ComponentOrientation.LEFT_TO_RIGHT;
          } else if (selected.equals(resources.getString("German"))) {
            Locale.setDefault(Locale.GERMANY);
            co = ComponentOrientation.LEFT_TO_RIGHT;
          } else if (selected.equals(resources.getString("Italian"))) {
            Locale.setDefault(Locale.ITALY);
            co = ComponentOrientation.LEFT_TO_RIGHT;
          } else if (selected.equals(resources.getString("French"))) {
            Locale.setDefault(Locale.FRANCE);
            co = ComponentOrientation.LEFT_TO_RIGHT;
```

*Example 9-16. Displaying Items That Adhere to Locale-Specific
Conventions and Formatting (continued)*

```
    } else if (selected.equals(resources.getString("Hebrew"))) {
      Locale.setDefault(new Locale("iw", "IL"));
      co = ComponentOrientation.RIGHT_TO_LEFT;
    } else if (selected.equals(resources.getString("Chinese"))) {
      Locale.setDefault(Locale.CHINA);
      co = ComponentOrientation.LEFT_TO_RIGHT;
    } else if (selected.equals(resources.getString("Japanese"))) {
      Locale.setDefault(Locale.JAPAN);
      co = ComponentOrientation.LEFT_TO_RIGHT;
    } else if (selected.equals(resources.getString("Russian"))) {
      Locale.setDefault(new Locale("ru", "RU"));
      co = ComponentOrientation.LEFT_TO_RIGHT;
    }
  }

  SimpleExample panel = new SimpleExample();
  SimpleExample.frame.setVisible(false);
  SimpleExample.frame.getContentPane().removeAll();
  SimpleExample.frame.setJMenuBar(panel.createMenuBar());
  SimpleExample.frame.getContentPane().add("Center", panel);
  SimpleExample.frame.pack();
  SimpleExample.frame.show();
  applyComponentOrientation(SimpleExample.getFrame(), co);
  }
}

public static void main(String [] argv) {

  SimpleExample panel = new SimpleExample();

  frame = new JFrame("Simple Example");
  frame.addWindowListener(new WindowAdapter() {
    public void windowClosing(WindowEvent e) {System.exit(0);}
  });
  frame.setJMenuBar(panel.createMenuBar());
  frame.getContentPane().add("Center", panel);
  frame.pack();
  frame.setVisible(true);
  }
}
```

We've also included a few of the sample *.properties* files required to run this example, as shown in Example 9-17. Again, you can find the source code to the examples in this book online at *http://www.oreilly.com/catalog/javaint/*.

Example 9-17. Simple.Properties

```
Hello = Hello World!
HelloToolTip = Hey there!
One = One
OneMnemonic = o
Two = Two
TwoMnemonic = t
Three = Three
ThreeMnemonic = h
Dates = Dates
Numbers = Numbers
Formats = Formats

# Menus
FileMenu = File
FileMenuMnemonic = F

FileMenuExit = Exit
FileMenuExitMnemonic = x

LanguageMenu = Language
LanguageMenuMnemonic = L

Arabic = Arabic
Chinese = Chinese
English = English
French = French
German = German
Hebrew = Hebrew
Italian = Italian
Japanese = Japanese
Korean = Korean
Russian = Russian

WarningMsg = There were {0,number,integer} spelling mistakes in file {1}
WarningTitle = Warning
OK = OK
CANCEL = CANCEL
```

Example 9-18 is a localized *.properties* file for German.

Example 9-18. Simple_de.properties

```
Hello = Guten label Welt!
HelloToolTip = Hallo!
One = Eins
OneMnemonic = e
Two = Zwei
TwoMnemonic = z
Three = Drei
ThreeMnemonic = d
Dates = Daten
```

Example 9-18. Simple_de.properties (continued)

```
Numbers = Anzahlen

# Menus
FileMenu = Datei
FileMenuMnemonic = D

FileMenuExit = Ende
FileMenuExitMnemonic = e

LanguageMenu = Sprachen
LanguageMenuMnemonic = S

Arabic = Arabisch
Chinese = Chinesisch
English = Englisch
French = Franz\u00f6sisch
German = Deutsch
Hebrew = Hebr\u00e4isch
Russian = Russisch
Japanese = Japanisch

WarningMsg = Datei {1} enth\u00e4lt {0,number,integer} Rechtschreibfehler.
WarningTitle = Warnung
OK = OK
CANCEL = CANCEL
```

Example 9-19 is a localized *.properties* file for Hebrew.

Example 9-19. Simple_iw.properties

```
Hello = \u05e9\u05dc\u05d5\u05dd \u05e2\u05d5\u05dc\u05dd!
HelloToolTip = \u05e9\u05dc\u05d5\u05dd
One = \u05d0\u05d7\u05ea
OneMnemonic = \u05d0
Two = \u05e9\u05ea\u05d9\u05d9\u05dd
TwoMnemonic = \u05e9
Three = \u05e9\u05dc\u05d5\u05e9
ThreeMnemonic = \u05dc
Dates = \u05ea\u05d0\u05e8\u05d9\u05db\u05d9\u05dd
Numbers = \u05de\u05e1\u05e4\u05e8\u05d9\u05dd

# Menus
FileMenu = \u05e7\u05d5\u05d1\u05e5
FileMenuMnemonic = \u05e7

FileMenuExit = \u05d9\u05e6\u05d9\u05d0\u05d4
FileMenuExitMnemonic = \u05d9

LanguageMenu = \u05e1\u05e4\u05d5\u05ea
LanguageMenuMnemonic = \u05e1

Arabic = \u05e2\u05e8\u05d0\u05d1\u05d9\u05ea
```

Example 9-19. Simple_iw.properties (continued)

```
Chinese = \u05e1\u05d9\u05e0\u05d9\u05ea
English = \u05d0\u05e0\u05d2\u05dc\u05d9\u05ea
French = \u05e6\u05e8\u05e4\u05ea\u05d9\u05ea
German = \u05d2\u05e8\u05de\u05e0\u05d9\u05ea
Hebrew = \u05e2\u05d1\u05e8\u05d9\u05ea
Russian = \u05e8\u05d5\u05e1\u05d9\u05ea
Italian = \u05d0\u05d9\u05d8\u05dc\u05e7\u05d9\u05ea
Japanese = \u05d9\u05e4\u05e0\u05d9\u05ea
```

Example 9-20 is a localized *.properties* file for Japanese.

Example 9-20. Simple_ja.properties

```
Hello = \u4eca\u65e5\u306f
HelloToolTip = \u4eca\u65e5\u306f
One = \u4e00
OneMnemonic = \u4e00
Two = \u4e8c
TwoMnemonic = \u4e8c
Three = \u4e09
ThreeMnemonic = \u4e09
Numbers=\u6570\u5b57
Dates=\u65e5\u6642

# Menus

FileMenu = \u30d5\u30a1\u30a4\u30eb (F)
FileMenuMnemonic = F

FileMenuExit = \u51fa\u5165\u308a\u53e3 (x)
FileMenuExitMnemonic = x

LanguageMenu = \u8a00\u8a9e (L)
LanguageMenuMnemonic = L

Arabic = \u30a2\u30e9\u30d3\u30a2\u8a9e
Chinese= \u4e2d\u56fd\u8a9e
English= \u82f1\u8a9e
French= \u30d5\u30e9\u30f3\u30b9\u8a9e
German= \u30c9\u30a4\u30c4\u8a9e
Hebrew = \u30d2\u30d6\u30e9\u30a4\u8a9e
Italian = \u4f0a\u8a9e
Japanese = \u65e5\u672c\u8a9e
Korean = \u97d3\u56fd\u8a9e
Russian = \u30ed\u30b7\u30a2\u8a9e

WarningMsg = \u30d5\u30a1\u30a4\u30eb\u306b\u306f
{0,number,integer}\u30a2\u30a4\u30c6\u30e0\u304c\u3042\u308a\u307e\u3059.
WarningTitle = \u8b66\u543f
OK = \u826f\u3044
CANCEL = \u53d6\u308a\u6d88\u3057
```

10

Input Methods

Most of the world's writing systems are composed of a relatively small set of characters, so they are easily displayed in a standard way on a computer keyboard. But some scripts, such as the East Asian ideographic system, have tens of thousands of individual characters. Imagine what it would be like trying to put all these characters on a keyboard! Worse yet, imagine what it would be like to a user trying to remember where all the characters were located! Obviously, we need a better approach for inputting text for these types of languages. The answer is a tool called an Input Method Editor (IME), also known as an Input Method.

This chapter provides a general overview of input methods and then moves quickly into the topic of writing input methods in Java. While Java 2 SDK, Standard Edition, Version 1.2 provided support for components to receive input from third party input methods, only after the release of Java 2 SDK, Standard Edition, Version 1.3 could input methods be written in Java. This chapter focuses on how to write input methods in Java; therefore, all examples are based on the Java 2 Platform, Standard Edition, Version 1.3.

What Are Input Methods?

Input methods are applications or software components that convert users' keystrokes into symbols, characters, or words. As each character is typed, the IME tries to determine what symbol the user actually wants to display. This process is known as *composition*. Typically, characters are keyed in phonetically, and the IME uses a dictionary lookup to display the closest matches. For example, to enter 日本語 (*nihongo*), the Japanese word for "Japanese language," we would type the word into the IME as it is pronounced, "ni hon go." Table 10-1 shows how the display changes as the keystrokes are entered. Since there is usually more than one correct result for any given pronunciation, pressing the spacebar tells the IME to choose the next match. Most IMEs display a scrollable list of possible matches if the spacebar is pressed more than once. To accept a match, the user typically presses the return key, at which point control is returned to the underlying application.

Table 10-1. Entering "nihongo" into a Japanese IME

Keystrokes	Display
n	n
ni	に
nih	に h
niho	にほ
nihon	にほ n
nihong	にほん g
nihongo	にほんご
nihongo[SPACE]	日本語
nihongo[SPACE][SPACE]	日本後

Input methods are available commercially from several vendors. Microsoft's Global IMEs (available for free download from Microsoft for the Windows platforms) are designed to work specifically with versions of Windows that were not designed to support the Asian languages (i.e., they allow Japanese text to be entered on a U.S. version of Windows).[1]

NOTE   Microsoft's Global IMEs are problematic because they only work with a limited set of applications that are designed to support them. The Global IME doesn't plug into the standard Input Method Manager in Windows, but uses its own API instead. When a Global IME is used with an application that does not support the Global IME API, the IME does not make itself available to the user. No support currently exists for Global IMEs in Java. Support is expected in future versions of the Java 2 Platform.

We talk about the Global IMEs here because they provide a good reference for readers who are unfamiliar with input methods. To gain a better understanding of how input methods work, we recommend downloading one and trying it. Figure 10-1 shows what the Global IME for Japanese control panel looks like when it is

---

[1] *http://www.microsoft.com/Windows/ie/Features/ime.asp*

selected from the taskbar. The menu shown allows users to choose which Japanese writing system they would like to use to spell the word phonetically (hiragana, katakana or rōmaji).

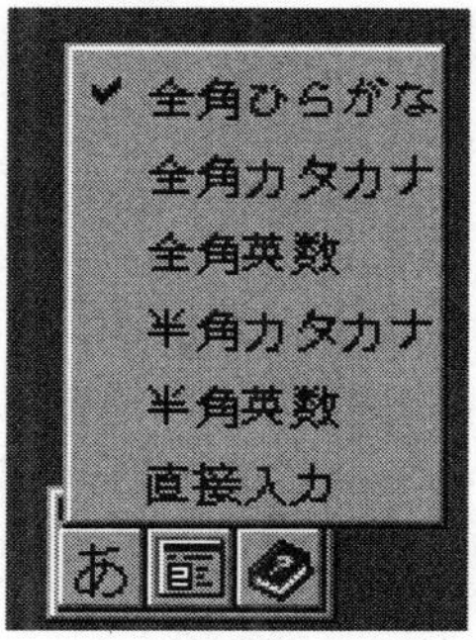

Figure 10-1. Microsoft's Global IME for Japanese control panel

Figure 10-2 shows the scrollable list that appears when typing *nihongo* into the Global IME for Japanese.

Figure 10-2. IME scrollable list

What Is the Java Input Method Framework?

The Java Input Method Framework supports APIs for two separate capabilities. The first capability is the Input Method Client API. Developers of text editing components wishing to support the use of input methods should use this interface. The second capability provided by the framework is the Input Method Engine Service

Provider Interface (SPI). Developers wishing to build their own input methods should use this interface. The client API has been available since Java 2 SDK, Standard Edition, Version 1.2, and the engine SPI has been available since Version 1.3. In this chapter, we summarize how to use the Input Method Engine SPI.

Why Use Java Input Methods?

So why would we want to use input methods written in Java? What's wrong with using input methods provided by Microsoft or other vendors? You might want to provide Java input methods to your end users for three reasons. First, if you provide a truly internationalized Java application, you can't predict what OS the end user will run. In particular, you won't know what language the OS was designed to support. Input methods are usually packaged with East Asian versions of operating systems or can be purchased as add-ons. Depending on the operating system vendor, input methods may not be provided with versions of the OS not designed for East Asian markets. To provide a complete solution, you should make sure that users have a way to enter text into your application. Providing your own input method is one guarantee.

Second, the input methods available for Microsoft's operating systems and Mac OS are typically more robust than those available for Unix. Implementing input methods in Java guarantees that the same features will be available across all platforms.

A third reason to develop your own input method is that you might want to provide input for languages that don't traditionally use IMEs. Input methods can be developed for all types of reasons, not just to support input of East Asian ideographs. For example, you might want to develop an input method that allows a user to enter Arabic text phonetically using a Latin keyboard.

Key Features of the Java Input Method Engine SPI

The Input Method Engine SPI allows developers to create their own input methods written entirely in Java. The SPI provides the following features:

- Input methods are packaged as Java extensions and are available to any application using the Java runtime.

- No recompilation of applications is needed to support new input methods.

- The SPI provides an interface that lets input methods interact with different text components via the framework. The framework is responsible for understanding differences between the text components.

- Input methods are platform independent. Complying with the "Write Once, Run Anywhere" model, the SPI allows input methods to be developed once and to run on any platform that hosts a Java runtime.

- Though input methods are typically used for East Asian languages, the SPI provides the flexibility for development of input methods to support any language.

- The SPI is input-device independent; input methods could be written to work with voice or handwriting recognition systems.

Selecting Input Methods

The input method framework allows selection of an input method either programmatically or through a user interface. A text editing component, also referred to as a *client component,* can call `InputContext.selectInputMethod()` to invoke an input method for a specific locale. The input method framework selects an input method whose `InputMethodDescriptor.getAvailableLocales()` returns the specified locale as one of its supported locales. If no installed input methods support the requested locale, the call to `InputContext.selectInputMethod()` returns `false`.

Typically, a user selects an input method through the user interface. The mechanism by which this is accomplished is implementation dependent; however, we explain how this selection is made in Sun's Java Runtime Environment. When one or more input methods are installed into the extension directory, a **Select Input Method** menu appears on the Windows System or Motif Window menu, as shown in Figure 10-3. Clicking on this menu causes a pop-up menu that shows the list of installed input methods to appear. Input methods that support more than one locale have a submenu that allows selection of the specific locale for that input method, as shown in Figure 10-4.

Using the Input Method Engine SPI

To build an input method, you must write classes that implement the interfaces defined in the `java.awt.im.spi` package. The two interfaces that you must implement are:

```
java.awt.im.spi.InputMethod
java.awt.im.spi.InputMethodDescriptor
```

The class files must then be packaged with a special file that tells the input method framework where to find the input method. In the rest of this chapter, we describe the essentials for writing the classes for each interface, and how to package and install the resulting input method.

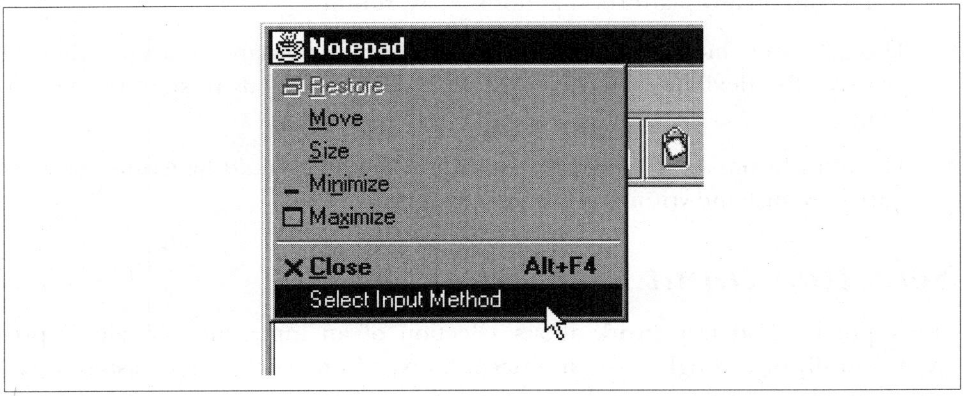

Figure 10-3. Selecting an input method

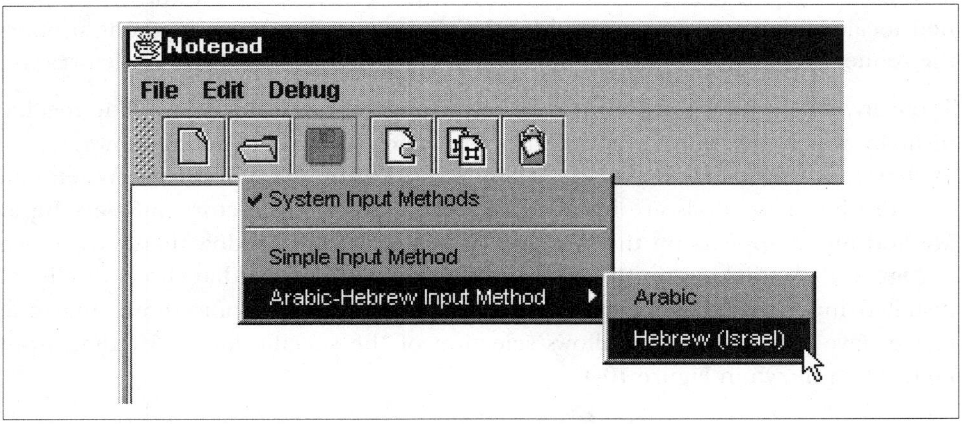

Figure 10-4. Selecting the input method's locale

java.awt.im.spi.InputMethodDescriptor

The input method framework becomes aware of each input method's capabilities through its associated InputMethodDescriptor. When an input method is selected (see the section "Selecting Input Methods" earlier in this chapter), the input method framework calls methods on the InputMethodDescriptor to learn more about it.

The input method framework determines the input method's name by calling `get-InputMethodDisplayName(Locale inputLocale, Locale displayLanguage)`. The input method can return a locale specific name by checking the `displayLanguage` parameter's value. The following code snippet demonstrates how to return such a name:

```
public String getInputMethodDisplayName(Locale inputLocale,
                                        Locale displayLanguage) {
  if (displayLanguage.equals(Locale.FRANCE)) {
    return "Simple Méthode D'Entrée";
  } else {
    return "Simple Input Method";
  }
}
```

When the user clicks on the **Select Input Method** menu, as shown in Figure 10-3, the name returned by `getInputMethodDisplayName()` subsequently appears on the next menu.

The member function `getAvailableLocales()` should return all locales the input method supports. When the user selects this input method from the **Select Input Method** menu, a submenu appears, allowing users to select which locale they want if more than one locale is returned in the array. In the following code snippet, the input method supports two locales:

```
public Locale[] getAvailableLocales() {
  Locale[] locales = { Locale.FRANCE, Locale.GERMANY };
  return locales;
}
```

Locale names are localized to the default locale for the application. In other words, if the input method supports French and German, as in our code sample, and the default locale for the application is set to French, then the locales displayed would appear as "français (France)" and "allemand (Allemagne)," as shown in Figure 10-5.

As the developer, you have no control over the translation of the displayed locale names. The name is the string returned by `Locale.getDisplayName()`. If the resource bundle distributed with your Java Runtime Environment for the applications default locale does not have a translation for a locale that your input method supports, then the locale name defaults to English. For example, Figure 10-6 shows the two locales for the input method with the default locale set to German. Notice that the locale for Germany displays correctly in German, but the locale for France appears in English.

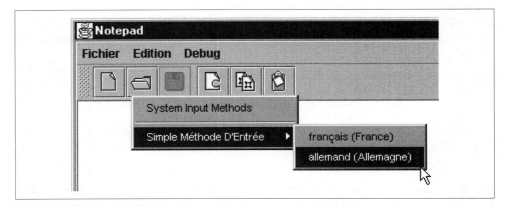

Figure 10-5. An input method displays its locales in a locale-sensitive manner

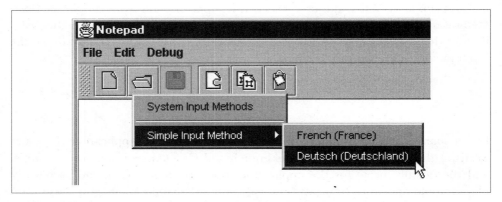

Figure 10-6. The same input method as in Figure 10-5 with the default locale set to German

Building an input method whose set of supported locales can dynamically change at runtime is possible. If the input method defines `hasDynamicLocaleList()` to return `true`, the input method framework does not cache the locale list and calls `getAvailableLocales()` every time the input method is selected. If `hasDynamicLocaleList()` returns `false`, then the input method framework might choose to cache the locale list (but it is not required to do so). As of Java 2 SDK, Standard Edition, Version 1.3, Sun's implementation of the input method framework always calls `getAvailableLocales()`, independent of `hasDynamicLocaleList()`'s value.

java.awt.im.spi.InputMethod

Once the input method is selected, the input method framework calls the Input-
MethodDescriptor.createInputMethod() member function to create an instance of
its associated input method. The framework calls setLocale() on the input
method instance. If the input method supports the locale passed in, it should
make the necessary modifications to support the new locale and return true. If the
input method does not support the locale that is passed in, it should return false.
After calling setLocale(), the framework then calls setInputMethodContext() and
passes an InputMethodContext object.

The InputMethodContext is the interface by which the input method
communicates with the framework. The input method should not attempt to
access the client component directly because the input method does not know
what type of client component it is dealing with. All communication with the client
component should be made via the input method framework, which seamlessly
interfaces between the various client component types. The input method can call
dispatchInputMethodEvent() to send the client component information about the
text being composed within the input method. The input method can make calls
to member functions inherited from InputMethodRequests to ascertain
information about the client component. For example, getSelectedText() returns
the currently selected text from the text-editing component.

When the input method is activated, it is notified via the activate() method.
Events are typically sent directly to the client component. However, when an input
method is active, instances of InputEvent or its subclasses (KeyEvent and
MouseEvent), are redirected to the input method through the dispatchEvent()
member function. For each event that arrives, the input method must decide if it
wishes to handle it. For events it chooses to handle, it calls the event's consume()
method so the event is not passed on to the client component's event listener:

```
public void dispatchEvent(AWTEvent event) {
  if (event.getID() == KeyEvent.KEY_TYPED) {
    KeyEvent e = (KeyEvent) event;
    char c = e.getKeyChar();

    // if we are going to handle the event, call e.consume()
    if (handleChar(c)) {
      e.consume();
    }
  }
}
```

If either the input method framework or the client component determine that the current composition must end, they notify the input method by calling `endComposition()`. The input method must then decide if it wishes to cancel all composed text or commit what was already composed.

As we described earlier, sometimes popping up a lookup window during composition is desirable. The window typically displays a list of candidate words that could match the interpretation of the inputted text. To create a pop up window, you should call `InputMethodContext.createInputMethodWindow()`. The method takes two parameters. The first parameter is the title of the window; the second, `attachToInputContext`, is a `boolean` parameter. If `attachToInputContext` is `true`, it indicates that the window is transient, as it should be for a lookup window. All events received by the pop-up window are sent to the input method automatically. If `attachToInputContext` is `false`, it indicates that the window is persistent and will receive its own events. An input method might want to use a persistent window to display a control panel that allows the user to change the input method's behavior.

Developing a Simple Input Method

We will now build a very simple input method called `SimpleInputMethod` to demonstrate how to use the SPI. The input method allows a user with an English keyboard to enter Hebrew text phonetically.[2] The input method does not need to deal with the complexities of on-the-fly composition or lookup windows. It simply needs to handle key events and map the Latin characters to their phonetic Hebrew equivalent.

The first task is to implement the `InputMethodDescriptor` interface as shown in Example 10-1.

Example 10-1. SimpleInputMethodDescriptor.java

```
package com.ora.intl.ime;

import java.awt.Image;
import java.awt.im.spi.InputMethod;
import java.awt.im.spi.InputMethodDescriptor;
import java.util.Locale;

public class SimpleInputMethodDescriptor
    implements InputMethodDescriptor {
```

---

[2] Some Hebrew characters, such as HEBREW LETTER TSADI (צ) (pronounced "ts," as in "cats"), don't map well to a single English character. Also, some Hebrew characters have a final form. We tried to map as many characters as we could to their equivalent English letter, but where we couldn't, we improvised.

Example 10-1. SimpleInputMethodDescriptor.java (continued)

```
    private static Locale HEBREW = new Locale("iw", "IL");

    public SimpleInputMethodDescriptor() {
    }

    public InputMethod createInputMethod() throws Exception {
        return new SimpleInputMethod();
    }

    // This input method supports only one locale.
    public Locale[] getAvailableLocales() {
        Locale[] locales = { HEBREW };

        return locales;
    }

    public boolean hasDynamicLocaleList() {
        return false;
    }

    public String getInputMethodDisplayName(Locale inputLocale,
                                    Locale displayLanguage) {
        // Make it simple. Ignore the parameters and simply return the
        // same name, independent of locale.
        return "Hebrew Input Method";
    }

    public Image getInputMethodIcon(Locale inputLocale) {
        return null;
    }
}
```

Most work of the input method is done in the implementation of `InputMethod`. Our class, `SimpleInputMethod`, is shown in Example 10-2.

Example 10-2. SimpleInputMethod.java

```
package com.ora.intl.ime;

import java.awt.*;
import java.awt.event.*;
import java.awt.font.TextHitInfo;
import java.awt.im.InputMethodHighlight;
import java.awt.im.spi.InputMethod;
import java.awt.im.spi.InputMethodContext;
import java.text.AttributedString;
import java.util.Locale;

public class SimpleInputMethod implements InputMethod {
```

Example 10-2. SimpleInputMethod.java (continued)

```java
    // The status window will be displayed
    // when the input method is active
    private static Window statusWindow;

    private InputMethodContext inputMethodContext;
    private Locale locale;

    public SimpleInputMethod() {
      // Set locale to Hebrew
      locale = new Locale("iw", "IL");
    }

    // When the input method is informed it has been activated,
    // display the status window.
    public void activate() {
      if (!statusWindow.isVisible()) {
        statusWindow.setVisible(true);
      }
    }

    // We do not want to hide the window when the input method
    // is deactivated because it might get activated almost
    // immediately by another client component. If another
    // input method is activated, this input method's hideWindows()
    // method will be called first.
    public void deactivate(boolean isTemporary) {
    }

    // Any characters that we handle via handleCharacter must be
    // consumed so they aren't passed on to the client component.
    public void dispatchEvent(AWTEvent event) {
      if (event.getID() == KeyEvent.KEY_TYPED) {
        KeyEvent e = (KeyEvent) event;
        if (handleCharacter(e.getKeyChar())) {
          e.consume();
        }
      }
    }

    public void dispose() {
    }

    public void endComposition() {
    }

    public Object getControlObject() {
      return null;
    }
```

Example 10-2. SimpleInputMethod.java (continued)

```java
public Locale getLocale() {
  return locale;
}

public void hideWindows() {
  statusWindow.hide();
}

public boolean isCompositionEnabled() {
  return true;
}

public void removeNotify() {
}

public void setCharacterSubsets(Character.Subset[] subsets) {
}

public void setCompositionEnabled(boolean enable) {
  throw new UnsupportedOperationException();
}

public void notifyClientWindowChange(Rectangle location) {
}

public void reconvert() {
  throw new UnsupportedOperationException();
}

// Once we have been given the InputMethodContext, we can create
// the status window as a persistent window (the second parameter,
// attachToInputContext is false). In this case, we simply display
// the locale of the input method and indicate that it is active.
public void setInputMethodContext(InputMethodContext context) {
  inputMethodContext = context;
  if (statusWindow == null) {
    statusWindow = context.createInputMethodWindow("Simple Input Method",
                                                   false);
    Label label = new Label();
    label.setBackground(Color.lightGray);
    label.setText(locale.getDisplayName() + "Input Method Active");
    statusWindow.add(label);
    label.setSize(200, 50);
    statusWindow.add(label);
    statusWindow.pack();
    Dimension d = Toolkit.getDefaultToolkit().getScreenSize();
    statusWindow.setLocation(
        d.width - statusWindow.getWidth(),
        d.height - statusWindow.getHeight());
  }
}
```

Example 10-2. SimpleInputMethod.java (continued)

```java
// If we support the locale passed in to us, return true;
// otherwise, return false.
public boolean setLocale(Locale locale) {
  return (locale.equals(this.locale));
}

// This method maps Latin keys to Hebrew letters via a large
// switch statement. If we wanted to generalize this, it would
// be better to use a property file that is loaded based on the
// locale. This way, we could create input methods for other types
// of scripts such as Arabic, Greek, etc.
private boolean handleCharacter(char ch) {
  switch(ch) {
    case 'a':
      write('\u05D0'); // Hebrew Letter Aleph
      return true;
    case 'b':
      write('\u05D1'); // Hebrew Letter Bet
      return true;
    case 'g':
      write('\u05D2'); // Hebrew Letter Gimmel
      return true;
    case 'd':
      write('\u05D3'); // Hebrew Letter Dalet
      return true;
    case 'h':
      write('\u05D4'); // Hebrew Letter He
      return true;
    case 'v':
      write('\u05D5'); // Hebrew Letter Vav
      return true;
    case 'z':
      write('\u05D6'); // Hebrew Letter Zayin
      return true;
    case 'k':
      write('\u05D7'); // Hebrew Letter Het
      return true;
    case 'j':
      write('\u05D8'); // Hebrew Letter Tet
      return true;
    case 'y':
      write('\u05D9'); // Hebrew Letter Yod
      return true;
    case '\'':
      write('\u05DA'); // Hebrew Letter Final Chaf
      return true;
```

Example 10-2. SimpleInputMethod.java (continued)

```
      case 'c':
        write('\u05DB'); // Hebrew Letter Chaf
        return true;
      case 'l':
        write('\u05DC'); // Hebrew Letter Lamed
        return true;
      case '.':
        write('\u05DD'); // Hebrew Letter Final Mem
        return true;
      case 'm':
        write('\u05DE'); // Hebrew Letter Mem
        return true;
      case ',':
        write('\u05DF'); // Hebrew Letter Final Nun
        return true;
      case 'n':
        write('\u05E0'); // Hebrew Letter Nun
        return true;
      case 's':
        write('\u05E1'); // Hebrew Letter Samekh
        return true;
      case 'i':
        write('\u05E2'); // Hebrew Letter Ayin
        return true;
      case 'p':
        write('\u05E3'); // Hebrew Letter Final Pe
        return true;
      case 'f':
        write('\u05E4'); // Hebrew Letter Pe
        return true;
      case ';':
        write('\u05E5'); // Hebrew Letter Final Tsadi
        return true;
      case 'x':
        write('\u05E6'); // Hebrew Letter Tsadi
        return true;
      case 'q':
        write('\u05E7'); // Hebrew Letter Qof
        return true;
      case 'r':
        write('\u05E8'); // Hebrew Letter Resh
        return true;
      case 'w':
        write('\u05E9'); // Hebrew Letter Shin
        return true;
      case 't':
        write('\u05EA'); // Hebrew Letter Tav
        return true;
    }
  return false;
}
```

Example 10-2. SimpleInputMethod.java (continued)

```
// write() is a helper method that takes a character and immediately
// commits it. The third parameter of dispatchInputMethodEvent indicates
// how many characters should be committed.
private void write(char ch) {
  AttributedString as =
      new AttributedString(String.valueOf(ch));

  inputMethodContext.dispatchInputMethodEvent(
          InputMethodEvent.INPUT_METHOD_TEXT_CHANGED,
          as.getIterator(),
          1,
          null,
          null);
  }
}
```

How to Package and Install Input Methods

Once you have compiled your input method classes, you need to package the contents as an *installed extension* so the JVM can find the input method when your application is running. This package takes the form of a JAR file containing the classes for the input method, and a text file whose contents point to the *Input-MethodDescriptor.class* file.

Example 10-3 shows the contents of a simple JAR file that contains the minimum files needed for an input method package.

Example 10-3. Contents of SimpleIM.jar

```
com/ora/intl/ime/SimpleInputMethod.class
com/ora/intl/ime/SimpleInputMethodDescriptor.class
META-INF/services/java.awt.im.spi.InputMethodDescriptor
```

The file *META-INF/services/java.awt.im.spi.InputMethodDescriptor* is a UTF-8 encoded text file that lists the full path to each compiled implementation of the *java.awt.im.spi.InputMethodDescriptor* interface in the JAR file.[3] During AWT initialization, the input method framework loads only the InputMethodDescriptor classes. Loading of the InputMethod classes occurs only when they are needed. This deferred loading approach reduces unnecessary overhead when the user never invokes the input method.

---

[3] Remember that UTF-8 looks like ASCII for all code points below \u007F.

In our simple example, the contents of the *java.awt.im.spi.InputMethodDescriptor* file are shown in Example 10-4. Comments can be included in the file by using the comment character (#). All text appearing after the comment character on the same line is ignored.

Example 10-4. META-INF/services/java.awt.im.spi.InputMethodDescriptor

```
# list fully qualified name of each InputMethodDescriptor
# class in this input method

com.ora.intl.ime.SimpleInputMethodDescriptor
```

Assuming you have the directory structure shown in Figure 10-7, place the two class files *SimpleInputMethod.class* and *SimpleInputMethodDescriptor.class* in the *com/ora/intl/ime* directory. Next, place the file *java.awt.im.spi.InputMethodDescriptor* in the *META-INF/services* directory.

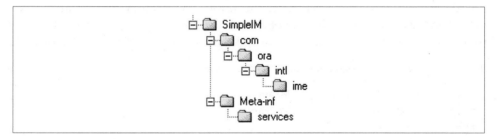

Figure 10-7. Directory structure for SimpleIM

To create the JAR file, make sure you are in the directory just above META-INF and com, in this case *C:\SimpleIM*, and issue the following command:

```
C:\SimpleIM>jar cvf SimpleIM.jar META-INF com
```

To install the input method so the runtime environment can detect it, place the JAR file you created in the standard extensions directory. Depending on whether you are running the JVM from the runtime environment or from the SDK, the extension directory is in a slightly different location, as shown in Table 10-2.

Table 10-2. Installed Extension Directory

Directory	Java Installation Type
lib/ext	Java 2 Runtime Environment
jre/lib/ext	Java 2 SDK

Developing a More Complex Input Method

Now that you have learned how to create and package a simple input method, we will develop a more complex example. While input methods are not usually used for Arabic and Hebrew, we will build one to demonstrate some of Java's Input Method Engine SPI capabilities. First, we start by providing a little background.

Describing the Scenario

Arabic and Hebrew have more in common than the direction in which they are both written. They are also both Semitic languages. One attribute of Semitic languages is that all words in the language are derived from either a three- or four-letter root. Once the root is known, it is possible to form many different words based on the root, even if you have never seen the word. For example, Table 10-3 lists words that can be derived from the three-letter Hebrew root lamed, mem, dalet (למד). Notice the common theme in the words' meaning and that the three root letters appear in order in each word, though not necessarily contiguously.

Table 10-3. Hebrew Words Derived from the Three-Letter Root למד

Word	Transliteration	Meaning
ללמוד	Lilmod	To learn
לומד	Lomed	Learner
תלמיד	Talmid	Student
לימוד	Limood	Learning
תלמוד	Talmud	Talmud
למדן	Lumdun	Scholar
למדנות	Lumdunoot	Scholarship
למוד	Lumood	Taught

Arabic words are derived in a similar manner. In fact, many roots are shared between the two languages. The Arabic root kaaf, ta, ba (كتب), appears in words related to writing, while the Hebrew root chaf, tet, bet (כתב) is also the basis for words related to writing. Many other similarities can be found between the two languages. We will take advantage of this commonality to build an input method that supports both Arabic and Hebrew.

Input Method Features

We will build an input method with the following features:

- Supports both Arabic and Hebrew locales.

- Allows a root to be entered using Latin letters.

- Upon pressing the spacebar, converts the Latin letters to their corresponding (phonetic equivalent) Arabic or Hebrew root letters.

- Upon pressing the spacebar a second time, displays a lookup window with various words derived from the root.

- After the lookup window has been displayed, pressing the spacebar cycles through the candidate matches.

- Pressing the return key selects the currently highlighted selection and closes the lookup window.

Figure 10-8 shows the input method in action, with the Hebrew locale selected. The user has typed the three Latin letters "ktb," which are converted upon the press of the spacebar to the three-letter root chaf, tet, bet (כתב). The user then pressed the spacebar again to display the lookup window, which shows five Hebrew words that are all derived from the root. The user then pressed the spacebar two more times to highlight the third item in the list (מכתב - michtav), the Hebrew word for "letter."[4]

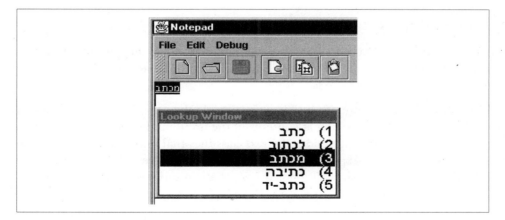

Figure 10-8. Hebrew input method lookup window

---

[4] The kind you put in an envelope and mail someone, not the word indicating a unit of the alphabet.

Figure 10-9 shows the input method with the Arabic locale selected. Again, the user has typed the three Latin letters "ktb," which are converted upon the press of the spacebar to the three Arabic letters kaaf, ta, ba (كتب). The user then pressed the spacebar again to display the lookup window, which shows five Arabic words all derived from the root. Pressing the spacebar two more times, the user highlighted the third word in the list (الكتاب – al kitaab), the Arabic word meaning "the book."

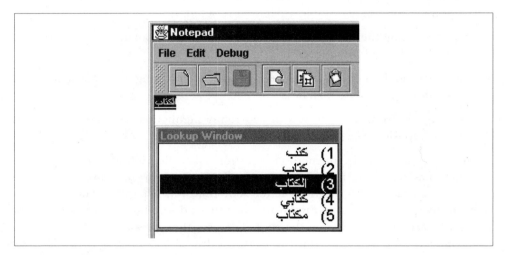

Figure 10-9. The lookup window for the Arabic locale

How It Works

We developed the Arabic-Hebrew Input Method by using the City Input Method sample from the Input Method Framework's SPI tutorial as a starting point, and modifying it to meet our needs.[5]

The Arabic-Hebrew Input Method is more flexible than the Simple Input Method we developed earlier. Looking at contents of the input method's JAR file, shown in Example 10-5, we see that besides the two class files that implement the interfaces `InputMethod` and `InputMethodDescriptor` and the file *java.awt.im.spi. InputMethodDescriptor*, we have a file called *LookupList.class* and several property files.

---

[5] The SPI tutorial is available with Sun's Java 2 documentation and can be found in the directory *docs/guide/imf.* We would like to thank Norbert Lindenberg of Sun Microsystems for his permission to use the code.

Example 10-5. The Contents of ArabicHebrewIM.jar

```
META-INF/services/java.awt.im.spi.InputMethodDescriptor
com/ora/intl/ime/arabichebrewim/ArabicHebrewInputMethod.class
com/ora/intl/ime/arabichebrewim/LookupList.class
com/ora/intl/ime/arabichebrewim/ArabicHebrewInputMethodDescriptor.class
com/ora/intl/ime/arabichebrewim/ktb_iw_IL.properties
com/ora/intl/ime/arabichebrewim/names.properties
com/ora/intl/ime/arabichebrewim/spr_iw_IL.properties
com/ora/intl/ime/arabichebrewim/kbtz_iw_IL.properties
com/ora/intl/ime/arabichebrewim/kra_iw_IL.properties
com/ora/intl/ime/arabichebrewim/qra_ar.properties
com/ora/intl/ime/arabichebrewim/ktb_ar.properties
```

Example 10-6 shows the contents of the file *java.awt.im.spi.InputMethodDescriptor*.

Example 10-6. java.awt.im.spi.InputMethodDescriptor

```
# fully-qualified name of the java.awt.im.spi.InputMethodDescriptor
# implementation class

com.ora.intl.ime.arabichebrewim.ArabicHebrewInputMethodDescriptor
```

Example 10-7 shows the source code for the `ArabicHebrewInputMethodDescriptor`. The main difference between this code and the version we developed for the simple input method is the `getAvailableLocales()` method, which now returns two locales instead of just one.

Example 10-7. ArabicHebrewInputMethodDescriptor.java

```java
package com.ora.intl.ime.arabichebrewim;

import java.awt.Image;
import java.awt.im.spi.InputMethod;
import java.awt.im.spi.InputMethodDescriptor;
import java.util.Locale;

public class ArabicHebrewInputMethodDescriptor
    implements InputMethodDescriptor {

  private static Locale HEBREW = new Locale("iw", "IL");
  private static Locale ARABIC = new Locale("ar", "");

  public ArabicHebrewInputMethodDescriptor() {
  }

  public Locale[] getAvailableLocales() {
    Locale[] locales = { ARABIC, HEBREW };

    return locales;
  }
```

Example 10-7. ArabicHebrewInputMethodDescriptor.java (continued)

```
public boolean hasDynamicLocaleList() {
  return false;
}

public InputMethod createInputMethod() throws Exception {
  return new ArabicHebrewInputMethod();
}

public String getInputMethodDisplayName(Locale inputLocale,
                                        Locale displayLanguage) {
  return "Arabic-Hebrew Input Method";
}

public Image getInputMethodIcon(Locale inputLocale) {
  return null;
}
}
```

The `LookupList` class contains the logic to handle the input method's lookup window behavior. The code for the `LookupList` class is located in the file called *ArabicHebrewInputMethod.java*, shown in Example 10-17, and is almost identical to the code provided with the City Input Method, except for some minor modifications.[6]

The `ArabicHebrewInputMethod` class uses the file *names.properties* to lookup roots entered using Latin letters and return the root converted to the Arabic or Hebrew alphabet. The code that performs the lookup is shown in Example 10-15. The contents of *names.properties* are shown in Example 10-8.

Example 10-8. names.properties

```
ktb_iw=\u05DB\u05EA\u05D1
kra_iw=\u05E7\u05E8\u05D0
spr_iw=\u05E1\u05E4\u05E8
kbtz_iw=\u05E7\u05D1\u05E5

ktb_ar=\u0643\u062A\u0628
qra_ar=\u0642\u0631\u0623
```

Each remaining properties file contains the list of derived words for a particular root. The name of each file matches a Latin transliterated root, followed by the locale. One file should exist for each key-value pair in the *names.properties* file. The code that looks up the derived words is shown in Example 10-16 and described later. The properties file contents are shown in Examples 10-9 through 10-14.

---

[6] We needed to right align the candidate matches in the lookup window for Arabic and Hebrew. We also changed the look of the highlight bar used for showing the currently selected candidate.

Example 10-9. ktb_ar.properties

```
1=\u0643\u062A\u0628
2=\u0643\u062A\u0627\u0628
3=\u0627\u0644\u0643\u062A\u0627\u0628
4=\u0643\u062A\u0627\u0628\u064A
5=\u0645\u0643\u062A\u0627\u0628
```

Example 10-10. ktb_iw_IL.properties

```
1=\u05DB\u05EA\u05D1
2=\u05DC\u05DB\u05EA\u05D5\u05D1
3=\u05DE\u05DB\u05EA\u05D1
4=\u05DB\u05EA\u05D9\u05D1\u05D4
5=\u05DB\u05EA\u05D1-\u05D9\u05D3
```

Example 10-11. kra_iw_IL.properties

```
1=\u05E7\u05E8\u05D0
2=\u05DC\u05E7\u05E8\u05D5\u05D0
3=\u05E7\u05E8\u05D9\u05D0\u05D4
4=\u05E7\u05E8\u05D9\u05D0
```

Example 10-12. qra_ar.properties

```
1=\u0642\u0631\u0623
2=\u0627\u0644\u0642\u0631\u0627\u0646
3=\u0645\u0642\u0631\u0648
4=\u0642\u0631\u0627\u0629
```

Example 10-13. kbtz_iw_IL.properties

```
1=\u05E7\u05D1\u05E5
2=\u05E7\u05D5\u05D1\u05E5
3=\u05DC\u05E7\u05D1\u05E5
4=\u05E7\u05D1\u05D5\u05E6\u05D4
5=\u05E7\u05D9\u05D1\u05D5\u05E5
```

Example 10-14. spr_iw_IL.properties

```
1=\u05E1\u05E4\u05E8
2=\u05DC\u05E1\u05E4\u05E8
3=\u05E1\u05E4\u05E8\u05D9\u05D9\u05D4
4=\u05E1\u05D9\u05E4\u05D5\u05E8
5=\u05E1\u05E4\u05E8\u05DF
```

The Arabic-Hebrew input method must interpret key presses differently for three separate states as follows:

Initial state

The user enters Latin characters representing the Arabic or Hebrew root.

Transliterated state

The Latin letters are converted to their Arabic or Hebrew equivalents.

Lookup window state

The user can select from a list of candidate words derived from the root.

When the input method is in the initial state and the user presses the spacebar, we attempt to transliterate the Latin letters the user typed into Arabic or Hebrew letters, depending upon the current locale. The code that performs this task is in the `transliterateLatinToRoot()` method, which we show in Example 10-15.

Example 10-15. tranliterateLatinToRoot()

```
1:  private void transliterateLatinToRoot() {
2:      String lookupName;
3:      lookupName = rawText.toString();
4:      String localeLookupName = lookupName + "_" + locale;
5:      while (true) {
6:          transText = (String) arabichebrewNames.get(localeLookupName);
7:          if (transText != null) {
8:              break;
9:          }
10:         int index = localeLookupName.lastIndexOf("_");
11:         if (index == -1) {
12:             break;
13:         }
14:         localeLookupName = localeLookupName.substring(0, index);
15:     }
16:     if (transText != null) {
17:         transliterated = true;
18:         sendText(false);
19:     } else {
20:         Toolkit.getDefaultToolkit().beep();
21:     }
22: }
```

Let's now look at this method in a little more detail. On line 3, the text the user enters before pressing the spacebar is copied from a `StringBuffer` (`rawText`) to the `String` variable `lookupName`. We then construct a `localeLookupName` on line 4 by appending the current locale to the `lookupName`. For example, if the user enters the three letters "ktb" and the locale is Arabic, the variable `localeLookupName` would contain the value `ktb_ar`.

The `while` loop that begins on line 5 and ends on line 15 attempts to find the `localeLookupName` in the *names.properties* file, which is shown in Example 10-8.[7] The actual lookup occurs on line 6. If we find it (line 7), the result is stored in the variable `transText` and we exit the loop on line 8. If we get to line 10 in the loop, then the lookup failed. Lines 10 through 14 adjust the contents of `localeLookupName` by

---

[7] The variable `arabichebrewNames` is a `Properties` object that was loaded with the *names.properties* file at construction time.

making the locale less specific. We accomplish this adjustment by searching for the last underscore in the string and truncating everything beyond it. For example, if the user enters "ktb" and the locale is Hebrew as spoken in Israel (iw_IL), then the localeLookupName would have the value ktb_iw_IL on line 4. The *names.properties* file does not have a key with ktb_iw_IL, so the lookup would fail on line 6. On line 10, we would find the last underscore in the string and we would truncate the string on line 14, leaving us with the value ktb_iw. The code then loops around and this time we find a match when we perform the lookup on line 6. If ktb_iw doesn't appear in *names.properties*, we repeat the truncation, this time looking for "ktb." The loop continues until a match is found, or no more underscores are found in the string (lines 11 and 12).

On line 16, we check to see if the text was transliterated. If it was, we assign the value true to the variable transliterated, indicating a state change, and call the method sendText(). sendText() uses the InputMethodContext to display the transliterated string on the client component.

Once the input method is in the transliterated state, if the user presses the spacebar again, we need to display a lookup window containing a list of words that derive from the transliterated root. The logic for determining the list of candidate words is found in the method showDerivedWords(), shown in Example 10-16.

Example 10-16. showDerivedWords()

```
1:  private void showDerivedWords() {
2:     String lookupName;
3:     lookupName = rawText.toString() + "_" + locale + ".properties";
4:
5:     Properties lookupList;
6:     String lookupString;
7:     try {
8:        lookupList = loadProperties(lookupName);
9:     } catch (IOException e) {
10:       // no lookup information
11:       return;
12:    }
13:
14:    lookupCandidates = new Vector();
15:    lookupCandidateCount = 1;
17:    while (true) {
18:       lookupString = (String) lookupList.getProperty(
19:         String.valueOf(lookupCandidateCount));
20:       if (lookupString == null) {
21:         lookupCandidateCount--;
22:         break;
23:       }
```

Example 10-16. showDerivedWords() (continued)

```
24:      lookupCandidates.add(lookupString);
25:      lookupCandidateCount++;
26:    }
27:
28:    lookupSelection = 0;
29:    openLookupWindow();
30: }
```

On line 3, we build the name of the properties file that contains the list of derived words. The name of each file is the Latin transliterated root (what the user entered) followed by the locale with a *.properties* extension. For example, if the user enters the three letters "ktb" and the locale is Hebrew as spoken in Israel (iw_IL), then the name of the file would be *ktb_iw_IL.properties*.

Lines 5 through 12 load the properties file. If the file cannot be found, then we return on line 11.

The while loop that begins on line 17 and ends on line 26 loads a Vector with the derived words. The key for each value in the properties file begins with a number indexed starting from 1. The variable lookupCandidateCount maintains the index, and the value is loaded into the Vector on lines 18 and 19. If no more words are found, we exit the loop on line 22.

On line 29 we call openLookupWindow() to display the list of words in the Vector.

Example 10-17 shows the complete listing of the file *ArabicHebrewInputMethod.java*.

Example 10-17. ArabicHebrewInputMethod.java

```
package com.ora.intl.ime.arabichebrewim;

import java.awt.*;
import java.awt.event.*;
import java.awt.font.*;
import java.awt.im.*;
import java.awt.im.spi.*;
import java.io.*;
import java.text.*;
import java.util.*;

public class ArabicHebrewInputMethod implements InputMethod {

  private static Locale HEBREW = new Locale("iw", "IL");
  private static Locale ARABIC = new Locale("ar", "");

  private static Locale[] SUPPORTED_LOCALES = {ARABIC, HEBREW};

  // lookup table - shared by all instances of this input method
  private static Properties arabichebrewNames;
```

Example 10-17. ArabicHebrewInputMethod.java (continued)

```java
// windows - shared by all instances of this input method
private static Window statusWindow;

// lookup information - per instance
private Vector lookupCandidates;
private int lookupCandidateCount;
private LookupList lookupList;
private int lookupSelection;

// per-instance state
private InputMethodContext inputMethodContext;
private Locale locale;
private boolean transliterated;
private StringBuffer rawText;
private String transliteratedText;

public ArabicHebrewInputMethod() throws IOException {
  if (arabichebrewNames == null) {
    arabichebrewNames = loadProperties("names.properties");
  }
  rawText = new StringBuffer();
}

public void setInputMethodContext(InputMethodContext context) {
  inputMethodContext = context;
  if (statusWindow == null) {
    statusWindow = context.createInputMethodWindow(
      "ArabicHebrew Input Method", false);
    Label label = new Label();
    label.setBackground(Color.white);
    statusWindow.add(label);
    updateStatusWindow(locale);
    label.setSize(200, 50);
    statusWindow.pack();
    Dimension d = Toolkit.getDefaultToolkit().getScreenSize();
    statusWindow.setLocation(d.width - statusWindow.getWidth(),
                             d.height - statusWindow.getHeight());
  }
}

public boolean setLocale(Locale locale) {
  for (int i = 0; i < SUPPORTED_LOCALES.length; i++) {
    if (locale.equals(SUPPORTED_LOCALES[i])) {
      this.locale = locale;
      if (statusWindow != null) {
        updateStatusWindow(locale);
      }
      return true;
    }
  }
```

Example 10-17. ArabicHebrewInputMethod.java (continued)

```java
    return false;
  }

  public Locale getLocale() {
    return locale;
  }

  public boolean isCompositionEnabled() {
    return true;
  }

  void updateStatusWindow(Locale locale) {
    Label label = (Label) statusWindow.getComponent(0);
    String localeName =
        locale == null ? "null" : locale.getDisplayName();
    label.setText(localeName + " IME Active");
  }

  public void setCharacterSubsets(Character.Subset[] subsets) {
  }

  public void setCompositionEnabled(boolean enable) {
    throw new UnsupportedOperationException();
  }

  public void notifyClientWindowChange(Rectangle location) {
  }

  public void dispatchEvent(AWTEvent event) {
    if (event.getID() == KeyEvent.KEY_TYPED) {
      KeyEvent e = (KeyEvent) event;
      if (handleCharacter(e.getKeyChar())) {
        e.consume();
      }
    }
  }

  public void activate() {
    if (!statusWindow.isVisible()) {
      statusWindow.setVisible(true);
    }
    updateStatusWindow(locale);
  }

  public void deactivate(boolean isTemporary) {
    closeLookupWindow();
  }

  public void hideWindows() {
```

Example 10-17. ArabicHebrewInputMethod.java (continued)

```
      closeLookupWindow();
      statusWindow.hide();
    }

  public void removeNotify() {
    }

  public void endComposition() {
      if (rawText.length() != 0) {
        acceptSelection();
      }
      closeLookupWindow();
    }

  public void dispose() {
      closeLookupWindow();
    }

  public Object getControlObject() {
      return null;
    }

  public void reconvert() {
      throw new UnsupportedOperationException();
    }

  private Properties loadProperties(String fileName)
        throws IOException {
      Properties props = new Properties();
      InputStream stream = this.getClass()
                             .getResourceAsStream(fileName);
      props.load(stream);
      stream.close();
      return props;
    }

  private boolean handleCharacter(char ch) {
      // if the lookup window is active...
      if (lookupList != null) {
        if (ch == ' ') {
          if (++lookupSelection == lookupCandidateCount) {
            lookupSelection = 0;
          }
          selectCandidate(lookupSelection);
          return true;
        } else if (ch == '\n') {
          acceptSelection();
          closeLookupWindow();
          return true;
        }
      // otherwise, if the Latin letters have already been
```

Example 10-17. ArabicHebrewInputMethod.java (continued)

```
      // transliterated to Arabic or Hebrew (transliterated state)
      } else if (transliterated) {
        if (ch == ' ') {
          showDerivedWords();
          return true;
        } else if (ch == '\n') {
          acceptSelection();
          return true;
        } else {
          Toolkit.getDefaultToolkit().beep();
          return true;
        }
      // initial state - we need to transliterate from Latin to Hebrew
      } else {
        if (ch == ' ') {
          transliterateLatinToRoot();
          return true;
        } else if (ch == '\n') {
          if (rawText.length() != 0) {
            acceptSelection();
            return true;
          }
        } else if (ch == '\b') {
          if (rawText.length() != 0) {
            rawText.setLength(rawText.length() - 1);
            sendText(false);
            return true;
          }
        // if a Latin letter is entered...
        } else if (Character.UnicodeBlock.of(ch) ==
          Character.UnicodeBlock.BASIC_LATIN && Character.isLetter(ch)) {
          rawText.append(ch);
          sendText(false);
          return true;
        // if we are already in the middle of composition, don't allow a
        // character other than a Latin letter to be entered.
        } else if (rawText.length() != 0) {
          Toolkit.getDefaultToolkit().beep();
          return true;
        }
      }
    return false;
  }

  private void transliterateLatinToRoot() {
    String lookupName;
    lookupName = rawText.toString();
    String localeLookupName = lookupName + "_" + locale;
    while (true) {
      transliteratedText = (String) arabichebrewNames.get(localeLookupName);
```

Example 10-17. ArabicHebrewInputMethod.java (continued)

```
    if (transliteratedText != null) {
      break;
    }
    int index = localeLookupName.lastIndexOf("_");
    if (index == -1) {
      break;
    }
    localeLookupName = localeLookupName.substring(0, index);
  }
  if (transliteratedText != null) {
      transliterated = true;
      sendText(false);
  } else {
    Toolkit.getDefaultToolkit().beep();
  }
}

private void showDerivedWords() {
  String lookupName;
  lookupName = rawText.toString() + "_" + locale + ".properties";

  Properties lookupList;
  String lookupString;
  try {
    lookupList = loadProperties(lookupName);
  } catch (IOException e) {
    // no lookup information
    return;
  }

  lookupCandidates = new Vector();
  lookupCandidateCount = 1;
  while (true) {
    lookupString = (String)lookupList.getProperty(
    String.valueOf(lookupCandidateCount));
    if (lookupString == null) {
      lookupCandidateCount--;
      break;
    }
    lookupCandidates.add(lookupString);
    lookupCandidateCount++;
  }

  lookupSelection = 0;
  openLookupWindow();
}

private void acceptSelection() {
  sendText(true);
  rawText.setLength(0);
```

Example 10-17. ArabicHebrewInputMethod.java (continued)

```java
    transliteratedText = null;
    transliterated = false;
  }

  private void sendText(boolean committed) {
    String text;
    InputMethodHighlight highlight;
    int committedCharacterCount = 0;
    TextHitInfo caret = null;

    if (transliterated) {
      text = transliteratedText;
      highlight = InputMethodHighlight.SELECTED_CONVERTED_TEXT_HIGHLIGHT;
    } else {
      text = new String(rawText);
      highlight = InputMethodHighlight.SELECTED_RAW_TEXT_HIGHLIGHT;
    }
    AttributedString as = new AttributedString(text);
    if (committed) {
      committedCharacterCount = text.length();
    } else if (text.length() > 0) {
      as.addAttribute(TextAttribute.INPUT_METHOD_HIGHLIGHT, highlight);
      caret = TextHitInfo.leading(text.length());
    }
    inputMethodContext.dispatchInputMethodEvent(
              InputMethodEvent.INPUT_METHOD_TEXT_CHANGED,
              as.getIterator(),
              committedCharacterCount,
              caret,
              null);
  }

  void selectCandidate(int candidate) {
    lookupSelection = candidate;
    lookupList.selectCandidate(lookupSelection);
    transliteratedText =(String)lookupCandidates.elementAt(lookupSelection);
    sendText(false);
  }

  void openLookupWindow() {
    lookupList = new LookupList(this, inputMethodContext, lookupCandidates);
    lookupList.selectCandidate(lookupSelection);
  }

  void closeLookupWindow() {
    if (lookupList != null) {
      lookupList.setVisible(false);
      lookupList = null;
    }
  }
}
```

Example 10-17. ArabicHebrewInputMethod.java (continued)

```java
class LookupList extends Canvas {

  ArabicHebrewInputMethod inputMethod;
  InputMethodContext context;
  Window lookupWindow;
  Vector candidates;          // list of candidates
  int candidateCount;         // number of candidates in the vector
  int selected;               // the currently select candidate

  final int INSIDE_INSET = 4;
  final int LINE_SPACING = 18;
  final int LINE_WIDTH = 200;

  LookupList(ArabicHebrewInputMethod inputMethod,
            InputMethodContext context, Vector candidates) {
    this.inputMethod = inputMethod;
    this.context = context;
    this.candidates = candidates;
    this.candidateCount = candidates.size();

    lookupWindow = context.createInputMethodWindow("Lookup Window", true);
    setFont(new Font("LucidaSans", Font.PLAIN, 18));
    setSize(LINE_WIDTH, candidateCount * LINE_SPACING + 2 * INSIDE_INSET);
    setForeground(Color.black);
    setBackground(Color.white);

    enableEvents(AWTEvent.KEY_EVENT_MASK);

    lookupWindow.add(this);
    lookupWindow.pack();
    updateWindowLocation();
    lookupWindow.setVisible(true);
  }

  /**
   * Positions the lookup window near (usually below) the
   * insertion point in the component where composition occurs.
   */
  private void updateWindowLocation() {
    Point windowLocation = new Point();
    Rectangle caretRect = context.getTextLocation(
        TextHitInfo.leading(0));
    Dimension screenSize = Toolkit.getDefaultToolkit()
                                  .getScreenSize();
    Dimension windowSize = lookupWindow.getSize();
    final int SPACING = 2;

    if (caretRect.x + windowSize.width > screenSize.width) {
      windowLocation.x = screenSize.width - windowSize.width;
    } else {
```

Example 10-17. ArabicHebrewInputMethod.java (continued)

```java
        windowLocation.x = caretRect.x;
    }

    if (caretRect.y + caretRect.height + SPACING +
        windowSize.height > screenSize.height) {
      windowLocation.y = caretRect.y - SPACING - windowSize.height;
    } else {
      windowLocation.y = caretRect.y + caretRect.height + SPACING;
    }

    lookupWindow.setLocation(windowLocation);
  }

  void selectCandidate(int candidate) {
    selected = candidate;
    repaint();
  }

  public void paint(Graphics g) {
    FontMetrics metrics = g.getFontMetrics();
    int descent = metrics.getDescent();
    int ascent = metrics.getAscent();
    String outString;
    Dimension size = getSize();
    g.fillRect(INSIDE_INSET / 2,
               LINE_SPACING * (selected + 1) + INSIDE_INSET - (descent + ascent + 1),
               size.width - INSIDE_INSET,
               descent + ascent + 2);
    g.setColor(Color.black);
    for (int i = 0; i < candidateCount; i++) {
      outString = (i + 1) + ")   " + (String)candidates.elementAt(i);
      if (i == selected) {
        g.setColor(Color.white);
      }
      g.drawString(outString,
                   (LINE_WIDTH - 4) - metrics.stringWidth(outString),
                   LINE_SPACING * (i + 1) + INSIDE_INSET - descent);
      if (i == selected) {
        g.setColor(Color.black);
      }
    }
    g.drawRect(0, 0, size.width - 1, size.height - 1);
  }

  public void setVisible(boolean visible) {
    if (!visible) {
      lookupWindow.setVisible(false);
      lookupWindow.dispose();
      lookupWindow = null;
    }
```

Example 10-17. ArabicHebrewInputMethod.java (continued)

```
    super.setVisible(visible);
  }

  protected void processKeyEvent(KeyEvent event) {
    inputMethod.dispatchEvent(event);
  }
}
```

11

Internationalized Web Applications

Until now, we have focused on internationalized applications in which the program code resides on the user's machine. However, in an increasing trend toward the use of thin client architectures, the program code for an application resides on a server and the user interacts with the server using a client application. The web browser is typically used as the application interface, and CGI programs on the server take input from the user and perform required processing. The server is also responsible for generating the user interface. As we saw from Chapter 9, *Internationalized Graphical User Interfaces*, a good deal of effort is required to make a user interface internationalized so that it can be easily localized.

Internationalization needs to be designed into three areas of a web application: how data is passed to the web application, how data is stored in the web application, and how data is presented to the user. In this chapter, we will focus on the presentation aspects of internationalized web applications, but you must understand how to handle the first two aspects correctly in an internationalized web application.

A user typically submits data to a server using an HTML form, in which the data is encoded properly into an HTTP request and sent to the server for processing. The data can be read in a Unicode format and then manipulated accordingly. Databases are typically used as the data store in web applications. Most modern databases allow you to store data in an encoding such as UTF-8. You should consult your database vendor to determine whether data can be stored in such a format.

Also, if you're using JDBC to interact with your database, then you should verify with the JDBC driver vendor that the vendor supports the given character encoding you would like to use.

Recently, several Java-specific server-side extensions were introduced to facilitate the development of cross-platform web applications. These extensions include Java Servlets and Java Server Pages. Java Servlets are the Java equivalent of traditional CGI programs written in C or Perl. JavaServer Pages are a way of separating the presentation interface from the underlying system that generates dynamic content.

Applets

We are discussing applets in this chapter to see how their locale can be set automatically for the user, based on the user's browser language preferences. Applets can run with a different default locale in a number of ways. You can certainly provide an interface in your applet to allow the change of locale. First, we'll show you the hard way (and the most unattractive from the user's standpoint), since it requires users to change settings in the operating system.

We already know what you're going to say, "Applets run on the client's desktop." Our answer is: applets originate from a server and are downloaded onto the client's desktop when you load up an HTML page with a set of <APPLET></APPLET> tags. Applets may need to be run using a locale specific to the client's machine or specified by the user.

Let's start out with an example demonstrating where you may run into problems using the Locale class when deploying your application using an applet. Although you may use other locales in applets, you are not allowed to set a new default locale because this setting violates security restrictions placed on applets.

Try running Example 11-1 and see what happens.

Example 11-1. Trying to Set a New Default Locale in an Applet

```
import java.awt.*;
import java.applet.*;
import java.util.Locale;

public class LocaleApplet extends Applet {

  TextField LocaleDisplayField = new TextField();

  public void init() {
    setLayout(null);
    setSize(250,96);
    add(LocaleDisplayField);
    LocaleDisplayField.setBounds(24,36,205,24);
```

Example 11-1. Trying to Set a New Default Locale in an Applet (continued)

```
    // Display the default locale
    System.out.println(Locale.getDefault().getDisplayName());
    LocaleDisplayField.setText(Locale.getDefault().toString());

    // Let's try and reset the locale
    Locale.setDefault(Locale.JAPAN);

    // And now display the new default locale
    System.out.println(Locale.getDefault().toString());
    LocaleDisplayField.setText(Locale.getDefault().toString());
  }
}
```

Example 11-2 shows the HTML used to run the applet. Try it for yourself if you have access to a web server.

Example 11-2. HTML File for Running the LocaleApplet Applet

```
<HTML>

<HEAD>
<TITLE>Locales and Applets</TITLE>
</HEAD>

<BODY>
<H3>Locale Applet</H3>

<P>
<APPLET CODE="LocaleApplet.class" WIDTH=250 HEIGHT=100>
</APPLET>

</BODY>
</HTML>
```

Figure 11-1 is a screenshot of the Java console in Netscape. The browser's status bar should give you an error, such as `Applet LocaleApplet can't start: ERROR`.

One way to resolve this issue is to change the regional settings in your operating system (Windows, in this example) to a different locale. Example 11-3 is a trimmed-down version of Example 11-1 and is meant to illustrate that, by changing the regional settings in Windows, you change the default locale for the JVM in Netscape or Internet Explorer.

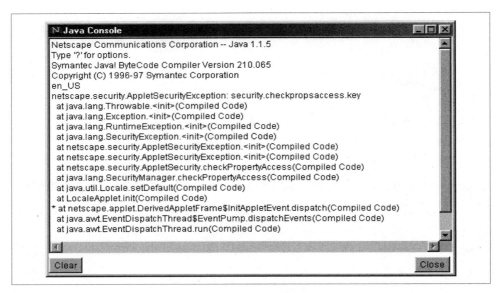

Figure 11-1. Java console in Netscape when trying to run LocaleApplet

Example 11-3. Modified LocaleApplet to Display Only the Default Locale

```java
import java.awt.*;
import java.applet.*;
import java.util.Locale;

public class ModifiedLocaleApplet extends Applet {

  TextField LocaleDisplayField = new TextField();

  public void init() {
    setLayout(null);
    setSize(250,96);
    add(LocaleDisplayField);
    LocaleDisplayField.setBounds(24,36,205,24);

    // Display the default locale
    System.out.println(Locale.getDefault().getDisplayName());
    LocaleDisplayField.setText(Locale.getDefault().toString());
  }
}
```

To change your regional settings in Windows, navigate to the Control Panel. Here you should see a window similar to the one in Figure 11-2.

Figure 11-2. Regional settings in the Windows Control Panel

In our example, we change the settings from English (United States) to English (Canadian). Figure 11-3 shows the new setting in the regional settings dialog. The "Servlets" section later in this chapter shows that this step is not an ideal way to allow users to run your applet using a different locale. In that section, we develop an example you can use to configure the user's browser's settings automatically.

That's it! You should see en_CA printed in the applet's text field if you've changed your regional settings correctly. You may also verify the output (see Figure 11-4) by looking at the Java console, since we also print the default locale to System.out

We'll now discuss Java Servlets and JavaServer Pages. Example 11-6 shows how we can utilize the servlet API to determine the locale that the user prefers and output an applet with locale-specific parameters. This locale can be used within applets as the default locale instead of a locale setting dictated by the operating system. You can also use it as a mechanism to initialize an applet with locale-specific startup messages. On the server, a default locale should only be used for things like log file messages and, as a last resort, to present locale-specific information to a user.

Servlets

Servlets can be thought of as applications that reside on an application server or web server. To interact with a user, server-side applications are accessed through other applications, typically a web browser. Their primary use is to enhance and extend a web server's functionality. Servlets are the Java equivalent of traditional CGI programs, with many attractive features. They are:

- Component-based so servlets can be developed to perform specific tasks

- Fast, providing significant performance improvement over traditional CGI programs

- Platform- and server-independent because they are written in Java

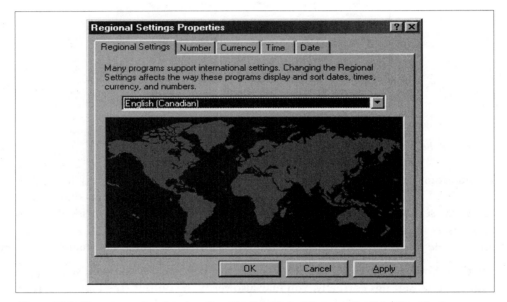

Figure 11-3. Changing regional settings from English (United States) to English (Canadian)

If you would like to read more about their benefits and how to program them, refer to O'Reilly's *Java Servlet Programming* by Jason Hunter.[1] It even devotes a chapter to internationalization.

So, why are we discussing servlets as part of this book? We will not rehash what other authors have already discussed. However, we'd like to present other uses of servlets in internationalized web application development. The examples that we

---

[1] You can also check out Jason Hunter's web site, *http://www.servlets.com*, which is devoted to the book *Java Servlet Programming* (O'Reilly, 1998). It is an excellent resource to learn about servlets and an excellent reference for servlet-related technologies.

cover in this chapter were tested under Allaire's JRun servlet engine.[2] To run the examples in this section, you need a servlet engine that is compliant with the Servlet 2.2 API specification.[3]

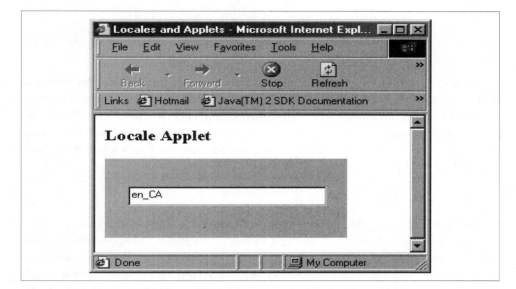

Figure 11-4. Modified LocaleApplet output after changing regional settings in Windows

Changes to the Servlet API for Internationalization

Several changes that affect internationalization have been made to the Servlet 2.2 specification, particularly the `ServletRequest` and `ServletResponse` interfaces. Before the Servlet 2.2 API was released, you had to worry about parsing the headers of a request to determine locale-specific information. The client sends this information in the `Accept-Language` header. The `Accept-Language` header may be sent using one of two formats, one without *q-values*:

```
en, en-GB, fr, es, kr
```

and one with *q-values*:

```
en, en-GB;q=0.9, fr;q=0.5, es;q=0.2, kr;q=0.1
```

---

[2] JRun is available from Allaire at *http://www.allaire.com.*

[3] Tomcat, available at *http://jakarta.apache.org,* and the Orion Application Server, available at *http://www.orionserver.com,* are two robust engines used to run servlets and JSPs.

q-values estimate the user's preference on a scale from 0.0 to 1.0 for the particular locale. A value of 1.0 indicates the strongest preference, so in the sample above, en-GB is preferred over es. This information is useful for web sites that can deliver content to a user in multiple languages. The user sets the order of the locale preferences, and the locales do not need any particular order of specification. For example, a user could have the following preferences for language: en, zh, en-US, which would correspond to a preference for English, then Chinese, and finally U.S. English.

If you want to send locale-specific information to a user, grab this header from the ServletRequest, parse the information, grab the locale-specific information from a resource bundle, and then write the information back to the client. Or, as described in *Java Servlet Programming*, the authors developed a LocaleNegotiator class to handle parsing and resource bundle lookup for you. We'll talk a bit more about this topic later.

Changes to ServletRequest

In the Servlet 2.2 API, two methods were introduced in the ServletRequest interface to remove the burden of having to parse the Accept-Language header yourself. The two methods are getLocale() and getLocales().getLocale() returns a single Locale object and indicates the client's preferred locale. If the browser making the request to the servlet doesn't send the Accept-Language header, then the returned Locale object will be the default locale for the servlet engine.

As we saw, the Accept-Language header may contain more than one language preference. If you are interested in determining all the locales the user prefers, you may use the getLocales() method. It returns an Enumeration of Locale objects. This information can be used to find a best match between the locale-specific resource bundles that exist on the server and the preferred locales given by the user's browser. As with the getLocale() method, if the user's browser does not send the Accept-Language header, this method will return an Enumeration that contains a single Locale object. This Locale object is the default locale for the servlet engine.

Example 11-4 illustrates how both these methods can be used.

Example 11-4. Using the getLocale() and getLocales() Methods

```
import java.io.*;
import java.util.*;
import javax.servlet.*;
import javax.servlet.http.*;

public class LocaleInformationServlet extends HttpServlet {
```

Example 11-4. Using the getLocale() and getLocales() Methods (continued)

```
public void doGet(HttpServletRequest request, HttpServletResponse response) throws
    IOException, ServletException {

  response.setContentType("text/html");
  PrintWriter out = response.getWriter();

  Locale userPreferredLocale = request.getLocale();
  Enumeration userPreferredLocales = request.getLocales();

  out.println("");
  out.println("");
  out.println("");
  out.println("Preferred Locale: " + userPreferredLocale.toString());
  out.println("");
  out.print("Preferred Locales: ");

  while (userPreferredLocales.hasMoreElements()) {
    userPreferredLocale = (Locale)userPreferredLocales.nextElement();
    out.print(userPreferredLocale.toString() + ", ");
  }
  out.println();
  out.println("");
 }
}
```

Running this example using out browser settings produces the following output:

```
Preferred Locale: en_US
Preferred Locales: en_US, en_GB, en_CA,
```

Notice that the locale information is in the `language_country_variant` format we saw in Chapter 3, *Locales*.

Changing your language preferences

The latest versions of Internet Explorer (5.0) and Netscape Communicator (4.7) allow you to change your language preferences. Web sites with content available in multiple languages use the information from the `Accept-Language` header to serve the pages in the language you prefer. If content in that language isn't available, the site uses the other language preferences to determine a best match with respect to your preferences and the available content.

You can access the language preferences settings in Internet Explorer from the **Tools → Internet Options → Languages** menu. The screen looks similar to the one in Figure 11-5. The displayed languages differ, depending on the language preferences set by default or that you added or removed yourself.

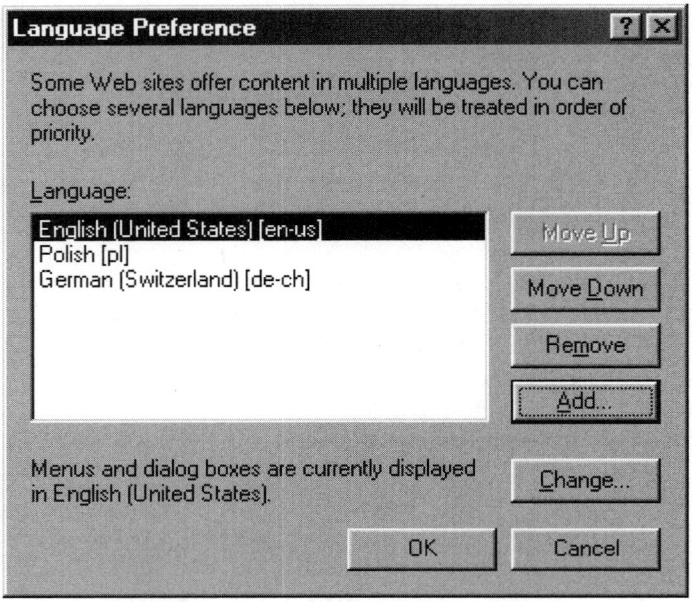

Figure 11-5. Language preference settings in Internet Explorer

In Netscape, the language preferences can be changed from the **Edit → Prefer-ences → Navigator → Languages** menu. Your screen will be similar to the one in Figure 11-6.

Changes to ServletResponse

Two methods, `getLocale()` and `setLocale(Locale locale)`, were also added to the `ServletResponse` interface. These methods allow you to get and set the locale of the response that is sent back to the client making the request of the servlet.

As you may have guessed, `getLocale()` returns a `Locale` object representing the locale assigned to the response object. The response object initially gets set with the servlet engine's default locale. The default character set assigned to the `charset` portion of the `Content-Type` header is ISO-8859-1. This character set can be set in one of two ways. First, you can call the `setContentType(String type)` method as follows:

```
response.setContentType("text/html; charset=ISO-8859-1");
```

Why, then, is the character set or `charset` portion of the `Content-Type` header necessary? The browser uses this value to render the page with the proper font that can display characters in a given character set. Suppose you wanted to write characters from one of the CJK character sets using ISO-8859-1 or the Latin-1 script. Since the CJK characters are not present in this character set, your browser cannot render them properly.

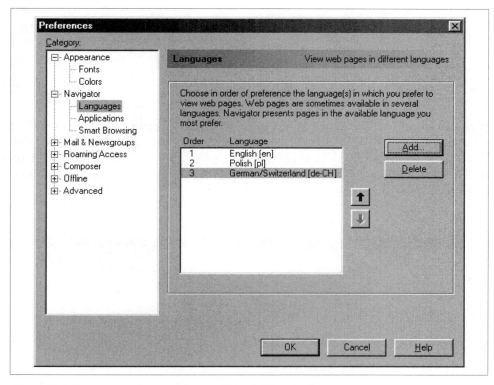

Figure 11-6. Language preference settings in Netscape Communicator

The second way to set the `charset` used in the response sent back to the client is to use the `setLocale(Locale locale)` method on `ServletResponse`. This method takes a `Locale` object and sets the appropriate headers in the response back to the client. This method is particularly useful when you need to set the `charset` portion of the `Content-Type` header, but you don't know the character set identifier's exact name. This method handles that mapping for you.

You have two alternatives when setting the character set of the response. The preferred method for setting this value in the `Content-Type` header is to use the `set-Locale(Locale locale)` method. Example 11-5 illustrates how things can go awry if you don't use this method.

Example 11-5. Invalid Character Encoding Specified for the Servlet Response

```java
import java.io.*;
import java.util.*;
import javax.servlet.*;
import javax.servlet.http.*;

public class UnknownEncodingServlet extends HttpServlet {

  public void doGet(HttpServletRequest request, HttpServletResponse response) throws
      IOException, ServletException {

    response.setContentType("text/html; charset=ISO-8850-1");
    PrintWriter out = response.getWriter();
  }
}
```

If you try running this servlet, you should get a similar error message depending on the servlet engine in which you run the example. This message occurs because ISO-8850-1 is not a recognized character encoding. We tried to send back a response with the ISO-8859-1 character encoding. Figure 11-7 illustrates the resulting error message when running Example 11-5.

Figure 11-7. Error message displayed when running UnknownEncodingServlet

When setting the appropriate character set, you must use either the setContentType(String type) or setLocale(Locale locale) method before any call to the `getWriter()` method on the `ServletResponse`; the call to `getWriter()` uses the `charset` tag to construct the proper `PrintWriter` object. If the `content-type` was not set before the call to `setLocale(Locale locale)`, it is set to a default of `text/plain`.

Example 11-6 illustrates how to use the `setLocale(Locale locale)` method to set the proper character set for writing out "Hello World" in Japanese.

Example 11-6. Hello World in Japanese

```java
import java.io.*;
import java.util.*;
import javax.servlet.*;
import javax.servlet.http.*;

public class JapaneseHelloWorldServlet extends HttpServlet {

  public void doGet(HttpServletRequest request, HttpServletResponse response) throws
      IOException, ServletException {

    response.setContentType("text/html");
    response.setLocale(Locale.JAPANESE);
    PrintWriter out = response.getWriter();
    out.println("<FONT SIZE=+2>");
    out.println("\u4eca\u65e5\u306f\u4e16\u754c");
    out.println("</FONT>");
  }
}
```

Figure 11-8 shows what this example looks like when the servlet is compiled and running.

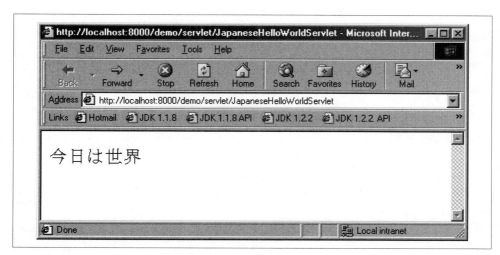

Figure 11-8. JapaneseHelloWorldServlet servlet running

The book *Java Servlet Programming* demonstrates a set of classes to handle locale negotiation and mappings from locale to character sets.[4] These classes were written before changes for internationalization were added to the Servlet 2.2 API. Locale-Negotiator scans the Accept-Language header in the request to the servlet and then allows you to retrieve a ResourceBundle for the locale that best matches the user's preferences and the available resource bundles on the server. LocaleToCharsetMap, on the other hand, maps all locales available in JDK 1.1 to their corresponding character set. This mapping allows you to set the charset value in the Content-Type header of the response sent back to the browser.

The LocaleNegotiator class is particularly useful because it removes much of the coding you would have to write yourself to determine the proper locale from the Accept-Language header and then to retrieve the proper resource bundle based on the user's preferred language settings. We use the class in Example 11-7.

Using Servlets to Control an Applet's Locale

Earlier in the discussion on applets, we presented all the steps a Windows user takes to change their default locale. On Windows, changing system settings is not an isolated change, and affects other things such as the system date and time, which the user may not want changed. Other ways to allow users to run your applet using a different locale certainly exist.

There is a better way to accomplish the same task. You can set the default locale for the servlet without requiring user intervention, and base this setting on the user's language preference settings. We can use a servlet to determine the user's language preferences and then set the locale for an applet accordingly.

Example 11-7. AppletLocaleServlet

```
import java.io.*;
import java.util.*;
import javax.servlet.*;
import javax.servlet.http.*;
import com.oreilly.servlet.*;

public class AppletLocaleServlet extends HttpServlet {

  public void doGet(HttpServletRequest request, HttpServletResponse response) throws
      IOException, ServletException {

    String appletName = request.getParameter("Applet");
    String bundleName = request.getParameter("Bundle");
```

---

[4] The com.oreilly.servlet package is available at *http://www.servlets.com/resources/com.oreilly.servlet/index.html.*

Example 11-7. AppletLocaleServlet (continued)

```
    String acceptLanguage = request.getHeader("Accept-Language");
    String acceptCharset = request.getHeader("Accept-Charset");

    LocaleNegotiator negotiator =
      new LocaleNegotiator(bundleName, acceptLanguage, acceptCharset);

    Locale locale = negotiator.getLocale();
    String charset = negotiator.getCharset();
    ResourceBundle bundle = negotiator.getBundle();

    response.setContentType("text/plain; charset=" + charset);
    response.setHeader("Content-Language", locale.getLanguage());

    PrintWriter out = response.getWriter();
    out.println("<HTML>");
    out.println();
    out.println("<HEAD>");
    out.println("  <TITLE>AppletLocale servlets</TITLE>");
    out.println();
    out.println("<BODY>");
    out.println();
    out.println("<APPLET CODE=\"" + appletName + "\" WIDTH=\""
                  + bundle.getString("Width")
                  + "\" HEIGHT=\"" + bundle.getString("Width")
                  + "\"> ");
    out.println("<PARAM NAME=\"language\" VALUE=\"" + locale.getLanguage() + "\">");
    out.println("<PARAM NAME=\"country\" VALUE=\"" + locale.getCountry() + "\">");
    out.println("<PARAM NAME=\"variant\" VALUE=\"" + locale.getVariant() + "\">");
    Enumeration parameters = bundle.getKeys();
    String key;
    while (parameters.hasMoreElements()) {
      key = (String)parameters.nextElement();
      out.println("<PARAM NAME=\"" + key + "\" VALUE=\""
                    + bundle.getString(key) + "\">");
    }
    out.println("</APPLET>");
    out.println();
    out.println("</BODY>");
    out.println();
    out.println("</HTML>");
  }
}
```

In Example 11-8, we've isolated a set of specific resource strings that we want to generate <PARAM> tags for when we create the HTML to invoke the applet. Generating a localized "Applet loading …" message is one example of using these tags.

Example 11-8. AppletResources_en_US.properties File Used to Run AppletLocaleServlet

```
# Sample resources for an applet
# Locale: en_US
Width=250
Height=100
LoadingMessage=Applet loading ... Please Wait!
```

Note that the HTML source generated for our applet contains the proper language, country, and variant, given the preferred locale from the servlet request:

```
<HTML>

<HEAD>
    <TITLE>AppletLocale servlet</TITLE>

<BODY>

<APPLET CODE="HelloWorldApplet" WIDTH="250" HEIGHT="250">
<PARAM NAME="language" VALUE="en">
<PARAM NAME="country" VALUE="US">
<PARAM NAME="variant" VALUE="">
<PARAM NAME="Height" VALUE="100">
<PARAM NAME="LoadingMessage" VALUE="Applet loading ... Please Wait!">
<PARAM NAME="Width" VALUE="250">
</APPLET>

</BODY>

</HTML>
```

Keeping Track of a User's Locale Preference

Generating localized content for your users can be accomplished in a number of different ways. One way permits users to set their locale preference by submitting this information to the servlet using parameters encoded in the URL.

Figure 11-9 illustrates that the three components to a Locale object can be encoded in the URL.

Figure 11-9. Encoding the user's language preferences in the URL

Example 11-9 illustrates how this information can be parsed into a Locale object that is placed in the user's Session object.

Example 11-9. Storing the Locale in the User's Session Object Based on the User's Explicit Preference

```
import java.io.*;
import java.util.*;
import javax.servlet.*;
import javax.servlet.http.*;

public class ParameterizedLocaleSessionServlet extends HttpServlet {

  public String nullToEmpty(String input) {
    if (input == null)
      return "";
    else
      return input;
  }

  public void doGet(HttpServletRequest request, HttpServletResponse response) throws
      IOException, ServletException {

    HttpSession userSession = request.getSession();
    Locale userLocale = null;

    if (userSession.isNew()) {
      String language = request.getParameter("language");
      language = nullToEmpty(language);
      String country = request.getParameter("country");
      country = nullToEmpty(country);
      String variant = request.getParameter("variant");
      variant = nullToEmpty(variant);
      userLocale = new Locale(language, country, variant);
      userSession.setAttribute("userLocale", userLocale);
    } else {
      userLocale = (Locale)userSession.getAttribute("userLocale");
    }
  }
}
```

Example 11-10 illustrates how we could store the user's language preference in a session object. However, this time we use the user's preference in the Accept-Language header to automatically determine their locale. When designing your web application using this method, make sure that locales you don't support are handled properly. If your web application supports English, French, Hebrew, and Spanish, and a user's language preference is set to only Russian, this preference should be handled properly. One way of ensuring proper handling would be to fall back on a default language for the application and output an error message to the users, letting them know that your web application does not support their preferred language.

Example 11-10. Storing the Locale in the User's Session Object, Based on the Accept-Language Header

```
import java.io.*;
import java.util.*;
import javax.servlet.*;
import javax.servlet.http.*;

public class LocaleSessionServlet extends HttpServlet {

  public void doGet(HttpServletRequest request, HttpServletResponse response) throws
      IOException, ServletException {

    HttpSession userSession = request.getSession();
    if (userSession.isNew()) {
      userSession.setAttribute("userLocale", request.getLocale());
    }
  }
}
```

JavaServer Pages

JavaServer Page technology allows you to create dynamic content without having intimate knowledge of Java programming. JavaServer Pages, usually referred to as JSPs, are nothing more than text files that contain:

- All necessary information or content to render a page using a markup language such as HTML. JSPs are not restricted to generating HTML, but could also generate Wireless Markup Language (WML) or eXtensible Markup Language (XML). Thus, the page can be designed independently of your dynamic content.

- Different JSP *elements* and *scriptlets*. JSP elements are XML-like tags, which tell the JSP to perform a certain action; for example, to set a page property. Scriptlets are small code fragments written in Java. Scriptlets can be as simple or as complex as you want, but the simpler, the better. For complex tasks, a JSP can use other enterprise components such as Enterprise JavaBeans (EJBs).

Before we get into the internationalization aspects of JSPs, you need to understand how JSPs work. JSPs are compiled into a servlet the first time they are executed. Like servlets, the compiled JSP remains in memory in the servlet engine. Not only can they handle dynamic content generation, but they're fast as well.

In the canonical three-tier web application architecture depicted in Figure 11-10, JSPs reside in the presentation layer. Therefore, like standalone GUI applications, you need to design your JSPs with internationalization and localization in mind.

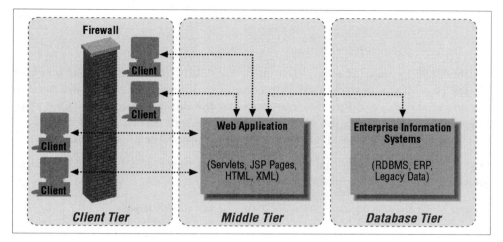

Figure 11-10. Three-tier web application

There is a page directive tag in the JSP specification that defines attributes that apply to an entire JSP page. If you develop an internationalized web application that uses JSPs, you need to be concerned with this tag since it may contain information regarding the character set that applies to a JSP page.

Example 11-11 shows how this step might be included in a JSP file.

Example 11-11. Applying a Specific Character Set to a JSP Page

```
<%@ include file="page_top.jsp" %>
<%@ page contentType="text/html; charset=ISO-8859-1" %>

<HTML>

<HEAD>
<TITLE>
<%
if(request.getParameter("pagetitle")==null) {

...
```

If the `contentType` attribute is left out of the `<%@ page ... %>` directive, then `text/html` is used as the default content-type attribute and ISO-8859-1 is used as the default for the character set attribute. The first occurrence of the `contentType` attribute is the one used to create the proper output stream that the JSP uses to deliver content back to the client. If you had the following code in a JSP:

```
<%@ include file="page_top.jsp" %>
<%@ page contentType="text/html; charset=ISO-8859-1" %>

...

<%@ page contentType="text/html; charset=UTF8" %>
```

the ISO-8859-1 character set is used. At compile time, the page directive is set for the JSP page; if you develop a JSP with content in different languages, you need to use one character encoding that can represent the different languages. One character encoding supported by many of today's browsers that can fulfill this role is UTF-8. Specifically, UTF-8 allows representation of any Unicode character.

Example 11-12 is a servlet that can be used to direct users to a JSP page specific to their browser's language preference settings.

Example 11-12. Servlet to Negotiate the Proper JSP Page Given a Browser Request

```
import java.io.*;
import java.util.*;
import javax.servlet.*;
import javax.servlet.http.*;

public class JSPLocaleNegotiatorServlet extends HttpServlet {

  private static final String defaultJSP = "/jsp/default_en_US.jsp";
  private static final String jspExtension = ".jsp";

  public void doGet(HttpServletRequest request, HttpServletResponse response) throws
      IOException, ServletException {

    Locale usersLocale = request.getLocale();

    StringBuffer jspWithLocale = new StringBuffer();
    if (request.getParameter("jsppage") != null) {
      jspWithLocale.append(request.getParameter("jsppage"));
      jspWithLocale.append("_");
      jspWithLocale.append(usersLocale.toString());
      jspWithLocale.append(jspExtension);
    } else
      jspWithLocale.append(defaultJSP);

    response.setLocale(usersLocale);
    getServletConfig().getServletContext()
        .getRequestDispatcher(jspWithLocale.toString())
        .forward(request,response);
  }
}
```

The JSP page created to display "Hello World" in English is rather simple, as shown in Example 11-13. Set the content type and the title of the page, and then print out your message in an increasingly large font.

Example 11-13. JSP Page Used to Display Hello World in English (hello_en.jsp)

```
<%@ page contentType="text/html; charset=ISO-8859-1" %>

<HTML>

<HEAD>
<TITLE>Hello World in English</TITLE>
</HEAD>

<BODY>

<%  for(int i = 1; i < 7;i++) { %>

    <FONT SIZE=<%=i%>>Hello World</FONT><BR>

<%  } %>

</BODY>
</HTML>
```

Example 11-14 is our JSP page used to display "Hello World" in Hebrew. Note that you explicitly tell the browser to use a character set capable of displaying the Hebrew characters. Beyond that, the page is almost exactly the same as the English example, except that you need to print out the message in Hebrew.

Example 11-14. JSP Page Used to Display Hello World in Hebrew (hello_iw.jsp)

```
<%@ page contentType="text/html; charset=UTF-8" %>

<HTML>

<HEAD>
<TITLE>Hello World in Hebrew</TITLE>
</HEAD>

<BODY DIR="rtl">

<%  for(int i = 1; i < 7;i++) { %>

    <FONT SIZE=<%=i%>> <% out.println("\u05E9\u05DC\u05D5\u05DD "+
                                "\u05E2\u05D5\u05DC\u05DD");
%>></FONT><BR>

<%  } %>

</BODY>
</HTML>
```

Figures 11-11 and 11-12 illustrate that you only need to change the language preference in our browser, and the JSPLocaleNegotiatorServlet servlet takes care of directing us to the proper JSP page for our language preference.

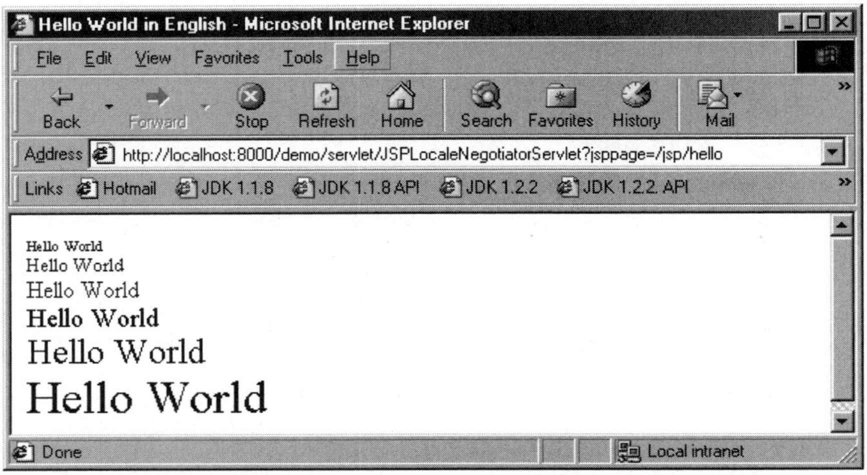

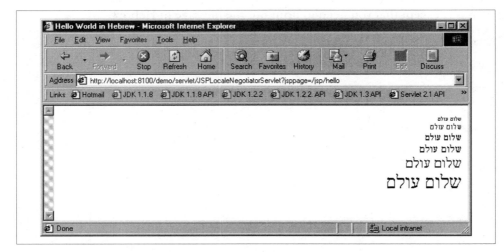

Figure 11-11. Using JSPLocaleNegotiator with a language preference set to English

Figure 11-12. Using JSPLocaleNegotiator with a language preference set to Hebrew

Note that in the JSP page for the Hello World in Hebrew you set the text direction attribute for the text contained within the body. Possible values for this attribute are "ltr" and "rtl." These values tell the browser that the text should be rendered left to right or right to left, respectively.

In Example 11-15, we develop JSPs to create the beginnings of an internationalized bookstore. The example uses English, French, and German. Previously, we said that for JSPs writing out more than one character set, you should use a character encoding that supports all the character sets you need. Since we use characters in our resource bundles that can be written using the ISO-8859-1 character encoding (the default character encoding for JSPs and servlets), we're okay for this example.

In the following example, we add all the locale-specific strings into the user's session based on the user's preferred locale. We also store the user's preferred locale in their session to determine the proper bookstore logo to display and the proper currency format to use.

Example 11-15. Login JSP That Can Add Locale-Specific Resources into the User's Session (loginpage.jsp)

```
<%@ page import="java.util.*" %>

<%
  Locale userLocale = request.getLocale();

  ResourceBundle bookstoreBundle = ResourceBundle.getBundle("Bookstore", userLocale);
    session.setAttribute("userLocale", userLocale);

  Enumeration bookstoreProperties = bookstoreBundle.getKeys();
  while (bookstoreProperties.hasMoreElements()) {
    String key = (String)bookstoreProperties.nextElement();
    String value = bookstoreBundle.getString(key);
    session.setAttribute(key, value);
  }

  Hashtable shoppingCart = (Hashtable)session.getAttribute("shoppingcart");

  if (shoppingCart != null) {
    session.setAttribute("shoppingcart", null);
  }
%>

<HTML>

<HEAD>
<TITLE><%=session.getValue("store.title")%></TITLE>
</HEAD>

<BODY>

<CENTER>
```

*Example 11-15. Login JSP That Can Add Locale-Specific Resources into
the User's Session (loginpage.jsp) (continued)*

```
<IMG SRC="<%=session.getValue("logo.image")+"_"+userLocale.getLanguage()
    +session.getValue("logo.image.extension")%>">

<H2><%=session.getValue("store.title")%></H2>

<BR>

<FORM ACTION="shoporeilly.jsp" METHOD="POST">

<TABLE BORDER="1">
<TR><TD><%=session.getValue("store.login")%></TD> <TD><INPUT TYPE="Text"
    NAME="login" SIZE="30"><BR></TD></TR>
<TR><TD>Password</TD> <TD><INPUT TYPE="Password" NAME="password"
    SIZE="10"></TD></TR>
</TABLE>

<P>

<INPUT TYPE="Submit" VALUE="<%=session.getValue("store.login")%>">

</FORM>

</CENTER>

</BODY>

</HTML>
```

Example 11-16 is the JSP to which the login JSP page posts its information after the
user clicks the login button. Note that at the top of the JSP we have a function that
determines the proper monetary format to use, based on the locale stored from
the user's session. See Chapter 5, *Formatting Messages*, for a review of message and
number formats. This example illustrates one aspect of developing internationalized web applications, but money units, dates, and times are often overlooked.

Example 11-16. Main Page for the Bookstore (shoporeilly.jsp)

```
<%@ page import="java.util.*" %>
<%@ page import="java.text.*" %>

<%!
  public String computeExchangeRate(double bookPrice, HttpSession session) {
    Locale userLocale = (Locale)session.getAttribute("userLocale");

    NumberFormat nf = NumberFormat.getInstance(userLocale);
    double exchangeRate = 0.0;
    try {
      exchangeRate =
```

Example 11-16. Main Page for the Bookstore (shoporeilly.jsp) (continued)

```
            ((Number)nf.parse((String)session.getValue("exchangerate"))).doubleValue();
      } catch (ParseException pe) {
        exchangeRate = 1.0;
      }

      NumberFormat localizedBookPrice = NumberFormat.getCurrencyInstance(userLocale);
      double convertedPrice = bookPrice * exchangeRate;
      return localizedBookPrice.format(convertedPrice);
  }
%>

<HTML>

<HEAD>
<TITLE><%=session.getValue("store.title")%></TITLE>
</HEAD>

<BODY>

<CENTER>

<H2><%=session.getValue("store.title")%></H2>

<BR>

<FORM NAME="oreillybookscatalog" ACTION="shoppingcart.jsp" METHOD="GET">

<SELECT NAME="books">

<OPTION VALUE="1-56592-206-9;34.95">Java Distributed Computing, Jim Farley,
      1-56592-206-9, 384 <%=session.getValue("book.pages") %>,
<%=computeExchangeRate(34.95,session) %></OPTION>
<OPTION VALUE="1-56592-483-5;29.95">Java Enterprise in a Nutshell,
      David Flanagan-Jim Farley-William Crawford-Kris Magnusson, 1-56592-483-5, 622
<%=session.getValue("book.pages") %>, <%=computeExchangeRate(29.95,session) %></OPTION>
<OPTION VALUE="1-56592-487-8;29.95">Java In A Nutshell-3rd Edition,
      David Flanagan, 1-56592-487-8, 668 <%=session.getValue("book.pages") %>,
<%=computeExchangeRate(29.95,session) %></OPTION>
<OPTION VALUE="1-56592-391-X;36.95">Java Servlet Programming,
      Jason Hunter with William Crawford, 1-56592-391-X, 528
<%=session.getValue("book.pages") %>, <%=computeExchangeRate(36.95,session) %></OPTION>
<OPTION VALUE="1-56592-455-X;44.95">Java Swing,
      Robert Eckstein-Marc Loy-Dave Wood, 1-56592-455-X, 1252
<%=session.getValue("book.pages") %>, <%=computeExchangeRate(44.95,session) %>
</OPTION>

</SELECT>

<BR>
```

Example 11-16. Main Page for the Bookstore (shoporeilly.jsp) (continued)

```
<%=session.getValue("add.quantity")%>: <INPUT TYPE="text" NAME="quantity"
   VALUE="1" SIZE="1" MAXLENGTH="1">

<INPUT NAME="submit" TYPE="Submit" VALUE="<%=session.getValue("add.book")%>">

</FORM>

<P><A HREF="loginpage.jsp"><%=session.getValue("store.return")%></A> |
   <A HREF="shoppingcart.jsp"><%=session.getValue("store.shoppingcart")%></A>

</CENTER>

</BODY>

</HTML>
```

The shopping cart page that displays the total purchase price for all books ordered is given in Example 11-17.

Example 11-17. Shopping Cart Page (shoppingcart.jsp)

```
<%@ page import="java.util.*" %>
<%@ page import="java.text.*" %>

<%!

  Hashtable shoppingCart;
  double totalPurchase;
  String totalPurchaseString;

%>

<%
  shoppingCart = (Hashtable)session.getAttribute("shoppingcart");

  if (shoppingCart == null) {
    shoppingCart = new Hashtable();
  }

  Integer purchaseQuantity;
  try {
    if ((request.getParameter("quantity")) != null
        && (request.getParameter("books") != null)) {
      purchaseQuantity = Integer.decode(request.getParameter("quantity"));
      if (purchaseQuantity.intValue() == 0) {
        shoppingCart.remove(request.getParameter("books"));
      } else {
        shoppingCart.put(request.getParameter("books"), purchaseQuantity);
      }
```

Example 11-17. Shopping Cart Page (shoppingcart.jsp) (continued)

```
      session.setAttribute("shoppingcart", shoppingCart);

      Enumeration keys = shoppingCart.keys();
      String bookAndPrice, price;
      Integer quantity;
      totalPurchase = 0.0;

       while (keys.hasMoreElements()) {
         bookAndPrice = (String)keys.nextElement();
         StringTokenizer st = new StringTokenizer(bookAndPrice, ";");
         st.nextToken();
         price = (String)st.nextToken();
         quantity = (Integer)shoppingCart.get(bookAndPrice);
         double dPrice = Double.parseDouble(price);
         double exchangeRate =
           Double.parseDouble((String)session.getValue("exchangerate"));
         totalPurchase += (dPrice * exchangeRate * quantity.intValue());
       }

      Locale userLocale = (Locale)session.getAttribute("userLocale");
      NumberFormat localizedTotalPrice =
        NumberFormat.getCurrencyInstance(userLocale);
      totalPurchaseString = localizedTotalPrice.format(totalPurchase);
    }
  } catch (NumberFormatException nfe) {
  }

%>

<HTML>

<HEAD>
<TITLE><%=session.getValue("checkout.label")%></TITLE>
</HEAD>

<BODY>

<CENTER>

<% if ((shoppingCart != null) && (shoppingCart.size() > 0)) { %>

  <P>
  <%=session.getValue("checkout.total")%> <%=totalPurchaseString%>.

<% } else { %>

  <%-- No items in the shopping cart --%>

<% } %>
```

Example 11-17. Shopping Cart Page (shoppingcart.jsp) (continued)

```
<P><A HREF="shoporeilly.jsp"><%=session.getValue("store.return")%></A>

</CENTER>

</BODY>

</HTML>
```

Example 11-18 is the default properties file we use as a fallback.

Example 11-18. Default Properties File for the O'Reilly Bookstore (Bookstore.properties)

```
#
# This properties file will be used for the default locale
#
add.book=Add Book
add.quantity=Quantity
book.author=Author
book.description=Description
book.ISBN=ISBN
book.pages=Pages
book.price=Purchase Price
book.title=Title
exchangerate=1.0
checkout.label=Purchase books
checkout.total=Total:
logo.image=oreilly_logo
logo.image.extension=.gif
store.login=Login
store.password=Password
store.return=Back to the bookstore
store.shoppingcart=View shopping cart
store.title=Welcome to O'Reilly & Associates
```

Example 11-19 is the properties resource bundle used for a German locale.

Example 11-19. Default Properties File for the O'Reilly Bookstore (Bookstore_de.properties)

```
# Properties file for the O'Reilly Internationalized Bookstore
#
# This properties file will be used for the German locale (de)
#
add.book=F\u00fcgen Sie Buch Hinzu
add.quantity=Quantit\u00e4t
book.author=Autor
book.description=Beschreibung
book.ISBN=ISBN
book.pages=Seiten
book.price=Kaufpreis
book.title=Name
checkout.label=Erwerb b\u00fccher
checkout.total=Gesamtmenge:
```

Example 11-19. Default Properties File for the O'Reilly Bookstore (Bookstore_de.properties) (continued)

```
exchangerate=2.2032
shoppingcart.view=
store.login=Anmeldung
store.password=Kennwort
store.return=Wechselt zur vorherigen Seite
store.shoppingcart=Ansicht einkaufswagen
store.title=Willkommen beim O'Reilly Verlag
```

Finally, Example 11-20 shows the properties resource bundle used for the French locale.

Example 11-20. Default Properties File for the O'Reilly Bookstore (Bookstore_fr.properties)

```
# Properties file for the O'Reilly Internationalized Bookstore
#
# This properties file will be used for the French locale (fr)
#
add.book=Ajoutez Le Livre
add.quantity=Quantit\u00e9
book.author=Auteur
book.description=Description
book.ISBN=ISBN
book.pages=Pages
book.price=Prix d'achat D'Achat
book.title=Titre
checkout.label=Journaux d'achats
checkout.total=Total:
exchangerate=7.3886
shoppingcart.view=Afficher votre panier
store.login=Connexion
store.password=Mot de passe
store.return=Retourne \u00e0 la page pr\u00e9c\u00e9dente
store.shoppingcart=Votre panier
store.title=Site des \u00c9ditions O'Reilly
```

Figure 11-13 shows you the main login page on which the browser is set using English as the preferred language.

Figure 11-14 shows what the bookstore looks like when the browser is set using English as the preferred language.

Figure 11-13. O'Reilly Bookstore when English is set as the preferred locale

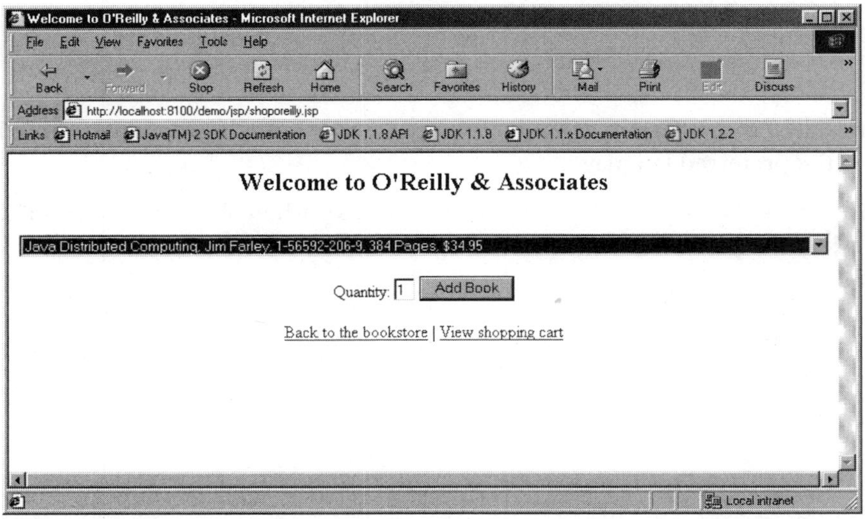

Figure 11-14. Book selection page when English is set as the preferred locale

Figure 11-15 shows the user's shopping cart, which contains the total purchase price for the books added to the shopping cart.

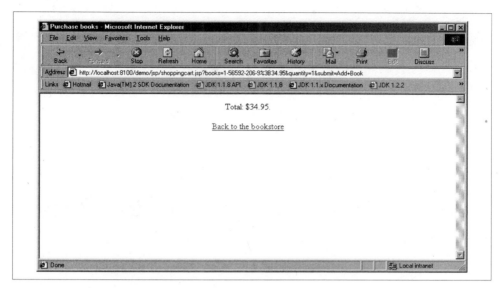

Figure 11-15. Displaying the total purchase price for books in the user's shopping cart

Figure 11-16 shows the login page when the user is using, or has changed, the language preference to German. Notice that the O'Reilly logo, the welcome title, and the login button have changed accordingly.

Figure 11-17 illustrates that things such as the book's price are now in German marks and not U.S. dollars. The number's representation has also changed.[5]

Finally, Figure 11-18 shows the user's shopping cart total, but this time the total is in German marks.

---

[5] Be sure to check the current exchange rates, as this example's localized exchange rates will surely change. You can check the PACIFIC Exchange Rate Service for up-to-date rates. Its web site is located at *http://pacific.commerce.ubc.ca/xr/*.

Figure 11-16. O'Reilly Bookstore when German is set as the preferred locale

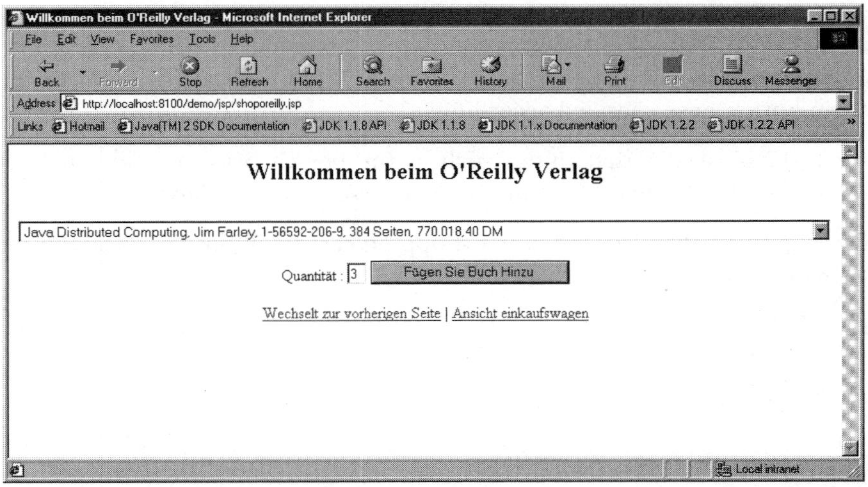

Figure 11-17. Book selection page when German is set as the preferred locale

Figure 11-18. Displaying the total purchase price for books in the user's shopping cart

12

Future Enhancements to the Internationalization Support in Java

While the current version of Sun's Java provides significant support for software internationalization and localization, many more features could still be added in future versions. This chapter explores some of the capabilities Sun's Internationalization team is considering for addition to future versions of their implementation of the Java platform.

Unicode 3.0 Support

As we discussed in Chapter 6, *Character Sets and Unicode,* Java is based on the Unicode Standard Version 2.1. In February 2000, the Unicode Consortium released the Unicode Standard Version 3.0. An additional 10,307 characters are included in the new version, bringing the total number of characters to 49,194. Several new blocks were added to the Unicode Standard, as shown in Table 12-1.

Table 12-1. Additional Blocks Added to the Unicode Standard Version 3.0

Block Name	Description
Syriac	A descendant of Aramaic.
Thanna	A script used for Dhivehi, spoken in the Republic of the Maldives.
Sinhala	A script used to write Sinhalese, spoken in Sri Lanka.
Myanmar	The official script of the Burmese language.
Ethiopic	The syllabic script used to write the Ethiopian languages Ge'ez, Amharic, Tigre, and Oromo.

Table 12-1. Additional Blocks Added to the Unicode Standard Version 3.0 (continued)

Block Name	Description
Cherokee	The syllabic script used for the Cherokee language.
Unified Canadian Aboriginal Syllabics	A unification of the syllabic symbols used by several aboriginal groups in Canada.
Ogham	A script used to write Irish. It appears on monuments throughout the British Isles.
Runic	An extinct script used to write various forms of Anglo-Saxon, German and Scandinavian runes from the first century.
Khmer	The script used to write Khmer, the official language of Cambodia.
Mongolian	The script used to write the Mongolian language. Mongolian is cursive and is written vertically from top to bottom starting at the left of the page and moving toward the right.
Braille Patterns	All possible combinations of eight-dot Braille patterns.
CJK Radicals Supplement	Alternate forms of the KangXi radicals.
KangXi Radicals	The 214 radicals that are the basis of all Chinese ideographs.
Ideographic Description Characters	Provides a way to describe ideographic characters by combining existing characters into a defined pattern. It should be used to represent ideographic characters that are not yet defined by Unicode.
Bopomofo Extended	Additional Bopomofo characters used to input Chinese.
CJK Unified Ideographs Extension A	Rare ideographs unified from Chinese, Japanese, Korean, and Vietnamese standards.
Yi Syllables	The Yi syllabary used to write the Yi language spoken in Western China.
Yi Radicals	The radicals that make up the Yi syllabary.

Besides the addition of characters to existing scripts and support for new scripts, the Unicode Standard Version 3.0 provides updated character properties (i.e., bidirectional, case, East-Asian width, etc.).

To support the new Unicode Standard, future versions of Java need to be upgraded in the following ways:

- The `java.lang.Character` and `java.lang.Character.UnicodeBlock` classes need updating to provide access to the new characters and blocks.

- The normalization algorithm, used by the `Collator` object, needs modification so that collation and string comparison are carried out correctly.

- The case mapping rules used to perform case mappings between upper- and lowercase letters need upgrading to handle new characters.

- The encoding converters need updating to support character conversion into and out of Unicode. Unicode Version 2.1 did not include many characters that are part of supported encodings, but they now exist in Unicode Version 3.0. The character encoding converters need modification to support these new characters.

Surrogate Pairs

In Chapter 6, we mentioned that a Surrogates Area that allows allocation of an additional 1,048,576 code points has been set aside. Although no characters in the Unicode Standard Version 3.0 are allocated in the surrogate range, characters are expected to appear there within the near future. As a result, future versions of Java need to support surrogate pairs to handle new characters added in this range.

The biggest problem in supporting surrogate pairs in the current version of Java is that char is a 16-bit base type, only capable of holding a Unicode value in the range of \u0000 through \uFFFF. Changing the size of char to a 32-bit value is not an acceptable option because it would cause incompatibilities in existing applications and in the Java platform itself.

Several options to overcome this problem are being considered, including: [1]

- Overloading the use of int to represent a UTF-32 character and provide supporting methods.

- Adding a new base type called char32, a corresponding Character32 class, and supporting methods.

- Creating an abstract representation of a Unicode character so that an object always represents each Unicode character. One obvious downside of this approach is that characters become heavyweight.

- Combining char pairs to represent low and high surrogates.

---

[1] Taken from *Java Internationalization Roadmap*, by Brian Beck, Stuart Gill, Norbert Lindenberg, and John O'Conner, Sixteenth International Unicode Conference.

Enhanced Complex Text

South and South East Asian Scripts

As we described in Chapter 8, *Fonts and Text Rendering,* Java provides support for rendering complex writing system text, such as Arabic and Hebrew. Future releases of Java will incorporate the work done at IBM to support rendering of Thai and Indic scripts. Support of these scripts requires enhancements to Java's rendering engine to perform the layout correctly. The Indic scripts use ligatures heavily, requiring the Lucida Sans font included with Sun's Java 2 Runtime Environment to be amended with the set of additional necessary ligatures.

Thai has some special text processing requirements that need support. Specifically, Thai does not use spaces to separate words, so `BreakIterator` and its subclasses need enchancement. The IBM team has already done this work and Sun is expected to adopt much of their work.

Component Orientation

Support for `ComponentOrientation` was added to Java in JDK 1.2.2, with additional functionality provided in JDK 1.3. The `ComponentOrientation` class is a marker used by certain component classes to indicate how they should lay out text and subcomponents. The following Swing components do not currently support right-to-left layout:

- `javax.swing.JTable`

- `javax.swing.JSplitPane`

- `javax.swing.JOptionPane`

- `javax.swing.JColorChooser`

- `javax.swing.JFileChooser`

- `javax.swing.BoxLayout`

Support for right-to-left layout is expected to be added to these components in a future release. Support for right-to-left layout will probably be added to the following AWT layout managers, too:

- `java.awt.GridLayout`

- `java.awt.GridBagLayout`

When Swing components are first instantiated, their `ComponentOrientation` is set to `ComponentOrientation.UNKNOWN`. In the future, the default orientation will be set appropriately depending on the locale. Support will also be provided to set the orientation for a group of components, rather than having to set the orientation for each individual component within the group.

Character Converter Framework

The character encoding converters provided with Sun's Java Runtime Environment are useful for many applications. A few drawbacks exist, however.

- Not all encodings are guaranteed to be supported in all implementations of the Java 2 platform. Table 12-2 lists the encodings that implementations of the Java 2 platform, Standard Edition Version 1.3 are required to support.[2]

- If an encoding isn't supported, no mechanism is in place to provide a custom character converter.

- The user has no control over how conversion of undefined characters is handled; if a character in one encoding cannot be mapped to a character in another encoding because no such mapping exists, a developer might want to handle this issue in a special way (e.g., throw an exception, skip the character, map it to a generic substitute character, etc.).

Table 12-2. Character Encodings Guaranteed to Exist in J2SE, Version 1.3

Encoding	Description
US-ASCII	Seven-bit ASCII, a.k.a. ISO646-US, a.k.a. the Basic Latin block of the Unicode character set
ISO-8859-1	ISO Latin Alphabet No. 1, a.k.a. ISO-LATIN-1
UTF-8	Eight-bit Unicode Transformation Format
UTF-16BE	Sixteen-bit Unicode Transformation Format, big-endian byte order
UTF-16LE	Sixteen-bit Unicode Transformation Format, little-endian byte order
UTF-16	Sixteen-bit Unicode Transformation Format, byte order specified by a mandatory initial byte-order mark (either order accepted on input, big-endian used on output)

To alleviate these issues, plans to develop a Character Converter Framework that provides a public API and SPI are underway.

The API will give developers fine-grain control over the character conversion process. Through a set of public interfaces, an application can get a converter object

---

[2] *http://java.sun.com/j2se/1.3/docs/guide/intl/encoding.doc.html*

and set parameters on that object to change its behavior during conversion. The API will also provide methods to allow querying of the Java Runtime Environment for supported character encodings.

The SPI will allow developers to provide customized character converters that can be subsequently accessed via the API. The SPI will support two separate models: in the first model, an application can create its own converter for private use; in the second model, converters can be created, packaged, and installed as extensions in a manner similar to that used for input methods. The installed converter is then available to any application using that JVM.

Improving the Input Method Framework

Several enhancements to the input method framework are being considered, including:

- Improving the mechanism by which input methods are selected is a priority. Currently, the user must select the input method from a pop-up menu, as described in Chapter 10, *Input Methods*. It is expected that in the next release of the JDK, input methods could be selected using a hot key (e.g., pressing the F1 key).

- In the current implementation of the input method framework, once an input method has been selected, it is selected for the current VM session only. Future enhancements will validate the input method selection across multiple VM instantiations.

- Further down the road, changes to the input method framework will allow SPI-compliant input methods to interact with one another via chaining or some other mechanism. This change will enable creation of more complex input methods by combining simpler input methods.

A

Language and Country Codes

This appendix consists of two large tables. Table A-1 lists the ISO-639 language codes; Table A-2 lists the ISO-3166 country codes.

Table A-1: ISO-639 Language Codes[1]

Language	ISO Code	Language	ISO Code
Abkhazian	ab	Bulgarian	bg
Afar	aa	Burmese	my
Afrikaans	af	Byelorussian	be
Albanian	sq	Cambodian	km
Amharic	am	Catalan	ca
Arabic	ar	Chinese	zh
Armenian	hy	Corsican	co
Assamese	as	Croatian	hr
Aymara	ay	Czech	cs
Azerbaijani	az	Danish	da
Bashkir	ba	Dutch	nl
Basque	eu	English	en
Bengali (Bangla)	bn	Esperanto	eo
Bhutani	dz	Estonian	et
Bihari	bh	Faeroese	fo
Bislama	bi	Farsi	fa
Breton	br	Fiji	fj

[1] Derived from *http://www.unicode.org/unicode/onlinedat/languages.html*

Table A-1: ISO-639 Language Codes (continued)

Language	ISO Code	Language	ISO Code
Finnish	fi	Latvian (Lettish)	lv
French	fr	Lingala	ln
Frisian	fy	Lithuanian	lt
Galician	gl	Macedonian	mk
Georgian	ka	Malagasy	mg
German	de	Malay	ms
Greek	el	Malayalam	ml
Greenlandic	kl	Maltese	mt
Guarani	gn	Manx Gaelic	gv^2
Gujarati	gu	Maori	mi
Hausa	ha	Marathi	mr
Hebrew	iw, he	Moldavian	mo
Hindi	hi	Mongolian	mn
Hungarian	hu	Nauru	na
Icelandic	is	Nepali	ne
Indonesian	in, id	Norwegian	no
Interlingua	ia	Occitan	oc
Interlingue	ie	Oriya	or
Inuktitut	iu	Oromo (Afan)	om
Inupiak	ik	Pashto (Pushto)	ps
Irish	ga	Polish	pl
Italian	it	Portuguese	pt
Japanese	ja	Punjabi	pa
Javanese	jw	Quechua	qu
Kannada	kn	Rhaeto-Romance	rm
Kashmiri	ks	Romanian	ro
Kazakh	kk	Russian	ru
Kinyarwanda	rw	Samoan	sm
Kirghiz	ky	Sangro	sg
Kirundi	rn	Sanskrit	sa
Korean	ko	Scots Gaelic	gd
Kurdish	ku	Serbian	sr
Laotian	lo	Serbo-Croatian	sh
Latin	la	Sesotho	st

---

[2] Proposed

Table A-1: ISO-639 Language Codes (continued)

Language	ISO Code	Language	ISO Code
Setswana	tn	Tigrinya	ti
Shona	sn	Tonga	to
Sindhi	sd	Tsonga	ts
Singhalese	si	Turkish	tr
Siswati	ss	Turkmen	tk
Slovak	sk	Twi	tw
Slovenian	sl	Uighur	ug
Somali	so	Ukrainian	uk
Spanish	es	Urdu	ur
Sundanese	su	Uzbek	uz
Swahili	sw	Vietnamese	vi
Swedish	sv	Volapük	vo
Tagalog	tl	Welsh	cy
Tajik	tg	Wolof	wo
Tamil	ta	Xhosa	xh
Tatar	tt	Yiddish	ji, yi
Telugu	te	Yoruba	yo
Thai	th	Zulu	zu
Tibetan	bo		

Table A-2: ISO-3166 Country Codes[3]

Country	Two Character ISO Code	Three Character ISO Code
Afghanistan	AF	AFG
Albania	AL	ALB
Algeria	DZ	DZA
American Samoa	AS	ASM
Andorra	AD	AND
Angola	AO	AGO
Anguilla	AI	AIA
Antarctica	AQ	ATA
Antigua and Barbuda	AG	ATG
Argentina	AR	ARG

[3] Derived from *http://www.unicode.org/unicode/onlinedat/countries.html*

Table A-2: ISO-3166 Country Codes (continued)

Country	Two Character ISO Code	Three Character ISO Code
Armenia	AM	ARM
Aruba	AW	ABW
Australia	AU	AUS
Austria	AT	AUT
Azerbaijan	AZ	AZE
Bahamas	BS	BHS
Bahrain	BH	BHR
Bangladesh	BD	BGD
Barbados	BB	BRB
Belarus	BY	BLR
Belgium	BE	BEL
Belize	BZ	BLZ
Benin	BJ	BEN
Bermuda	BM	BMU
Bhutan	BT	BTN
Bolivia	BO	BOL
Bosnia and Herzegovina	BA	BIH
Botswana	BW	BWA
Bouvet Island	BV	BVT
Brazil	BR	BRA
British Indian Ocean Territory	IO	IOT
Brunei Darussalam	BN	BRN
Bulgaria	BG	BGR
Burkina Faso	BF	BFA
Burundi	BI	BDI
Cambodia	KH	KHM
Cameroon	CM	CMR
Canada	CA	CAN
Cape Verde	CV	CPV
Cayman Islands	KY	CYM
Central African Republic	CF	CAF
Chad	TD	TCD
Chile	CL	CHL
China	CN	CHN
Christmas Island	CX	CXR

Table A-2: ISO-3166 Country Codes (continued)

Country	Two Character ISO Code	Three Character ISO Code
Cocos (Keeling) Islands	CC	CCK
Colombia	CO	COL
Comoros	KM	COM
Congo	CG	COG
Cook Islands	CK	COK
Costa Rica	CR	CRI
Côte d'Ivoire	CI	CIV
Croatia (Local Name: Hrvatska)	HR	HRV
Cuba	CU	CUB
Cyprus	CY	CYP
Czech Republic	CZ	CZE
Denmark	DK	DNK
Djibouti	DJ	DJI
Dominica	DM	DMA
Dominican Republic	DO	DOM
East Timor	TP	TMP
Ecuador	EC	ECU
Egypt	EG	EGY
El Salvador	SV	SLV
Equatorial Guinea	GQ	GNQ
Eritrea	ER	ERI
Estonia	EE	EST
Ethiopia	ET	ETH
Falkland Islands (Malvinas)	FK	FLK
Faroe Islands	FO	FRO
Fiji	FJ	FJI
Finland	FI	FIN
France	FR	FRA
France, Metropolitan	FX	FXX
French Guiana	GF	GUF
French Polynesia	PF	PYF
French Southern Territories	TF	ATF
Gabon	GA	GAB
Gambia	GM	GMB
Georgia	GE	GEO

Table A-2: ISO-3166 Country Codes (continued)

Country	Two Character ISO Code	Three Character ISO Code
Germany	DE	DEU
Ghana	GH	GHA
Gibraltar	GI	GIB
Greece	GR	GRC
Greenland	GL	GRL
Grenada	GD	GRD
Guadeloupe	GP	GLP
Guam	GU	GUM
Guatemala	GT	GTM
Guinea	GN	GIN
Guinea-Bissau	GW	GNB
Guyana	GY	GUY
Haiti	HT	HTI
Heard and McDonald Islands	HM	HMD
Honduras	HN	HND
Hong Kong	HK	HKG
Hungary	HU	HUN
Iceland	IS	ISL
India	IN	IND
Indonesia	ID	IDN
Iran (Islamic Republic of)	IR	IRN
Iraq	IQ	IRQ
Ireland	IE	IRL
Israel	IL	ISR
Italy	IT	ITA
Jamaica	JM	JAM
Japan	JP	JPN
Jordan	JO	JOR
Kazakhstan	KZ	KAZ
Kenya	KE	KEN
Kiribati	KI	KIR
Korea, Democratic People's Republic of	KP	PRK
Korea, Republic of	KR	KOR
Kuwait	KW	KWT
Kyrgyzstan	KG	KGZ

Table A-2: ISO-3166 Country Codes (continued)

Country	Two Character ISO Code	Three Character ISO Code
Lao People's Democratic Republic	LA	LAO
Latvia	LV	LVA
Lebanon	LB	LBN
Lesotho	LS	LSO
Liberia	LR	LBR
Libyan Arab Jamahiriya	LY	LBY
Liechtenstein	LI	LIE
Lithuania	LT	LTU
Luxembourg	LU	LUX
Macao	MO	MAC
Macedonia, The Former Yugoslav Republic of	MK	MKD
Madagascar	MG	MDG
Malawi	MW	MWI
Malaysia	MY	MYS
Maldives	MV	MDV
Mali	ML	MLI
Malta	MT	MLT
Marshall Islands	MH	MHL
Martinique	MQ	MTQ
Mauritania	MR	MRT
Mauritius	MU	MUS
Mayotte	YT	MYT
Mexico	MX	MEX
Micronesia, Federated States of	FM	FSM
Moldova, Republic of	MD	MDA
Monaco	MC	MCO
Mongolia	MN	MNG
Montserrat	MS	MSR
Morocco	MA	MAR
Mozambique	MZ	MOZ
Myanmar	MM	MMR
Namibia	NA	NAM
Nauru	NR	NRU
Nepal	NP	NPL

Table A-2: ISO-3166 Country Codes (continued)

Country	Two Character ISO Code	Three Character ISO Code
Netherlands	NL	NLD
Netherlands Antilles	AN	ANT
New Caledonia	NC	NCL
New Zealand	NZ	NZL
Nicaragua	NI	NIC
Niger	NE	NER
Nigeria	NG	NGA
Niue	NU	NIU
Norfolk Island	NF	NFK
Northern Mariana Islands	MP	MNP
Norway	NO	NOR
Oman	OM	OMN
Pakistan	PK	PAK
Palau	PW	PLW
Panama	PA	PAN
Papua New Guinea	PG	PNG
Paraguay	PY	PRY
Peru	PE	PER
Philippines	PH	PHL
Pitcairn	PN	PCN
Poland	PL	POL
Portugal	PT	PRT
Puerto Rico	PR	PRI
Qatar	QA	QAT
Réunion	RE	REU
Romania	RO	ROM
Russian Federation	RU	RUS
Rwanda	RW	RWA
Saint Kitts and Nevis	KN	KNA
Saint Lucia	LC	LCA
Saint Vincent and the Grenadines	VC	VCT
Samoa	WS	WSM
San Marino	SM	SMR
Sao Tome and Principe	ST	STP
Saudi Arabia	SA	SAU

Table A-2: ISO-3166 Country Codes (continued)

Country	Two Character ISO Code	Three Character ISO Code
Senegal	SN	SEN
Seychelles	SC	SYC
Sierra Leone	SL	SLE
Singapore	SG	SGP
Slovakia (Slovak Republic)	SK	SVK
Slovenia	SI	SVN
Solomon Islands	SB	SLB
Somalia	SO	SOM
South Africa	ZA	ZAF
Spain	ES	ESP
Sri Lanka	LK	LKA
St. Helena	SH	SHN
St. Pierre and Miquelon	PM	SPM
Sudan	SD	SDN
Suriname	SR	SUR
Svalbard and Jan Mayen Islands	SJ	SJM
Swaziland	SZ	SWZ
Sweden	SE	SWE
Switzerland	CH	CHE
Syrian Arab Republic	SY	SYR
Taiwan, Province of China	TW	TWN
Tajikistan	TJ	TJK
Tanzania, United Republic of	TZ	TZA
Thailand	TH	THA
Togo	TG	TGO
Tokelau	TK	TKL
Tonga	TO	TON
Trinidad and Tobago	TT	TTO
Tunisia	TN	TUN
Turkey	TR	TUR
Turkmenistan	TM	TKM
Turks and Caicos Islands	TC	TCA
Tuvalu	TV	TUV
Uganda	UG	UGA
Ukraine	UA	UKR

Table A-2: ISO-3166 Country Codes (continued)

Country	Two Character ISO Code	Three Character ISO Code
United Arab Emirates	AE	ARE
United Kingdom	GB	GBR
United States	US	USA
United States Minor Outlying Islands	UM	UMI
Uruguay	UY	URY
Uzbekistan	UZ	UZB
Vanuatu	VU	VUT
Vatican City State	VA	VAT
Venezuela	VE	VEN
Vietnam	VN	VNM
Virgin Islands (British)	VG	VGB
Virgin Islands (U.S.)	VI	VIR
Wallis and Futuna Islands	WF	WLF
Western Sahara	EH	ESH
Yemen	YE	YEM
Yugoslavia	YU	YUG
Zaire	ZR	ZAR
Zambia	ZM	ZMB
Zimbabwe	ZW	ZWE

B

Character Encodings Supported by Java

This appendix provides a list of the character encodings supported by Sun's Java 2 Platform, Standard Edition, Version 1.3. For a list of the encodings supported by other implementations of Java, consult the documentation provided by the vendor.[1] For each table, the "Encoding Keyword" is the name of the `file.encoding` property as well as the string that should be used in Java methods that request an encoding. Table B-1 shows the character encodings that all implementations of the Java 2 platform, Standard Edition, Version 1.3 are required to support.

Table B-1. Character Encodings All Java Implementations Must Support

Encoding Keyword	Description
ASCII	Seven-bit ASCII
ISO8859_1	ISO Latin Alphabet No. 1
UTF8	8-bit Unicode Transformation Format
UnicodeBigUnmarked	Sixteen-bit Unicode Transformation Format, big-endian byte order
UnicodeLittleUnmarked	Sixteen-bit Unicode Transformation Format, little-endian byte order
UTF-16	Sixteen-bit Unicode Transformation Format, byte order specified by a mandatory initial byte-order mark

---

[1] The encodings supported by Sun's JDK Version 1.1 are available online at *http://java.sun.com/products/ jdk/1.1/docs/guide/intl/encoding.doc.html*. The character encodings supported by Sun's J2SE Version 1.2 are available online at *http://java.sun.com/products/jdk/1.2/docs/guide/internat/encoding.doc.html*.

The Microsoft Windows version of Sun's Java 2 Runtime Environment, Standard Edition, Version 1.3 comes in two flavors: the US-only version and the international version. Table B-2 lists all character encodings provided in the US-only version. These character encodings are located in *lib/rt.jar*.

Table B-2. Character Encodings Found in the US-only Version of Sun's Java 2 Runtime Environment, Standard Edition, Version 1.3

Encoding Keyword	Description
ASCII	Seven-bit ASCII
Cp1252	Windows Latin-1
ISO8859_1	ISO Latin Alphabet No. 1
UnicodeBig	Sixteen-bit Unicode Transformation Format, big-endian byte order, with byte-order mark
UnicodeBigUnmarked	Sixteen-bit Unicode Transformation Format, big-endian byte order
UnicodeLittle	Sixteen-bit Unicode Transformation Format, little-endian byte order, with byte-order mark
UnicodeLittleUnmarked	Sixteen-bit Unicode Transformation Format, little-endian byte order
UTF8	8-bit Unicode Transformation Format
UTF-16	Sixteen-bit Unicode Transformation Format, byte order specified by a mandatory initial byte-order mark

Sun's Java 2 SDK, Standard Edition, Version 1.3 for Windows or Solaris and the Java 2 Runtime Environment, Standard Edition, Version 1.3 for Solaris support the character encodings listed in Table B-2 and the character encodings listed in Table B-3. In addition, the character encodings shown in Table B-3 are available in the international version of the Runtime Environment for Windows found in *lib/i18n.jar*.

Table B-3. Extended Character Encodings

Encoding Keyword	Description
Big5	Big5, Traditional Chinese
Cp037	USA, Canada (Bilingual, French), Netherlands, Portugal, Brazil, Australia
Cp273	IBM Austria, Germany
Cp277	IBM Denmark, Norway
Cp278	IBM Finland, Sweden
Cp280	IBM Italy

Table B-3. Extended Character Encodings (continued)

Encoding Keyword	Description
Cp284	IBM Catalan/Spain, Spanish Latin America
Cp285	IBM United Kingdom, Ireland
Cp297	IBM France
Cp420	IBM Arabic
Cp424	IBM Hebrew
Cp437	MS-DOS United States, Australia, New Zealand, South Africa
Cp500	EBCDIC 500V1
Cp737	PC Greek
Cp775	PC Baltic
Cp838	IBM Thailand extended SBCS
Cp850	MS-DOS Latin-1
Cp852	MS-DOS Latin-2
Cp855	IBM Cyrillic
Cp857	IBM Turkish
Cp860	MS-DOS Portuguese
Cp861	MS-DOS Icelandic
Cp862	PC Hebrew
Cp863	MS-DOS Canadian French
Cp864	PC Arabic
Cp865	MS-DOS Nordic
Cp866	MS-DOS Russian
Cp868	MS-DOS Pakistan
Cp869	IBM Modern Greek
Cp870	IBM Multilingual Latin-2
Cp871	IBM Iceland
Cp874	IBM Thai
Cp875	IBM Greek
Cp918	IBM Pakistan (Urdu)
Cp921	IBM Latvia, Lithuania (AIX, DOS)
Cp922	IBM Estonia (AIX, DOS)
Cp930	Japanese Katakana-Kanji mixed with 4370 UDC, superset of 5026
Cp933	Korean Mixed with 1880 UDC, superset of 5029
Cp935	Simplified Chinese Host mixed with 1880 UDC, superset of 5031
Cp937	Traditional Chinese Host mixed with 6204 UDC, superset of 5033
Cp939	Japanese Latin Kanji mixed with 4370 UDC, superset of 5035
Cp942	Japanese (OS/2) superset of 932

Table B-3. Extended Character Encodings (continued)

Encoding Keyword	Description
Cp942C	Variant of Cp942
Cp943	IBM OS/2 Japanese, superset of Cp932 and Shift-JIS
Cp943C	Variant of Cp943
Cp948	OS/2 Chinese (Taiwan) superset of 938
Cp949	PC Korean
Cp949C	Variant of Cp949
Cp950	PC Chinese (Hong Kong, Taiwan)
Cp964	AIX Chinese (Taiwan)
Cp970	AIX Korean
Cp1006	IBM AIX Pakistan (Urdu)
Cp1025	IBM Multilingual Cyrillic: Bulgaria, Bosnia, Herzegovinia, Macedonia (FYR)
Cp1026	IBM Latin-5, Turkey
Cp1046	IBM Arabic (Windows)
Cp1097	IBM Iran (Farsi)/Persian
Cp1098	IBM Iran (Farsi)/Persian (PC)
Cp1112	IBM Latria, Lithuania
Cp1122	IBM Estonia
Cp1123	IBM Ukraine
Cp1124	IBM AIX Ukraine
Cp1140	Variant of Cp037 with Euro Character
Cp1141	Variant of Cp273 with Euro Character
Cp1142	Variant of Cp277 with Euro Character
Cp1143	Variant of Cp278 with Euro Character
Cp1144	Variant of Cp280 with Euro Character
Cp1145	Variant of Cp284 with Euro Character
Cp1146	Variant of Cp285 with Euro Character
Cp1147	Variant of Cp297 with Euro Character
Cp1148	Variant of Cp500 with Euro Character
Cp1149	Variant of Cp871 with Euro Character
CP1250	Windows Eastern European
Cp1251	Windows Cyrillic
Cp1253	Windows Greek
Cp1254	Windows Turkish
Cp1255	Windows Hebrew
Cp1256	Windows Arabic

Table B-3. Extended Character Encodings (continued)

Encoding Keyword	Description
Cp1257	Windows Baltic
Cp1258	Windows Vietnamese
Cp1381	IBM OS/2, DOS People's Republic of China (PRC)
Cp1383	IBM AIX People's Republic of China (PRC)
Cp33722	IBM-eucJP - Japanese (superset of 5050)
EUC_CN	GB2312, EUC Encoding, simplified Chinese
EUC_JP	JIS0201, 0208, 0212, EUC Encoding, Japanese
EUC_KR	KS C 5601, EUC Encoding, Korean
EUC_TW	CNS11643 (Plane 1-3), T. Chinese, EUC Encoding
GBK	GBK, Simplified Chinese
ISO2022CN	ISO 2022 CN, Chinese
ISO2022CN_CNS	CNS 11643 in ISO-2022-CN form, T. Chinese (conversion from Unicode only)
ISO2022CN_GB	GB 2312 in ISO-2022-CN form, S. Chinese (conversion from Unicode only)
ISO2022JP	JIS0201, 0208, 0212, ISO2022 Encoding, Japanese
ISO2022KR	ISO 2022 KR, Korean
ISO8859_2	ISO 8859-4, Latin alphabet No. 2
ISO8859_3	ISO 8859-4, Latin alphabet No. 3
ISO8859_4	ISO 8859-4, Latin alphabet No. 4
ISO8859_5	ISO 8859-5, Latin/Cyrillic alphabet
ISO8859_6	ISO 8859-6, Latin/Arabic alphabet
ISO8859_7	ISO 8859-7, Latin/Greek alphabet
ISO8859_8	ISO 8859-8, Latin/Hebrew alphabet
ISO8859_9	ISO 8859-9, Latin alphabet No. 5
ISO8859_13	ISO 8859-13, Latin alphabet No. 7
ISO8859_15_FDIS	ISO 8859-15, Latin alphabet No. 9
JIS0201	JIS 0201, Japanese
JIS0208	JIS 0208, Japanese
JIS0212	JIS 0212, Japanese
JISAutoDetect	Detects and converts from Shift-JIS, EUC-JP, ISO 2022 JP (conversion to Unicode only)
Johab	Johab, Korean
KOI8_R	KOI8-R, Russian
MS874	Windows Thai
MS932	Windows Japanese
MS936	Windows Simplified Chinese

Table B-3. Extended Character Encodings (continued)

Encoding Keyword	Description
MS949	Windows Korean
MS950	Windows Traditional Chinese
MacArabic	Macintosh Arabic
MacCentralEurope	Macintosh Latin-2
MacCroatian	Macintosh Croatian
MacCyrillic	Macintosh Cyrillic
MacDingbat	Macintosh Dingbat
MacGreek	Macintosh Greek
MacHebrew	Macintosh Hebrew
MacIceland	Macintosh Iceland
MacRoman	Macintosh Roman
MacRomania	Macintosh Romania
MacSymbol	Macintosh Symbol
MacThai	Macintosh Thai
MacTurkish	Macintosh Turkish
MacUkraine	Macintosh Ukraine
SJIS	Shift-JIS, Japanese
TIS620	TIS620, Thai

C

Unicode Character Blocks

Table C-1 lists the Unicode character blocks.

Table C-1. Unicode Character Blocks

Block	Range
BASIC_LATIN	\u0000 … \u007F
LATIN_1_SUPPLEMENT	\u0080 … \u00FF
LATIN_EXTENDED_A	\u0100 … \u017F
LATIN_EXTENDED_B	\u0180 … \u024F
IPA_EXTENSIONS	\u0250 … \u02AF
SPACING_MODIFIER_LETTERS	\u02B0 … \u02FF
COMBINING_DIACRITICAL_MARKS	\u0300 … \u036F
GREEK	\u0370 … \u03FF
CYRILLIC	\u0400 … \u04FF
ARMENIAN	\u0530 … \u058F
HEBREW	\u0590 … \u05FF
ARABIC	\u0600 … \u06FF
DEVANAGARI	\u0900 … \u097F
BENGALI	\u0980 … \u09FF
GURMUKHI	\u0A00 … \u0A7F
GUJARATI	\u0A80 … \u0AFF
ORIYA	\u0B00 … \u0B7F
TAMIL	\u0B80 … \u0BFF
TELUGU	\u0C00 … \u0C7F

Table C-1. Unicode Character Blocks (continued)

Block	Range
KANNADA	\u0C80 … \u0CFF
MALAYALAM	\u0D00 … \u0D7F
THAI	\u0E00 … \u0E7F
LAO	\u0E80 … \u0EFF
TIBETAN	\u0F00 … \u0FBF
GEORGIAN	\u10A0 … \u10FF
HANGUL_JAMO	\u1100 … \u11FF
LATIN_EXTENDED_ADDITIONAL	\u1E00 … \u1EFF
GREEK_EXTENDED	\u1F00 … \u1FFF
GENERAL_PUNCTUATION	\u2000 … \u206F
SUPERSCRIPTS_AND_SUBSCRIPTS	\u2070 … \u209F
CURRENCY_SYMBOLS	\u20A0 … \u20CF
COMBINING_MARKS_FOR_SYMBOLS	\u20D0 … \u20FF
LETTERLIKE_SYMBOLS	\u2100 … \u214F
NUMBER_FORMS	\u2150 … \u218F
ARROWS	\u2190 … \u21FF
MATHEMATICAL_OPERATORS	\u2200 … \u22FF
MISCELLANEOUS_TECHNICAL	\u2300 … \u23FF
CONTROL_PICTURES	\u2400 … \u243F
OPTICAL_CHARACTER_RECOGNITION	\u2440 … \u245F
ENCLOSED_ALPHANUMERICS	\u2460 … \u24FF
BOX_DRAWING	\u2500 … \u257F
BLOCK_ELEMENTS	\u2580 … \u259F
GEOMETRIC_SHAPES	\u25A0 … \u25FF
MISCELLANEOUS_SYMBOLS	\u2600 … \u26FF
DINGBATS	\u2700 … \u27BF
CJK_SYMBOLS_AND_PUNCTUATION	\u3000 … \u303F
HIRAGANA	\u3040 … \u309F
KATAKANA	\u30A0 … \u30FF
BOPOMOFO	\u3100 … \u312F
HANGUL_COMPATIBILITY_JAMO	\u3130 … \u318F
KANBUN	\u3190 … \u319F
ENCLOSED_CJK_LETTERS_AND_MONTHS	\u3200 … \u32FF
CJK_COMPATIBILITY	\u3300 … \u33FF
CJK_UNIFIED_IDEOGRAPHS	\u4E00 … \u9FFF
HANGUL_SYLLABLES	\uAC00 … \uD7A3

Table C-1. Unicode Character Blocks (continued)

Block	Range
SURROGATES_AREA	\uD800 ... \uDFFF
PRIVATE_USE_AREA	\uE000 ... \uF8FF
CJK_COMPATIBILITY_IDEOGRAPHS	\uF900 ... \uFAFF
ALPHABETIC_PRESENTATION_FORMS	\uFB00 ... \uFB4F
ARABIC_PRESENTATION_FORMS_A	\uFB50 ... \uFDFF
COMBINING_HALF_MARKS	\uFE20 ... \uFE2F
CJK_COMPATIBILITY_FORMS	\uFE30 ... \uFE4F
SMALL_FORM_VARIANTS	\uFE50 ... \uFE6F
ARABIC_PRESENTATION_FORMS_B	\uFE70 ... \uFEFF
HALFWIDTH_AND_FULLWIDTH_FORMS	\uFF00 ... \uFFEF
SPECIALS	\uFFF0 ... \uFFFF

D

Programmer's Quick Reference

In this appendix, we have tried to identify all classes in the Java 2 SDK, Standard Edition, Version 1.3 that are directly related to supporting internationalization. We list the core classes in this area, but left out classes that use the functionality available in these core classes. For example, the `java.awt.ComponentOrientation` class is listed, but a class using the `ComponentOrientation` class, such as a subclass of `java.awt.Component`, is not.

You can view the full documentation for these classes online at *http://java.sun.com/ j2se/1.3/docs/api/index.html.*

java.awt Package

ComponentOrientation

Synopsis

Class Name:	`java.awt.ComponentOrientation`
Superclass:	`java.lang.Object`
Immediate Subclasses:	None
Interfaces Implemented:	`java.io.Serializable`

Class Summary

```
pubic final class ComponentOrientation extends Object implements Serializable

    //Constants
    public static final ComponentOrientation LEFT_TO_RIGHT;
```

```
public static final ComponentOrientation RIGHT_TO_LEFT;
public static final ComponentOrientation UNKNOWN;

// Methods
public static ComponentOrientation getOrientation(Locale locale);
public static ComponentOrientation getOrientation(ResourceBundle bdl);
public boolean isHorizontal()
public boolean isLeftToRight();
}
```

Font

Synopsis

Class Name:	`java.awt.Font`
Superclass:	`java.lang.Object`
Immediate Subclasses:	`javax.swing.plaf.FontUIResource`
Interfaces Implemented:	`java.io.Serializable`

Class Summary

```
public class Font implements java.io.Serializable {

    // Constants
    public static final int BOLD;
    public static final int CENTER_BASELINE;
    public static final int HANGING_BASELINE;
    public static final int ITALIC;
    public static final int PLAIN;
    public static final int ROMAN_BASELINE;
    public static final int TRUETYPE_FONT;

    // Constructors
    public Font(Map attributes);
    public Font(String name, int style, int size);

    // Methods
    public boolean canDisplay(char c);
    public int canDisplayUpTo(String str);
    public int canDisplayUpTo(char[] text, int start, int limit);
    public int canDisplayUpTo(CharacterIterator iter, int start, int limit);
    public static Font createFont ( int fontFormat, InputStream fontStream )
            throws java.awt.FontFormatException, java.io.IOException;
    public GlyphVector createGlyphVector(FontRenderContext frc, String str);
    public GlyphVector createGlyphVector(FontRenderContext frc, char[] chars);
    public GlyphVector createGlyphVector(FontRenderContext frc,
                                         CharacterIterator ci);
    public GlyphVector createGlyphVector(FontRenderContext frc,
                                         sint [] glyphCodes);
    public static Font decode(String str);
    public Font deriveFont(int style, float size);
```

```
        public Font deriveFont(int style, AffineTransform trans);
        public Font deriveFont(float size);
        public Font deriveFont(AffineTransform trans);
        public Font deriveFont(int style);
        public Font deriveFont(Map attributes);
        public Map getAttributes();
        public Attribute[] getAvailableAttributes();
        public byte getBaselineFor(char c);
        public String getFamily();
        public String getFamily(Locale l);
        public static Font getFont(String nm);
        public static Font getFont(String nm, Font font);
        public String getFontName();
        public String getFontName(Locale l);
        public float getItalicAngle();
        public LineMetrics getLineMetrics( String str, FontRenderContext frc);
        public LineMetrics getLineMetrics( String str,
                                        int beginIndex, int limit,
                                        FontRenderContext frc);
        public LineMetrics getLineMetrics(char [] chars,
                                        int beginIndex, int limit,
                                        FontRenderContext frc);
        public LineMetrics getLineMetrics(CharacterIterator ci,
                                        int beginIndex, int limit,
                                        FontRenderContext frc);
        public Rectangle2D getMaxCharBounds(FontRenderContext frc);
        public int getMissingGlyphCode();
        public String getName();
        public String getPSName();
        public int getNumGlyphs();
        public int getSize();
        public float getSize2D();
        public Rectangle2D getStringBounds(String str, FontRenderContext frc);
        public Rectangle2D getStringBounds(String str,
                                        int beginIndex, int limit,
                                        FontRenderContext frc);
        public Rectangle2D getStringBounds(char [] chars,
                                        int beginIndex, int limit,
                                        FontRenderContext frc);
        public Rectangle2D getStringBounds(CharacterIterator ci,
                                        int beginIndex, int limit,
                                        FontRenderContext frc);
    public int getStyle();
    public AffineTransform getTransform();
    public boolean hasUniformLineMetrics();
    public boolean isBold();
    public boolean isItalic();
    public boolean isPlain();
}
```

GraphicsEnvironment

Synopsis

Class Name: java.awt.GraphicsEnvironment
Superclass: java.lang.Object
Immediate Subclasses: None
Interfaces Implemented: None

Class Summary

```
public abstract class GraphicsEnvironment {

    // Methods
    public abstract Graphics2D createGraphics(BufferedImage img);
    public abstract Font[] getAllFonts();
    public abstract String[] getAvailableFontFamilyNames();
    public abstract String[] getAvailableFontFamilyNames(Locale l);
    public abstract GraphicsDevice getDefaultScreenDevice();
    public static synchronized GraphicsEnvironment getLocalGraphicsEnvironment();
    public abstract GraphicsDevice[] getScreenDevices();
}
```

java.awt.font Package

TextLayout

Synopsis

Class Name: java.awt.font.TextLayout
Superclass: java.lang.Object
Immediate Subclasses: None
Interfaces Implemented: java.lang.Cloneable

Class Summary

```
public final class TextLayout implements Cloneable {

    // Constants
    public static final CaretPolicy DEFAULT_CARET_POLICY;

    // Constructors
    public TextLayout(String string, Font font, FontRenderContext frc);
    public TextLayout(String string, Map attributes, FontRenderContext frc);
    public TextLayout(AttributedCharacterIterator text, FontRenderContext frc);
```

```
    // Methods
    public void draw(Graphics2D g2, float x, float y);
    public boolean equals(Object obj);
    public boolean equals(TextLayout rhs);
    public float getAdvance();
    public float getAscent();
    public byte getBaseline();
    public float[] getBaselineOffsets();
    public Shape getBlackBoxBounds(int firstEndpoint, int secondEndpoint);
    public Rectangle2D getBounds();
    public float[] getCaretInfo(TextHitInfo hit);
    public float[] getCaretInfo(TextHitInfo hit, Rectangle2D bounds);
    public Shape getCaretShape(TextHitInfo hit);
    public Shape getCaretShape(TextHitInfo hit, Rectangle2D bounds);
    public Shape[] getCaretShapes(int offset);
    public Shape[] getCaretShapes(int offset, Rectangle2D bounds);
    public Shape[] getCaretShapes(int offset, Rectangle2D bounds, CaretPolicy policy);
    public int getCharacterCount();
    public byte getCharacterLevel(int index);
    public float getDescent();
    public TextLayout getJustifiedLayout(float justificationWidth);
    public int[] getLogicalRangesForVisualSelection(TextHitInfo firstEndpoint,
                                                    TextHitInfo secondEndpoint);
    public TextHitInfo getNextLeftHit(TextHitInfo hit);
    public TextHitInfo getNextLeftHit(int offset);
    public TextHitInfo getNextLeftHit(int offset, CaretPolicy policy);
    public TextHitInfo getNextRightHit(TextHitInfo hit);
    public TextHitInfo getNextRightHit(int offset);
    public TextHitInfo getNextRightHit(int offset, CaretPolicy policy);
    public float getLeading();
    public Shape getLogicalHighlightShape(int firstEndpoint, int secondEndpoint);
    public Shape getLogicalHighlightShape(int firstEndpoint,
                                          int secondEndpoint,
                                          Rectangle2D bounds);
    public Shape getOutline(AffineTransform tx);
    public float getVisibleAdvance();
    public Shape getVisualHighlightShape(TextHitInfo firstEndpoint,
                                         TextHitInfo secondEndpoint);
    public Shape getVisualHighlightShape(TextHitInfo firstEndpoint,
                                         TextHitInfo secondEndpoint,
                                         Rectangle2D bounds);
    public TextHitInfo getVisualOtherHit(TextHitInfo hit);
    public int hashCode();
    public TextHitInfo hitTestChar(float x, float y);
    public TextHitInfo hitTestChar(float x, float y, Rectangle2D bounds);
    public boolean isLeftToRight();
    public boolean isVertical();
    public String toString();
}
```

CaretPolicy

Synopsis

Class Name: `java.awt.font.TextLayout.CaretPolicy`
Superclass: `java.lang.Object`
Immediate Subclasses: None
Interfaces Implemented: None

Class Summary

```
public static class CaretPolicy {

    // Constructors
    public CaretPolicy();

    // Methods
    public TextHitInfo getStrongCaret(TextHitInfo hit1, TextHitInfo hit2,
                                      TextLayout layout);

}
```

java.awt.im Package

InputContext

Synopsis

Class Name: `java.awt.im.InputContext`
Superclass: `java.lang.Object`
Immediate Subclasses: None
Interfaces Implemented: None

Class Summary

```
public class InputContext {

    // Methods
    public void dispatchEvent(AWTEvent event);
    public void dispose();
    public void endComposition();
    public Object getInputMethodControlObject();
    public static InputContext getInstance();
    public Locale getLocale();
    public boolean isCompositionEnabled();
    public void reconvert();
    public boolean selectInputMethod(Locale locale);
```

```
      public void setCharacterSubsets(Subset[] subsets);
      public void setCompositionEnabled(boolean enable);
      public void removeNotify(Component client);
  }
```

InputMethodRequests

Synopsis

Interface Name:	java.awt.im.InputMethodRequests
Superinterface:	None
Immediate Subinterfaces:	java.awt.im.spi.InputMethodContext
Interfaces Implemented:	None

Class Summary

```
  public interface InputMethodRequests {

    // Methods
    AttributedCharacterIterator cancelLatestCommittedText(Attribute[] attributes);
    AttributedCharacterIterator getCommittedText(int beginIndex, int endIndex,
                                          Attribute[] attributes);
    int getCommittedTextLength();
    int getInsertPositionOffset();
    TextHitInfo getLocationOffset(int x, int y);
    AttributedCharacterIterator getSelectedText(Attribute[] attributes);
    Rectangle getTextLocation(TextHitInfo offset);
  }
```

InputMethodHighlight

Synopsis

Class Name:	java.awt.im.InputMethodHighlight
Superclass:	java.lang.Object
Immediate Subclasses:	None
Interfaces Implemented:	None

Class Summary

```
  public class InputMethodHighlight {

    // Constants
    public final static int CONVERTED_TEXT;
    public final static int RAW_TEXT;
    public final static InputMethodHighlight SELECTED_CONVERTED_TEXT_HIGHLIGHT;
    public final static InputMethodHighlight SELECTED_RAW_TEXT_HIGHLIGHT;
    public final static InputMethodHighlight UNSELECTED_CONVERTED_TEXT_HIGHLIGHT;
    public final static InputMethodHighlight UNSELECTED_RAW_TEXT_HIGHLIGHT;
```

```
    // Constructors
    public InputMethodHighlight(boolean selected, int state);
    public InputMethodHighlight(boolean selected, int state, int variation);
    public InputMethodHighlight(boolean selected, int state, int variation, Map style);

    // Methods
    public int getState();
    public Map getStyle();
    public int getVariation();
    public boolean isSelected();
}
```

InputSubset

Synopsis

Class Name:	java.awt.im.InputSubset
Superclass:	java.lang.Character.Subset
Immediate Subclasses:	None
Interfaces Implemented:	None

Class Summary

```
    public final class InputSubset extends Character.Subset {

    // Constants
    public static final InputSubset FULLWIDTH_DIGITS;
    public static final InputSubset FULLWIDTH_LATIN;
    public static final InputSubset HALFWIDTH_KATAKANA;
    public static final InputSubset HANJA;
    public static final InputSubset KANJI;
    public static final InputSubset LATIN;
    public static final InputSubset LATIN_DIGITS;
    public static final InputSubset SIMPLIFIED_HANZI;
    public static final InputSubset TRADITIONAL_HANZI;
}
```

java.awt.im.spi Package

InputMethod

Synopsis

Interface Name:	java.awt.im.spi.InputMethod
Superinterface:	None
Immediate Subinterfaces:	None
Interfaces Implemented:	None

Class Summary

```
public interface InputMethod {

    // Methods
    public void activate();
    public void deactivate(boolean isTemporary);
    public void dispatchEvent(AWTEvent event);
    public void dispose();
    public void endComposition();
    public Object getControlObject();
    public Locale getLocale();
    public void hideWindows();
    public boolean isCompositionEnabled();
    public void notifyClientWindowChange(Rectangle bounds);
    public void reconvert();
    public void removeNotify();
    public void setCharacterSubsets(Subset[] subsets);
    public void setCompositionEnabled(boolean enable);
    public void setInputMethodContext(InputMethodContext context);
    public boolean setLocale(Locale locale);
}
```

InputMethodContext

Synopsis

Interface Name:	java.awt.im.spi.InputMethodContext
Superinterface:	java.awt.im.InputMethodRequests
Immediate Subinterfaces:	None
Interfaces Implemented:	None

Class Summary

```
public interface InputMethodContext extends InputMethodRequests {

    // Methods
    public Window createInputMethodWindow(String title, boolean attachToInputContext);
    public void dispatchInputMethodEvent(int id,
                AttributedCharacterIterator text, int committedCharacterCount,
                TextHitInfo caret, TextHitInfo visiblePosition);
    public void enableClientWindowNotification(InputMethod inputMethod, boolean enable);
}
```

InputMethodDescriptor

Synopsis

Interface Name:	`java.awt.im.spi.InputMethodDescriptor`
Superinterface:	None
Immediate Subinterfaces:	None
Interfaces Implemented:	None

Class Summary

```
public interface InputMethodDescriptor {

    // Methods
    InputMethod createInputMethod() throws Exception;
    Locale[] getAvailableLocales() throws AWTException;
    String getInputMethodDisplayName(Locale inputLocale, Locale displayLanguage);
    Image getInputMethodIcon(Locale inputLocale);
    boolean hasDynamicLocaleList();
}
```

java.io Package

InputStreamReader

Synopsis

Class Name:	`java.io.InputStreamReader`
Superclass:	`java.io.Reader`
Immediate Subclasses:	`java.io.FileReader`
Interfaces Implemented:	None

Class Summary

```
public class InputStreamReader extends Reader {

    // Constructors
    public InputStreamReader(InputStream in);
    public InputStreamReader(InputStream in, String enc);

    // Methods
    public void close() throws IOException;
    public String getEncoding();
    public int read() throws IOException;
    public int read(char cbuf[], int off, int len) throws IOException;
    public boolean ready() throws IOException;
}
```

OutputStreamWriter

Synopsis

Class Name: `java.io.OutputStreamWriter`
Superclass: `java.io.Writer`
Immediate Subclasses: `FileWriter`
Interfaces Implemented: None

Class Summary

```
public class OutputStreamWriter extends Writer {

    // Constructors
    public OutputStreamWriter(OutputStream out);
    public OutputStreamWriter(OutputStream out, String enc);

    // Methods
    public void close() throws IOException;
    public void flush() throws IOException;
    public String getEncoding();
    public void write(int c) throws IOException;
    public void write(char cbuf[], int off, int len) throws IOException;
    public void write(String str, int off, int len) throws IOException;
}
```

java.lang Package

Character

Synopsis

Class Name: `java.lang.Character`
Superclass: `java.lang.Object`
Immediate Subclasses: None
Interfaces Implemented: `java.io.Serializable`
                        `java.lang.Comparable`

Class Summary

```
public final class Character extends Object
    implements java.io.Serializable, Comparable {

    // Constants
    public static final byte COMBINING_SPACING_MARK;
    public static final byte CONNECTOR_PUNCTUATION;
    public static final byte CONTROL;
    public static final byte CURRENCY_SYMBOL;
    public static final byte DASH_PUNCTUATION;
```

```
public static final byte DECIMAL_DIGIT_NUMBER;
public static final byte ENCLOSING_MARK;
public static final byte END_PUNCTUATION;
public static final byte FORMAT;
public static final byte LETTER_NUMBER;
public static final byte LINE_SEPARATOR;
public static final byte LOWERCASE_LETTER;
public static final byte MATH_SYMBOL;
public static final int MAX_RADIX;
public static final int MIN_RADIX;
public static final char MAX_VALUE;
public static final char MIN_VALUE;
public static final byte MODIFIER_LETTER;
public static final byte MODIFIER_SYMBOL;
public static final byte NON_SPACING_MARK;
public static final byte OTHER_LETTER;
public static final byte OTHER_NUMBER;
public static final byte OTHER_PUNCTUATION;
public static final byte OTHER_SYMBOL;
public static final byte PARAGRAPH_SEPARATOR;
public static final byte PRIVATE_USE;
public static final byte SPACE_SEPARATOR;
public static final byte START_PUNCTUATION;
public static final byte SURROGATE;
public static final byte TITLECASE_LETTER;
public static final Class TYPE;
public static final byte UNASSIGNED;
public static final byte UPPERCASE_LETTER;

// Constructors
public Character(char value);

// Methods
public char charValue();
public int compareTo(Object o);
public int compareTo(Character anotherCharacter);
public static int digit(char ch, int radix);
public boolean equals(Object obj);
public static char forDigit(int digit, int radix);
public static int getNumericValue(char ch);
public static int getType(char ch);
public int hashCode();
public static boolean isDigit(char ch);
public static boolean isLowerCase(char ch);
public static boolean isDefined(char ch);
public static boolean isIdentifierIgnorable(char ch);
public static boolean isISOControl(char ch);
public static boolean isLetter(char ch);
public static boolean isLetterOrDigit(char ch);
public static boolean isJavaLetter(char ch);
public static boolean isJavaLetterOrDigit(char ch);
public static boolean isJavaIdentifierStart(char ch);
public static boolean isJavaIdentifierPart(char ch);
```

```
    public static boolean isSpace(char ch);
    public static boolean isSpaceChar(char ch);
    public static boolean isTitleCase(char ch);
    public static boolean isUnicodeIdentifierStart(char ch);
    public static boolean isUnicodeIdentifierPart(char ch);
    public static boolean isUpperCase(char ch);
    public static boolean isWhitespace(char ch);
    public static char toLowerCase(char ch);
    public String toString();
    public static char toTitleCase(char ch);
    public static char toUpperCase(char ch);
}
```

Character.Subset

Synopsis

Class Name: `java.lang.Character.Subset`

Superclass: `java.lang.Object`

Immediate Subclasses: `java.awt.im.InputSubset`
                             `java.lang.Character.UnicodeBlock`

Interfaces Implemented: None

Class Summary

```
    public static class Subset {

        // Constructors
        protected Subset(String name)

        // Methods
        public final boolean equals(Object obj);
        public final int hashCode();
        public final String toString();
    }
```

Character.UnicodeBlock

Synopsis

Class Name: `java.lang.Character.UnicodeBlock`

Superclass: `java.lang.Character.Subset`

Immediate Subclasses: None

Interfaces Implemented: None

Class Summary

```
    public static final class UnicodeBlock extends Subset {

        // Constants
        public static final UnicodeBlock ALPHABETIC_PRESENTATION_FORMS;
```

```
public static final UnicodeBlock ARABIC;
public static final UnicodeBlock ARABIC_PRESENTATION_FORMS_A;
public static final UnicodeBlock ARABIC_PRESENTATION_FORMS_B;
public static final UnicodeBlock ARMENIAN;
public static final UnicodeBlock ARROWS;
public static final UnicodeBlock BASIC_LATIN;
public static final UnicodeBlock BENGALI;
public static final UnicodeBlock BLOCK_ELEMENTS;
public static final UnicodeBlock BOX_DRAWING;
public static final UnicodeBlock BOPOMOFO;
public static final UnicodeBlock CJK_COMPATIBILITY_IDEOGRAPHS;
public static final UnicodeBlock CJK_COMPATIBILITY;
public static final UnicodeBlock CJK_COMPATIBILITY_FORMS;
public static final UnicodeBlock CJK_SYMBOLS_AND_PUNCTUATION;
public static final UnicodeBlock CJK_UNIFIED_IDEOGRAPHS;
public static final UnicodeBlock COMBINING_DIACRITICAL_MARKS;
public static final UnicodeBlock COMBINING_HALF_MARKS;
public static final UnicodeBlock COMBINING_MARKS_FOR_SYMBOLS;
public static final UnicodeBlock CONTROL_PICTURES;
public static final UnicodeBlock CURRENCY_SYMBOLS;
public static final UnicodeBlock CYRILLIC;
public static final UnicodeBlock DEVANAGARI;
public static final UnicodeBlock DINGBATS;
public static final UnicodeBlock ENCLOSED_ALPHANUMERICS;
public static final UnicodeBlock ENCLOSED_CJK_LETTERS_AND_MONTHS;
public static final UnicodeBlock GEOMETRIC_SHAPES;
public static final UnicodeBlock GEORGIAN;
public static final UnicodeBlock GENERAL_PUNCTUATION;
public static final UnicodeBlock GREEK;
public static final UnicodeBlock GREEK_EXTENDED;
public static final UnicodeBlock GUJARATI;
public static final UnicodeBlock GURMUKHI;
public static final UnicodeBlock HALFWIDTH_AND_FULLWIDTH_FORMS;
public static final UnicodeBlock HANGUL_COMPATIBILITY_JAMO;
public static final UnicodeBlock HANGUL_JAMO;
public static final UnicodeBlock HANGUL_SYLLABLES;
public static final UnicodeBlock HEBREW;
public static final UnicodeBlock HIRAGANA;
public static final UnicodeBlock IPA_EXTENSIONS;
public static final UnicodeBlock KANBUN;
public static final UnicodeBlock KANNADA;
public static final UnicodeBlock KATAKANA;
public static final UnicodeBlock LAO;
public static final UnicodeBlock LATIN_EXTENDED_ADDITIONAL;
public static final UnicodeBlock LATIN_1_SUPPLEMENT;
public static final UnicodeBlock LATIN_EXTENDED_A;
public static final UnicodeBlock LATIN_EXTENDED_B
public static final UnicodeBlock LETTERLIKE_SYMBOLS;
public static final UnicodeBlock MALAYALAM;
public static final UnicodeBlock MATHEMATICAL_OPERATORS;
public static final UnicodeBlock MISCELLANEOUS_SYMBOLS;
```

```
    public static final UnicodeBlock MISCELLANEOUS_TECHNICAL;
    public static final UnicodeBlock NUMBER_FORMS;
    public static final UnicodeBlock OPTICAL_CHARACTER_RECOGNITION;
    public static final UnicodeBlock ORIYA;
    public static final UnicodeBlock PRIVATE_USE_AREA;
    public static final UnicodeBlock SMALL_FORM_VARIANTS;
    public static final UnicodeBlock SPACING_MODIFIER_LETTERS;
    public static final UnicodeBlock SPECIALS;
    public static final UnicodeBlock SUPERSCRIPTS_AND_SUBSCRIPTS;
    public static final UnicodeBlock SURROGATES_AREA;
    public static final UnicodeBlock TAMIL;
    public static final UnicodeBlock TELUGU;
    public static final UnicodeBlock THAI;
    public static final UnicodeBlock TIBETAN;

    // Methods
    public static UnicodeBlock of(char c);
}
```

java.text Package

AttributedCharacterIterator

Synopsis

Interface Name:	java.text.AttributedCharacterIterator
Superinterface:	java.text.CharacterIterator
Immediate Subinterfaces:	None
Interfaces Implemented:	java.lang.Cloneable

Class Summary

```
    public interface AttributedCharacterIterator extends CharacterIterator {

        // Methods
        public Set getAllAttributeKeys();
        public Map getAttributes();
        public Object getAttribute(Attribute attribute);
        public int getRunLimit();
        public int getRunLimit(Attribute attribute);
        public int getRunLimit(Set attributes);
        public int getRunStart();
        public int getRunStart(Attribute attribute);
        public int getRunStart(Set attributes);
    }
```

AttributedCharacterIterator.Attribute

Synopsis

Class Name: `java.text.AttributedCharacterIterator.`
                               `Attribute`
Superclass: `java.text.AttributedCharacterIterator`
Immediate Subclasses: `java.awt.font.TextAttribute`
Interfaces Implemented: `java.io.Serializable`

Class Summary

```
public static class Attribute implements Serializable {

    // Constants
    public static final Attribute INPUT_METHOD_SEGMENT;
    public static final Attribute LANGUAGE;
    public static final Attribute READING;

    // Constructors
    protected Attribute(String name);

    // Methods
    public final boolean equals(Object obj);
    protected String getName();
    public final int hashCode();
    public String toString();
}
```

BreakIterator

Synopsis

Class Name: `java.text.BreakIterator`
Superclass: `java.lang.Object`
Immediate Subclasses: None
Interfaces Implemented: `java.lang.Cloneable`

Class Summary

```
public abstract class BreakIterator implements Cloneable {

    // Constants
    public static final int DONE;

    // Constructors
    protected BreakIterator();
```

```
    // Methods
    public Object clone();
    public abstract int current();
    public abstract int first();
    public abstract int following(int offset);
    public static synchronized Locale[] getAvailableLocales;
    public static BreakIterator getCharacterInstance();
    public static BreakIterator getCharacterInstance(Locale where);
    public static BreakIterator getLineInstance();
    public static BreakIterator getLineInstance(Locale where);
    public static BreakIterator getSentenceInstance();
    public static BreakIterator getSentenceInstance(Locale where);
    public abstract CharacterIterator getText();
    public static BreakIterator getWordInstance();
    public static BreakIterator getWordInstance(Locale where);
    public boolean isBoundary(int offset);
    public abstract int last();
    public abstract int next(int n);
    public abstract int next();
    public int preceding(int offset);
    public abstract int previous();
    public void setText(String newText);
    public abstract void setText(CharacterIterator newText);
}
```

CharacterIterator

Synopsis

Interface Name:	`java.text.CharacterIterator`
Superinterface:	`java.lang.Cloneable`
Immediate Subinterfaces:	`java.text.AttributedCharacterIterator`
Interfaces Implemented:	`java.lang.Cloneable`
Implementing Classes:	`java.text.StringCharacterIterator` `javax.swing.text.Segment`

Class Summary

```
    public interface CharacterIterator extends Cloneable {

        // Constants
        public static final char DONE;

        // Methods
        public Object clone();
        public char current();
        public char first();
        public int getBeginIndex();
        public int getEndIndex();
        public int getIndex();
        public char last();
        public char next();
```

```
    public char previous();
    public char setIndex(int position);
}
```

ChoiceFormat

Synopsis

Class Name: `java.text.ChoiceFormat`
Superclass: `java.text.NumberFormat`
Immediate Subclasses: None
Interfaces Implemented: `java.io.Serializable`
                               `java.lang.Cloneable`

Class Summary

```
    public class ChoiceFormat extends NumberFormat {

        // Constructors
        public ChoiceFormat(String newPattern);
        public ChoiceFormat(double[] limits, String[] formats);

        // Methods
        public void applyPattern(String newPattern);
        public Object clone();
        public boolean equals(Object obj);
        public StringBuffer format(long number, StringBuffer toAppendTo,
                            FieldPosition status);
        public StringBuffer format(double number, StringBuffer toAppendTo,
                            FieldPosition status);public Object[] getFormats();
        public double[] getLimits();
        public int hashCode();
        public static final double nextDouble (double d);
        public static double nextDouble (double d, boolean positive);
        public Number parse(String text, ParsePosition status);
        public static final double previousDouble (double d);
        public void setChoices(double[] limits, String formats[]);
        public String toPattern();
    }
```

CollationElementIterator

Synopsis

Class Name: `java.text.CollationElementIterator`
Superclass: `java.lang.Object`
Immediate Subclasses: None
Interfaces Implemented: None

Class Summary

```
public final class CollationElementIterator {

    // Constants
    public final static int NULLORDER;

    // Methods
    public int getOffset();
    public int getMaxExpansion(int order);
    public int next();
    public int previous();
    public final static int primaryOrder(int order);
    public void reset();
    public final static short secondaryOrder(int order);
    public void setText(String source);
    public void setText(CharacterIterator source);
    public void setOffset(int newOffset);
    public final static short tertiaryOrder(int order);
}
```

CollationKey

Synopsis

Class Name:	`java.text.CollationKey`
Superclass:	`java.lang.Object`
Immediate Subclasses:	**None**
Interfaces Implemented:	`java.lang.Comparable`

Class Summary

```
public final class CollationKey implements Comparable {

    // Methods
    public int compareTo(CollationKey target);
    public int compareTo(Object o);
    public boolean equals(Object target);
    public String getSourceString();
    public int hashCode();
    public byte[] toByteArray();
}
```

Collator

Synopsis

Class Name: java.text.Collator
Superclass: java.lang.Object
Immediate Subclasses: java.text.RuleBasedCollator
Interfaces Implemented: java.lang.Cloneable
                        java.util.Comparator

Class Summary

```
public abstract class Collator implements Comparator, Cloneable {

    // Constants
    public final static int CANONICAL_DECOMPOSITION;
    public final static int FULL_DECOMPOSITION;
    public final static int IDENTICAL;
    public final static int NO_DECOMPOSITION;
    public final static int PRIMARY;
    public final static int SECONDARY;
    public final static int TERTIARY;

    // Constructors
    protected Collator();

    // Methods
    public Object clone();
    public abstract int compare(String source, String target);
    public int compare(Object o1, Object o2);
    public boolean equals(String source, String target);
    public boolean equals(Object that);
    public static synchronized Locale[] getAvailableLocales();
    public abstract CollationKey getCollationKey(String source);
    public synchronized int getDecomposition();
    public static synchronized Collator getInstance(Locale desiredLocale);
    public synchronized int getStrength();
    public abstract int hashCode();
    public synchronized void setDecomposition(int decompositionMode);
    public synchronized void setStrength(int newStrength);
}
```

DateFormat

Synopsis

Class Name: java.text.DateFormat
Superclass: java.text.Format

Immediate Subclasses: `java.text.SimpleDateFormat`

Interfaces Implemented: `java.io.Serializable`
`java.lang.Cloneable`

Class Summary

```
public abstract class DateFormat extends Format {

    // Constants
    public final static int AM_PM_FIELD;
    public final static int DATE_FIELD;
    public final static int DAY_OF_WEEK_FIELD;
    public final static int DAY_OF_WEEK_IN_MONTH_FIELD;
    public final static int DAY_OF_YEAR_FIELD;
    public static final int DEFAULT;
    public final static int ERA_FIELD;
    public static final int FULL;
    public final static int HOUR_OF_DAY0_FIELD;
    public final static int HOUR_OF_DAY1_FIELD;
    public final static int HOUR0_FIELD;
    public final static int HOUR1_FIELD;
    public static final int LONG;
    public static final int MEDIUM;
    public final static int MILLISECOND_FIELD;
    public final static int MINUTE_FIELD;
    public final static int MONTH_FIELD;
    public static final int SHORT;
    public final static int TIMEZONE_FIELD;
    public final static int WEEK_OF_MONTH_FIELD;
    public final static int WEEK_OF_YEAR_FIELD;
    public final static int YEAR_FIELD;


    // Constructors
    protected DateFormat();


    // Methods
    public Object clone();
    public boolean equals(Object obj);
    public final String format(Date date);
    public final StringBuffer format(Object obj, StringBuffer toAppendTo,
                               FieldPosition fieldPosition);
    public abstract StringBuffer format(Date date, StringBuffer toAppendTo,
                               FieldPosition fieldPosition);
    public static Locale[] getAvailableLocales();
    public Calendar getCalendar();
    public final static DateFormat getDateInstance();
    public final static DateFormat getDateInstance(int style);
    public final static DateFormat getDateInstance(int style, Locale aLocale);
    public final static DateFormat getDateTimeInstance();
    public final static DateFormat getDateTimeInstance(int dateStyle, int timeStyle);
    public final static DateFormat
          getDateTimeInstance(int dateStyle, int timeStyle, Locale aLocale);
    public final static DateFormat getInstance();
```

```
    public NumberFormat getNumberFormat();
    public final static DateFormat getTimeInstance();
    public final static DateFormat getTimeInstance(int style);
    public final static DateFormat getTimeInstance(int style, Locale aLocale);
    public TimeZone getTimeZone();
    public int hashCode();
    public boolean isLenient();
    public Date parse(String text) throws ParseException;
    public abstract Date parse(String text, ParsePosition pos);
    public Object parseObject (String source, ParsePosition pos);
    public void setCalendar(Calendar newCalendar);
    public void setLenient(boolean lenient);
    public void setNumberFormat(NumberFormat newNumberFormat);
    public void setTimeZone(TimeZone zone);
}
```

DateFormatSymbols

Synopsis

Class Name:	java.text.DateFormatSymbols
Superclass:	java.lang.Object
Immediate Subclasses:	None
Interfaces Implemented:	java.io.Serializable
	java.lang.Cloneable

Class Summary

```
    public class DateFormatSymbols implements Serializable, Cloneable {

        // Constructors
        public DateFormatSymbols();
        public DateFormatSymbols(Locale locale);

        // Methods
        public Object clone();
        public boolean equals(Object obj);
        public String[] getAmPmStrings();
        public String[] getEras();
        public String getLocalPatternChars();
        public String[] getMonths();
        public String[] getShortMonths();
        public String[] getShortWeekdays();
        public String[] getWeekdays();
        public String[][] getZoneStrings();
        public int hashCode();
        public void setAmPmStrings(String[] newAmpms);
        public void setEras(String[] newEras);
        public void setLocalPatternChars(String newLocalPatternChars);
        public void setMonths(String[] newMonths);
```

```
    public void setShortMonths(String[] newShortMonths);
    public void setShortWeekdays(String[] newShortWeekdays);
    public void setWeekdays(String[] newWeekdays);
    public void setZoneStrings(String[][] newZoneStrings);
}
```

DecimalFormat

Synopsis

Class Name:	`java.text.DecimalFormat`
Superclass:	`java.text.NumberFormat`
Immediate Subclasses:	None
Interfaces Implemented:	`java.io.Serializable` `java.lang.Cloneable`

Class Summary

```
    public class DecimalFormat extends NumberFormat {

        // Constructors
        public DecimalFormat();
        public DecimalFormat(String pattern);
        public DecimalFormat(String pattern, DecimalFormatSymbols symbols);

        // Methods
        public void applyPattern( String pattern );
        public void applyLocalizedPattern( String pattern );public Object clone();
        public boolean equals(Object obj);
        public StringBuffer format(double number, StringBuffer result,
                                FieldPosition fieldPosition);
        public StringBuffer format(long number, StringBuffer result,
                                FieldPosition fieldPosition);
        public DecimalFormatSymbols getDecimalFormatSymbols();
        public int getGroupingSize ();
        public int getMultiplier ();
        public String getNegativePrefix ();
        public String getPositivePrefix ();
        public String getPositiveSuffix ();
        public int hashCode();
        public boolean isDecimalSeparatorAlwaysShown();
        public Number parse(String text, ParsePosition parsePosition);
        public void setDecimalFormatSymbols(DecimalFormatSymbols newSymbols);
        public void setDecimalSeparatorAlwaysShown(boolean newValue);
        public void setGroupingSize (int newValue);
        public void setMaximumFractionDigits(int newValue);
        public void setMinimumFractionDigits(int newValue);
        public void setMaximumIntegerDigits(int newValue);
        public void setMinimumIntegerDigits(int newValue);
        public void setMultiplier (int newValue);
        public void setNegativePrefix (String newValue);
        public void setNegativeSuffix (String newValue);
```

```
        public void setPositivePrefix (String newValue);
        public void setPositiveSuffix (String newValue);
        public String toLocalizedPattern();
        public String toPattern();
    }
```

DecimalFormatSymbols

Synopsis

Class Name: `java.text.DecimalFormatSymbols`

Superclass: `java.lang.Object`

Immediate Subclasses: None

Interfaces Implemented: `java.io.Serializable`
                             `java.lang.Cloneable`

Class Summary

```
    public final class DecimalFormatSymbols implements Cloneable, Serializable {

        // Constructors
        public DecimalFormatSymbols();
        public DecimalFormatSymbols( Locale locale );

        // Methods
        public Object clone();
        public boolean equals(Object obj);
        public String getCurrencySymbol();
        public char getDecimalSeparator();
        public char getDigit();
        public char getGroupingSeparator();
        public String getInfinity();
        public String getInternationalCurrencySymbol();
        public char getMinusSign();
        public char getMonetaryDecimalSeparator();
        public String getNaN();
        public char getPatternSeparator();
        public char getPercent();
        public char getPerMill();
        public char getZeroDigit();
        public int hashCode();
        public void setCurrencySymbol(String currency);
        public void setDecimalSeparator(char decimalSeparator);
        public void setDigit(char digit);
        public void setGroupingSeparator(char groupingSeparator);
        public void setInfinity(String infinity);
        public void setInternationalCurrencySymbol(String currency);
        public void setMinusSign(char minusSign);
        public void setMonetaryDecimalSeparator(char sep);
        public void setNaN(String NaN);
        public void setPatternSeparator(char patternSeparator);
        public void setPercent(char percent);
```

```
        public void setPerMill(char perMill);
        public void setZeroDigit(char zeroDigit);
    }
```

FieldPosition

Synopsis

Class Name:	`java.text.FieldPosition`
Superclass:	`java.lang.Object`
Immediate Subclasses:	None
Interfaces Implemented:	None

Class Summary

```
    public class FieldPosition {

        // Constructors
        public FieldPosition(int field);

        // Methods
        public boolean equals(Object obj);
        public int getBeginIndex();
        public int getEndIndex();
        public int getField();
        public int hashCode();
        public void setBeginIndex(int bi);
        public void setEndIndex(int ei);
        public String toString();
    }
```

Format

Synopsis

Class Name:	`java.text.Format`
Superclass:	`java.lang.Object`

Immediate Subclasses:	`java.text.DateFormat`
	`java.text.MessageFormat`
	`java.text,NumberFormat`

Interfaces Implemented:	`java.io.Serializable` `java.lang.Cloneable`

Class Summary

```
    public abstract class Format implements Serializable, Cloneable {

        // Constructors
        public Format();
```

```
    // Methods
    public Object clone();
    public final String format (Object obj);
    public abstract StringBuffer format(Object obj,
                    StringBuffer toAppendTo,
                    FieldPosition pos);
    public Object parseObject(String source) throws ParseException;
    public abstract Object parseObject(String source, ParsePosition status);
}
```

MessageFormat

Synopsis

Class Name:	`java.text.MessageFormat`
Superclass:	`java.text.Format`
Immediate Subclasses:	None
Interfaces Implemented:	`java.io.Serializable` `java.lang.Cloneable`

Class Summary

```
public class MessageFormat extends Format {

    // Constructors
    public MessageFormat(String pattern);

    // Methods
    public void applyPattern(String newPattern);
    public Object clone();
    public boolean equals(Object obj);
    public static String format(String pattern, Object[] arguments);
    public final StringBuffer format(Object source, StringBuffer result,
                                     FieldPosition ignore);
    public final StringBuffer format(Object[] source, StringBuffer result,
                                     FieldPosition ignore);
    public Format[] getFormats();
    public Locale getLocale();
    public int hashCode();
    public Object[] parse(String source) throws ParseException;
    public Object[] parse(String source, ParsePosition status);
    public Object parseObject (String text, ParsePosition status);
    public void setFormats(Format[] newFormats);
    public void setFormat(int variable, Format newFormat);
    public void setLocale(Locale theLocale);
    public String toPattern();
}
```

NumberFormat

Synopsis

Class Name: `java.text.NumberFormat`

Superclass: `java.text.Format`

Immediate Subclasses: `java.text.ChoiceFormat`
                               `java.text.DecimalFormat`

Interfaces Implemented: `java.io.Serializable`
                               `java.lang.Cloneable`

Class Summary

```java
public abstract class NumberFormat extends Format {

    // Constants
    public static final int FRACTION_FIELD;
    public static final int INTEGER_FIELD;

    // Constructors
    public NumberFormat();

    // Methods
    public final StringBuffer format(Object number,
                                     StringBuffer toAppendTo,
                                     FieldPosition pos);
    public final Object parseObject(String source,
                                    ParsePosition parsePosition);
    public final String format (double number);
    public final String format (long number);
    public abstract StringBuffer format(double number,
                                        StringBuffer toAppendTo,
                                        FieldPosition pos);
    public abstract StringBuffer format(long number,
                                        StringBuffer toAppendTo,
                                        FieldPosition pos);
    public abstract Number parse(String text, ParsePosition parsePosition);
    public Number parse(String text) throws ParseException;
    public boolean isParseIntegerOnly();
    public void setParseIntegerOnly(boolean value);
    public final static NumberFormat getInstance();
    public static NumberFormat getInstance(Locale inLocale);
    public final static NumberFormat getNumberInstance();
    public static NumberFormat getNumberInstance(Locale inLocale);
    public final static NumberFormat getCurrencyInstance();
    public static NumberFormat getCurrencyInstance(Locale inLocale);
    public final static NumberFormat getPercentInstance();
    public static NumberFormat getPercentInstance(Locale inLocale);
    public static Locale[] getAvailableLocales();
    public int hashCode();
    public boolean equals(Object obj);
```

```
    public Object clone();
    public boolean isGroupingUsed();
    public void setGroupingUsed(boolean newValue);
    public int getMaximumIntegerDigits();
    public void setMaximumIntegerDigits(int newValue);
    public int getMinimumIntegerDigits();
    public void setMinimumIntegerDigits(int newValue);
    public int getMaximumFractionDigits();
    public void setMaximumFractionDigits(int newValue);
    public int getMinimumFractionDigits();
    public void setMinimumFractionDigits(int newValue);
}
```

ParsePosition

Synopsis

Class Name: `java.text.ParsePosition`
Superclass: `java.lang.Object`
Immediate Subclasses: None
Interfaces Implemented: None

Class Summary

```
public class ParsePosition {

    // Constructors
    public ParsePosition(int index);

    // Methods
    public boolean equals(Object obj);
    public int getErrorIndex();
    public int getIndex();
    public int hashCode();
    public void setErrorIndex(int ei);
    public void setIndex(int index);
    public String toString();
}
```

RuleBasedCollator

Synopsis

Class Name: `java.text.RuleBasedCollator`
Superclass: `java.text.Collator`
Immediate Subclasses: None
Interfaces Implemented: `java.lang.Cloneable`
                                `java.util.Comparator`

Class Summary

```
public class RuleBasedCollator extends Collator {

    // Constructors
    public RuleBasedCollator(String rules) throws ParseException;

    // Methods
    public Object clone();
    public synchronized int compare(String source, String target);
    public boolean equals(Object obj);
    public CollationElementIterator getCollationElementIterator(String source);
    public CollationElementIterator getCollationElementIterator(
                                        CharacterIterator source);
    public synchronized CollationKey getCollationKey(String source);
    public String getRules();
    public int hashCode();
}
```

SimpleDateFormat

Synopsis

Class Name:	java.text.SimpleDateFormat
Superclass:	java.text.DateFormat
Immediate Subclasses:	None
Interfaces Implemented:	java.io.Serializable
	java.lang.Cloneable

Class Summary

```
public class SimpleDateFormat extends DateFormat {

    // Constructors
    public SimpleDateFormat();
    public SimpleDateFormat(String pattern);
    public SimpleDateFormat(String pattern, Locale loc);
    public SimpleDateFormat(String pattern, DateFormatSymbols formatData);

    // Methods
    public void applyLocalizedPattern(String pattern);
    public void applyPattern (String pattern);
    public Object clone();
    public boolean equals(Object obj);
    public StringBuffer format(Date date, StringBuffer toAppendTo, FieldPosition pos);
    public Date get2DigitYearStart();
    public DateFormatSymbols getDateFormatSymbols();
    public int hashCode();
    public Date parse(String text, ParsePosition pos);
    public void set2DigitYearStart(Date startDate);
    public void setDateFormatSymbols(DateFormatSymbols newFormatSymbols);
    public String toLocalizedPattern();
    public String toPattern();
}
```

StringCharacterIterator

Synopsis

Class Name:	`java.text.StringCharaterIterator`
Superclass:	`java.lang.Object`
Immediate Subclasses:	None
Interfaces Implemented:	`java.lang.Cloneable` `java.text.CharacterIterator`

Class Summary

```
public final class StringCharacterIterator implements CharacterIterator {

    // Constructors
    public StringCharacterIterator(String text);
    public StringCharacterIterator(String text, int pos);
    public StringCharacterIterator(String text, int begin, int end, int pos);

    // Methods
    public Object clone();
    public char current();
    public boolean equals(Object obj);
    public char first();
    public int getBeginIndex();
    public int getEndIndex();
    public int getIndex();
    public int hashCode();
    public char last();
    public char next();
    public char previous();
    public char setIndex(int p);
    public void setText(String text);
}
```

java.util Package

Calendar

Synopsis

Class Name:	`java.util.Calendar`
Superclass:	`java.lang.Object`
Immediate Subclasses:	`java.util.GregorianCalendar`
Interfaces Implemented:	`java.lang.Cloneable` `java.io.Serializable`

Class Summary

```
public abstract class Calendar implements Serializable, Cloneable {

    // Constants
    public final static int AM;
    public final static int AM_PM;
    public final static int APRIL;
    public final static int AUGUST;
    public final static int DATE;
    public final static int DAY_OF_MONTH;
    public final static int DAY_OF_WEEK;
    public final static int DAY_OF_WEEK_IN_MONTH;
    public final static int DAY_OF_YEAR;
    public final static int DECEMBER;
    public final static int DST_OFFSET;
    public final static int ERA;
    public final static int FEBRUARY;
    public final static int FIELD_COUNT;
    public final static int FRIDAY;
    public final static int HOUR;
    public final static int HOUR_OF_DAY;
    public final static int JANUARY;
    public final static int JUNE;
    public final static int JULY;
    public final static int MARCH;
    public final static int MAY;
    public final static int MILLISECOND;
    public final static int MINUTE;
    public final static int MONDAY;
    public final static int MONTH;
    public final static int NOVEMBER;
    public final static int OCTOBER;
    public final static int PM;
    public final static int SATURDAY;
    public final static int SECOND;
    public final static int SEPTEMBER;
    public final static int SUNDAY;
    public final static int THURSDAY;
    public final static int TUESDAY;
    public final static int UNDECIMBER;
    public final static int YEAR;
    public final static int WEDNESDAY;
    public final static int WEEK_OF_MONTH;
    public final static int WEEK_OF_YEAR;
    public final static int ZONE_OFFSET;

    // Constructors
    protected Calendar();
    protected Calendar(TimeZone zone, Locale aLocale);

    // Methods
    abstract public void add(int field, int amount);
```

```
        public boolean after(Object when);
        public boolean before(Object when);
        public final void clear();
        public final void clear(int field);
        public Object clone();
        public boolean equals(Object obj);
        public static synchronized Locale[] getAvailableLocales();
        public final int get(int field);
        public int getActualMaximum(int field);
        public int getActualMinimum(int field);
        public int getFirstDayOfWeek();
        abstract public int getGreatestMinimum(int field);
        public static synchronized Calendar getInstance();
        public static synchronized Calendar getInstance(TimeZone zone);
        public static synchronized Calendar getInstance(Locale aLocale);
        public static synchronized Calendar getInstance(TimeZone zone,
                                                        Locale aLocale);
        abstract public int getLeastMaximum(int field);
        abstract public int getMaximum(int field);
        public int getMinimalDaysInFirstWeek();
        abstract public int getMinimum(int field);
        public final Date getTime();
        public TimeZone getTimeZone();
        public int hashCode();
        public boolean isLenient();
        public final boolean isSet(int field);
        abstract public void roll(int field, boolean up);
        public void roll(int field, int amount);
        public final void set(int field, int value);
        public final void set(int year, int month, int date);
        public final void set(int year, int month, int date, int hour, int minute);
        public final void set(int year, int month, int date, int hour, int minute,
                              int second);
        public void setFirstDayOfWeek(int value);
        public void setLenient(boolean lenient);
        public void setMinimalDaysInFirstWeek(int value);
        public final void setTime(Date date);
        public void setTimeZone(TimeZone value);
        public String toString();
    }
```

GregorianCalendar

Synopsis

Class Name:	`java.util.GregorianCalendar`
Superclass:	`java.util.Calendar`
Immediate Subclasses:	None
Interfaces Implemented:	`java.lang.Cloneable` `java.io.Serializable`

Class Summary

```
public class GregorianCalendar extends Calendar {

    // Constants
    public static final int AD;
    public static final int BC;

    // Constructors
    public GregorianCalendar();
    public GregorianCalendar(TimeZone zone);
    public GregorianCalendar(Locale aLocale);
    public GregorianCalendar(TimeZone zone, Locale aLocale);
    public GregorianCalendar(int year, int month, int date);
    public GregorianCalendar(int year, int month, int date, int hour, int minute);
    public GregorianCalendar(int year, int month, int date, int hour, int minute,
                                                                int second);

    // Methods
    public void add(int field, int amount);
    public boolean equals(Object obj);
    public int getActualMaximum(int field);
    public int getActualMinimum(int field);
    public final Date getGregorianChange();
    public int getGreatestMinimum(int field);
    public int getLeastMaximum(int field);
    public int getMaximum(int field);
    public int getMinimum(int field);
    public int hashCode();
    public boolean isLeapYear(int year);
    public void roll(int field, boolean up);
    public void roll(int field, int amount);
    public void setGregorianChange(Date date);
}
```

ListResourceBundle

Synopsis

Class Name:	`java.util.ListResourceBundle`
Superclass:	`java.util.ResourceBundle`
Immediate Subclasses:	`javax.accessability.AccessibleResourceBundle`
Interfaces Implemented:	None

Class Summary

```
public abstract class ListResourceBundle extends ResourceBundle {

    // Constructors
    public ListResourceBundle();
```

```
    // Methods
    protected abstract Object[][] getContents();
    public Enumeration getKeys();
    public final Object handleGetObject(String key);
}
```

Locale

Synopsis

Class Name: `java.util.Locale`
Superclass: `java.lang.Object`
Immediate Subclasses: None
Interfaces Implemented: `java.io.Serializable`
                          `java.lang.Cloneable`

Class Summary

```
public final class Locale implements Cloneable, Serializable {

    // Constants
    static public final Locale CANADA;
    static public final Locale CANADA_FRENCH;
    static public final Locale CHINA;
    static public final Locale CHINESE;
    static public final Locale ENGLISH;
    static public final Locale FRANCE;
    static public final Locale FRENCH;
    static public final Locale GERMAN;
    static public final Locale GERMANY;
    static public final Locale ITALIAN;
    static public final Locale ITALY;
    static public final Locale JAPAN;
    static public final Locale JAPANESE;
    static public final Locale KOREA;
    static public final Locale KOREAN;
    static public final Locale PRC;
    static public final Locale SIMPLIFIED_CHINESE;
    static public final Locale TAIWAN;
    static public final Locale TRADITIONAL_CHINESE;
    static public final Locale UK;
    static public final Locale US;

    // Constructors
    public Locale(String language, String country);
    public Locale(String language, String country, String variant);

    // Methods
    public Object clone();
    public boolean equals(Object obj);
    public static Locale[] getAvailableLocales();
    public String getCountry();
```

```
    public static Locale getDefault();
    public final String getDisplayCountry();
    public String getDisplayCountry(Locale inLocale);
    public final String getDisplayLanguage();
    public String getDisplayLanguage(Locale inLocale);
    public final String getDisplayName();
    public String getDisplayName(Locale inLocale);
    public final String getDisplayVariant();
    public String getDisplayVariant(Locale inLocale);
    public static String[] getISOCountries();
    public static String[] getISOLanguages();
    public String getISO3Country() throws MissingResourceException;
    public String getISO3Language() throws MissingResourceException;
    public String getLanguage();
    public String getVariant();
    public synchronized int hashCode();
    public static synchronized void setDefault(Locale newLocale);
    public final String toString();
}
```

PropertyResourceBundle

Synopsis

Class Name:	`java.util.PropertyResourceBundle`
Superclass:	`java.util.ResourceBundle`
Immediate Subclasses:	None
Interfaces Implemented:	None

Class Summary

```
public class PropertyResourceBundle extends ResourceBundle {

    // Constructors
    public PropertyResourceBundle(InputStream stream) throws IOException;

    // Methods
    public Enumeration getKeys();
    public Object handleGetObject(String key);
}
```

ResourceBundle

Synopsis

Class Name:	`java.util.ResourceBundle`
Superclass:	`java.lang.Object`
Immediate Subclasses:	`java.util.ListResourceBundle` `java.util.PropertyResourceBundle`
Interfaces Implemented:	None

Class Summary

```
public abstract class ResourceBundle {

    // Constructors
    public ResourceBundle();

    // Methods
    public abstract Enumeration getKeys();
    public static final ResourceBundle getBundle(String baseName)
        throws MissingResourceException;
    public static final ResourceBundle getBundle(String baseName,
                                                 Locale locale);
    public static ResourceBundle getBundle(String baseName, Locale locale,
                                           ClassLoader loader)
        throws MissingResourceException;
    public Locale getLocale();
    public final Object getObject(String key) throws MissingResourceException;
    public final String getString(String key) throws MissingResourceException;
    public final String[] getStringArray(String key)
        throws MissingResourceException;
    protected abstract Object handleGetObject(String key)
        throws MissingResourceException;
}
```

SimpleTimeZone

Synopsis

Class Name:	`java.util.SimpleTimeZone`
Superclass:	`java.util.TimeZone`
Immediate Subclasses:	**None**
Interfaces Implemented:	`java.lang.Cloneable` `java.io.Serializable`

Class Summary

```
public class SimpleTimeZone extends TimeZone {

    // Constructors
    public SimpleTimeZone(int rawOffset, String ID);
    public SimpleTimeZone(int rawOffset, String ID,
                          int startMonth, int startDay, int startDayOfWeek,
                          int startTime, int endMonth, int endDay,
                          int endDayOfWeek, int endTime);
    public SimpleTimeZone(int rawOffset, String ID,
                          int startMonth, int startDay, int startDayOfWeek,
                          int startTime, int endMonth, int endDay,
                          int endDayOfWeek, int endTime, int dstSavings);
```

```
    // Methods
    public Object clone();
    public boolean equals(Object obj);
    public int getDSTSavings();
    public int getOffset(int era, int year, int month, int day, int dayOfWeek,
                                                           int millis);
    public int getRawOffset();
    public synchronized int hashCode();
    public boolean hasSameRules(TimeZone other);
    public boolean inDaylightTime(Date date);
    public void setDSTSavings(int millisSavedDuringDST);
    public void setEndRule(int month, int dayOfMonth, int time);
    public void setEndRule(int month, int dayOfWeekInMonth, int dayOfWeek,
                                                           int time);
    public void setEndRule(int month, int dayOfMonth, int dayOfWeek, int time,
                                                       boolean after);
    public void setRawOffset(int offsetMillis);
    public void setStartRule(int month, int dayOfMonth, int time);
    public void setStartRule(int month, int dayOfWeekInMonth, int dayOfWeek, int time);
    public void setStartRule(int month, int dayOfMonth, int dayOfWeek, int time,
                                                       boolean after);
    public void setStartYear(int year);
    public String toString();
    public boolean useDaylightTime();
}
```

TimeZone

Synopsis

Class Name:	`java.util.TimeZone`
Superclass:	`java.lang.Object`
Immediate Subclasses:	`java.util.SimpleTimeZone`
Interfaces Implemented:	`java.lang.Cloneable` `java.io.Serializable`

Class Summary

```
    public abstract class TimeZone implements Serializable, Cloneable {

    // Constants
    public static final int LONG;
    public static final int SHORT;

    // Constructors
    public TimeZone();

    // Methods
    public Object clone();
    public static synchronized String[] getAvailableIDs();
    public static synchronized String[] getAvailableIDs(int rawOffset);
    public static synchronized TimeZone getDefault();
```

```
    public final String getDisplayName();
    public final String getDisplayName(Locale locale);
    public final String getDisplayName(boolean daylight, int style);
    public String getDisplayName(boolean daylight, int style, Locale locale);
    public String getID();
    abstract public int getOffset(int era, int year, int month, int day,
                                  int dayOfWeek, int milliseconds);
    abstract public int getRawOffset();
    public static synchronized TimeZone getTimeZone(String ID);
    public boolean hasSameRules(TimeZone other);
    abstract public boolean inDaylightTime(Date date);
    public static synchronized void setDefault(TimeZone zone);
    public void setID(String ID);
    abstract public void setRawOffset(int offsetMillis);
    abstract public boolean useDaylightTime();
}
```

E

Internationalization Enhancements Across Versions of the JDK

This appendix outlines the bug fixes, changes, or enhancements made to the internationalization support that exists across versions of Sun's Java Runtime Environment. We start with JDK 1.1 beta and progress to Java 2 SDK, Standard Edition, Version 1.3. As we stated in the Preface, much of the existing internationalization support was introduced with the release of JDK 1.1.

Detailed information about specific bugs can be obtained from the Java Developer Connection Bug Database. This site is available at *http://developer.java.sun.com/ developer/bugParade/*.

Changes from JDK 1.1 beta1 to JDK 1.1 beta2

Bug number 4018252 was fixed. If any format or parse methods were called on `java.text.DecimalNumberFormat`, an exception would be thrown.

A number of classes were moved into the `sun.io` package: the `ByteToCharConverter` and `CharToByteConverter` classes. The `ConversionBufferFullException`, `MalformedInputException`, and `UnknownCharacterException` classes were also moved. Because of this move, they are no longer part of the public API.

Changes from JDK 1.1beta3 to JDK 1.1_Final

Almost all problems related to internationalization. Numerous bug fixes and enhancements were made.

Changes from JDK 1.1_Final to JDK 1.1.1

Bug number 4036076 was fixed. The `getMenu` and `getMenuBar` methods were removed from the `java.util.ResourceBundle` class. These methods were left in the final release accidentally. This change removed dependencies on the AWT package. The field, `java.awt.Component.locale`, was changed from `protected` to `private`.

Changes from JDK 1.1.2 to JDK 1.1.3

Two bugs, 4049223 and 4055084, were fixed to resolve a localization bug in JDK 1.1.2. Characters from non-ISO8859-1 code sets would not display properly in text display areas.

Bug number 4059684 was fixed and resolved an issue with the `InputStreamReader` class if a UTF8 encoding was used. The problem was that the character stream would miss characters.

Changes from JDK 1.1.3 to JDK 1.1.4

Bug number 4031620, affecting the `DateFormat.parse()` method, was fixed. This method is only supposed to throw a `FormatException`, but sometimes a `StringIndexOutOfBoundsException` would be thrown.

A bug affecting the AWT input methods on Solaris under JDK 1.1.1 was fixed. The bug number is 4041569. The input method status region was created inside an AWT window and would affect the layout of the window.

Bug number 4053637 affected the `zh_TW` locale where a BIG5 character encoding was used. Users were unable to input Chinese into a text area.

Changes from JDK 1.1.5 to JDK 1.1.6

As some of the documentation describes, numerous performance and support enhancements were introduced in JDK 1.1.6.

Unicode code point `\u301c` was not mapped correctly. This problem was reported in bug number 4023097.

Before JDK 1.1.6, if a resource bundle were not found in attempting to load a particular bundle, a large number of error messages would be produced. This issue was reported in bug number 4050902 and has been fixed to limit the messages produced if a search for a bundle is unsuccessful.

Prior to the release of JDK 1.1.6, the name of the default ISO 8859-1 character encoding was "8859_1." The name of the character encoding was changed to "ISO8859_1."

Changes from JDK 1.1.6 to JDK 1.1.7

Support for the European Union currency, the euro, was added to the Solaris JDK. A number of new locale resources were added. Unicode support was upgraded from 2.0.14 to 2.1.2 to support the euro currency character correctly.

Many bug fixes affecting a large number of the internationalization classes were made.

A change was made to the default character encoding on Windows systems. It is now called Cp1252, or Windows Latin-1, for western locales. Under Solaris, the default encoding remains ISO8859_1 for western locales.

Changes from JDK 1.1.7 to JDK 1.1.7A

Support for the European Union currency, the euro, was added to the Windows JDK. Variant locale resources were provided for the countries adopting the euro.

Bug number 4182062 affected locale names in the Solaris JDK. This problem occurred because the names did not match up with the locale names provided in a patch to Solaris that added these locales. This bug has been fixed with proper mapping of locale names in the JDK to the Solaris patch locale names.

A *font.properties* file, which supports the euro symbol, was added to the JDK under Solaris. This file was referenced in bug number 4181915.

Changes from JDK 1.1.7B to JDK 1.1.8

As with other releases, numerous bug fixes were made in internationalization support in this release of the JDK.

Bug number 4059431 prevented some time zones from proper interpretation, and it was fixed in this release.

Changes from JDK 1.1 to Java 2 SDK 1.2 Beta 2

The Input Method Framework was added in the 1.2 release of the Java platform. Chapter 10, *Input Methods*, discusses the Input Method Framework in more detail.

Changes from Java 2 SDK 1.2 Beta 2 to Java 2 SDK 1.2 Beta 3

Swing controls can now take advantage of the Input Method Framework. Numerous enhancements were made in this area. Support was added for the Internet-Intranet Input Method Protocol (IIIMP).

Changes from Java 2 SDK 1.2 Beta 3 to Java 2 SDK 1.2 Beta 4

A couple of new methods were added to classes in the `java.awt.im` package.

Two new methods were added to `java.text.BreakIterator`: `isBoundary` and `preceding`.

Two new methods were added to the `java.text.SimpleDateFormat` class: set2DigitYearStart and get2DigitYearStart. This addition allows the entry of two-digit years.

Numerous methods were added to the `java.text.DecimalFormatSymbols` class. These methods allow independent get and set of currency formatting symbols.

Changes from Java 2 SDK 1.2 Beta 4 to Java 2 SDK 1.2 Release Candidate 1

`javax.swing.JOptionPane` was made localizable; however, as we said in Chapter 9, *Internationalized* Graphical *User Interfaces*, these strings in resource files within the *rt.jar* file are not easily modified. Previously, the strings used in a `JOptionPane` were hardcoded in the class.

The `java.lang.Character.Subset` class was redefined to no longer contain constants for character subsets. Constants representing Unicode 2.0 character blocks were added to a static inner class called `Character.UnicodeBlock`.

Some localization support was added to the `javax.swing.JFileChooser` class with the setApproveButtonText method.

Changes from Java 2 SDK 1.2 Release Candidate 1 to Java 2 SDK 1.2 Release Candidate 2

No changes affecting internationalization were introduced in Release Candidate 2.

Changes from Java 2 SDK 1.2.1 to Java 2 SDK 1.2.2

Two clarifications were made in documentation to the `java.util.Calendar` and `java.util.Date` classes. Documentation changes were made in the class-level specification for the Calendar class, while documentation changes were made to the parse methods in the Date class to describe the behavior of dealing with two-digit dates.

Bug number 4208960 affected the `getOffset` method in the `java.util.SimpleTimeZone` class. An `IllegalArgumentException` would be thrown if its argument were February 29 in a leap year. This bug was fixed.

If you use Japanese Solaris 2.5.1, you can't print Kanji or other Japanese characters. More recent versions of the operating system are not affected.

The ja_JP.UTF-8 locale on the Solaris 7 operating environment does not work with the Java 2 SDK. This problem is an in progress request for enhancement and its bug number is 4198131.

Under the Japanese version of Windows NT 4.0 Service Pack 3, an application crashes the system if the `getGlyphOutline` method in the `java.awt.font.GlyphVector` class is called. Microsoft posted a fix at the web site *http://www.microsoft.com/japan/products/ntupdate/nt4sp3/glyphfix.htm*.

The first release of the Microsoft Windows 95 for Traditional Chinese Version 2.0 does not include certain fonts referenced in the *font.properties* files. However, the second release of Microsoft Windows 95 for Traditional Chinese Version 2.0 does contain the required fonts. Without the second release, traditional Chinese characters will not display correctly in Swing components. The bug number for this problem is 4181857.

If you would like to see a full list of bugs fixed in Java 2 SDK, Standard Edition, Version 1.2.2, check out *http://java.sun.com/products/jdk/1.2/fixedbugs /index.html.*

Changes from Java 2 SDK 1.2.2 to Java 2 SDK 1.3

An Input Method Engine Service Provider Interface (SPI) was added. The SPI is described in detail at the web site *http://java.sun.com/j2se/1.3/ docs/guide/imf/spi-reference.html.* Chapter 10 discusses the Input Method Framework.

Chinese and Japanese characters may not display properly under Windows 2000. These display problems can be fixed by setting the "System Locale" rather than the "User Locale." This issue is detailed on Microsoft's web site at *http://www.microsoft.com/globaldev/faqs/locales.asp.*

If you would like to see a full list of bugs fixed in Java 2 SDK, Standard Edition, Version 1.3, check out *http://java.sun.com/products/jdk/1.3/fixedbugs/index.html.*

Glossary

AD

Acronym for Anno Domini (meaning "In the year of our Lord" in Latin). Used in conjunction with BC. See *BC* and *CE*.

Alphabet

A collection of characters used in a writing system that represent the sounds of particular language. See also *writing system*.

ASCII

Acronym for American Standard Code for Information Interchange.

Base character

A character that can stand alone and cannot combine with a preceding character. See also *combining character*.

BC

Acronym for Before Christ. Used in conjunction with AD. See also *AD* and *BCE*.

BCE

Acronym for Before the Common Era. Used in conjunction with CE. See also *CE* and *BC*.

Bidirectional text

In writing systems such as Arabic and Hebrew, the text is written horizontally from right to left except for numbers and embedded Latin text, which is written from left to right.

BIDI

An acronym for bidirectional text. See *bidirectional text*.

Bopomofo

ㄅㄆㄇㄈ. See *zhuyin*.

Boustrophedon

Literally meaning "turning like the oxen's plow." The writing of alternate lines in opposite directions (i.e., from left to right and from right to left).

CE

Acronym for Common Era. Used in conjunction with BCE. See also *BCE* and *AD*.

Character

The smallest unit of a writing system.

Character encoding

The mapping from a coded character set to a sequence of bits.

Choseong

The 19 jamo consonants in Hangul writing that can begin a syllable. See also *jongseong*, *jungeong*, and *jamo*.

CJK

Acronym for "Chinese, Japanese, and Korean" and is typically used when referring to the issues associated with computing in these languages.

Coded character set

A collection of characters in which each character is been assigned a unique numerical value.

Code element

The smallest unit defined in the Unicode Standard; equivalent to a code point.

Code point

An index into a coded character set.

Code set

See *coded character set.*

Collation

The process of sorting text.

Combining character

A character (typically a diacritical mark) used to combine with a preceding base character to form a new character. See also *base character.*

Component orientation

The positioning of various GUI components in an application that is appropriate for the locale in which the application runs. See also *bidirectional text.*

Composed character

A character consisting of a base character and at least one combining character. See *base character* and *combining character.*

Composition

The process of composing text in an input method as the user types on the keyboard.

Dagesh

A Hebrew vowel sign used to indicate that the letter should be pronounced with a hard sound.

Daylight saving time

A technique used by many countries to increase the amount of daylight hours by moving the clock ahead by an hour in the summer. Also called *summer time* in much of the world. See also *standard time.*

Decomposition

The breaking down of a precomposed character into a base character and one or more combing characters.

Diacritic

Special marks used for accents, tones, and vowels or to uniquely identify a character. In some writing systems, such as Indic and Thai, diacritics can span multiple characters. Also called diacritical marks.

Diaeresis

Two dots placed over a vowel to indicate that the vowel should be pronounced as a separate syllable, as in "naïve." See *umlaut.*

Encoding

A method of assigning numerical values to characters in a coded character set.

Encoding method

See *character encoding.*

Font

A collection of glyphs (typically of the same weight and style). See also *glyph.*

G11N

Abbreviation for globalization. See *globalization.*

Glyph

The shape drawn to represent a character. For example, "g" and "**g**" are two glyphs representing the same underlying character.

Globalization

The term that refers to the process of both internationalization and localization.

GMT

Greenwich mean time. The time in Greenwich, England, from which all other time zones are given an offset.

Guillemet

Quotation marks used in French and other languages that resemble small less-than and greater-than signs (e.g., «Français»).

Han Unification

The process undertaken by the Unicode Consortium to find duplicate Chinese characters among the Chinese, Japanese, and Korean writing systems.

Hangul

The native name for the Korean writing system. Also the name of the script's syllabic

Hangul (continued)

elements. Each hangul is composed of two or three elements called jamo. See also jamo.

Hanja

The Korean name for Chinese ideographic characters.

Hànzì

The Chinese name for ideographic characters.

Harakat

A set of marks used to represent short vowels in the Arabic writing system.

High-Surrogate

A Unicode code point in the range \uD800–\uDBFF. The first half of a surrogate pair. See also *surrogate pair.*

Hiragana

One of two syllabic scripts used in Japanese writing. Hiragana is typically used for native Japanese words and grammar particles.

Ideograph

A symbol used to represent an idea rather than a sound. Ideographs are commonly associated with Chinese writing.

I18N

Abbreviation for internationalization. See *internationalization.*

IME

Acronym for Input Method Editor. A software component or program that converts keystrokes to characters based on dictionary lookup.

Internationalization

The concept of developing software in a generic manner so it can later be localized for different markets without having to modify or recompile source code.

Jamo

The basic elements of the Hangul writing system. Jamo are equivalent to letters in an alphabet, representing either a consonant or a vowel. They are combined to form syllables. See also *Hangul.*

Jongseong

The 27 jamo consonants in Hangul writing that can end a syllable. See also *choseong, jungeong,* and *jamo.*

Jungeong

The 21 jamo median vowels that can form a hangul syllable. See also *choseong, jongseong,* and *jamo.*

Kana

The term used for hiragana and katakana, the syllabic scripts used in Japanese writing.

Kanji

The Japanese name for the Chinese ideographic characters.

Katakana

One of two syllabic scripts used in Japanese writing. Katakana is typically used to spell foreign loan words.

Kokuji

The Japanese word meaning "national characters" and referring to ideographic characters of Japanese origin.

L10N

Abbreviation for localization. See *localization.*

Ligature

A glyph whose shape is formed by combining two or more characters. An example is the laam-alif ligature "لا" formed by combining the letter laam "ل" with the letter alif "ا." In Arabic and Indic scripts, the use of ligatures is mandatory.

Locale

The encapsulation of language, formatting rules, and cultural nuances for a specific region of the world.

Locale-sensitive

A class or method that modifies its behavior based on the locale's specific requirements. See also *locale.*

Localization

The process of adapting an internationalized piece of software for a specific locale.

Logical order

The order in which text is typed on a keyboard. See also *visual order*.

Low-surrogate

A Unicode code point in the range \uDC00–\uDFFF. The second half of a surrogate pair. See also *surrogate pair*.

Nekudot

The Hebrew word for "dots," indicating vowels used with Hebrew letters.

Noncoded character set

A collection of characters that have not been coded. The English alphabet is an example of a noncoded character set.

Normalization

Conversion of data to a normal form. In Unicode, it typically refers to a process used prior to collating text.

Nuqat

The Arabic word for dots or diacritic marks used to distinguish characters with a similar base shape. For example, the Arabic letters ba "ب", ta "ت", and tha "ث".

Pictograph

A character whose shape represents a concrete concept.

Pinyin

The standard system for romanization of Chinese based on Mandarin pronunciation.

Precomposed character

A character that is equivalent to a base character and one or more combining characters. See also *base character* and *combining character*.

Radical

The 214 building blocks of Chinese ideographs.

Rōmaji

The Japanese term for the use of Latin letters in Japanese writing.

Round-trip conversion

The ability to convert text from one encoding method to another, and back again, without loss of data.

Script

See *writing system*.

Simplified Chinese

The form of Chinese writing used in the People's Republic of China that has been modified by removing strokes from characters. See also *Traditional Chinese*.

Standard time

The offset from GMT that is used during the winter months for regions that observe daylight saving time. See also *daylight saving time*.

Stroke

The basic element of a Chinese character.

Summer time

See *daylight saving time*.

Surrogate pair

A sequence of two 16-bit Unicode code points (one called the *high-surrogate*, the other called the *low-surrogate*) that combine to form a character.

Syllabary

A set of characters from which each character represents a syllable. Hiragana and Katakana are examples of syllabaries.

Titlecase

For characters that are composed of two letters (e.g., the Serbo-Croation character "dz"), a third case is needed in addition to upper and lower case. The titlecase of "dz" is "Dz," whereas the uppercase of "dz" is "DZ."

Traditional Chinese

The set of Chinese characters used outside the People's Republic of China that have been used for thousands of years.

Translation

The process of converting (translating) one language into another.

Transliteration

The process of representing text using a nonnative writing system (e.g., using Latin to write Russian).

UCS

Acronym for Universal Character Set, a term defined and used by the International Standard ISO/IEC 10646.

UCS-2

Universal Character Set encoded in two bytes and equivalent to the default Unicode encoding form.

Umlaut

The two dots that are placed above vowels in German and other European languages (e.g., ä, ë, ö, and ü). See also *diaereses*.

Unicode

A fixed-width 16-bit character encoding used to encode the world's writing systems. Unicode is maintained by the Unicode Consortium.

UTC

Acronym for universal time coordinate, equivalent to GMT. See also *GMT*.

UTF-8

Unicode (or UCS) Transformation Format, eight-bit encoding.

Visual Order

The order in which characters are displayed for reading, as opposed to logical order. See also *logical order*.

Writing system

A collection of characters and a set of rules that specify how a language should be written.

Zhuyin

A phonetic script developed in 1913 for Chinese, used mainly in Taiwan. Also known as bopomofo for the first four sounds of the script: b, p, m, and f.

Bibliography

Books

Chang, Raymond and Chang Margaret Scrogin. *Speaking of Chinese.* W. W. Norton & Company, Inc. 1978. ISBN 0-393-04503-X

Comrie, Bernard (Editor), Matthews, Stephen (Editor), and Polinsky, Maria (Editor). *The Atlas of Languages: The Origin and Development of Languages Throughout the World.* Quatro, Inc. 1996. ISBN 0-8160-3388-9

Eckstein, Robert, Loy, Marc, and Wood, Dave. *Java Swing.* O'Reilly & Associates, Inc. 1998. ISBN 1-56592-455-X

Firmage, Richard A. *The Alphabet Abecedarium: Some Notes on Letters.* David R. Gondine, Publisher, Inc. 1993. ISBN 0-87923-987-5

Giblin, James Cross. *The Riddle of the Rosetta Stone: Key to Ancient Egypt.* Harper & Row, Publishers, Inc. 1990. ISBN 0-06446-137-8

Graham, Tony. *Unicode: A Primer.* M&T Books. 2000. ISBN 0-7645-4625-2

Harold, Elliotte Rusty. *Java I/O.* O'Reilly & Associates, Inc. 1999. ISBN 1-56592-485-1

Harz Jorden, Eleanor and Ito Chaplin, Hamako. *Reading Japanese.* Yale University Press. 1976. ISBN 0-300-01913-0

Hunter, Jason. *Java Servlet Programming.* O'Reilly & Associates, Inc. 1998. ISBN 1-56592-391-X

Kano, Nadine. *Developing International Software for Windows 95 and Window NT.* Microsoft Press. 1995. ISBN 1-55615-840-8

Katzner, Kenneth. *The Languages of the World.* Funk & Wagnalls. 1975. ISBN 0-41511-809-3

Knudsen, Jonathan B. *Java 2D Graphics.* O'Reilly & Associates, Inc. 1999. ISBN 1-56592-484-3

Lunde, Ken. *CJKV Information Processing.* O'Reilly & Associates, Inc. 1999. ISBN 1-56592-224-7

Luong, Tuoc V., Lok, James S. H., Taylor, David J., and Driscoll, Kevin. *Internationalization: Developing Software for Global Markets.* John Wiley & Sons, Inc. 1995. ISBN 0-471-07661-9

O'Donnell, Sandra Martin. *Programming for the World: A Guide to Internationalization.* Prentice Hall. 1994. ISBN 0-13-722190-8

Samoyault, Tiphaine, and Pulver, Kathryn M. *Alphabetical Order: How the Alphabet Began.* Viking. 1998. ISBN 0-6708-7808-1

Scott, Joseph and Scott, Lenore. *Egyptian Hieroglyphs for Everyone: An Introduction to the Writing of Ancient Egypt.* Barnes & Noble, Inc. 1998. ISBN 1-56619-068-1

Tsirpanlis, Constantine N. *Modern Greek Idiom and Phrase Book.* Barons Educational Series, Inc. 1978. ISBN 0-81200-476-0

Unicode Consortium, The. *The Unicode Standard 2.0.* Addison-Wesley. 1996. ISBN 0-201-48345-9

Wightwick, Jane and Gaafar, Mahmoud. *Mastering Arabic.* Hippocrene Books. 1996. ISBN 0-87052-922-6

Wolff, Diane and Chien, Jeanette. *Chinese Writing: An Introduction.* Holt, Rinehart & Winston. 1975. ASIN: 0030489466

Articles and Papers

Andrews, Whit. "Tomorrow the World." *Internet World.* July 15, 1999, pp 35–39.

Beck, Brian. "Complex Text Rendering in Java™ 2." Fourteenth International Unicode Conference, Boston, Massachusetts, March 24–25, 1999.

Beck, Brian, Gill, Stuart, Lindenberg, Norbert, and O'Conner, John. "Java Internationalization Roadmap and Panel Q&A." Sixteenth International Unicode Conference, Amsterdam, The Netherlands, March 2730, 2000.

Davis, Mark, Felt, Doug and Raley, John. "International Text in JDK 1.2." *Java Report.* April 1998, Volume 3, Number 4, pp 25–38.

Freytag, Asmus. "Introducing Unicode 2.1: A Tutorial." Fourteenth International Unicode Conference, Boston, Massachusetts, March 24–25, 1999.

Freytag, Asmus. "Introduction to Unicode 3.0." Sixteenth International Unicode Conference, Amsterdam, The Netherlands, March 27–30, 2000.

Gillam, Richard. "Text Boundary Analysis in Java." Fourteenth International Unicode Conference, Boston, Massachusetts, March 24–25, 1999.

Gillam, Richard. "Developing Global Applications in Java." Fifteenth International Unicode Conference, San Jose, California, August 30 – September 2, 1999.

Ishida, Richard. "Non-Latin Writing Systems: Characteristics and Impact on Multinational Product Design." Thirteenth International Unicode Conference, San Jose, California, September 8–11, 1998.

Ishida, Richard. "Making Your Product Translatable." Thirteenth International Unicode Conference, San Jose, California, September 8–11, 1998.

Lindenberg, Norbert and Okutsu, Masayoshi. "Java Input Method Framework." Fourteenth International Unicode Conference, Boston, Massachusetts, March 24–25, 1999.

MacFarland, Thomas. "Developing Internationalized Software with JDK 1.1." Fourteenth International Unicode Conference, Boston, Massachusetts, March 24–25, 1999.

Milo, Thomas. "Authentic Arabic—Backgrounds." Thirteenth International Unicode Conference, San Jose, California, September 8–11, 1998.

O'Conner, John. "Java Localization with Resource Bundles." *Multilingual Computing & Technology*. Volume 9, Issue 5, pp 49–53.

O'Conner, John. "International Character Set Conversions in Java." *Multilingual Computing & Technology*. Volume 10, Issue 2, pp 58–62.

O'Conner, John. "Displaying Unicode with Java's Composite Fonts." Fourteenth International Unicode Conference, Boston, Massachusetts, March 24–25, 1999.

Shih, Helena. "The Java International API, JDK 1.1 and Beyond." Fourteenth International Unicode Conference, Boston, Massachusetts, March 24–25, 1999.

Vine, Andrea. "Demystifying Character Sets." *Multilingual Computing & Technology*. Volume 10, Issue 4, pp 48–52.

Werner, Laura A. "Unicode Text Searching in Java." Fourteenth International Unicode Conference, Boston, Massachusetts, March 24–25, 1999.

Web Sites

Arabic

http://members.aol.com/gnhbos/meissues.htm
> A good overview on the issues of developing software for Arabic speaking markets.

Currency

http://currency.xe.net/gen/iso4217.htm
> This site contains the list of ISO 4217 codes.

Chinese

http://www.zhongwen.com
> An excellent resource for learning about Chinese characters. Any Chinese character on the web site can be clicked on to learn more about the character. It even has cross-links to the Unicode site so that you learn the Unicode code point for any character.

http://www.ocrat.com
> A web site designed for English speakers who want to learn more about Chinese. It includes several useful links, including a section that teaches how to write Chinese characters.

http://www.chinesecomputing.com
> A page dedicated to Chinese computing with Java.

http://www.mandarintools.com
> Several tools for Chinese computing, including source code for various Java applets and applications.

http://www.uiowa.edu/~chinese/pinyin
> A web page that focuses on the Pinyin romanization system.

Hangul

http://catcode.com/kintro/index.htm
> An introduction to the Korean language and the Hangul writing system.

Indic

http://www.ukindia.com
> This web site has links to several tutorials on reading the various Indic writing systems.

http://www.geocities.com/Athens/Academy/9594
> This web site, maintained by Eden Golshani, is a good reference to the scripts of South Asia, including those from the Indian subcontinent.

http://www.clas.ufl.edu/users/gthursby/ind/shabda.htm
> An index of Indic language-related web sites.

Internationalization

http://www.xerox-emea.com/globaldesign
> Richard Ishida maintains a nice site that discusses general issues associated with software internationalization and localization.

Java

http://java.sun.com/j2se/1.3/docs
> The Java 2 SDK, Standard Edition, Version 1.3 online documentation.

http://java.sun.com/j2se/1.3/docs/guide/intl/faq.html
> Sun's Internationalization Frequently Asked Questions page.

http://forum.java.sun.com/list/discuss.sun.internationalization
> Sun's Java discussion forum on internationalization issues.

http://oss.software.ibm.com/icu4j
> The web site that hosts the International Components for Unicode for Java; a collaborative open source project for extending Java's internationalization features.

Time

http://www.webexhibits.org/daylightsaving
> A good overview of daylight savings time. The site includes a list of countries that observe daylight savings time and when they make the switch from standard time.

http://www.worldtimeserver.com
> Contains accurate local times for cities around the world. This site notes differences based on local observance of daylight savings time.

Unicode

http://www.unicode.org

    The official web site of the Unicode Consortium.

http://www.hclrss.demon.co.uk/unicode

    A Unicode resources web site with links to useful utilities. This site also includes freely available Unicode fonts.

http://czyborra.com/unicode/characters.html

    A good overview of Unicode.

Index

We'd like to hear your suggestions for improving our indexes. Send email to *index@oreilly.com*.

About the Author

Andrew Deitsch is a software engineer who manages an e-business group at GE's Corporate Research and Development Center in Niskayuna, New York. Andrew was fortunate enough to be involved in the beta release of Java in 1995 and has been programming in the language ever since. The inspiration for this book came from his efforts to use Java effectively to build internationalized applications and his frustrations in not finding any books related to this important topic.

David Czarnecki is a computer scientist in the Internet and Software Technology Laboratory at the GE Corporate Research and Development Center. He is involved with various e-commerce initiatives and projects, and in recent months has been increasingly involved in providing expertise on how to properly internationalize software. David holds both B.S. and M.S. degrees in computer science.

Colophon

Our look is the result of reader comments, our own experimentation, and feedback from distribution channels. Distinctive covers complement our distinctive approach to technical topics, breathing personality and life into potentially dry subjects.

Ann Schirmer was the production editor and the copyeditor for *Java*™ *Internationalization*. Claire Cloutier, Linley Dolby, and Jeffrey Holcomb provided quality control. Mary Sheehan proofread the book. Bruce Tracy wrote the index. Joe Wizda and Judy Hoer reviewed the index. Tim Atalla, Paolo De Coppi, Tatiana Diaz, Cliff Dyer, Byung-Soo Kim, Brenda Miller, Lenny Muellner, Nik Udompanyanan, Anne-Marie Vaduva, and Melanie Wang proofread the language sections.

Hanna Dyer designed the cover of this book, based on a series design by Edie Freedman. The image of a beachball globe on the cover of *Java*™ *Internationalization* was photographed by Kevin Thomas and manipulated in Adobe Photoshop by Michael Snow. Emma Colby produced the cover layout with QuarkXPress 4.1 using the Bodoni Black font from URW Software and the Bodoni Bold Italic font from Bitstream.

David Futato and Melanie Wang designed the interior layout based on a series design by Nancy Priest. Lenny Muellner and Mike Sierra implemented the design in Microsoft Word 2000. The heading font is Bodoni BT, the text font is New

Baskerville, and the code font is Courier. The illustrations that appear in the book were produced by Robert Romano using Macromedia FreeHand 8 and Adobe Photoshop 5.

Whenever possible, our books use a durable and flexible lay-flat binding. If the page count exceeds this binding's limit, perfect binding is used.

How to stay in touch with O'Reilly

1. Visit Our Award-Winning Web Site

http://www.oreilly.com/

★ "Top 100 Sites on the Web" —*PC Magazine*
★ "Top 5% Web sites" —*Point Communications*
★ "3-Star site" —*The McKinley Group*

Our web site contains a library of comprehensive product information (including book excerpts and tables of contents), downloadable software, background articles, interviews with technology leaders, links to relevant sites, book cover art, and more. File us in your Bookmarks or Hotlist!

2. Join Our Email Mailing Lists

New Product Releases

To receive automatic email with brief descriptions of all new O'Reilly products as they are released, send email to:
ora-news-subscribe@lists.oreilly.com
Put the following information in the first line of your message (*not* in the Subject field):
subscribe ora-news

O'Reilly Events

If you'd also like us to send information about trade show events, special promotions, and other O'Reilly events, send email to:
ora-news-subscribe@lists.oreilly.com
Put the following information in the first line of your message (*not* in the Subject field):
subscribe ora-events

3. Get Examples from Our Books via FTP

There are two ways to access an archive of example files from our books:

Regular FTP

- ftp to:
  ftp.oreilly.com
  (login: anonymous
  password: your email address)
- Point your web browser to:
  ftp://ftp.oreilly.com/

FTPMAIL

- Send an email message to:
  ftpmail@online.oreilly.com
  (Write "help" in the message body)

4. Contact Us via Email

order@oreilly.com
To place a book or software order online. Good for North American and international customers.

subscriptions@oreilly.com
To place an order for any of our newsletters or periodicals.

books@oreilly.com
General questions about any of our books.

software@oreilly.com
For general questions and product information about our software. Check out O'Reilly Software Online at **http://software.oreilly.com/** for software and technical support information. Registered O'Reilly software users send your questions to: **website-support@oreilly.com**

cs@oreilly.com
For answers to problems regarding your order or our products.

booktech@oreilly.com
For book content technical questions or corrections.

proposals@oreilly.com
To submit new book or software proposals to our editors and product managers.

international@oreilly.com
For information about our international distributors or translation queries. For a list of our distributors outside of North America check out:
http://www.oreilly.com/distributors.html

5. Work with Us

Check out our website for current employment opportunites:
http://jobs.oreilly.com/

O'Reilly & Associates, Inc.
101 Morris Street, Sebastopol, CA 95472 USA
TEL   707-829-0515 or 800-998-9938
          (6am to 5pm PST)
FAX   707-829-0104

International Distributors

http://international.oreilly.com/distributors.html

UK, EUROPE, MIDDLE EAST AND AFRICA (EXCEPT FRANCE, GERMANY, AUSTRIA, SWITZERLAND, LUXEMBOURG, AND LIECHTENSTEIN)

INQUIRIES

O'Reilly UK Limited
4 Castle Street
Farnham
Surrey, GU9 7HS
United Kingdom
Telephone: 44-1252-711776
Fax: 44-1252-734211
Email: information@oreilly.co.uk

ORDERS

Wiley Distribution Services Ltd.
1 Oldlands Way
Bognor Regis
West Sussex PO22 9SA
United Kingdom
Telephone: 44-1243-843294
UK Freephone: 0800-243207
Fax: 44-1243-843302 (Europe/EU orders)
or 44-1243-843274 (Middle East/Africa)
Email: cs-books@wiley.co.uk

FRANCE

INQUIRIES & ORDERS

Éditions O'Reilly
18 rue Séguier
75006 Paris, France
Tel: 1-40-51-71-89
Fax: 1-40-51-72-26
Email: france@oreilly.fr

GERMANY, SWITZERLAND, AUSTRIA, LUXEMBOURG, AND LIECHTENSTEIN

INQUIRIES & ORDERS

O'Reilly Verlag
Balthasarstr. 81
D-50670 Köln, Germany
Telephone: 49-221-973160-91
Fax: 49-221-973160-8
Email: anfragen@oreilly.de (inquiries)
Email: order@oreilly.de (orders)

CANADA (FRENCH LANGUAGE BOOKS)

Les Éditions Flammarion ltée
375, Avenue Laurier Ouest
Montréal (Québec) H2V 2K3
Tel: 00-1-514-277-8807
Fax: 00-1-514-278-2085
Email: info@flammarion.qc.ca

HONG KONG

City Discount Subscription Service, Ltd.
Unit A, 6th Floor, Yan's Tower
27 Wong Chuk Hang Road
Aberdeen, Hong Kong
Tel: 852-2580-3539
Fax: 852-2580-6463
Email: citydis@ppn.com.hk

KOREA

Hanbit Media, Inc.
Chungmu Bldg. 210
Yonnam-dong 568-33
Mapo-gu
Seoul, Korea
Tel: 822-325-0397
Fax: 822-325-9697
Email: hant93@chollian.dacom.co.kr

PHILIPPINES

Global Publishing
G/F Benavides Garden
1186 Benavides Street
Manila, Philippines
Tel: 632-254-8949/632-252-2582
Fax: 632-734-5060/632-252-2733
Email: globalp@pacific.net.ph

TAIWAN

O'Reilly Taiwan
1st Floor, No. 21, Lane 295
Section 1, Fu-Shing South Road
Taipei, 106 Taiwan
Tel: 886-2-27099669
Fax: 886-2-27038802
Email: mori@oreilly.com

INDIA

Shroff Publishers & Distributors Pvt. Ltd.
12, "Roseland", 2nd Floor
180, Waterfield Road, Bandra (West)
Mumbai 400 050
Tel: 91-22-641-1800/643-9910
Fax: 91-22-643-2422
Email: spd@vsnl.com

CHINA

O'Reilly Beijing
SIGMA Building, Suite B809
No. 49 Zhichun Road
Haidian District
Beijing, China PR 100080
Tel: 86-10-8809-7475
Fax: 86-10-8809-7463
Email: beijing@oreilly.com

JAPAN

O'Reilly Japan, Inc.
Yotsuya Y's Building
7 Banch 6, Honshio-cho
Shinjuku-ku
Tokyo 160-0003 Japan
Tel: 81-3-3356-5227
Fax: 81-3-3356-5261
Email: japan@oreilly.com

SINGAPORE, INDONESIA, MALAYSIA AND THAILAND

TransQuest Publishers Pte Ltd
30 Old Toh Tuck Road #05-02
Sembawang Kimtrans Logistics Centre
Singapore 597654
Tel: 65-4623112
Fax: 65-4625761
Email: wendiw@transquest.com.sg

ALL OTHER ASIAN COUNTRIES

O'Reilly & Associates, Inc.
101 Morris Street
Sebastopol, CA 95472 USA
Tel: 707-829-0515
Fax: 707-829-0104
Email: order@oreilly.com

AUSTRALIA

Woodslane Pty., Ltd.
7/5 Vuko Place
Warriewood NSW 2102
Australia
Tel: 61-2-9970-5111
Fax: 61-2-9970-5002
Email: info@woodslane.com.au

NEW ZEALAND

Woodslane New Zealand, Ltd.
21 Cooks Street (P.O. Box 575)
Waganui, New Zealand
Tel: 64-6-347-6543
Fax: 64-6-345-4840
Email: info@woodslane.com.au

ARGENTINA

Distribuidora Cuspide
Suipacha 764
1008 Buenos Aires
Argentina
Phone: 5411-4322-8868
Fax: 5411-4322-3456
Email: libros@cuspide.com

O'REILLY®